D0705560

RECEIVED
SEP 2 8 2011
BY: ....

How to Run a Successful Design Business

For Don.
Without him, none of this would be possible.

NEWARK CAMPUS LIBRARY - COTC

How to Run a Successful Design Business

The New Professional Practice

Shan Preddy

WITH CONTRIBUTIONS FROM OTHER DESIGN EXPERTS

GOWER

© Shan Preddy and Contributors 2011

All rights reserved. No part of this publication may be reproduced, stored in a retrieval system or transmitted in any form or by any means, electronic, mechanical, photocopying, recording or otherwise without the prior permission of the publisher.

Published by
Gower Publishing Limited
Wey Court East
Union Road
Farnham
Surrey
GU9 7PT
England

Gower Publishing Company
Suite 420
101 Cherry Street
Burlington
VT 05401-4405
USA

www.gowerpublishing.com

Shan Preddy has asserted her moral right under the Copyright, Designs and Patents Act, 1988, to be identified as the editor of this work.

British Library Cataloguing in Publication Data
How to run a successful design business : the new
   professional practice.
   1. Design services--Management.
   I. Preddy, Shan.
   745.4'068-dc22

   ISBN: 978-0-566-09189-6 (pbk)
        978-1-4094-1763-7 (ebk)

Library of Congress Cataloging-in-Publication Data
Preddy, Shan.
   How to run a successful design business : the new professional practice / Shan Preddy.
      p. cm.
   Includes index.
   ISBN 978-0-566-09189-6 (hardback) -- ISBN 978-1-4094-1763-7 (ebook)
   1. Industrial management. 2. Success in business. 3. Industrial design. I. Title.
   HD31.P668 2011
   745.2068--dc22

                                                           2010032973

Printed and bound in Great Britain by the
MPG Books Group, UK

Important Notice

The material contained in *How to Run a Successful Design Business* has been provided by a number of authors. The Editor and Publishers have taken care to check its content but they cannot be held responsible for the views and opinions of the authors or for the accuracy of their information. Several of the chapters address legal and financial issues and while the guidance and examples given will help you prepare for consultations they should not be treated as substitutes for specialist advice in specific situations. Make sure that the plans you make and the decisions you take are appropriate for your own business and within the current law of the country (or countries) in which you operate.

Contents

SECTION SIX   THE DESIGNERS

SECTION SEVEN   THE CLIENTS

SECTION EIGHT   THE DESIGN BODIES

SECTION NINE   THE REFERENCE LIBRARY

SECTION TEN   THE CONTRIBUTORS

Reviews of
How to Run a Successful Design Business

Occasionally a book is published that you know you will keep not in the bookcase but on the top of your desk. A book that will get well-thumbed and dirty with use, with pages curled up, the spine broken, passages and phrases underlined, re-read many times, copied, quoted and memorised. This is such a book! Shan Preddy has brought together some of the brightest minds in the design industry and distilled a lifetime's experience as consultant and coach to the stars of our profession. The result is a vital reference tool for anyone who works in the field of design, stuffed with clear and practical advice. This is a book you cannot afford to be without.

- Rowland Heming, Business Development Director, Design Board, Belgium

Doing creative work with impact needs headspace and optimism. Without the underpinning of a well-managed business, design business owners – the creative linchpins – are lost to circular conversations about office supplies and what went wrong. It's never too soon to take your business seriously. Help is at hand from a dream team of experienced practitioners. Don't anyone let them go into business together.

- Joe Heapy, Director, Engine Service Design, UK

Shan Preddy's new publication is a bible for design business practice. She and her contributors cover all the basics for growing your firm, avoiding pitfalls and offering some surprising insights that might otherwise be lost. Everyone in the industry should read this invaluable contribution to success. It will put pounds in your pocket!

- Celestine Phelan, Chairman, Event Communications, UK

This is an uplifting affirmation of the power of design in business, combining a clear view of the big picture with a strong focus on the important details that make design such a great business to be in. As always, Shan Preddy gets right to the heart of the matter; with exactly the kind of insightful business advice that designers need to know and, more importantly, put into practice.

- Jim Orkney, Managing Director, Kinneir Dufort, UK

It's not very often a book comes along that is as relevant as this one. It is packed with information and guidance on every aspect of running a design business. Its success lies in the variety and cross-section of information provided by the specialist practitioners Shan Preddy has invited to contribute to the book. Their in-depth knowledge delivers great nuggets of consultancy advice that would take you years to accumulate. The book does a great job of reminding you of all the good things you've ever learnt; it provides reassurance that much of what you've implemented (or tried to) is right; most importantly, it provides the inspiration and confidence to go on to achieve ever greater things.

- Caroline Hagen, Managing Director, Reach, UK

Reviews of
How to Run a Successful Design Business

A well informed – and at times surprising – wealth of information which, whilst acknowledging extremely well the traits of the design sector, provides sound advice for any modern business. The book explores so many important facets, which you can easily dip in and out of, and the use of quotes at the start of each chapter add an interesting mix of humour and philosophy.

- Adryan Bell, workplace consultant and adviser, formerly Director, DEGW

Maintaining an equilibrium between customers, team work and design quality is a delicate balancing act at which many fail and few master brilliantly. A book that explains how these elements are connected was long overdue; Shan Preddy has now written it. Please read it. It belongs on every designer's bedside table.

- Jean Jacques Schaffner, Founder, Schaffner & Conzelmann, Switzerland

The more we designers understand and value the business world, the more impact we can make with our ideas. This book has some very impressive contributors. It is an interesting read and a useful book to have on your shelf for ongoing reference.

- Deborah Szebeko, Founder, Think Public, UK

A 'must read' for anyone who wants to follow their passion in design whilst putting food on the table. Shan Preddy has managed to collect the hard-learned experiences of some of the best in the business. I wish I'd had this years ago when I started out: it would have saved a lot of grief.

- John Corcoran, Director, Wire Design, UK

Foreword

When you're getting to grips with graphic design software, honing your modelling capabilities and mastering 3D drawing, no one mentions hiring and firing, profit and loss and client meetings. But maybe they should. Design Council research suggests the average design business is a little like a butterfly – very eye-catching while it lasts but prone to a short lifespan. In some of the disciplines we surveyed, as many as 45 per cent had been trading for under three years, and most lacked a long-term perspective, which tells its own story.

When design businesses shut up shop, it might be because key people move on and can't be replaced. But often they close because they have to. And the reason they have to is a simple lack of business skills. All that carefully nurtured design craft goes unused until the next opportunity to open a studio comes along. Very draining, very frustrating.

Office leases, accounts and billing are boring compared to the crackle of creativity, but unfortunately you can't get by without a working knowledge of them. They're part of being a professional designer. Knowing how to pitch ideas, bring a project in on budget and manage a client's whims are all vital too.

But don't mistake business savvy for drudgery. It makes you a better designer. The more you know about business, the better you'll be at seeing the world from your clients' point of view, working out what they need and spotting opportunities for them. Do enough of that and you will win their confidence and form a really effective partnership where everyone wins.

So this book is good news. Whether you're starting out or an experienced veteran, the wisdom in these pages will help to make being in business a positive experience.

David Kester
Chief Executive, Design Council
www.designcouncil.org.uk

Preface

How do you run a successful design business? That's the question this book aims to answer. It contains advice, information, suggestions, guidelines and top tips, not to mention a number of thought-provoking opinions.

It's a big subject, so I asked a big group of people to help me to write about it. They are all experts in their different fields. Some, like me, are advisers and consultants to the design sector. Others are clients, practitioners or representatives of design organisations. A huge thank you to all of them.

I would also like to thank the Design Council for their continuous support; the editorial and production teams at Gower for their expertise; and my husband and business partner, Don Preddy, who worked on the book with me throughout its life from initial idea to final implementation.

Louis Hellman has generously allowed us to use some of his wonderful cartoons; they originally appeared in Design Week. And this book would not have been possible without Preddy&Co's clients worldwide who, over the years, have demonstrated to me how to run successful design businesses: thank you.

This book will give you the knowledge and tools you need to run a successful design business. I hope you enjoy reading it as much as we did writing it.

Shan Preddy
Partner, PREDDY&CO
www.preddy.co.uk

Section One:
The Industry

1.1 The arrival

Jeremy Myerson

Art without industry is guilt; industry without art is brutality.
- John Ruskin (1819–1900), art critic and social thinker

DESIGN AND THE HUMAN DIMENSION

Every object and experience in our world today has been designed. Professional designers make fundamental decisions about function, shape, colour, form, style, material, layout, assembly and production to enable us to understand, use and enjoy modern products, communications and environments. Knowledge and skills may vary between different design fields but, essentially, the work of designers can be defined as influencing the relationship between people and the objects, messages and places they encounter every day.

This 'human dimension' to design is highly significant. It explains why design is such an important business tool for company profitability, and why it is a social lever to improve the quality of life. It accounts for the prominent role of design businesses in Britain, which today has one of the largest and most sophisticated design industries in the world.

But how did a country which has leaned more to the literary than the visual throughout its cultural history develop such a breadth and depth of design expertise? For answers, we need to look back to the roots of the design industry and explore the pioneers of the past.

CRADLE OF THE INDUSTRIAL REVOLUTION

British design owes its illustrious position to deep historical roots stretching right back to the tradition of craft creativity evident in the stained glass windows, royal regalia, flags, heraldry and tapestries of medieval times. However, the true origins of the modern design industry can be traced to the first stirrings of the Industrial Revolution in the mid-eighteenth century, to the foundation of the Royal Society for the Encouragement of Arts, Manufactures and Commerce, the RSA, in 1754, and to the pioneering work of ceramics manufacturer Josiah Wedgwood (1730–95).

Wedgwood's family ceramics business was the first in the world to mass-produce goods. It pioneered production techniques and a division of labour that anticipated Henry Ford's model of manufacture by 150 years. Wedgwood used simple, practical design to target a new consumer group: the expanding middle class. His famous Black Basalt teapot, for example, was produced to show off the bleached white hands in vogue among women at that time.

In the same period, the commercial and cultural impact of professional interior design was being felt for the first time through the activities of the Classicist architect Robert Adam (1728–92). During the 1770s, Adam's design business employed 2,000 people. According to records of the time, his senior craftsmen – cabinet-makers, sculptors and decorative artists – did rather well financially out of his patronage by the royal and the rich. Some of Adam's ornate interior designs survive today at Osterley Park and Syon Park in west London. His reputation is of a British designer who combined creative flair with business acumen. Many great British design names were destined to follow in his footsteps.

THE 1851 GREAT EXHIBITION

A century later, following rapid industrialisation and the consolidation of Wedgwood's achievements, design attention was focused on the 1851 Great Exhibition in Hyde Park, as Britain embarked on a period in which its mastery of industrial techniques would famously make it 'the workshop of the world'. Prominent in this period was Christopher Dresser (1834–1904), widely acknowledged as the first industrial design consultant of the modern age.

Dresser was a Glasgow-born botanist who turned to design after an unsuccessful application for the Chair of Botany at University College, London. From 1862 onwards, he gradually built up a large and thriving freelance practice, designing glass, ceramics, tableware and wallpapers for popular use. Tile maker Doulton's, a supplier to Liberty's of London, and Sheffield silver plate company Elkington's were among his clients.

Within a decade, Dresser was able to boast that 'there is not a branch of manufacture I do not design patterns for'. He can be seen today as an early example of a designer who was commissioned to create new designs specifically to boost sales for a company. Although his work was largely based on the metaphors of botany, he became increasingly interested in geometric forms and in the possibilities of the machine-made rather than handcrafted design.

As a counter-balance to this, another great designer of the late-nineteenth century, William Morris (1834–96), led the Arts & Crafts Movement in defiance of the machine and argued for a return to the medieval craft guild. Morris was ultimately to be disappointed. The machine was to dominate design thinking in the early years of the twentieth century, at a time when artistic movements were subject to intense change.

THE MODERN MOVEMENT

Increasingly, design in Britain began to divorce itself from arts and crafts and became an activity associated with mass production and mass marketing. This change was reinforced by the impact of the Modern Movement in design after World War One, with its emphasis on machine-like forms to sweep away the bourgeois ornament of the old order and express a new, egalitarian social purpose.

Professional designers saw their role as interpreting and refining the new industrial technologies of the era for commercial use. They became as fascinated and inspired by man-made automobiles and turbines as Victorian artists had been by studying the natural environment.

Modernist design was an import from influential Bauhaus art school in Germany in the 1930s, as Bauhaus pioneers such as Walter Gropius and Marcel Breuer fled to Britain from the Nazis. The Bauhaus would go on to claim an impact on post-war British design practice and education in terms of promoting a core ideology. But this wasn't the only external catalyst to development. During the twentieth century, British designers synthesised a range of historical and international influences – including American and Scandinavian design – to create their own special mix of design.

Technical developments, especially in new materials, were also a key factor, from early plastics such as Bakelite in the 1920s and 1930s, which gave designers an expressive new material, to new prefabricated building techniques, which acted as a catalyst for modern architectural ideas.

INFLUENCE OF THE NEW YORK PIONEERS

When two UK designers Milner Gray (1899–1997) and Misha Black (1910–77) established Britain's first modern design consultancy, Design Research Unit, in 1943, they freely acknowledged their debt not only to the material technology rapidly advanced during World War Two, but also to the pioneering New York design firms of Raymond Loewy, Henry Dreyfuss, Walter Dorwin Teague and Norman Bel Geddes which had thrived during the 1930s.

In America, a design industry with distinctive characteristics had already emerged; publicity-conscious design consultants charged companies substantial fees to devise new products, environments and communications. Their methods entailed linking consumer psychology and advancing technology to the traditional design skills of thinking, drawing and visualising. Their approach was unashamedly commercial, in sharp contrast to the more purist and elevated concerns of the Bauhaus masters.

Design Research Unit (which created the landmark British Rail corporate identity programme) was based on this American model and anticipated the future multidisciplinary shape of the British design industry. Importantly, its emergence coincided with an era after World War Two in which sleepy British industry slowly began to realise that it could no longer rely on large, captive Empire markets and be aloof from design trends from across the Atlantic.

POST-WAR OPTIMISM

The 1951 Festival of Britain set an optimistic post-war tone for Britain's design potential, showcasing the vibrant work of young designers and architects. Names such as Hugh Casson, James Gardner and a very young Terence Conran emerged from this event. But this proved a false dawn during the often grey and gloomy 1950s and it was not until the 1960s that Britain fully shook off a period of austerity to become a world centre for Pop art, design and music.

Many of the consultancies destined to lead Britain's design industry – for example, Wolff Olins, and the forerunner to Pentagram, Fletcher Forbes Gill – were first established during that exciting decade. Much design work previously done by technicians, printers and shopfitters was at last in the hands of professional designers dedicated to developing and publicising their skills.

In the 1970s, British designers began to sell their design expertise overseas, although with mixed success, against a background of economic uncertainty at home and abroad. The world's first global design firm, American-owned Unimark International, created the corporate identity for Ford before collapsing amid the repercussions of industrial unrest of the early 1970s.

DESIGN BOOM OF THE 1980s

Despite such setbacks, the trend towards globalisation accelerated in the 1980s as British design companies set up international networks to meet demand from multinational clients. The background this time was of more dynamic and sustained economic growth: rapid growth in property prices, high street spending and corporate mergers and acquisitions all helped to fuel a British design boom.

Several UK designers became wealthy entrepreneurs, their design firms publicly listed on the Stock Market, among them Rodney Fitch and Michael Peters. By 1988,

British design had expanded spectacularly, even investing more than £70 million in the US design market through a series of takeovers of American design firms. Before long, the entire sector began to overheat.

In the recession that followed, there was painful contraction in the design industry. The 100 largest design firms in the UK trimmed their workforces by nearly half. Yet fee income was not similarly reduced; by the early 1990s, the use of new labour-saving computer technology was enabling design practices to produce more work with fewer people.

POWER OF THE CREATIVE INDUSTRIES

Gradually, during the 1990s, the design industry nursed itself back to robust health. A combination of a common digital platform and the rise of global brands allowed British design consultants back into the game on favourable terms. Design was essential to the marketing mix and at the same time important to broader cultural debates about the future of our cities, the environmental cost of production and social inclusion. By the late 1990s, the Labour Government could claim that Britain was a 'design workshop for the world', its historical echo sending a message about the growing economic power of the creative industries.

From 2000 onwards, all of these themes would be developed at breakneck speed with sustainable and inclusive design rising to the fore in the face of growing social challenges. Today, the core business areas of product, graphic and environmental design are reframed in the context of new digital technology, which makes interaction design central to product development, web communication an essential part of the graphic armoury and a digital layer part of every environmental project.

There is also an industry-wide concern to measure the effectiveness of design, to isolate and monitor its impact on business performance, in much the same way that marketing and advertising agencies track their commercial effectiveness.

FORGED FROM DISPARATE ROOTS

With the benefit of hindsight, it is possible to see that today's British design industry is forged from disparate roots in art, craft, architecture, marketing and engineering. It has distilled the best qualities of the adjacent professions from which its core disciplines have emerged.

Design draws its:

- skill, vision, form-giving and lateral thinking from art and craft;
- focus on planning, project management and social responsibility from architecture;
- boldness of communication, spirit of entrepreneurship, consumer psychology and emphasis on meeting business objectives from advertising and marketing;

- commitment to invention, technique, process and use of materials from engineering and science.

Design is a hybrid profession, freely borrowing techniques and vocabularies from other areas, but that is what makes it such a fascinating field in which to work. The design industry in Britain is not just built on the rich pattern of historical experience: it is supported by the largest and most comprehensive system of design education and training in the world.

Pentagram co-founder Alan Fletcher once described design as 'a mental utensil', a practical tool but also a way of thinking. The pioneers of Britain's design business have been true to that idea.

1.2 The present

Shan Preddy

I'm looking for a lot of men who have an infinite capacity to not know what can't be done.
• Henry Ford (1863–1947), automobile industrialist

WHAT SHAPE ARE WE IN?

We can be accused in the UK of being blinkered and over-confident about our design prowess. We sometimes imagine that we are above comparison with the rest of the world, that we are as good as it gets. We are not; we face many genuine and robust threats from other countries, and we are nowhere near as strong and inviolable as we like to think we are. But we are not a cottage industry either. We are a significant, growing and rapidly maturing business sector.

Mapping design can be problematic, and the available data can be a bit muddy: our still relatively young and rapidly changing industry doesn't always fit neatly into existing categories, and reports inevitably lag some time behind data collection. We also have to deal with the ongoing problem of what exactly constitutes 'design'. However, even if the picture isn't quite crystal clear yet, visibility is certainly improving.

Just how big is the UK design industry today? Are we growing or shrinking? How many consultancies are there? How many people work in design? Statistics don't always provide the most gripping reading, but here are some that are worth knowing and using when you talk to your clients, your colleagues and the bank manager.

TAKING MEASUREMENTS

The UK creative industries are valued at almost £60 billion with average growth over the ten-year period 1997–2007 running at 5 per cent a year compared with 3 per cent for the economy as a whole.[1] This data excludes design; if it was included, the figure would be substantially higher.

Design itself contributes an estimated £6.8 billion Gross Value Added (GVA) to the UK economy each year.[2] It is a substantial and growing business sector in its own right. Including consultancies, freelancers and in-house units, our total 2009 income totalled £15 billion; in 2005, a turnover figure of £11.6 billion was reported. This indicates a growth of 29 per cent while, for comparison, general inflation for the same period was 15 per cent. Design consultancies accounted for 51 per cent (£7.6 billion) of income, freelancers 24 per cent (£3.6 billion) and in-house units 25 per cent (£3.8 billion).[3]

We are well-populated, and getting more so. Total design employment is 232,000, with 82,500 in consultancies, 65,900 freelancers and 83,600 in in-house units. This is a 29 per cent increase on the equivalent 2005 figure.[4]

We have a lot of consultancies. There are 10,800 design consultancies in the UK alone,[5] and although this represents a 13 per cent fall from the equivalent 2005 figure of 12,450, overall fee income and employment numbers are up; this suggests that, on average, consultancies are each employing more people than before.

We are a dynamic sector, constantly launching new firms and merging others. Just under a quarter of design consultancies, 24 per cent, have been in business for fewer than three years; 37 per cent if freelancers and in-house units are included. However, to counter-balance that, almost 20 per cent have been in operation for more than 15 years.[6]

We have a consultancy sector composed largely of very small businesses. 60 per cent employ fewer than five people; 27 per cent between five and nine, and 11 per cent between ten and 49. Only 2 per cent employ more than 50 people.[7] Some clients have departments which are bigger than many of our consultancies. We are, however, broadly in line with the national picture of all employers in all industries: BIS, the Department for Business Innovation and Skills, estimates that 95 per cent of all enterprises in the UK employ fewer than ten people, and 99 per cent fewer than 50.[8]

We also have a lot of in-house design units. At an estimated 6,500, over a quarter of organisations which employ more than 100 people have such in-house teams. 59 per cent of them are in the private sector, with the remainder in the public and not-for-profit sectors.[9]

---

1   DCMS (Department for Culture, Media and Sport) *Creative Industries Economic Estimates February 2010*, using 2007 data. GVA is a measure of the contribution to the economy of each individual producer, industry or sector in the UK. It is used in estimating Gross Domestic Product (GDP)

2   Creative and Cultural Skills Design: *Impact and Footprint 2008–2009*

3   *Design Council Design Industry Survey* 2010 and *The Business of Design*: Design Industry Research, 2005

4   Ibid.

5   Ibid.

6   Ibid.

7   Ibid.

8   BIS (Department for Business Innovation and Skills) *Small and Medium Enterprises Statistics*: UK Whole Economy Table 2a, 2008

9   *Design Council Design Industry Survey* 2010 and *The Business of Design*: Design Industry Research, 2005

We are diverse in our skills. Some 62 per cent of us report competencies in communications, and 48 per cent in digital and multimedia. 16 per cent offer interior and exhibition design, 11 per cent product and industrial and around 1 per cent service design. The natural overlap between some of these disciplines, by the way, results in these percentages adding to more than 100.[10]

We are geographically uneven. 40 per cent of us are based in London and the South East of England, with all other regions ranging between 1 per cent and 10 per cent.[11] This compares with an overall UK population percentage of 26 per cent in London and the South East.[12]

We have clients who are predominantly UK based. Only 10 per cent of design consultancies' clients are based outside the UK; the figure for freelancers is lower.[13]

We are largely a fee-based business. However, other sources of income include retainers, royalties and a combination of fixed-fee plus percentage-of-profit. These models are not mutually exclusive; several might be in use concurrently.[14]

And, on average, we are earning money from our employees. Financial experts Kingston Smith W1 publishes an annual survey of the financial performance of marketing services companies, including branding and design. Based on a detailed analysis of 30 businesses to the end of 2008, the design sector's average annual operating profit per head ran at £9,494, or 9.9 per cent of gross income per employee. This was higher than digital, which Kingston Smith W1 treats as a separate category from design, at 5.7 per cent (£4,037) and higher than direct marketing and sales promotion combined at 7.7 per cent (£6,440). Don't cheer too loudly, though. We are beaten resoundingly by advertising at 12.6 per cent (£13,442), PR at 16.6 per cent (£17,123) and media buying at 22.2 per cent (£25,492); of the three, PR operates on the most similar financial model to the design sector, in that it is largely fee-based. In fact, we shouldn't be cheering at all. Kingston Smith W1 believes that a well run marketing services firm should be generating an operating profit per head of at least £15,000 a year. The same could apply to design firms of all disciplines but, at under £10,000, we have some way to go yet.[15]

MORPHING AND MATURING

The UK design industry is fortunate to have in it a number of world-class consultancies, many of them leaders in their respective fields. Both large and small in size, they are sought-after and respected internationally by clients, and they are

---

10   Ibid.

11   Ibid.

12   *Office for National Statistics Census,* 2001

13   *Design Council Design Industry Research Survey,* 2010 and *The Business of Design*: Design Industry Research, 2005

14   Ibid.

15   Kingston Smith W1 *Financial Performance of Marketing Services Companies,* 2009

an inspiration to other design businesses. You can find several of them in Section Six of this book, *The Designers*.

And yet design businesses are not big businesses. Many thousands employ fewer than five people and only a very small minority enjoy an annual fee income of over £1 million. Around a quarter of design consultancies earn less than £100,000 a year.[16] While some of these businesses are undoubtedly profitable, remaining small in size over the years through choice, others work on projects with tiny budgets, returning very low profits to their owners. As in any business sector, the less successful firms will eventually vanish without trace unless their owners close the gap in their business skills.

Overall, there are many reasons to be optimistic about the prognosis for the UK design industry's future. One advantage of being a dynamic, growing industry is that we have people with ambition, enthusiasm, passion and energy. One advantage of micro-businesses[17] is that they can be flexible, and can change rapidly to meet market or economic circumstances. And there is a great advantage of being a design firm in the UK: compared with many countries, we have a lot of help, information, advice and support to help new and ambitious design businesses of today become the global players of tomorrow.

For example, within the wider business arena, we have our Chambers of Commerce and the Federation of Small Businesses as well as government-funded Business Link with its aid to small and medium-sized businesses;[18] this category includes all but a tiny handful of design firms. We have Creative and Cultural Skills, whose vision is to make the UK the world's creative hub. We have a very proactive Design Council, the national strategic body for design, which is predominantly funded through government grant-in-aid. We have the UK Design Alliance and its Good Design Practice campaign, which addresses the gap in business and professional skills in design firms. It also supports design teaching and learning in schools, colleges and universities to ensure tomorrow's designers are ready for new challenges. And we have more membership-based design associations and networks, both national and regional, than anyone could ever be an active member of in a lifetime.

The UK design industry is now maturing in a number of important ways. It is settling from fragmentation to segmentation, from an amorphous mixture where it is hard to tell one brand or sub-sector from another, to clear marketplace differentiation. We are learning that the way forward, the route to success, is to make sure we have the right professional and business skills in place. We are beginning to focus our offers not on what we can do, but on what clients want now and will want in the future. We are pursuing specialisms in whichever fields we have chosen, while understanding the bigger picture. We are working in strategic alliances with other experts when appropriate instead of missing out on opportunities or trying

---

16   Creative and Cultural Skills Design: *Impact and Footprint 2008–09* and *Design Council Design Industry Survey,* 2010

17   The EU (European Union) defines 'micro-enterprises' as those which employ fewer than 10 people and whose annual turnover and/or annual balance sheet total does not exceed €2 million

18   The EU definition of small and medium-sized enterprises (SMEs) is those employing fewer than 250 people and whose annual turnover does not exceed €50 million or whose annual balance sheet total does not exceed €43 million

to do it all ourselves. And we know more and more about what design is, and what it does, increasingly having the courage to measure and prove the effectiveness of our design interventions in the marketplace. All in all, the UK design industry is a very exciting place.

1.3   The global context

Michael Thomson

A journey of a thousand miles must begin with a single step.
• Lao Tzu (sixth century BC), philosopher

THE INTERNATIONAL DESIGN BUSINESS

The design business is global. It is a distinctive form of economic activity that for many economies represents an important tradable, intangible and exportable asset. Many nations now categorise design within the creative industries as an important aspect of the cultural economy and the link between design and innovation is increasingly recognised in innovation policy.

As a global business, the distinctive characteristics of design consulting companies across the world appear to be similar. These include the average size of the companies, their business models, methods of working and the training backgrounds of the creative, professionally qualified, talented people that are attracted to work in them.

DESIGN IS A NANOTECHNOLOGY

Studies from a number of sources demonstrate that the design industry is structured principally of small companies operating in specialist discipline niches.

As an example, research completed for the European Commission on the service industries across Europe in 2005 revealed that some 70 per cent of all design companies across 27 Member States are between one and five people in size, with only 6 per cent of companies employing more than 50 people. Of that 70 per cent, a total of 38 per cent are businesses of only one or two people.[1]

NUMBERS OF DESIGN FIRMS IN DIFFERENT COUNTRIES

The *International Design Scoreboard: Initial indicators of international design capabilities* (see Table 1.3.1), produced by Cambridge University in 2009, provides an indication of the number of design firms in different countries according to the most recently available statistics.

Table 1.3.1   International Design Scoreboard: Initial indicators of international design capabilities, Cambridge University 2009

	Number of design firms	Design firms per million population
USA	30,485	105.7
UK	12,450	206.8
Canada	12,411	380.4
Sweden	8,459	947.8
Singapore	3,657	888.9
Korea	2,500	51.8
Japan	2,349	18.4
Hong Kong	1,797	26.7
Norway	927	203.1
Finland	921	176.2
Denmark	450	82.3
Iceland	82	283.5

The USA is attributed 30,485 design firms and the UK 12,450. Canada is close to the UK with 12,411 firms. The smallest in the sample of 12 countries is Iceland with 82 companies.

These numbers make more sense relative to population size, and the report also provides these figures.

---

1   *Innovation in Services: Issues at Stake and Trends*, J Howells and B Tether, 2004. A report for the European Commission, Directorate General for Enterprise and Industry

CONTRIBUTION TO NATIONAL ECONOMIES

If measured by size alone, it is clear that design is a very small component of any national economy. This is a barrier to policy formation, as design falls below the 'policy radar'. And yet, time and again, through different studies in different parts of the world, design's impact on national economic performance is revealed as being larger than could be assumed according to its scale. Design brings considerable added value to the economy.

In the UK, British Design Innovation (BDI) lists 4,500 design companies generating a turnover of some £4.4bn, with 65,000 employees and overseas income of £0.8bn.[2] In Denmark, recent research indicates that in 2005 the turnover of the design industry was some €740 million, four times more than it was in 1995.[3] Equally, the export figures showed a six-fold increase during the same time period, representing about twice the growth experienced by other consultancy sectors in Denmark.

A GLOBAL COMPETITIVENESS RANKING FOR DESIGN

In 2002, the New Zealand Institute of Economic Research (NZIER) assessed countries' design competitiveness[4] by selecting indexes from the World Economic Forum (WEF)'s *Global Competitiveness Report*.[5] These included: 'Extent of Branding'; 'Capacity for Innovation'; 'Uniqueness of Product Designs'; 'Production Process Sophistication'; and 'Extent of Marketing'. Despite some variations in the indicators from year to year,[6] these features were aggregated in 2007 into the WEF's *Sophistication of Company Operations and Strategy Index* to create a so-called *Design Index* (see Figure 1.3.2). Based on these indicators, it was possible to plot the national competitiveness ranking of leading countries against their 'design ranking' to show a correlation between national competitiveness and levels of design.

Building upon this work, Designium, the Design Innovation Centre at the University of Art and Design in Helsinki, produced in 2008 its third *Global Design Watch*.[7] This latest report utilises a new combination of seven rather than five WEF indicators including three from the original NZIER 2002 *Design Index*. The new indicators have been added to take into account the impact of indirect spending on design competitiveness and include 'Company spending on research and

---

2   *BDI Valuation Survey*, 2008

3   *A Picture of Danish Design – Challenges and Perspectives*, Danish Enterprise and Construction Authority, 2007

4   *Building a Case for Added Value through Design*, NZIER, 2002

5   *The Global Competitiveness Report 2007–08*, World Economic Forum, October 2008, Palgrave Macmillan

6   'Uniqueness of product design' was dropped from the WEF list after the 2001/2002 competitiveness report and 'Extent of branding' was last included in the WEF report for 2004/2005

7   *Global Design Watch* 2008, Katja Sorvali and Eija Nieminen, Designium, the Design Innovation Centre at the University of Art and Design in Helsinki. The previous two reports were published in 2003 and 2006

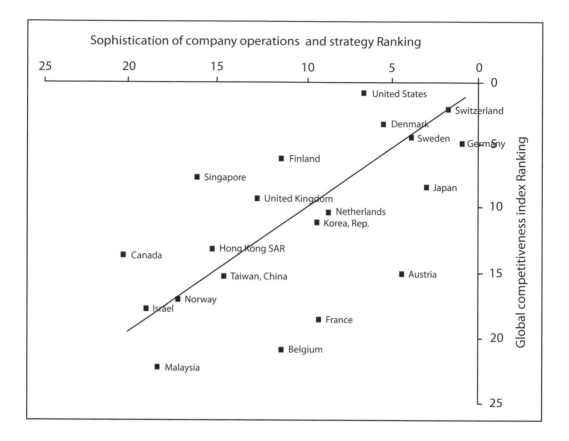

Figure 1.3.2   'Sophistication of company operations and strategy' ranked with 'global competitiveness ranking', 2007, as quoted in INNO-GRIPS Mini Study 05 – Design[a]

Source: With kind permission of Pierre Bitard and the Publications Office of the European Union

[a]   Mini Study 04 – Design, Pierre Bitard and Julie Basset, June 2008. Work package 3 for INNO–GRIPS, (Global Review of Innovation Intelligence and Policy Studies), EU Commission.

development', 'Nature of competitive advantage', 'Value chain process' and 'Degree of customer orientation'.[8]

DESIGN PROMOTION AND DESIGN SUPPORT

In many countries, governments support design through funding design promotion and design support organisations. These exist in a number of different formats and can operate at regional, national and international levels. The commitment of

---

8   Ibid. p. 14

governments to these design organisations also differs from country to country, ranging from little or no interest to supportive engagement over decades.

In the UK, the national authority for design is the Design Council. Although only one of a number of different organisations working in the area, (including for example, The British Council, Invest Northern Ireland, Design Wales and Design Partners to name but a few), the Design Council is by far the largest in the UK when measured in terms of funding received from Government.

Alongside government-funded design promotion, the impact should not be underestimated of the non-government-funded design promotion organisations, for example Design Exchange in Canada, and the national professional bodies or associations, such as Industrial Designers Society of America (IDSA) in the US, the Design Business Association (DBA) and Chartered Society of Designers (CSD) in the UK, and Danish Designers in Denmark. These organisations play a complementary role at the national level in creating organisational infrastructure and activities that facilitate the development of the professional practice of design.

THE NEED FOR COHERENT ACTION IN EUROPE

In any case, when viewed from a pan-European perspective, it is clear that the regional and national design support and promotion organisations are both diverse and fragmented.[9] Some organisations have very low funding levels; others have only part-funding. Within Europe, some Member States such as the Czech Republic have closed down their established Design Centres whilst others, such as Norway, are currently increasing their commitment to design as a component of innovation strategy. In competitor nations outside Europe, in particular in the Far East including South Korea and Taiwan, the levels of government commitment to design are much higher. In short, the picture is very mixed.

Driven by this realisation amongst others, the Bureau of European Design Associations (BEDA) met with the President of the European Commission, José Manuel Barroso, in October 2007 to push for a strategic approach to design at the European level. BEDA presented the case for better statistical evidence of design's impact on the European economy, and requested a mapping of the pan-European design promotion sector and coherent action at the European level for design, incorporating a permanent dialogue for design with the European Commission.

As a direct consequence of that meeting, the European Commission embarked on the development of a design strategy as a component of Europe's strategy for innovation. This work led to the publication in 2009 of the Commission's Staff Working Document entitled *Design as a Driver of User-centred Innovation*.[10] Following a successful public consultation that received over 500 responses during May/June

---

9   *The European Design Report*, BEDA, 2006

10   Commission Staff Working Document, *Design as a Driver of User-centred Innovation*, SEC(2009) 501 final, Brussels, 07 April 2009

2009, the intention is that design can be included within Europe's Innovation policy, post-Lisbon Agenda 2010.

COMPETITOR NATIONS – AGGRESSIVE DESIGN POLICIES

Returning to the picture at the national level, many countries are now competing hard with the UK's design capability as a consequence of aggressive policies offering support at the micro – and macro – economic levels to push design as a strategy for innovation. South Korea's current target is for its design industries to be at 95 per cent of the capability of that of the Western industrialised nations by 2013.

Indeed, South Korea has been implementing five-year plans since the 1990s and it is clear that determination and tenacity are paying off. A number of companies have transformed themselves from Original Equipment Manufacturers (OEMs), making products or components for other companies, into global brands in their own right. LG and Samsung in Korea are powerful examples of companies taking design as a strategy to change their vision; both these companies extensively use design talent from the UK.

As reflected elsewhere in this book, the BRIC countries (Brazil, Russia, India and China) will continue to develop their creative talent and are putting in place policies to support design. India's Union Cabinet published the first national design policy in February 2008. Actions such as these will continue to accelerate the development of design competence in developing economies and this will lead to the availability of competent creative design services at fee levels far below those of Western industrialised economies.

STAYING AHEAD

At the international level the design game is changing. There are many new entrants coming to market with sophisticated consulting offers. Research conducted over the past years by the Danish Government identifies the emergence of a larger and more sophisticated form of design firm that represents what they believe to be a development in the sector.[11] These companies, which have been labelled as 'Concept' or 'Strategic Design Companies', are emerging in 'concept design hubs' including London, New York, the San Francisco Bay area and The Netherlands. These companies offer more strategic responses to the changing innovation and business needs of global clients.

For the UK design sector facing increasing competition, it may be possible to take some comfort from the fact that our education system and heritage of design

---

11   Research conducted by FORA, Centre for Industrial Economics Research, Danish Ministry of Economic and Business Affairs

excellence continue to keep us ahead of the game. But this position will continue to be challenged.

In an ocean of design companies that all claim creativity, innovation, user-centred design and design thinking as unique qualities, it will be increasingly vital to build sophisticated international competence in order to survive. Only those consultancies that achieve both insight and foresight into the changing international marketplace for design will be able to stay ahead. For design firms that are ambitious, connected, flexible, mobile, networked and talented, the world will be their oyster.

1.4   The client perspective

Shan Preddy

Greater creativity is key to greater productivity, whether by way of higher-value products and services, better processes, more effective marketing, simpler structures or better use of people's skills. Every business needs to be cost-conscious, but that's insufficient for enduring success. No company ever cut its way to greatness.

- Sir George Cox, former Chairman, UK Design Council

THE IMPACT OF DESIGN

For clients, the purpose of design is to provide businesses or organisations with solutions to problems, challenges and opportunities in order to get results. Everything else, including working with interesting and inspirational design professionals, is just a bonus. It doesn't matter whether the clients are experienced or inexperienced design buyers, nor whether they are entrepreneurs, business people or public sector employees. It's results they are after.

Design works. Regular tracking studies carried out by the UK Design Council demonstrate that clients who use design out–perform their rivals consistently. The *Value of Design Factfinder*[1] not only assesses the attitudes and behaviour of design-buying clients, but also evaluates the impact of design on a number of performance measures, including market share, growth, productivity, share price and competitiveness.

Here are a few headline facts and figures; they are worth using when you need to make the case for design to any reluctant clients you might encounter:

- Design can help to increase turnover. For every £100 a 'design alert business' (the Design Council's term for those which have observed a direct impact from the use of design) spends on design, turnover increases by £225.[2]

---

1   UK Design Council *Value of Design Factfinder* contains research from a number of sources, mainly the ongoing *National Survey of Firms* and *Added Value Research 2007*

2   Ibid.

- Design can help to increase profit. For every £100 a design alert business spends on design, profit increases by £83.[3]
- Design can help to improve share prices. Design-led companies' share prices outperformed the FTSE by 200 per cent over ten years.[4]
- Design can help to increase market share. On average, design alert businesses increased their market share by 6.3 per cent through design. Those in the retail, wholesale and leisure services and manufacturing sectors saw the biggest increases: 6.9 per cent and 7.2 per cent respectively. Some manufacturers increased their market share by 100 per cent, with design helping them to either take over a market or create a new one.[5]
- Design can help to produce and launch new products. On average, design alert businesses develop 25 new products a year through design and over two-thirds (71 per cent) launch at least one. 83 per cent of businesses which see design as integral to their operation have launched new products or services, compared with just 40 per cent of all businesses.[6]
- Design can help to increase employment. Design alert businesses with more than 250 employees are most likely to increase staff numbers as a result of using design; on average, such businesses hired 13 new people in a year.[7]
- Design can help a business to grow. Rapidly growing businesses are six times likelier than static ones to see design as integral to their operation.[8]

This research demonstrates a clear link between the use of design and improved performance in commercial businesses, and there is no reason to believe that an equivalent link doesn't exist in, say, public services, or education, or the not-for-profit sectors of the economy.

BARRIERS TO BUYING DESIGN

Design is a powerful and valuable tool. So why don't clients feel more assured about using it? It's not primarily a question of price, but of perceived need and perceived value.

There are four main barriers to purchase:

- poor knowledge and understanding about what design is, and what it does;
- little confidence in an investment in design having the desired effect;
- difficulty in finding the right designers;
- anxiety about managing the design process.

---

3   Ibid.
4   Ibid.
5   Ibid.
6   Ibid.
7   Ibid.
8   Ibid.

Poor knowledge and understanding

As an industry and as individual consultancies, we're already doing a lot to promote design and the benefits it can bring to clients' organisations. However, we don't always make it easy for ourselves. Part of the difficulty lies in the term 'design'. It covers such a wide range of activities that it's not surprising that clients find it hard to define; we sometimes find it hard ourselves. The rapid growth of the industry since the 1970s and its continuous development into new areas has left us with a dazzling number of 'design specialism' descriptions. Additionally, we don't make it easy when we constantly invent new ones.

Then there's the relationships and inter-relationships between the design industry and its closely related cousins. Is service design closer to management consultancy than it is to, say, industrial design? Does a branding consultant relate more to a marketing consultant than to a museum designer? Where does architecture stop and interior design start? No wonder clients are confused. We need to be clear ourselves before we can communicate what we do clearly to other people.

Little confidence in investment in design

We know that design provides value for money, and we are able to prove it. Not only do we have the Design Council's *Value of Design Factfinder* research and many, freely available results-based case studies, but we also have the DBA (Design Business Association) Design Effectiveness Awards scheme. Launched in 1989, it has demonstrated year after year the return on investment that a coherent, well-thought-out and professionally executed design programme can achieve.

In their marketing materials and in meetings with prospective clients, design firms tend to describe what they have done: identities, packs, brochures, websites, interiors, products. However, these are simply the facts of their interventions; they should be talking instead about the result. What was the effect of the design work? What impact did it make?

Put yourself in the shoes of a prospective client. Wouldn't you be reassured about planned expenditure on design if you were persuaded that it would provide a return?

Difficulty in finding the right designers

Clients will often use one design firm's services until something goes wrong; this is because finding a new one can be surprisingly difficult. Often, it's the designers who find the clients through their marketing activities, but clients are much more likely to base their decisions on other criteria: they will use their own past experience of working with a particular firm; they sometimes 'inherit' a designer from a previous holder of their job; they rely on suggestions from colleagues and friends; they might ask for recommendations from a respected source such as an industry body or a valued adviser; and they might use a professional search service. Clients see any one of these options as more likely to guarantee success than the lottery of responding to incoming sales approaches or looking at names in a directory; it's a damage limitation exercise.

Anxiety about managing the design process

For all but the most experienced design-buyers, the thought of managing a creative process can be a deterrent. The anticipated difficulty of working in an unfamiliar territory can be enough to put a stop to the idea of doing it at all. For example, an internet search on 'managing the design process' currently returns 17 million results; 'managing design' returns 79 million. Many contain useful guidelines and advice, but the sheer number is daunting. Professional guidelines and advice are available from some of the leading design membership and support bodies but, to access them, clients need to know where to look in the first place.

BREAKING DOWN THE BARRIERS

Whose fault is it that these barriers exist? It's ours, the design industry's, and it's our responsibility to demolish them.

We need to remove anxieties about return on investment by talking about the outcomes, or results, of our design interventions and not just the outputs, or what we've done. We need to think about alternative business models such as royalty agreements, 'shared risk, shared responsibility', and money-back guarantees against poor satisfaction. We need to encourage our trade organisations and design support bodies to promote design in the general business press, and to forge links to relevant client bodies. We need to make sure that design and its proven value are on the agenda of every business school. We need to be much better at marketing our services, so the right clients find the right designers at the right time. We need to reassure clients about the design process by explaining it more convincingly. And we need to stop giving our work away for free in pitches; if we don't value it, why would anyone else?

Finally, we need to communicate better. There is an old saying: 'Failure in communication is always the fault of the sender, not the receiver.' If we, the sellers of design services, aren't completely clear about what we are offering, how can we expect clients to be clear about what they are buying? As an industry, it's up to us to articulate our skills and benefits confidently and persuasively so that they are understood and believed.

Let's break down those barriers. Let's start right now.

1.5　The future

James Woudhuysen

To expect the unexpected shows a thoroughly modern intellect.
* Oscar Wilde (1854–1900), playwright, from 'An Ideal Husband'

ECONOMIC TRENDS AFFECTING DESIGN

The end of the first decade of the century brought a global recession, and economic uncertainty is now the New Normal. Future spending on design will remain constrained, and clients will be late to pay if their cashflows allow them to pay at all.

However, life will not be all 'downs' for client sectors or consumer spending; there will be 'ups' as well. Things will not be completely bleak for manufacturing in the West, for instance. Firstly, labour costs are not the only factor in the cost of products, or China would have completely triumphed long ago. Secondly, China's currency will continue to appreciate and, with that, its own costs will rise. Perhaps more importantly, few UK manufacturers are purely in the manufacturing business any more. Services, including financial services, will continue to form a key part of every major manufacturing business. Rolls Royce, for example, has for some time sold 'power by the hour', charging customers a fee for every hour that its engines run. Naturally, each arrangement includes the sale of an engine; but it also includes a guarantee to monitor, maintain, and – if necessary – replace that engine should it break down. In other words, rather than simply sell a sophisticated assembly of metal and carbon fibre, Rolls sells the purpose of that assembly: reliable, efficient propulsion and time in the sky.

The shift to services will persist. What the UK Government defines as 'service industries' take no fewer than 21.56 million, or nearly 84 per cent, of the 25.7 million employee jobs in Great Britain.[1] However, they account for just 76 per

---

1　Office for National Statistics, *Monthly Digest of Statistics*, 765, September 2009

cent of Gross Value Added (GVA), the measure of the value of goods and services produced.[2] It will remain hard, however, to raise productivity in services, especially in the public sector.

Persistent economic difficulties in the West will underline how important it will be for genuine innovation to triumph over new financial and business models. To the extent that it wins, innovation will encourage realism in design, and products and brands that deliver unimpeachable functional performance. Tough times will also produce design solutions that reduce costs, whether of production, operation or disposal.

DESIGN THINKING WILL CHANGE

The design of services will be more important. So will what Tim Brown, head of the innovation consultancy IDEO, calls 'design thinking': not just designing an artefact to a brief, but involving staff and users in video-recording, brainstorming, role-playing and rapid prototyping around new processes, services, interactions, forms of entertainment and ways of communicating and collaborating. Both privately delivered and public sector services will be subject to more of this treatment.

Additionally, designers will need to consider demographic changes in the population: the staff and the users consulted in design thinking will be older. The expansion of the over-65s group is particularly striking (see Figure 1.5.1).

FROM WEST TO EAST

Client work will not just shift further into services; it will shift further to the East. It will therefore be more orientated to technology than in the past, because technology is taken more seriously in the East than in the West. Design there will regain some of its historic role as the handmaiden of technological innovation.

Design will not always be sold as eco-friendly, as 'conspicuous non-consumption'. For the wealthy East in particular, design will still be aspirational. With the big proviso that it works well, people will continue to want design to relieve them from drabness. That will put a premium on aesthetics and emotions in design.

Chinese and Indian designers will become more self-confident; they will be the ones handling most of Asia's tasks in design. Brands indigenous to that continent will grow, too. To be a global brand, says Melanie McShane of consultancy Wolff Olins, you 'have to be number one in Asia'.[3]

Nevertheless, there will be a major market for Western design firms in Asia, if they build an Eastward-facing culture. It is notable that newspapers such as *China Daily* and *The Hindu* cover the West more than, say, *The Times* in the UK covers the East. Acquainting yourself fully with trends there will pay dividends.

---

2   Office for National Statistics, *Annual Abstract of Statistics*, No 145, 2009

3   McShane, quoted in Jenny Wiggins, 'World's Next Top Brands Set to Rise in the East', *Financial Times*, 19 July 2009

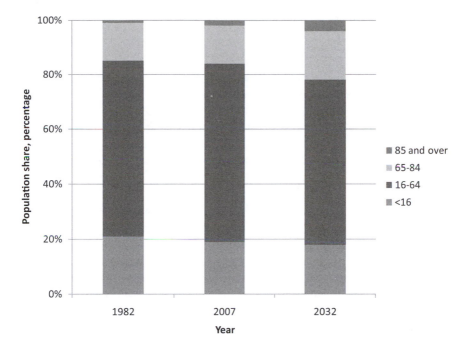

Figure 1.5.1   Population age structure, 1982–2032, UK[a]

[a] Karen Dunnell, 'Ageing and Mortality in the UK – National Statistician's Annual Article on the Population', Figure 5, p. 10, Population Trends, No 134, Winter 2008 (with kind permission of the National Archives)

THE GREEN ISSUE

The Green Economy and Green Jobs will be illusions more than real trends. In government, design and the wider culture, Green will arguably be the biggest game in town, until something radical changes that game. However, while the capitalist spirit is more than willing to go Green, the capitalist flesh finds it much more difficult. It is more likely that China and India will sell green technology to the West than countries like the UK will set an example to the world through their 'Low Carbon Economies'.

The ability of designers to be discriminating in sustainable design will do much to persuade clients. For example, people impulsively object to the export, by air, of Kenyan horticulture to Europe. However, most Kenyan produce travelling this way is, in fact, put in the holds of planes taking European tourists home from Nairobi.[4] Should Kenyan smallholders be penalised for this? Instead of fretting over different ways of calculating food miles and carbon footprints, it may be more worthwhile to design vehicles, receptacles, installation processes and educational materials to help Africa establish large-scale irrigation.

---

4   James Gikunju Muuru, 'Kenya's Flying Vegetables: Small Farmers and the Food Miles Debate', *Africa Research Institute*, 8 July 2009

THE IMPACT OF INFORMATION TECHNOLOGY

Information Technology (IT) will be more than simply 'virtual'. It will become more physical and controlling, as well as more visual. It will be about making sure that robots, wind turbines and solar panels run smoothly, and it will be about the projection of images in 3D. What the Paris-based Organisation for Economic Co-operation and Development (OECD) describes as sensors and displays'[5] will have a new prominence: sensor-based networks will facilitate the remote monitoring of patients, traffic, pollution and geological phenomena, while liquid crystal, 3D, wearable and holographic displays will multiply. More and more computers, too, will read faces, voices, gestures and handwriting.

The use of Enterprise 2.0 – Web 2.0 techniques within organisations – will grow, with Asian players setting much of the pace in consumer versions. Mobile applications will determine much of the future of other applications. Yet design studios need to avoid dumbing down their practices: facility with a mobile phone is not the Alpha and Omega of the future. The idea that young people inherently know more about IT because they are 'digital natives' – as opposed to old people, who are 'digital immigrants' – is longstanding, but misguided. To be able to play around with social media on a mobile handset is not the same as having a degree in computer science, nor is it the same as reading a book from cover to cover. The successful design leaders of the future will acquire those skills, and will encourage younger people to acquire them.

IMPLICATIONS FOR DESIGNERS

In new products and services, an orientation to realism and to engineering in its broadest sense will ensure that design's answers are substantive, not superficial. Designers will have to develop new skills in economics, business, services and technology, and this will mean understanding technologies relevant to:

- construction;
- cognitive science, medicine, biology, neuroscience;
- energy and adaptation to climate change;
- the environment (for example, agriculture, water, forests, pollution and waste).

In the future, good design will increasingly demonstrate effectiveness. A glance at the winners of the UK Design Business Association (DBA) awards for effectiveness shows that both the categories for awards and the criteria for giving them have changed over the years.

Finally, in this move to a more extensive, more advanced design offer, it will be vital not to confuse design with social engineering. To plan and develop better, more

---

5   OECD, *OECD Information Technology Outlook 2008*, 18 December 2008

effective products or services or surroundings is one thing; to take on the politicians' responsibility for solving deep-rooted social problems, however, will inevitably lead to ill-feeling if, as is likely, design alone cannot solve those problems.

Section Two:
The Business

2.1 The vision and values

Shan Preddy

You've got to have a dream; if you don't have a dream, how you gonna have a dream come true?
• Oscar Hammerstein (1898–1960), from 'South Pacific'

WHY YOU NEED A VISION

A business without a vision is a business without direction. Far too many design companies are reactive in their development and, even if they are growing and profitable, they have arrived where they are by accident. How does this happen? Very easily. Opportunities are pursued without enough questions being asked about their usefulness; projects appear from clients and are accepted, whether or not they are a good fit; senior people with specific skills and experience join or leave and this changes the company's capabilities.

Like boats without a destination and without navigation charts, businesses like this are drifting. They might have powerful engines and active crew members, but they are either going nowhere fast or heading for the wrong place. If they are lucky, they ride the high seas on favourable winds and find safe harbours when storms threaten. If they are unlucky, they circle aimlessly and sink without trace. The majority of visionless companies lie somewhere between these extremes, of course. They just dock in ports they don't like, on landmasses they never wanted to visit in the first place.

AND WHAT ABOUT VALUES?

Like nation states and individual people, businesses have values whether or not they are formally stated. Think of any market sector: one retailer, one airline, one accountancy firm or one architectural practice might have very different values from its competitors, even though some aspects of their vision, such as their commercial goals, might be identical.

Values are simply the things which are important to a business. They will not lightly be compromised, if at all, and they form an integral part of the vision. In some cases, a value can become a business's core proposition to its customers: examples of this would be an ethical, fair-trading stance, or an organic premise, or a no-questions-asked returns policy.

What's important to you right now? What do you think will be important in the future? If you own your firm as well as managing it, your business values will inevitably reflect those you and any co-owners hold in life in general.

THE BENEFIT, AND THE BUILDING BLOCKS

A good vision, and its accompanying values, will allow you to run your business more easily. Once they are in place, everything else – from major to minor decisions you will need to take – follows: finance policies; marketing strategies; recruitment criteria; IT investment; location and style of your workplace; choice of coffee and biscuit brands in the office kitchen.

They will also help you to construct your business strategy and plan. If you don't first lay down the foundations of vision and values, you will be building on quicksand.

Think of it as building blocks. Start with your vision and values and, from them, develop your overall business strategy. What will the business be doing in, say, three or five years' time? If you run a new or small company, or work in a rapidly-changing, emerging market such as digital, two years might be more realistic.

Once the two foundation building blocks of your vision and values and your business strategy are in place, you can work on strategies and plans for the separate elements in your business. Some typical design company elements (finance, product, marketing, people) are shown in Figure 2.1.1; they are explored in detail in the following chapters.

After the separate plans are completed, they can be combined to form your overall three (or five, or two) year business plan.

HOW TO DEFINE YOUR VISION AND VALUES

Get together with your management team and do a bit of imagineering. Think forwards, and then think again. One projective technique you could use is to imagine your company being written about in the press in three (or five, or two) years' time. How would it be described? Another is to imagine a fairy godmother or a genie giving you the wish to create the business exactly as you want it. The wish won't come true without a lot of input from you, but it's a good place to start.

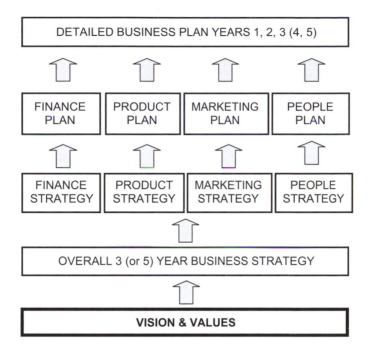

Figure 2.1.1   Strategic building blocks for business development

Source: © PREDDY&CO

To help define your vision, you could consider:

- The finances: what do you want the business's annual fee income and profit to be?
- Geographical location(s): where do you see the business being situated, in the same location as now, or somewhere else, and how many offices might you have?
- The type of work done: will it be the same as now, or different?
- The client list: who will you be doing the work for?
- Staff, if any: numbers, skills, quality, seniority.
- Your own role(s) in the business: what you, personally, will be doing.

To define your values, think about what's important to you; those are the things to work on. You could look at:

- intellectual satisfaction
- award-winning creativity
- maximising profit
- peer group recognition and respect
- market reputation
- brand image and profile

- design effectiveness
- the client sectors you will (or won't) work with
- the quality of client relationships
- your levels of client service
- staff development
- environmental sustainability
- community and charitable activities – design or broader
- leisure time
- fun.

Setting the vision and values for a business is the responsibility of the owner, Partners or Directors. Unless you work alone, it should be a team effort, but only up to a point. Employees, together with any shareholders or investors who are not directly involved in running the firm, only need to be informed – and inspired – once the full business strategy and plans have been developed. Democratic vision-setting-by-committee can be disastrous, leading to division of opinions and resulting in inactivity.

REALITY CHECKS

Once you've drafted your vision and values, you will need to ask yourself whether they are achievable. If necessary, ask a trusted external consultant or expert to work with you. Your vision needs to be ambitious, challenging and, ideally, exciting to the point of being just a little scary. But it also needs to be realistic. Otherwise, you will become frustrated and dispirited if you don't achieve it.

Your vision and values will change when external factors change and when unexpected opportunities or challenges occur. The market, the economy, your competitors and your clients will all influence them. Revisit and confirm them regularly, at least annually and preferably every six months; the newer the business, the more frequently you'll need to do it. In very volatile economic trading environments such as rapid market growth or economic recession, review them monthly.

You can tell if your vision and values are getting a bit murky when you can't describe them easily and convincingly to someone else, or when you just can't get excited about them anymore. And you'll know when they are clear. That's when you are brave enough to turn down work – any work, even the attractive and profitable stuff – which doesn't help you to achieve it. Voyage to Mombasa? No, thanks. This boat's heading for Rio.

2.2 The culture

Shan Preddy

The man ain't got no culture.
- Paul Simon (b. 1941) and Art Garfunkel (b. 1941) from 'A Simple Desultory Philippic'

PLANNED OR ACCIDENTAL?

Endlessly fascinating to outsiders and almost invisible to insiders, a business's culture develops from its vision and values. It is the job of the management team to make sure it is as it should be, influencing it as appropriate and correcting it whenever needed.

From the way you run your business and the tone of voice of your marketing materials, to your attitude to paying bills, to the way you identify your washrooms, everything you do – absolutely everything – says something about your business.

Some corporate cultures and personalities are planned and actively driven; others will grow organically. Most are, of course, a mixture of the two. If your business's culture is not as you want it to be, change it. If it is, make sure you maintain, grow and develop it as both you and external factors change. If your culture is exactly the same now as it was, say, ten years ago, it could be overdue for a refit.

If you don't know what your corporate culture really is, try asking an independent consultant to carry out an expert 360° survey among your clients, prospects, staff and suppliers. The results can be enlightening.

THEY'RE NOT MOVING, IT MUST'VE CRASHED

WHO CARES?

You and your management team, for a start. Are you proud of your business? Inspired by it? Leaping-out-of-bed excited by it? Would you want to work there if you didn't have to?

Your staff will be significantly influenced by your culture. Their work needs to be challenging and satisfying, of course, and they need to be in possession of the right remuneration package. But over and above that, your company's culture will either motivate them or demotivate them. To paraphrase Oscar Wilde's Lady Bracknell: to lose good staff because they win the lottery and decide to retire early may be regarded as a misfortune; to lose them because they don't like your culture looks like carelessness.

And what about recruiting new staff? It's not only your snazzy ads, animated website and the headhunter's recommendation that will influence possible future employees. The design sector is a very small world, and people – including your current and former staff – will talk. All it takes is 'it's not really a happy place at the moment' or 'it's not very professionally run' to dissuade people from applying for a job, let alone joining you.

Clients and prospects will be influenced by your culture as well as by your skills, capabilities and experience. In fact, if all things are equal at the selection stage – and when design buyers have done their job properly, all things should be equal – it will be the culture and personality of the relevant design businesses which influence the appointment.

Finally, your extended commercial network, including strategic alliances, freelancers and suppliers, will be affected by your culture and personality, even if it's only for a short time. They can, of course, escape whenever it suits them by simply being, 'with great regret, too busy to help'. And that's the problem: the best networkers and freelancers and suppliers will favour the businesses whose culture they like. They will prioritise working for them, and will be prepared to go that extra mile. If the people you want to work with are always mysteriously unavailable, or half-hearted in their work for you, it might be worth holding a mirror up to your own culture.

DOING IT YOUR WAY

Most design companies of any size will have a 'welcome pack' or manual for new joiners. They vary in content and style, but tend to cover things like company structure, staff details and examples of paperwork procedures such as how to complete time sheets, expenses forms and so on. Some also include useful local information, like the best place to buy sandwiches at lunchtime.

However, in every company of every size, there is also an unwritten rulebook: let's call it 'This Is The Way We Do Things Around Here'. These rules for behaviour – good or bad – are initially devised by the leaders of the business, and then demonstrated on a daily basis by their attitude and behaviour. They filter down through every team member, until the newest arrival turns to the person next to them and asks how something should be done.

Your unwritten rules will derive from example, not instruction. If, after a particularly difficult conversation with a client, a senior manager puts the phone down with a grimace and an expletive or two, he or she is hardly in a position to criticise a more junior staff member for inappropriate attitude towards client service. In business management, there is no place for 'do as I say but not what I do': it must be 'do as I say and also as I do'.

One problem we face in our sector is that it is inexpensive and easy to launch a design business, and many firms are run by young, ambitious, dynamic people who have had little experience of being an employee, let alone an employer. Or, if they have spent time working for other people, it was so many years ago that they've forgotten what it feels like. In addition, the owners of design businesses are, by definition, entrepreneurial in nature; they are initiative-takers and used to taking unilateral decisions. As a result, they sometimes find it hard to empathise with their employees and the issues they face. To them, the 'rules' are obvious; to their staff, however, they might seem unclear at best and, at worst, contradictory. If you fit into this category, take care with the unwritten messages you might be sending to your team members.

When investigating your rulebooks – both written and unwritten – there is no limit to the areas you might consider. There are the 'macro policies': staff welfare; what and how you charge clients for your work; your attitude to waste management; fire drill. And there are the 'micro policies': how the phone is answered; general time keeping; washing up; birthday conventions. Large or small, good or bad, planned or unplanned: if it relates to your business, it forms your culture.

THE COMPANY THAT PLAYS TOGETHER STAYS TOGETHER

The social elements of a business's culture are important; they help to reinforce and maintain team relationships and allow people to relax away from the working environment.

It's important to cover both the spontaneous trip to the pub to celebrate a new project win and the scheduled events which are an integral part of your business, such as a summer picnic or an annual winter party. Some companies organise weekend trips away. If you are asking people to give up their free time, you will need to take a policy decision about the inclusion or otherwise of social partners. If you decide on a staff-only invitation, make sure you don't penalise any partnered employees who choose not to come.

You can also spread invitations to parties and events to your clients, your alliance networkers and your suppliers as well as your staff. After all, these people make up a significant element of your business's culture and personality, and they all influence each other as well as you.

And then there are the sporting events. Could you have a champion baseball team just waiting to be discovered? Tiddlywinks? Quizzes? By sponsoring a team event, you can enjoy the benefits of teamwork training outside of the normal working environment without having to send everyone on a week's outward bound course. Make sure that anyone who doesn't want to play an active part in the team is encouraged to participate as a supporter, or organiser, or even just an observer. Aim for inclusivity and diversity.

BRAIN FOOD AND BODY FOOD

Does your business have a 'learning culture'? As well as formal training programmes, ongoing CPD (continuing professional development) is important, and CPD can include observing, analysing, thinking and sharing. Brain food keeps the grey cells – and the more colourful creative cells – refreshed and active.

Some design businesses have art galleries in their reception areas, which stimulate the team and attract visitors; they can even make a profit. Others organise staff trips to other cities or countries, using them as 'incentive-and-reward' for good performance as well as learning opportunities. Most firms can't afford the time and money to do this, but there is a lot you can do on a smaller scale. What about visits to museums, galleries and exhibitions? Or trips to films and concerts? Outings, perhaps: to shops if you work in retail or packaging; to businesses if in identity and service design; to hotels, restaurants and theme-parks if in leisure markets. One of the great drivers of creativity is a burning curiosity about everything. Why not throw a little fuel on the fire? Make sure you get your money's worth, however. Ask staff to report back afterwards with a presentation of what they have observed and learned in a 'show and tell' session, so that everyone else can learn something as well, and store any relevant materials in your central resource library.

Finally, don't forget body food. Some of the world's larger creative businesses have their own in-house cafés, where people can meet over good, nutritious food at subsidised costs at breakfast, coffee, lunch and tea, and occasionally evenings as well.

If you don't have a café but your business is large enough to have one, why not investigate the feasibility? You will need to work out the 'benefit-in-kind' tax implications with your financial advisers as well as the cost of the café itself. If you're not big enough to make a café realistic, how about dedicating an area of your offices to a place where people can munch their lunchtime sandwiches together instead of going out or sitting isolated at their desks checking their social media messages? Either option will return huge benefits of informal working and relationship-building, as well as encouraging a time-efficient and, in the case of a café, properly-fed workforce.

2.3   The product

Shan Preddy

If a man write a better book, preach a better sermon, or make a better mousetrap than his neighbour, though he build his house in the woods, the world will beat a path to his door.
• Ralph Waldo Emerson (1803–82), essayist, philosopher and poet

MOUSETRAPS AND MYTHS

The statement from Ralph Waldo Emerson above lingers on as a famous concept in business circles. It is known, unsurprisingly, as 'the better mousetrap'. If your product is better than anyone else's, it claims, that's all you need to do.

It is, however, something of a myth, and – like most good myths – it refuses to go away. The premise clearly doesn't hold water these days, and perhaps never did. There are many examples of successful businesses which have inferior products, and there have always been great products and services which don't succeed commercially.

Nevertheless, it is the case that you will be much more likely to fail if your product is poorer than your competitors' products. No disappointed customer ever bought an unsatisfactory product twice from the same source and, worse, no disappointed customer ever lied about it to someone else. We are many times more likely to tell others about our displeasure with a business or personal purchase than we are about our pleasure. Like it or not, humans are good at complaining.

Another lingering myth is that a business's greatest asset is its people. They are important, of course, but every individual – even the owner – is replaceable. A business's greatest asset is its good reputation, and while there are many elements which go to make up that reputation (including, of course, the behaviour and capabilities of its people), the 'product' or 'service' forms the core. No one sets out to make mistakes, but the truth is that if your product is impeccable, you're likely to be forgiven for them. If your basic product is poor, on the other hand, every tiny error will be held against you.

A high-quality product is a wonderful asset. It will help to attract new business prospects and satisfy existing clients. It will attract new staff and retain existing employees. In fact, it will almost do your marketing and recruitment for you. But, like all assets, it needs to be cared for, maintained and developed. Think of it like a living organism: without nurture, it will die.

THE NURTURING

So what are these 'organisms' in the design sector and how do you nurture them? Whichever design specialism you embrace, they are the three main elements of your work:

1. strategic thinking;
2. creativity and innovation;
3. production and delivery.

To be successful, each element needs to be equally strong as the others, and they all need to be wrapped up in expert client service, faultless business administration and inspirational leadership.

Here are a few 'product' questions you can raise with your management team:

- Are you paying as much attention to your product as you are to the rest of your business, such as finance, law and HR?
- When did you last invest the time, budget and energy in away-days or events for your teams with no other objective than product improvement?
- How much time and money are you investing in staff training and skills updating on your product?
- Are you encouraging your staff to get out to design events, lectures, exhibitions?
- Are you running regular 'show-and-tell' sessions internally, where all of your staff can hear about a project from one of their colleagues, and learn from it?
- Are you running regular 'creative inspiration' sessions, where colleagues talk to each other about what inspires them, perhaps over a beer or a breakfast?
- Whose job is it in your business to keep an eye on product quality?
- When did you last do a formal benchmarking analysis of how your product stacks up against that of your direct competitors?
- When did you last find out what your clients and prospects want and expect, so you can adjust your product to match?
- Are you keeping abreast of market trends and innovations? Or even overtaking them?

HURDLES AND EXPECTATIONS

The hurdles in product and service provision get higher and higher and, once they have been raised, they will never be lowered.

Imagine you ran a small hotel. Some years ago, you could get away without providing ensuite bathroom facilities: now, even the tiniest of B&Bs seem to offer individual toiletries, TVs with DVD players and in-room tea-making equipment. How long will it be before fluffy bathrobes and slippers become as normal as they are in luxury hotels? And then what will luxury hotels have to offer to earn their keep?

Your own 'hurdles' will be raised partly by your own actions, partly by clients' demands, partly by your competitors and partly by activities in the worldwide marketplace. Think about the three product elements mentioned earlier. In the design sector, there was a time when 'creativity and innovation' was enough. The clients did the 'strategic thinking' part, and a few slips in 'production and delivery' were not only accepted, but expected. In fact, wise clients always used to include time and budget contingencies in their plans. Now, they rightly expect perfection in all three. Why? Because that is how we have positioned ourselves, as consultants charging top fees.

We have set the expectations ourselves, and we have raised those hurdles. At the moment, perfection in the three product elements is just the basic entry-level for a serious design business. You and your management team should be keeping a very close eye on the levels of future hurdles, and making sure your product is fit for the race.

BENCHMARKING

There are a number of things you can do to benchmark your business against the marketplace. You can carry out desk research, such as reading books and publications. You can analyse creative and effectiveness award winners. You can investigate what related business sectors such as advertising, architecture and technology do. You can carry out a survey among your clients, prospects, employees, freelancers and suppliers to see how you compare with other design firms they know. You could even consider starting a formal benchmarking system with a similarly sized, but not directly competitive, company: if you work with an external business adviser, why not discuss this with them?

If, after analysis, you decide that your product isn't as good as it needs to be, you will need to decide whether you can improve it organically, or will need to form strategic alliances with other, differently skilled businesses.

Make a habit of constantly benchmarking your business, and make sure that you list product quality as a regular item on your management meeting's agenda. As well as thinking about new product development, you will raise internal awareness of the importance of actively driving existing product development.

Do what you do best. Then work on doing it even better.

2.4   The business journey

Adrian Rasdall

If you are going through Hell, keep going.
• Sir Winston Churchill (1874–1965), politician and statesman

BEYOND THE START-UP

The adrenalin rush of starting a company is likely to ebb as you realise you have created a sustainable business. From here the task is to build your agency to the size that matches your ambitions, through organic growth, merger and acquisition, and then eventually to make your exit.

By forming excellent relationships with a raft of clients and working hard to win new business, you have reduced your dependency on one or two customers. Now there is a stream of work flowing into the agency, with a balance of resource to manage the work to a very high standard. The right processes and strict financial controls are in place, and the business is generating a comfortable profit. It would not be unreasonable to feel less vulnerable and happier with the world.

This is when you have to be true to your ambition. It's possible to have a highly successful and fruitful career running a £1.5m, tightly managed business, aiming for very small growth and a constant team of committed staff. If that is your goal, then it is important to resist the pressures around you to grow for growth's sake. It's OK to be small and profitable.

However, for many people standing still in business isn't an option. Driving forward and building a bigger and better agency is perceived as simply the next stage of the business adventure.

HOW DO YOU GROW AND DEVELOP WHAT YOU HAVE?

The key word is plan. Just running helter-skelter for more business and recruiting more staff usually ends in tears.

Look at what effect more revenue would have on your annual budget. Say you plan to grow turnover by 20 per cent. What would be the effect on staff and office space? Growth needs financing, so is the company sufficiently capitalised?

Consider also if more work would put a strain on the team and endanger current client relationships. The risk is that you bring in 20 per cent more work but lose 20 per cent of your current client business.

So to plan for growth it is first necessary to increase resources, both in quantity and quality. This is a bold move and requires investment. In the short term you could see a fall in profits while you are growing and developing the company. This is the next stage in the business cycle-growth, followed by consolidation – as the business regains its equilibrium and maximises profits.

Quite often, though, growth is unplanned. A huge win can transform an agency overnight, putting stress on its infrastructure. This can be a threat as well as an exciting opportunity. When a company overheats and there is way more revenue than resource, the business can overtrade, and you could lose control.

It is critical to stand back and recognise what is going on. By acting swiftly to either bring in more resource, which impacts on your margin, or negotiate longer lead times with your clients, you can slow the company down and thereby regain control.

The idea is to grow and grow, not grow then shrink, then grow again. This puts too much strain on everyone.

MERGERS AND ACQUISITIONS

Mergers

As an alternative to organic growth, opportunities may arise to merge your agency with another business. If all goes well you can end up with a larger market presence, a stronger management team and a much enhanced balance sheet.

Mergers have worked very well in the worlds of law and accountancy, where clients and revenue are attached primarily to partners. A merger becomes a restructuring of the partnership arrangement under one name. This is highly democratic and should deliver greater value to clients with more disciplines available to them.

However, for many this approach is fraught with difficulty and not for the faint-hearted. The usual areas of contention are around the name and leadership of what should be an equal partnership. Generally the largest, longest established and best-known wins. The issue is more about emotions than realities and a pragmatic approach must be applied. If all else fails then an amalgamation of names may resolve the issue, although a combination of leaders seldom works and can lead to corporate schizophrenia.

Whenever you are considering a merger it wise to begin with the end. What would these two, streamlined operations look like merged and how will they appear to your clients? Does it really make sense? If cost saving is an issue, will it really deliver benefits?

Deals have a way of distorting the original plan as they progress. So, when all parties have agreed a model, keep referring back to that model throughout the merger process.

Acquisitions

A less democratic approach to non-organic growth is the acquisition. Here, there is a definite buyer and seller.

It is always wise to avoid buying a company just for the turnover and profit. There should be much deeper reasons, such as:

- clients you covet and would take ages to develop yourself;
- a geographic advantage;
- technology that would give you a competitive advantage.

When you have made the overtures to a company or someone has approached you, it is imperative that you select appropriate advisors to guide and protect you. The right lawyers and accountants can aid you through the nightmare of valuations, due diligence, negotiations, renegotiations, tax and employment issues.

If you have not yet formed solid relationships with professionals who specialise in mergers and acquisitions, then ask around for referrals and shortlist three law and accountancy firms. It's common practice to hold a 'beauty parade', where potential clients choose professionals with the most sector experience and a style that suits.

Not all deals reach completion, as problems can be thrown up at any stage. However, as your confidence grows that the deal will happen, start planning and even act as if the deal is done. Develop relationships with all the key managers in the target company, and try to resolve issues before you sign the papers. At all times concentrate on how this deal will be communicated to clients and staff. Nobody likes surprises!

SELLING YOUR BUSINESS TO OTHERS

Third-party acquisition

As you build up your business with a good team and effective client management, the core value of your company will increase. It should not be a surprise that your

NEWARK CAMPUS LIBRARY - COTC

business shows up on competitors' radar and becomes a target for acquisition itself.

When an approach comes from an agent or directly from the interested party it is very flattering and should be taken seriously. Be aware, though, that the process of talking about a sale is very time-consuming and can impact on the day-to-day running of the company.

If you are the sole shareholder the process is straightforward. If there is more than one owner, the situation is more complicated. It is important to acknowledge that people are at different stages of their lives and while the disruption of a sale of the company may be exciting to some, it can be threatening to others. Taking time to explore the needs of the individuals before the discussions begin ensures a united team.

First, ascertain the identity of the interested party and why they think there is a fit between the two companies. If your immediate reaction is negative, then it is better to say so at once. If you think the deal has potential, spend time with the principals and listen to their plans for your company. Remember that price is not everything. A deal that adversely affects staff morale will affect client relationships and therefore the future success of the business.

Your role in the agency may not end if the business is acquired. If you and other principals work in the business and have client relationships, a change of ownership could affect the value. Your company will be attractive because of your track record, but will be bought for its future earnings. That means most buyers will prefer to buy the company over a period of years to mitigate their risk. They pay an amount of cash up front, with agreed amounts released if certain targets are met. If the targets are missed then the payments are not made and therefore the sale price reduced.

This is called an 'earn out', with the principals being given a fixed-term service agreement to cover the earn out period. It ties the principals into the company for a number of years until the sale is complete.

As with all deals, it is your advisors who will guide you through this process and act for you to achieve the very best sales price with the most reasonable conditions.

Management buy out

The clever principal continually strives to hire the best people and invest in developing a strong management team. As the company grows the management team expects to play a more dynamic role in running the company.

Ultimately, there can come a time when the management feel ready to approach the principals with a suggestion that they would like to instigate a Management Buy Out (MBO).

This is a time for plain talking. An MBO can be a very successful route to a transfer of ownership, as long as the tricky question of value can be agreed. However, one of the most devastating occurrences a business can suffer is a failed MBO. When the management and owners fall out, there is a very serious schism, which can generally only be adjudicated by an outsider.

An alternative approach is a Buy In Management Buy Out (BIMBO) where an experienced outsider buys into the agency, and then controls the MBO from the inside and negotiates on behalf of the team.

YOUR OWN EXIT STRATEGY

Eventually you will want to leave the business – to take a new direction or to retire altogether. You will need to plan your exit strategy.

A business is made up of two entities: assets on the balance and a cash generator. While you consider how to decouple yourself from the assets, it's important to remember the day-to-day business of making money.

Much will depend on what sort of leader you are when you decide to move on – a player manager or as a sideline manager?

As a player manager you are completely involved in every aspect of the agency, which relies on you to win work, manage clients and/or produce killer creativity. Any reduction in your involvement will show up negatively in the figures. To move away from being a player manager takes time, courage and patience.

Being a sideline manger is all about building a team and letting them work together while you support their strengths and help them address their weaknesses.

As ever, this process relies as much on the quality of people you hire as your own attitude. You cannot remove yourself from responsibility in your business simply by delegating functions to others. The transfer of responsibility will only come if you surround yourself with people who actually crave that responsibility. By also creating an environment where people feel supported, you can grow the business beyond yourself.

As the strength of team grows, you can start to groom your successor. Choosing the right person is one of the most difficult processes and it is vital to put the needs of the agency first. In a family business, children may seem the obvious choice, but may not actually have the specific skills for running a business. Dividing your role into skill bites and spreading them across a management team may prove a more viable route.

Handing over the reins when you go on vacation offers candidates the opportunity to demonstrate their expertise, but be clear about what roles you are promising. To raise expectations only to change your mind can crush enthusiasm and disrupt the smooth running of the agency.

How quickly and how completely you leave the business is your choice. With effective planning, you can transfer management and ownership smoothly, assured that the business will continue to move forward with highly capable new leadership.

2.5 The business structure

Peers de Trensé

A place for everyone and everyone in their place.
- Adapted from congregational minister Charles A Goodrich's (1790–1862) motto 'Have a place for every thing, and keep every thing in its proper place'

WHO DOES WHAT?

A well-organised structure enables members of a design company to understand where they fit in, and what purpose they serve within the organisation. It provides the framework for companies to develop and deliver their offer in a timely, cost-effective manner, without destroying any of the raw energy and creativity. It allows companies with whom they do business, both clients and suppliers, to understand the company and who they relate to within it.

One definition of structure is: 'The organisation of a society or other group and the relation between its members determining its working.'

Design companies would not exist without clients, and it's obvious that the structure of such organisations should reflect the demands and requirements of the client base. Some clients want to deal directly with designers, others prefer a more formal and structured company, and require account handlers or project managers.

However, it's your agency. What you put in place has to deliver profit, create interesting careers and opportunities for the people who work with you, and operate efficiently to produce consistently high standards of work. Although clients are necessary, they should never be allowed to dictate to you how you operate your company.

Motivation and direction are two critical management tools that can help growth and build profitability. This process starts at the very top, from the managing director down to the intern, with every person in the business implicitly understanding what he or she should be doing and what is required of them. Not just for each project, but also in their wider roles as part of growing and developing the business. This is about involvement and team spirit.

Roles and responsibilities are evolutionary, require planning and need reviewing from time to time, at least once a year. The key word here is review because once you have set the targets and parameters and agreed them with each person, you have a basis on which to measure, judge and reward. You eliminate duplication of effort, and can play to strength and character rather than job title. Someone who is good with people may not be good with process and vice versa. Much can be learnt from upward reviews where staff take management to task.

Structure is essential whatever the size of the company. Structure equals efficiency and purpose. This is important for employees who will see a career path ahead of them, promotion and the rewards that go with it. It's also important for managers who can measure performance and judge ability, and identify training opportunities to bring people on, or to teach them new skills.

A good structure helps deliver a good return on investment and creates a highly motivated and energised team acting as one, rather than as individuals. This shows in the work that is produced and in the client meetings that are held where everyone has a voice and a function.

WHO RUNS THE SHIP, AN AUTOCRAT OR A DEMOCRAT?

At the head of every design company is a leader with a management style. Take any half dozen exemplary design consultancies and you will find as many different management and leadership styles, each claiming to be the model for a successful and dynamic business. Indeed they can be, but which works best, and for whom? The company or the employees, and are they all as good as each other? A designer moving from one consultancy to another could well experience all of them in a short space of time.

Leadership and management styles are either inherent in the psyche of the person, or have to be learnt very quickly, or bought and brought in. The different styles are not hard to identify.

There's the entrepreneur, or the creative, both of whom might want do what they are best at, rather than manage and lead. Then there's the professional manager, Master of Business Administration (MBA) or equivalently trained, full of process and procedure, and possibly slightly unemotional. Or the home grown manager, who's had to learn at the coal face, making it up as he or she goes along, and making mistakes too.

So what makes for a good management style? Would you rather work in a dictatorship, where everyone knows their place and there's that certain frisson when the boss strides in, or work in a relaxed, democratic environment, where everyone has a say about the place, and the boss ambles in?

The worst of each of these scenarios is anarchy in the dictatorship, and chaos in the democracy. The best are the authoritarian leader who is single-minded and has the best interests of the company at heart, driving it forward, and the democrat who can hold together, motivate and represent the wishes of the people to grow and develop the business.

There is also the 'Collective' which always seems to end in tears: oh, and would the last person out please turn the light off?

Some important characteristics of leadership are charisma and personality: not everyone is lucky enough to possess these qualities. The most important quality of all however, is respect, and this has to be earned, usually by leading from the front. Earn it, and you will gain respect for what you do and what you say. Frankly, people will be much more inclined to follow you whatever your leadership style.

IS THE SUM OF THE PARTS GREATER THAN THE WHOLE?

Which is best for an agency, designers who are all-rounders or teams of specialists?

How often have you heard this? 'One day I'm going to have my own design company, and it's going to be full of creative people producing bright ideas and stunning work for brands that share the same ideals.'

This is the dream that many designers have, which some have turned into reality. At this stage it's purely a creative enterprise. There are several design companies that have pursued this ideal relentlessly and successfully. The purity of the concept is a wonderful ideal and of course many clients just love dealing directly and only with creative people.

It's somewhat of a perverse and contrary idea, however, given that rather than devoting all their time and energy to creativity, designers have perforce to be their own account manager with all that it entails: part planner, part strategist, part accountant, part client service, part this, part that.

From a business point of view, having a purely creative team is possibly easier and more cost effective to manage, but recruiting a creative who is capable of multitasking as an all rounder is not always easy, and there is an inherent danger of creating a series of one-man bands, each operating in its own ivory tower.

This particular model works well in a start-up situation or in a collective. However, the design industry recognises, and clients generally demand, a three-stage delivery process of strategy, creativity and implementation, the latter more often than not with multichannel creative interpretations.

This process calls for teams with specialist skills; in larger agencies this can often consist of a triumvirate of planner, creative and account person each with very clearly defined roles. The creative should be in his/her element, not having to be involved with housekeeping, and being given what all creatives desire, a tight brief. With this model the sum of the parts are genuinely greater than the whole.

The designers are happy because, unless they work on a very large account, they are more likely to enjoy a varied diet of clients and they have colleagues to bounce ideas off. And the clients are happy, getting such professional attention from three specialists.

THE TEAM: PERMANENT OR FREELANCE?

A wise old financial guru once said, 'watch fixed overheads, keep them as low, and as flexible as is possible' but of course the biggest expense in a design company is its people.

Enter the freelance, the name that originates literally from a mercenary cavalry lancer, hired for a specific battle or war. The cavalry is always welcome in design companies: we are, after all, primarily a project-based industry having to deal with skirmish after skirmish.

Freelancers are hired for a number of reasons: specialist expertise; when times are busy; maternity relief; in times of uncertainty; or because the financial model forbids hiring any additional permanent staff. What do they bring to the party?

Flexibility is the big bonus and, although they can be more expensive, they can be turned on and off like a tap. No notice period, redundancy payment, and so on. They also bring a wealth of experience of working in other, possibly larger agencies, including your competitors. Learn from them, how they work and how they present their work. Freelancers bring intelligence. There's no suggestion here of broken confidences, but you'd be surprised at what you can pick up about people, clients and the levels of morale in other design companies where they have previously worked.

Freelancers will become more important for design companies that morph into other areas of communication: broadcast, computer generated imagery (CGI), research, sonic branding and so on, where specialist expertise needs to bought in. This is generally known as the 'Hollywood model', where you assemble around you the skills to deliver the project.

However, the real character of every design company lies in creating a dynamic, skilled and permanent team of experts, the people and personalities that make up your brand. Clients want a long-term relationship so they can build a rapport, have confidence and trust in the team and know that the team is acquiring vital brand and sector knowledge. This is unlikely to happen with new faces at every other meeting. Permanent staff are the lifeblood of the design company; they are responsible for its reputation and ultimately for other designers wanting to work there.

They have other responsibilities too, such as helping to build up morale, evangelising about the business, and, in all but the smallest of agencies, helping to create a hierarchy where seniors bring on the juniors and juniors aspire to be seniors, in one big happy family.

HOW BIG IS YOUR TEAM? HOW BIG DO YOU WANT IT TO BE?

Being part of an extended network or operating within a strategic partnership, allows a local and specialised design business to punch above its weight, extend its offer through wider skill sets, and reach out to the world.

The big advantage is that it gives you the ability to field anything that the client throws at you, anywhere. It allows you be involved with the whole project, rather than parts of it, local and global. If you offer pure design, who does the brand strategy? If your creative solution needs to work in Japan, who makes sure that it's a cultural fit and is understood? With links, partnerships, a network, all these things are possible. Being part of a network means you can refer the client to a trusted specialist. Word of mouth is the most powerful form of recommendation and so much more credible. Having a strategic partnership allows you to compete with the bigger design companies, which may have several specialist divisions and a global operation.

Perhaps the biggest benefit of an alliance or a closer tie is the opportunity of cross referral. If you are linked to, say, four complementary skills or regions, there is a fourfold chance of new business introductions. The companies to which you are linked will expect you to reciprocate.

Who to partner with? Look at your offer and top and tail. Which discipline comes before, and which after? Track your clients and projects to see what part of the process or project you are not being given. Many design companies have links with PR companies, a natural fit where each company can introduce business to the other.

What to expect financially? There's money to be made. Agree how successful business leads should be rewarded. A one-off introductory fee or a percentage of the fee value of the project? Agree how you might collaborate, and who will lead the project.

On another level, make good use of business colleagues and suppliers. Promote them on your website: writers, photographers, artists, gurus, printers, bloggers, animators, or just people who have inspired you. They will be thrilled to be included. Suddenly your design company looks twice the size and will appear three times as interesting and, hopefully, four times as successful.

2.6   The money (part one)

Mandy Merron

You only find out who's swimming naked when the tide goes out.
• Warren Buffet (b1930), investor and philanthropist

WHY PLAN YOUR FINANCES?

With a buoyant market and a good creative product, there are times when it is relatively easy to run a design business. Work comes in, clients approve budgets and pay bills, banks lend money when it's needed and the company can hire the right staff. In such times, management teams can jog along and turn in a modest profit without thinking too hard about the financial structure of the business. Does it matter that margins are not as high as they should be? Or that the assets in the business don't work as hard as they should? Or that the capital base of the business is not high enough? Yes, because the owners will not be getting the most out of their asset and, in more difficult economic circumstances, the business will be more likely than its professionally run peers to fail.

The three key aspects of managing profits in a business are: (i) planning, (ii) taking action and (iii) measuring the results (see Figure 2.6.1).

THE FAMOUS DESIGNER:

BUSINESS PLANNING

Planning gives a context within which to assess performance. If a design consultancy generates a profit of £200,000 when hoping for £200,000, the management team will have delivered on budget and will be happy. If they were hoping for £500,000, however, this will be a disappointing result.

Every business should have a business plan. This should be a working document used to set business and financial goals, to provide a context for evaluating

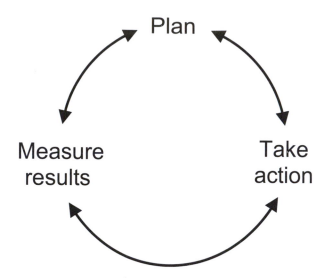

Figure 2.6.1   The profit management cycle

Source: © Kingston Smith W1

performance, to consider and plan for factors which will affect trade, to assess likely outcomes and responses and to identify key performance indicators (KPIs).

Not all KPIs will be financial, and it helps to bring them together in an executive summary, often referred to as a 'dashboard'.

Which financial performance measures matter? In a design business there are four key headings:

- *Income pipeline:* how far and how much known and likely business is coming through.
- *Profit margins:* comparing profit and costs with revenue.
- *Productivity statistics:* revenue and costs per head as well as utilisation rates, or the proportion of time spent on client work.
- *Balance sheet statistics:* cash balance versus overdraft level; cash resources versus overheads.

CREATING A BUSINESS PLAN

Although this chapter deals with financial plans, it's worth remembering that they sit within a broader business plan, which can be split into three 'M's:

- *Market*: the business offer; where the firm sits versus the competition; the state of the marketplace.
- *Manpower*: the people needed for delivery to clients, with roles and responsibilities; the resources (like premises and IT) needed to support them.

- *Money*: the pricing policy, and how clients will be charged (project fees, retainers); the mark-up on recharged costs; the hours which could be worked on client business, and how many hours are likely to be worked on client business; future business costs, revenue and cashflow.

PLANNING 'THE MONEY'

Financial forecasting is an iterative process. Costs are known and relatively easy to predict. Income is harder to predict, especially for designers. Separately estimating costs and income usually leads to a gap – often a forecasted loss. It is tempting to fill this gap with a new business target, but this can be dangerous and every income and cost assumption needs to be challenged and tested. Usually both forecast income and forecast costs are revised until an acceptable profit is predicted.

In producing forecasts, it is very important to run two or three versions which answer 'what if?' questions such as:

- What if fee income is 10 per cent lower than we think?
- What if we grow by 25 per cent not 15 per cent?
- What if clients take a month longer to pay us than we think?

By running spreadsheets which look at these different possibilities, management can get a good feel for what they would need to do in those circumstances.

PLANNING PROFIT

Once the first working plan has been produced the underlying assumptions need to be challenged. For example:

- Is productivity high enough?
- If not, why? And how can we change that?
- How else can we increase profit?
- Can efficiency and 'right first time' process be improved?
- Is it possible to charge more?
- Is there a line of work which is particularly profitable or unprofitable?
- Should the business focus more or less on those areas?
- Is the business dependent on one or two key clients and if so how can it diversify?

The action generated will be company-wide and will include looking at efficiencies in process, approaches to client handling, client contracts, estimation procedure and charging models among other areas.

Without the discipline of a business plan, significant opportunities to improve performance can be ignored.

PLANNING CASHFLOW

Cash is the oil which enables a business machine to keep turning, and design businesses can run out of cash before they run out of profit. Buying fixed assets, paying rent deposits and returning VAT payments won't affect profit, but they will have a significant impact on cash.

Producing a cashflow forecast helps to identify pressure points such as quarter ends when a rent payment might coincide with a VAT payment, and it will give management teams the chance to take actions like arranging a short-term overdraft extension with the bank to cover a peak need.

Growth needs cash, and faster growth needs more cash, to fund the gap between paying staff to do the work and eventually being paid by the client (see Figure 2.6.2).

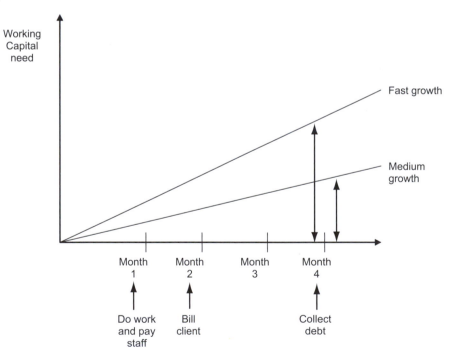

Figure 2.6.2   Growth and cash requirements

Source: © Kingston Smith W1

In a design business, there is only limited scope to manage cash. The two biggest overheads are people and premises, and it is not usually possible to extend payment terms for either. How clients are billed and managed does, however, have a significant impact. Many consultancies bill an element in advance, while others bill monthly based on progress: payment terms should be expressly discussed and agreed in the client contract.

Credit checks should always be run before credit is extended, and any clients where cash collection may be difficult – such as overseas clients – should be billed and the cash collected in advance of the work.

RAISING INVESTMENT FROM BANKS

Design consultancies can need significant cash for items such as buying capital assets, following business development opportunities, setting up abroad, company acquisitions or buying out departing shareholders.

There are various ways to raise funds but the basic rule is to match the type of funding to the type of expenditure. Companies shouldn't use cash to buy capital assets unless they are sitting on a cash mountain, and borrowing arrangements should match the type of expenditure. Just as people don't buy a house using an overdraft, companies shouldn't use short-term borrowing arrangements to buy long-term assets such as another company.

Working capital is the cash needed to fund day-to-day trading activities. This is the sort of finance provided by banks, either as an overdraft or as invoice-discounting. Typically an overdraft is less expensive but invoice-discounting can raise more cash for the business.

Overdrafts are generally well understood. Banks will need security in the form of good trade debts and usually want any lending they advance to be covered two and half to three times by trade debts. Often, banks will ask for additional security in the form of personal guarantees from the directors.

In undisclosed invoice-discounting, the bank effectively buys the company's debts for cash and the company then collects the cash on behalf of the bank. Disclosed invoice-discounting, or factoring, involves the bank or factor collecting the debts itself and so effectively running the design business's debtor book. Banks won't take on debts which are not contractually enforceable so invoices for stage payments, up-front payments or retainer fees can be difficult to invoice-discount.

For longer-term projects bank funding can be available in the form of loans. Banks need to understand how easily the business will be able to repay the loan interest, and when they can expect their money back. This should have been covered in the business plan and profit and cash forecasts. The economic climate has a significant impact on the terms on which banks are prepared to lend, but they will usually want to see that the interest cost is easily covered by profits. It is useful to speak to your accountant before approaching your bank to see what broad lending criteria are currently in operation and to ensure that any lending request is sensibly framed.

RAISING INVESTMENT FROM GOVERNMENT

It is worth investigating the Government-introduced measures designed to give small and medium-sized businesses (SMEs) access to guaranteed bank loan finance. Most banks will have information on how these schemes work. At the time of writing, there are also Government grants available to businesses in some parts of the UK: details are available from Business Link, a free business advice and support service.

RAISING INVESTMENT FROM OTHER SOURCES

If a business needs more long-term capital, and bank finance is unavailable or too costly, alternatives include individual angel investors, trade investors, venture capital and flotation, or public listing.

Angel investors will often be people who already know the management team and are prepared to back them. There are organisations which can introduce business angels to design firms, and a good place to start is the British Business Angels Network. The best business angels bring more to the table than cash, and will usually want to help the business as a non-executive director. Non-executive directors can be very useful in providing an objective perspective to the management team and in particular to help them focus on key issues and long-term strategy. They can also bring business experience which may be lacking in a less experienced management team.

Trade investors are companies operating in the same or similar field. They may want a stake in the business in order to secure a specialist offer for their clients, or to cement existing shared client relationships. A trade investor may take a minority stake (less than 50 per cent) although some will insist on a controlling stake. It is usual for the trade investor to want the right to buy the rest of the business at some point in the future, which means it is vital to be happy with that relationship.

Venture capital investors are interested in investing in businesses with good growth potential where they can see a high return for their investment. They are not usually interested in investing small amounts so this sort of investment suits larger businesses with fairly ambitious growth and acquisition plans. Venture capitalists will want to see their money back with a good return, typically over a three to five year period.

Becoming a *publicly listed* company is a fourth source of finance. This can assist in providing funds, usually for acquisition, and a market in the company's shares can make them more attractive when used to pay for acquisitions. This is suitable for only a few design businesses: to have a reasonably active market in the shares, a business needs to be generating profits of around £10 million.

INCOME MODELS, RETAINERS AND PROJECT FEES

How much designers charge for their work and how that income comes in both have a significant impact on the business's finances. Systems and processes should never obscure the opportunity for designers to charge what a project is worth, as opposed to what it might cost.

There are a number of income models used by designers. These are the most common:

- project fees
- retainers
- recharges on production costs
- performance-related fees
- royalty streams
- share-based payments.

Project fees are the most common income model. They have the advantage of being separately negotiated for every project, thus providing the opportunity to charge what the market will bear, which may be more than the resource cost. Conversely, they also give the client the opportunity to negotiate the price down. Project fees have other disadvantages. Psychologically, they reinforce a short-term client/supplier relationship. They also provide little certainty of income, and they are difficult to forecast which makes planning difficult and cashflow harder to manage.

Retainers reflect a longer-term relationship which is more of a partnership, and also provide more certainty of income and cashflow. The disadvantage is that they are difficult to negotiate. Containing the work requested within the scope of the retainer can be a struggle, and it can also be hard to invoice-discount debts for retainer fees.

Recharging production costs can still represent a significant element of income even though more clients are putting clauses in their contracts which prohibit mark-ups and which require designers to pass on any volume discounts. Where production income is significant, it should not subsidise creative fees. The core product is creative output and designers should be paid properly for this and not for, say, buying print.

Performance-related fees are less common in design than in other marketing disciplines. Clients will sometimes ask a design company to share their risk and take a smaller basic fee in exchange for an additional bonus fee based on the achievement of agreed targets. These may be delivery targets for the consultancy (client satisfaction ratings for example) or targets based around the outcome of the work. Performance fees can provide a welcome upside, but care is needed that the potential bonus is sufficient to compensate for the risk.

Royalties can happen when designer and clients work together to develop a new product, and a suitable deal negotiated.

Share payments can be offered by clients who have no cash, but offer shares in their business instead. If a design business has cash reserves to sustain work for which it will not be paid until the shares are sold, this can be worth doing. The question designers should ask themselves is: 'If we were paid in cash, would we then invest that cash in those shares?' If the answer is no, it's probably a bad idea to do it.

BUSINESS INSURANCES

It is important to plan for when things can go wrong, and insurance plays an important role. The usual insurances include the following:

- Professional Indemnity
- Public Liability
- Employer's Liability
- Directors' Insurance
- Buildings & Contents
- Legal Expenses
- Key Man Cover
- Shareholder Protection

Professional Indemnity Insurance protects the business against claims made by dissatisfied clients where they have suffered financial loss as a result of neglect, errors and omissions. This is probably the most important cover a designer should consider.

Public Liability Insurance protects against claims from third parties as a result of injury (or death) or harm done to property as a result of business activities.

Employer's Liability Insurance protects the business against claims from any employees, including claims for accidents and sickness. It is a legal requirement to have it.

Directors' Insurance protects directors from being sued. Even though the nature of running a limited company 'limits' claims against its directors, in some cases (for example, negligence), directors of limited companies can be sued. Non-executive directors will usually insist on this insurance being in place.

Buildings & Contents Cover is standard insurance to protect business property and fixtures/fittings.

Legal Expenses Insurance provides protection in the eventuality of legal action being taken against the business.

Key Man Cover protects the business against the loss through death or illness of its key people.

Shareholder Protection Insurance protects each of the shareholders. On the death or diagnosis of a critical illness of a shareholder, the other shareholders receive a cash lump sum which can then be used to buy the affected shareholder's shares. This ensures a swift resolution with minimum disruption to the company.

FROM PLANNING TO MANAGING

Planning helps management teams to anticipate what the business may throw at them, and to think about what to do before the heat of battle. It also provides opportunities to optimise performance and to build a business which, when followed with effective management action and the measurement of results, will be highly focused, efficient and profitable.

2.7   The money (part two)

Gary Baxter

As a general rule, the most successful man in life is the man who has the best information.
*   Benjamin Disraeli (1804–81), politician and statesman

WHO NEEDS FINANCIAL MANAGEMENT?

Design has come a long way in the last quarter of a century, but the fundamental qualities of successful design companies have changed little. It has always been true that a rigorous approach to financial management greatly improves the likelihood of business success. This is because the culture of a company with good financial management tends to be one in which the management is disciplined in all aspects of its business.

The success of any accounting system ultimately depends on whether the business owners and managers understand the information, and whether it is sufficient to enable them to make timely decisions, taking into account the company's financial circumstances and the wider economic environment.

Particularly in recessionary times, businesses need to pay very close attention to their finances, which means that there is little tolerance in slack or inadequate financial management. Accounting systems which may have been adequate in more buoyant times start to creak under the pressure of the demand to understand what is going on in the business.

It is possible to create a successful accounting system in the form of handwritten 'books', but owners and managers of design companies today can take advantage of sophisticated and affordable technology to produce timely financial information and reports. This ensures that the directors of the company have the opportunity to understand their performance and enables them to react quickly to information derived from analysis of the data.

FINANCIAL PLAN AND BUDGETING

Whatever the size or situation of your design company, you need to prepare a financial income and expenditure plan and budget for the year ahead. How?

Money in

Firstly, look at how much money you can bring in.

Evaluate the fee income potential of your team. To do this you need to work out the estimated 'achievable chargeable hours' for the fee earners in the year ahead, taking account of planned additions and departures. Experience suggests that designers should achieve 1,500 chargeable hours per year, and client services 1,200. The number of achievable chargeable hours for directors will be less because of their non-chargeable work in areas such as new business development, human resource management and so on. The chargeable hours plan for them is likely to be between 250 and 750.

Hourly charge-out rates should be established for each chargeable employee. By using published survey data, such as that provided to Design Business Association (DBA) members, it is possible to ensure that the hourly rates used are 'market-rates'. By multiplying the hourly rates by the estimated achievable chargeable hours, the 'potential fee income' can be established. Typically, about 25 per cent of this value will be 'written off' and not charged to clients, because of lost pitches or general inefficiencies. Having worked out your 'potential fee income', therefore, take 75 per cent of this to arrive at the fee income budget.

Using this as a basis, plan your team potential for each of the 12 months ahead. This will give you your budgeted fee income for each month against which you can measure actual performance. If you then apply the same charge-out rates used in this calculation to your quotes for each and every project, it will be possible to derive a meaningful analysis of the variances between your budgeted fee income and the actual fee income achieved.

Having arrived at the fee income budget, use historical data to estimate the amount of rechargeable expenses that will be billed to clients in addition to design fees. This will vary according to design discipline, but could be in the range 10–50 per cent of fee income.

Turnover is the sum of the fee income plus the recharged expenses. But for useful comparison with other businesses and for internal statistics you should use 'Gross Income' rather than turnover, because turnover can be greatly increased by items such as large print bills, whereas the mark-up on that item may only be 20 per cent. Gross income is defined as fee income plus the mark-up on recharged expenses. For the gross income budget, therefore, you need to use historical data to calculate the estimated mark-up on recharged expenses for the year ahead.

Money out

Next, you need to review your salaries and overheads and set budgets for the year ahead. In carrying out this review, take the opportunity to categorise the budget into levels 1–4, with 1 being the costs which could be cut most easily and 4 those where cuts would radically change the way the business operates.

For the expenditure plan, allocate costs into these categories:

- *Salaries*: include employers' National Insurance Contributions, planned dividends, freelancers.
- *People costs*: include training, pension scheme, staff social costs.
- *Premises*: include rent, utilities, maintenance, mortgage.
- *Technology and communications*: include IT, telephone, equipment.
- *Business development*: include entertaining, awards, website costs.
- *Professional fees*: include legal, accountancy, insurance, consultancy.
- *Studio costs*: include studio administration, stationery, reference material, postage.

In preparing the expenditure plan, it is essential to consider the detail within the above headings and create sub-headings to suit your particular circumstances. This will make cost control and monthly review much easier. It will be particularly important to prepare a detailed plan and allocate personal responsibility for the business development and technology budgets. This is because these two areas are typically where there is most choice – unlike rent or electricity, for example – so the budget needs to be planned and controlled by an individual.

Armed with this cost analysis, the 'break-even' figure can be computed. This is the level of fees which have to be achieved in order to pay for the total salaries and overheads. If done accurately, this gives business owners an instant feel of how the business is doing each month when the billing figures are reviewed. One of the best uses of the break-even figure is to compare it to the forecast gross income for the next three months. This is often the earliest warning sign of potential problems, and can be used to make timely, crucial decisions on cost cutting when they can be most effective.

Whilst owners and managers may employ the services of someone in the finance department or their accountant to help with the budget, its 'ownership' should be very much theirs so that they understand the content and implications.

FINANCIAL MANAGEMENT REPORTING

The budgets, as detailed above, should be compiled into a format which the owners and managers understand. Also, it is important to ensure that reports of actual results from the accounting system are easily compared to the budgets. Data entered into the report (sales and purchase invoices, for example) needs to be analysed into categories which exactly reflect the income and expenditure headings and sub-headings used when preparing the budgets.

The financial management reports will include:

- *Operating Report*: income and expenditure analysed into categories.
- *Balance Sheet*: showing investment in premises and equipment and what is owed by the company and what it owes to suppliers, HMRC and so on.

- *Cashflow Forecast*: based on expected money receivable and payable over the next 3–12 months, this is a forecast of the expected balance in the bank.
- *Billing Analysis*: by client and by job, showing billing and profitability.
- *Billing Forecast*: 3–12 months, 'known', 'prospective' and 'speculative'.[1]
- *Accounts Receivable Report*: aged debtors (amounts owed by clients), with comments on the 60–90 day columns.
- *Accounts Payable Report*: aged creditors (amounts owed to suppliers).

A summary extract from a simple operating report would look like this (Table 2.7.1). For detail to be included in the expenditure lines, see bullet points under 'Money Out' on the previous page.

Table 2.7.1   Summary extract from a simple operating report

	Current Month		
	Budget	Actual	Variance
Fee income			
Mark-up on expenses			
Gross Income			
Salaries & planned dividends			
People costs			
Premises			
Technology and communications			
Business development			
Professional fees			
Studio costs			
Total salaries and overheads			
Net profit (before taxation)			

---

1   From a CRM (Client Relationship Management) pipeline or other system, the potential for fee income over 3–12 months should be analysed into: (i) 'known' projects, normally those in the plan to be completed in the next 1–3 months and confirmed by the client; (ii) 'prospective', those for which proposals and/or quotes have been sent; (iii) 'speculative', the potential, based on estimates of projects and relationships yet to be developed.

BENCHMARKING AND KEY PERFORMANCE INDICATORS (KPIs)

To put your company's performance into context, you need to benchmark your performance against others in the industry.

On average over the last 25 years, well-run design companies would have spent 55 per cent of their gross income on salaries and 25 per cent on overheads, leaving a net profit margin of 20 per cent (before taxation). In recessionary times companies will have shifted their targets to 60 per cent, 30 per cent and 10 per cent respectively, in order to keep their team and structure in place in anticipation of an upturn.

Design companies' spend on overheads will vary from year to year depending on their particular circumstances. Based on UK survey data, realistically achievable targets would be as follows (Table 2.7.2).

Table 2.7.2   Overhead targets

Salaries	57%
People costs	4%
Premises	9%
Technology and communications	3%
Business development	4%
Professional fees and insurance	2%
Studio expenses	5%
Subtotal	84%
PROFIT MARGIN	16%

PROBLEM AVOIDANCE

The above is a useful guide to levels of reasonable expenditure, when the business remains profitable. When income starts to fall, the 'fixed' element of the costs will obviously start to impact upon these ratios. It is not easy to simply cut out sufficient costs instantly, to bring your ratios back in line.

As mentioned earlier, budgets should be categorised in the planning stage in order to prepare for the possibility of a need to make cuts. This preparation will prove invaluable in a situation where income is falling toward the break-even point.

As a rule, sufficient funds should have been retained in the business so that the amount of cash, plus debtors, less creditors, equates to at least four times the monthly running costs of the business. This would give a cushion of time to evaluate the situation and develop an action plan.

The extent to which funds have been retained will influence the required speed at which decisions need to be taken. For example, if only two months' salaries and overheads are covered, the decision to cut costs can't wait one more month.

In addition to the expenditure percentages described above, key balance sheet ratios should be compiled to reveal strengths and weaknesses in the company's finances.

The following are some useful ratios with typical targets:

1. *Debtor days:* the ratio of the total amount owed by debtors (excluding VAT) to turnover for the last two months.

    This calculation will give you the average number of days' credit period you are giving to your clients. You should aim to achieve average debtor days of around 45, and it would be a warning sign if the average were over 60.

    A hypothetical example of the calculation would be: 60 (average debtor days) divided by £100,000 (turnover for last two months) multiplied by £120,000 (debtors excluding VAT). It indicates average debtor days of 72, and potential cashflow problems on the horizon.

2. *Running costs cover:* the ratio of net current assets to monthly running costs.

    This ratio will indicate how long the company could continue to pay for its running costs (overheads plus salaries and loan repayments) if income dried up.

    In current times we would expect this ratio to exceed three (months) and be aiming at five.

    Other 'risk assessment' ratios would include:
    - 'Gearing' ratios, which compare the amount of loan finance to equity in the balance sheet, and the extent to which loan repayments are covered by after-tax profit.
    - The spread of income across the client base, the target being no more than 15 per cent from any one client, with warning signs if this reaches more than 30 per cent.

ACCOUNTING AND FINANCIAL PROJECT MANAGEMENT SYSTEMS

Avoid overly complicated project management systems, which purport to give you ratios and margins on just about every piece of data you can imagine. For projects, all you really need to know is if you are on time and on budget. Project management systems need to have a facility for recording the fees budget for a project, broken down into its natural stages. It should be capable of processing time sheets so that the value of the resources used – mostly time spent at charge-rate – can be monitored against the budget. Similarly, you need to record the budget for rechargeable expenses and monitor the expenditure via purchase orders, not via suppliers' invoices. By the time they arrive it's often too late!

With this basic data recorded, the system should be capable of producing reports which show how much of the budget has been used and profitability reports, once a project or stage has been billed to the client, to show whether the project was completed in accordance with the criteria set in the business plan. The financial target in the business plan will be achieved only if, on average, the completed projects comply with the chargeable hours, charge-rates and efficiency ratios implicit in the financial plan.

WHO'S IN CHARGE OF THE MONEY?

If necessary, owners and managers should know when they need to take a back seat and let someone else look after the details of the finances. However, as indicated already, it is important to remember that the responsibility for financial management rests with the businesses owners. This is true in law, but it also needs to be true in practice, in the way the business is run.

Whilst it is not possible or indeed desirable to turn designers into accountants, systems should be in place which are capable of producing reports and information, free of accounting jargon and mystery, and accessible.

This means that you need to find expert employees or specialist professional advisors who understand the industry, and who can introduce appropriate accounting and financial project management software which is intuitive and has good reporting capability.

2.8 The law

Jo Evans

Although our intellect always longs for clarity and certainty, our nature often finds uncertainty fascinating.
- Carl Von Clausewitz (1780–1831), soldier, historian and military theorist

BUSINESS TYPES, AND THE PROS AND CONS

The most common form of business entity in the UK is a private company limited by shares, identified by the word 'Limited' or 'Ltd' after its name. You may also see the suffix 'LLP', which identifies a limited liability partnership.

A limited company or an LLP is likely to be the most suitable vehicle for establishing a new design business. So why are they the most popular and which one is likely to suit you best?

Why a limited company and not a partnership or sole trader?

One reason why most people set up a limited company when starting a business, rather than operating as a sole trader or as a partnership, is to minimise risk. As a shareholder in a company, your risk is limited to the amount invested: the company has its own legal identity and is responsible for paying its own debts.

If you operate as a sole trader you are responsible for the debts of the business. Similarly, in a partnership the liability of each partner is unlimited and each partner is jointly liable for the debts of the other partners in connection with the business.

Another form of limited company is a public limited company, or plc. If you intend to offer shares in your company to the general public – by floating on the stock market, for example – then the company must be a plc. Whilst the risk to shareholders is still limited to the amount invested in the shares, a public limited company (plc) must have share capital of at least £50,000 of which £12,500 must be fully paid up before the company can trade. So whilst there is some kudos attached to having 'plc' after the company's name, the minimum capital requirement and additional corporate governance requirements to maintain a plc are usually dissuasive factors.

There are other forms of company: unlimited companies; companies limited by guarantee and community interest companies. However, unless your business has a social enterprise or charitable objective, these are unlikely to be the most suitable.

Whilst minimising risk is a key factor, there are other characteristics of limited companies which make them good business vehicles:

- *Tax*: a limited company structure may be more tax efficient.
- *Continuity*: a limited company continues even though the personnel changes.
- *Shares*: in a limited company, shares can be used to incentivise key employees as the company grows.
- *Finance*: companies can offer shares to third-party investors to raise funds and, if borrowing from a bank, can offer security in the form of a charge over its assets.

The quid pro quo for the limited liability of the shareholders is that, unlike a partnership and a sole trader, a company needs to file financial statements each year with Companies House and they appear on a publicly available record.

The rise of the Limited Liability Partnership (LLP)

For all of the above reasons, a limited company has been the natural choice of vehicle for many businesses. However, since 2001, it has been possible to incorporate a limited liability partnership in the UK. There are now over 40,000 limited liability partnerships registered at Companies House, so in a relatively short period of time they have become a popular business vehicle. As the name suggests, they are a partnership in which the liability of the partners (or members) is limited. This distinguishes them from a traditional partnership where the liability of the partners is unlimited. The LLP is a hybrid vehicle. Think of it as a partnership on the inside and a company on the outside. The key difference between an LLP and a limited company is that the LLP has no share capital. The members of the LLP themselves determine their rewards and returns outside of a share capital framework

An LLP has many of the advantages of a limited company: limited liability; continuity; tax efficiency, especially in the early growth years; and the ability to raise finance and offer security. These characteristics when coupled with the concept of a partnership between its participants – suggestive of collaborative working and equality between members and, importantly, with the ability to fix the rewards between members privately and flexibly – make them an attractive proposition for 'people' businesses.

Table 2.8.1 compares some of the key features of an LLP, a private limited company and a partnership/sole trader. Which is right for you will depend upon the needs and expectations of the participants and their plans for the growth and development of that business.

Table 2.8.1   Comparison of business types

	Limited company	LLP	Partnership/sole trader
Constitutional documents	Articles of association (filed at Companies House)	None required	None required
Annual Accounts	Filed at Companies House	Filed at Companies House	None required
Taxation	Taxed according to company principles: corporation tax on profits; income tax on salaries and dividends to shareholders	Taxed on partnership principles: no corporation tax, members taxed on shares of profits	Taxed on partnership principles: no corporation tax, partners/trader taxed on shares of profits/income
Liability to third parties	Liability of shareholders and directors limited	Liability of members limited	Unlimited liability
Interest of participants	Dividends and capital returns to shareholders governed by share rights in articles of association; directors and employees paid by salary	Members determine income and capital rights between themselves and can flex as required	Partners determine income and capital rights between themselves and can flex as required
Contractual arrangements between participants	Articles (see above). Shareholders agreement recommended (private document)	None required but LLP members agreement recommended (private document)	None required but partnership agreement recommended (private document)
Publicly filed returns	Annual accounts; annual return; names of directors and shareholders	Annual accounts; annual return; names of designated members	None
Registered name and registered office	Required and filed at Companies House	Required and filed at Companies House	None required

A final word on limited liability. It is increasingly the case that banks, landlords and suppliers are minimising their own risk in lending to smaller limited liability enterprises by seeking personal guarantees from the owners of such enterprises. This trend undermines the concept of limited liability, holding the owners personally accountable for liabilities of the business which ordinarily would stay with the business. The incidence and scope of those guarantees will be a matter of bargaining power in each case. Whilst you may not be able to avoid giving the guarantee in the first place, do keep it under review. As the business grows and the loan is repaid or the overdraft no longer used, you can seek to have the guarantee released.

CLIENT CONTRACTS

There is no need, as a matter of law, for there to be anything in writing in order to establish the existence of a binding contract. As any good law student will tell you, all you need to make a binding contract are an offer, an acceptance of that offer, some consideration (usually money) and an intention to create legal relations.

Litigation thrives on, and is fuelled by, uncertainty, and the main reason why contracts are usually reduced to writing is to establish certainty as to the precise terms agreed between the parties. Certainty is needed in the complex terms which might have been negotiated back and forth between the parties dealing with matters such as: payment; deliverables; obligations; responsibilities; rights and consequences in the event of breach; termination provisions; length of the contract; exclusions and exclusivity of arrangements.

Common law also imports terms, called 'implied terms', into contracts and the parties need to be clear in the explicit terms agreed between them which of the implied terms are to remain and which to be excluded.

Understanding that eventually a commercial relationship will end, and realising that the point of termination is probably not the best time to be arguing about notice provisions and the scope of ownership of intellectual property, is often a sufficient prompt to agree contract terms with clients in writing.

There are good design industry-specific standard terms for client/agency agreements which reflect a fair position between the contracting parties. Whilst these agreements should not be slavishly followed, they provide a good starting point for negotiations between your agency and its clients.

EMPLOYEES' CONTRACTS AND POLICIES

In whatever form your business is established, you will be taking on employees as it grows. You need to make sure that your prospective employees have permission to work in the UK. If you are in any doubt as to whether a visa stamp means the person is allowed to work then you should seek specialist help, for example from The UK Border Agency. You will also need to familiarise yourself with UK income tax and social security regulations.

All employees in the UK are entitled to receive a written statement of certain employment terms, covering things such as: place of work; start date; salary; notice period and holiday entitlement. Certain terms will also be implied into an employment contract by common law; these implied terms include a duty by the employee not to misuse confidential information or trade secrets of the employer and the mutual obligation of trust and confidence.

Whilst the provision of a written statement may satisfy your statutory employer obligations, you might find it advantageous to consider a longer agreement. This would allow you to clarify explicitly the common law implied terms, and also to include covenants to protect the goodwill of the business when the employment relationship ends. These post-termination provisions or 'restrictive covenants' allow you, for example, to prevent the employee from soliciting clients when they leave. If you have an employee who is producing creative work for clients and/or has a client-facing role, then it is perfectly legitimate to seek to protect the goodwill created in an employment contract. Enforcing such provisions is difficult but provided they are drafted carefully and with proper thought given to the nature of the business, the clients and the client relationships and are limited in scope, they are upheld by the courts.

Employment legislation is constantly evolving. The 1990s and early 2000s saw fundamental changes to employment rights reminiscent of the far reaching changes introduced in the 1970s when equal pay and race and sex discrimination were embedded in statute. Legislation now covers: minimum wages; health and safety; working hours; rights for part timers and maternity, paternity and adoption rights; grievance and disciplinary procedures; and discrimination on disability, sexual orientation, religion and belief and age.

Best practice dictates putting in place policies for dealing with these statutory obligations. Whilst it is not a legal obligation to have a policy covering all these issues in the event of, for example, a discrimination claim, the lack of an equal opportunities policy will make it appear that you, as an employer, are not committed to equal opportunities. That is a factor which a tribunal could take into account when deciding whether to draw an inference of discrimination.

SUPPLIERS AND FREELANCERS

Suppliers and freelancers engaged by design businesses are frequently providing creative work to the agency; this might include freelancers engaged to assist on a particular client brief or suppliers designing the agency's website.

In the case of employees, if there is any doubt as to ownership of the intellectual property rights (IPR) created by the employee in the course of their employment, the courts and relevant intellectual property statutes tend to favour the employer. This is not always the case where those intellectual property rights are created by freelancers and third-party suppliers.

In the absence of any contract dealing specifically with intellectual property rights, consultants or freelancers (that is, non-employees) will, by default, own the copyright in works they create. This means that computer programmers, photographers and artists will be the primary owners of the copyright in their work not the agency – or indeed the agency's client – for whom the work was created. But the rules applying to different forms of intellectual property are not the same. For example, in relation to design rights, it is the commissioner of the design (the agency or the client) rather than the designer him or herself who is entitled to any registered or unregistered design rights in a design.

The application of those two principles could lead to a situation where the copyright in a drawing or model belongs to the freelancer but the agency or client owns the registered or unregistered design rights. As most contracts between an agency and its clients will contain a warranty from the agency that it owns the intellectual property rights in the work created for the client, the agency might find itself in the awkward position of having to deliver rights in intellectual property to a client and being unable to so because the freelance owner of the right refuses to assign the rights over.

All of the above could be avoided by a clear contract between the agency and its freelancers and suppliers dealing with a comprehensive assignment of intellectual property rights to the agency.

PARTNERSHIP AND SHAREHOLDER AGREEMENTS

Many successful design businesses have sprung from the creative collaboration between two or more individuals: look at the top names on any industry league table. It is an overused cliché, but true nonetheless, that embarking on a business partnership is akin to a marriage. Many marriages are long and harmonious, but not all. And the same is true of creative business partnerships.

Let's continue the analogy and assume an early honeymoon period of business growth and prosperity and a roster of amazing work for an enviable list of clients. But, as time goes on, strains appear in the relationship, or something unexpected happens, like the death or illness of one of the founders. At that stage, the business itself could be a very valuable asset, and most would agree that is not the best time to embark upon the discussions about how the founding partners are going to deal with the new circumstances.

Far better, at the start of the relationship to have had a thorough discussion about the future plans and expectations of each of the founders; to have thought through what will happen if one of the partners wants to go part time, becomes ill, divorces or dies; or if one wants to sell all or some of their shares, or bring in a new partner, and the others don't like the prospective new shareholder or partner.

All of the above issues, having been discussed and agreed, can be set out in an agreement between you and your founding partners. If the business entity is a limited company, the principles will be enshrined in your company's articles of association and a shareholders' agreement. If your business is an LLP, you ought to have a partnership or members' agreement. As well as dealing with the 'big' questions mentioned above, the agreements can also clarify the roles and responsibilities of each of you and become a blueprint for good business practice and governance.

2.9   The intellectual property

Darrell Stuart-Smith

Don't worry about people stealing an idea. If it is original you will have to ram it down their throats.

- Howard H. Aiken (1900–73), computer pioneer

WHY ARE INTELLECTUAL PROPERTY RIGHTS SO IMPORTANT?

Intellectual Property Rights (IPR) protect work that is the expression of human intellectual creativity. They arise either automatically or through a process of registration.

All businesses own IPR even if it is just in the letters they write or their name, but for a creative business it can be its very life blood. Every design business needs to recognise, manage and protect its own IPR, whilst understanding what clients need to receive to use and exploit the creative work which they are buying.

If a design business does not address IPR in its dealings with clients, suppliers, agents, representatives and staff then the law will, to an extent, deal with it for them in a way that might fetter the future creativity of the business. It may also leave a design consultancy with a contractual obligation to deliver or license rights to a client which the consultancy does not, in fact, own.

WHAT IS INCLUDED IPR?

Copyright

Arises automatically and protects original literary (including computer programmes), dramatic, musical and artistic works as well as sound recordings and films. The owner of the copyright in a qualifying protected work has – subject to certain limited exceptions – the right to copy, publish, adapt or perform the work. It generally lasts for the life of the author plus a number of years, usually 70. Copyright is often asserted by the symbol ©, followed by the year of creation and the name of the owner. Whilst recommended, it is not a legal requirement to do this, and works that do not carry this assertion may still be protected by copyright.

Design right

Arises automatically and protects the original design of the shape and configuration (including patterns and aspects of surface decoration) of articles or parts thereof. The owner has the right to produce articles to that design. It lasts for a maximum of 15 years.

Unregistered trade marks

Arises automatically and protects aspects of the goodwill, usually the identity, of a business (such as name, logo, house style) against unfair use. This right, which, unlike copyright and design right, originates not from statute but through the decisions of the courts and their desire to control unfair competition, is protected through the law of 'passing off'.

Registered trade marks

A mark (including words, logos, design devices, strap lines and even smells, shapes and sounds) which meets qualifying criteria and which distinguish goods and services of one business from another can be registered. This confers an almost monopolistic right to use the mark in relation to the goods and/or services for which it has been registered. A registered mark can be challenged if it is not used, but otherwise can be renewed every ten years.

Patents

A registered right which protects by conferring a legal monopoly upon novel and not obvious inventive processes and features which make things work. A registered patent will last for up to 20 years.

Confidential information

Proprietary information that is not generally in the public domain. It is most effectively protected through the use of contractual confidentiality or non-disclosure agreements.

Know-how

Accumulated commercially sensitive business knowledge that is often protected through the retention of staff with particular expertise and, where it has to be disclosed in the course of business, through confidentiality agreements.

Moral right

The right of an author of a copyright work to be identified and to stop the work being treated in a derogatory way. This right cannot be transferred and must be asserted.

MANAGING CLIENTS' IPR EXPECTATIONS

Clients are concerned about the disclosure of their confidential information, whether it be plans to rebrand their business or to launch or relaunch a particular product or service or even to just freshen up an existing part of their business.
Clients often believe:

- that design work produced in response to a brief will somehow incorporate confidential information about their business;
- that they have bought a complete design process (rather than just a design solution);
- that all of the work arising in response to a brief has been created for them and paid for by them.

Many clients therefore conclude that all of the work arising in response to the brief and all IPR therein should and must belong to them, whereas the design process will invariably generate a vast amount of work that does not form any part of the final design solution.

Designers need to understand their clients' concerns and be able and prepared to explain why it may not be appropriate for such a large body of work and rights to pass, and that the focus should be on the final design solution.

The designer must also consider if it is necessary to transfer IPR to the client or merely grant a licence of IPR to allow the client to use the work for the purpose it was created. This requires balancing the clients' expectations against what is reasonable and appropriate in the circumstances.

As a general rule of thumb, the graphic, two-dimensional design business probably has nothing to be concerned about if it transfers IPR in the final selected design, whereas the three-dimensional designer, and those who work in areas where there are limited design solutions available because of functionality or other factors, is better off thinking in terms of a licence.

If IPR are to be licensed, then usage, exclusivity, duration, market sector and rights of adaptation should be addressed. If the licence terms are not stipulated, the court will impose such terms as are appropriate in the circumstances.

If a design consultancy agrees to transfer or exclusively license IPR to a client then it should consider if it needs to reserve rights to itself to enable it to work on similar projects in the future.

PITCHES AND IPR

A pitch (paid or unpaid) is a form of contract, with work being carried out in return for a fee and/or an opportunity to be considered for further work. The same considerations regarding IPR apply.

Where a consultancy is unsuccessful with a pitch (paid or unpaid) it may feel it inappropriate to pass to the prospective client any work and any IPR. It may also wish to protect, through written pitch terms, the ideas and concepts that have been presented as part of the pitch.

INFRINGEMENT OF IPR

Designers have a tendency to think that provided they do not actually copy another's work there will be no problem. At a certain level (specifically as regards copyright) this is generally true, although the designer needs to be alert to the possibility of subconscious or subliminal copying. It is also necessary to consider the possible infringement of registered rights. Searches are possible but the interpretation of the results is often complex and inconclusive.

Clients usually assume that their use of commissioned work will not infringe the rights of another person or business. If the client prepares the contract terms, it will often include a warranty from the designer to this effect and may require this to be supported by an indemnity against any infringement claims. This is usually unreasonable. Unless designers specifically agree, as part of the brief, to provide intellectual property clearance in relation to their work, responsibility should be limited to producing 'original' work that does not 'knowingly' infringe any other rights. It should also be made clear that, unless expressly agreed, the designer is not expected to carry out formal searches or enquiries.

SHOULD IPR EVER BECOME A DEAL BREAKER?

This depends upon the nature of the services being provided and the attitude of the client to legal clearance and liability. A brief that provides for all of the work arising (and IPR) to pass to the client, backed up by the passing of responsibility for legal clearance, topped up with an indemnity for claims and losses arising, may be a contract too far!

Each contract and its risks has to be considered in context with regard to the nature of the work, the reward and the ability of the consultancy to discharge its obligations. Most problems arise because the design firm either did not understand its obligations or did not address certain of those obligations and merely signed the contract believing, perhaps, that it had insurance if there was a problem.

In all contractual negotiations – and in particular when dealing with IPR and risks – it is important to put forward reasonable proposals which can be explained and supported. Professional and reasonable terms of trading will probably apply to the majority of contract work, and an understanding of how contracts are formed is helpful in this regard. However, contracts tabled by clients will invariably seek to claim ownership of all the rights in any work arising and place unreasonable burden and responsibility upon the design consultancy.

With a good working knowledge of IPR, an understanding of client expectations and a reasonable position to put forward, the design consultancy can maintain good client relations without taking on unreasonable and potentially business threatening risks.

2.10 The management issues

James Woudhuysen

My own business always bores me to death. I prefer other people's.
- Oscar Wilde (1854–1900), playwright, from 'Lady Windermere's fan'

TAKING THE HIGH GROUND

Clients buy designs, but they also buy individuals who clearly convey relevant, informed and surprising opinions. They buy the charismatic mind, not just the brilliant execution. While designers need to show that they understand clients and their businesses, they also need to show that they can anticipate developments in and beyond the sector those businesses are in.

There is no reason to have pretensions to be a management consultant, but there is a reason to differentiate your business from those run by design-only designers. That way, you can hope to achieve higher margins and to secure more durable client relationships. A critical attitude, mastery of facts, numeracy and real brain skills – in finding things out, writing and speaking about them – are the invaluable complement to the skills of hand and eye.

THIS IS THE FIRST BIODEGRADEABLE-MOBILE-INTERACTIVE-WIRELESS-RAPID DOWNLOADER-IT'S CALLED "A BOOK"!

Remember, too, that although a fierce intellectual approach doesn't guarantee a close attention to client briefs, it can help to create the right forensic skills and environment to allow such attention to flourish.

The management advantages of a practical, but also intellectual, stance don't end with client relationships. Your ability to motivate, retain and get the best out of staff will be improved if they believe that they will learn from you. Your relations with suppliers and regulators will get better, the more you understand where they are coming from and going to. Your ability to get into the mainstream media, and to win more respect from everyone, will depend on your taking the high ground.

To help in this, there are plenty of books and journals on economics, leadership, management and human resources. However, although designers need to know about the dynamics of the workplace, the supply chain and perhaps even corporate finance, the imperatives for them have more to do with understanding future trends, communicating their ideas with the maximum clarity and doing good research. Designers also need closely to follow developments in innovation and marketing.

UNDERSTANDING FUTURE TRENDS

There are many pitfalls in forecasting future trends.[1] Designers, as much as anyone, have a habit of impressionistically representing ideas they have picked up from the mass media as their own, freshly minted. They also have much to learn about the history of ideas: understanding the past is important to grasping the real outlines of tomorrow. The Web and sites like Wikipedia make the history of ideas a much easier subject to grasp than it was in the past.

The chief thing to remember when working on future trends for clients is that they grow out of both the present and history, but they never repeat them. Nor is the future just something that happens to people; it's something that people, including clients, make happen.

It is always hard to predict the timing of coming developments. However, a way to avoid mistakes is to collect more professional forecasts and, having collected them, suspect them more. In particular, there is a clear need to adopt a critical and independent stance towards breathless declarations about new trends, whose novelty, poor durability and weak force make them better described as fads.

COMMUNICATING WITH CLARITY

In 1963, the legendary British advertising guru, David Ogilvy, could insist that discipline was needed to write good ads. He admonished his readers that the then 'fashionable' word 'creativity' was 'not in the 12-volume *Oxford Dictionary*'.[2] His other rules included:

- what you say is more vital than how you say it;
- unless your campaign is built around a great idea, it will flop;
- give the facts;
- you can't bore people into buying.

---

1   See *Trends: Introducing Futures and Trends Research*, James Woudhuysen, Design Council

2   *Confessions of an Advertising Man*, David Ogilvy, 1963

Communication needs to be simple, incisive, and, as George Orwell said of good prose, like a windowpane.[3]

In all your communications with clients, you need to put yourself in their shoes. The key to that is to research their overall position and operating context.

DOING GOOD RESEARCH

Your business can only benefit by conducting a programme of research that runs independently from the different projects you have running with clients.

Make sure you build separate files on:

- sectors
- clients
- rivals
- issues.

With research, outcomes cannot be predicted in advance. It involves taking risks, accepting serendipity and, often, embracing the bizarre. It must have an inspiring goal. It must be comprehensive and done from every angle. It means learning about how other people have, historically, approached the problem you're looking at – what they've got right, and what they've got wrong.

Be prepared to suspend judgment, at least initially: don't take the problem as given. You will also find that it is particularly useful to start by thinking hard about the most topical, concrete and puzzling paradox about the issue you are researching.

For example, why is it that, despite all the interest in fashion and in mobile phones, few applications have yet emerged for what specialists have been talking about for some years: 'wearable media' – electronic textiles that can monitor your blood pressure, or adjust to different conditions of temperature and humidity? Part of the answer to this difficult question is that it is hard to make flexible electronic garments that can withstand the rigours of washing and drying. What the example shows is that, by selecting paradoxes, one is led both into useful directions for research, and into what to do next. In this case, the next thing to do would be to find out who is doing what in flexible and waterproof electronics. Makers of thin, bendy plastic electronic screens, and of underwater cameras, would be worth a look.

This broad approach to research is also relevant to how you present your ideas and your past work. Organise these things by topical and knotty theme, not by chronology. Start with the present dilemmas, explore their history from the standpoint of the present, and build design directions from scholarly, creative challenges to received opinion and the status quo.

---

3   Essay, *Why I Write*, George Orwell, 1946

INNOVATION AND MARKETING AMONG CLIENTS

Not a few clients are rather averse to taking risks and engaging in technological innovation. Activities related to accounting and finance ('business models'), human resources, regulation and environmentalism tend to win out against hard work, leadership and long-term programmes of basic research and development (R&D).[4]

An obsessive interest in the West in branding, customer segmentation and customer loyalty is the flip side of disdain for the messy business of developing and applying new technologies and designs. Indeed there are signs that the East, despite its continued commitment to new technology, is also beginning to revel in marketing as a low-cost, line-of-least-resistance route toward profitability.

A big trend in the West is to talk up any aspect of innovation that isn't technological. This is all too convenient at a time when business spending on R&D, and – even more – government spending on R&D is stagnant. R&D in energy, and in services, is particularly weak.

While clients and designers both have much to learn about users, the exaltation of users as the key to innovation only flatters the user-conscious designer. Just like conventional market research, it is unlikely to lead to groundbreaking innovations. Bill Gates, Google, Sony and James Dyson did not do what they did by fixating on consumers.

In fact, investing in daring, risky, supply- and expertise-led innovations contrary to the business cycle tends to make the biggest differences. Design should be a willing collaborator in such projects, and not a cheap alternative to them.

CONVINCING YOUR CLIENTS

After all these years, design is part of the mainstream, and is managed more professionally than in the past. However, for many board-level clients, it is still more about styling than about real practical benefits. To spell out those benefits convincingly, in terms of costs and time saved, ease of use, likely profitability and other factors, is the main task facing the managers of design today.

That is why you should broadly price your work by the benefits your design brings, not by the timesheets you have filled out. What clients are interested in paying for is not your blood, sweat and tears, but rather the difference you make to the bottom line. To compute that difference convincingly, you will need to understand the client's business and its future – in some ways, and without being arrogant, even better than the client.

That is also why, to give them the persuasive powers that are required, your staff need to be able to work in and feel comfortable with high professional standards of

---

4   See Chapter 7 of *Energise! A Future for Energy Innovation*, James Woudhuysen and Joe Kaplinsky, Beautiful Books, 2009

reading, writing and public presentation. Such skills can never substitute for creativity in solving design problems, but they are now the indispensable complement to professionalism in design.

2.11 The validation

Shan Preddy

The fight does not always go to the strongest, nor the race to the swiftest, but that's the way to bet.
• Damon Runyon (1880–1946), newspaperman and writer

THE PROOF OF THE PADDING

Unlike many other business sectors, including its close cousins architecture and advertising, the design world gets off lightly: we are not regulated and controlled, and we do not have compulsory validations or accreditations. Anyone with a laptop and the appropriate software can set themselves up as a design firm, regardless of their abilities, qualifications and experience. Many, of course, succeed in building very successful businesses and take their professional responsibilities seriously. Others work hard within the various design associations and bodies to improve the professionalism of the sector as a whole. But it is all voluntary.

Your own business might be perfect in every respect: processes and procedures; policies; accountability; due diligence; ethics; sustainability; staff training and development; health and safety. However, there will be times when you need to prove that perfection to others, particularly to clients and prospective clients from larger commercial companies and public sector bodies. If they operate rosters, frameworks or approved suppliers' lists, they might ask in their pre-qualification questionnaires (PQQs) whether you hold any accreditations from third parties. These might range from simple membership of professional organisations to official international standards certificates. If you don't hold them, it doesn't necessarily mean that your roster application or project bid will be rejected outright, but you might have to fight a bit harder to get on the list.

For clients and prospects who don't actively insist on accreditation, of course, the presence of some sort of validation will act as a reassurance of your professionalism.

WHAT VALIDATION IS THERE, AND HOW DO YOU DECIDE IF IT'S IMPORTANT?

There are several forms of validation which are relevant to the design sector, and which you might like to consider.

Refereed or qualified memberships

One of the benefits of being part of a recognised membership organisation is that it will underline your professionalism, especially when there are criteria for eligibility. In the UK, for example, the DBA (Design Business Association) stipulates that full membership is available to design consultancies and company in-house design teams which earn more than 50 per cent of their total income from providing design services, and that the contact details of three clients must be supplied for the DBA to approach for references[1]. There is also a Code of Conduct which members agree to follow. Other, but by no means all, membership bodies worldwide have similar arrangements. Organisations which require that members qualify to join are harder to enter, but much more worthwhile once you're there.

Awards

Some design-specific honours are given to individuals in recognition of lifetime achievements; they are awarded, not applied for. However, there are many application-based schemes for design firms, and listing the awards you have won is a powerful way to support your claim of professionalism. They act as an independent, prestigious endorsement of the quality of your company.

Firstly, there are the design sector awards. There are dozens, and there will almost certainly be one or more for your own design discipline and specialism. Winning creative awards which are based on peer-to-peer judgements is important and inspirational, and will help to attract and retain key creative staff. Winning design effectiveness awards, on the other hand, will impress clients and prospects, demonstrating that your design interventions have commercial value.

But what about looking beyond our immediate sector and applying for national recognition schemes for businesses, especially for small businesses? Contact your local or national government enterprise support service to see what might be available. Also, look out for schemes advertised or reviewed in the business press; new initiatives are being launched all the time. What about being 'best employer of the year', or 'greenest company in the county', or 'fastest growing firm in the region'?

What about the really premium awards? In the UK, for example, we have the Queen's Award for Enterprise with three categories: International Trade, Innovation and Sustainable Development. What a wonderful opportunity winning any of these would be to illustrate to your clients, suppliers and staff (not to mention your competitors) the success of your business.

And some clients have their own regular assessment schemes for suppliers and contractors, and issue awards to those which provide a particularly high-quality service. It's worth checking whether any of your clients run such schemes, and discussing with them how you might apply and qualify.

---

1   Source: DBA, January 2010

Official accreditation certificates

Finally, there are the official accreditation schemes which exist for all companies, regardless of business sector.

Of these, the ISO (International Organisation for Standardisation) certificates are probably the best-known. ISO, a non-government organisation with a Central Secretariat in Switzerland, is the world's largest developer and publisher of International Standards, and is a network of the national standards institutes of 163 countries. There are hundreds of standards relating to every aspect of business and public life, but within the design sector there are two which are most likely to be held by leading firms: ISO 9001, which relates to quality management, and ISO 14001, which relates to sustainability, or environmental management.

Additionally, in the UK many design successful firms – not all of them large – have qualified for the Investors in People (IIP) accreditation, a standard which covers the way businesses improve their performance through their people. By placing proper emphasis on your staff and their training and development, and being recognised for doing so, you will demonstrate that you are a serious contender in the business arena.

CHOOSING THEM, AND USING THEM

Qualifying for, and subsequently maintaining, the various types of validation can be expensive and time-consuming. It's worth remembering, particularly with the official accreditation schemes, that there are independent commercial organisations which specialise in helping companies through the maze.

The simplest way to decide which, if any, to pursue is to keep a weather-eye on what your clients and prospects are asking for, and on what your main competitors are offering. If the cost and effort involved in validation will, in your judgement, result in a commercial benefit, go for it.

And once you've got your validations, don't forget to use them to maximum effect in your marketing materials: brochures, website, stationery, credentials presentations, written proposals. It's surprising how many design businesses sweat blood to get an accreditation, and then forget to mention it to anyone.

2.12 The memberships

Shan Preddy

What good is sitting alone in your room?
- Fred Ebb (1933–2004), lyricist, from 'Cabaret'

COME HEAR THE MUSIC PLAY

Running a design business can be a lonely occupation and you can sometimes end up talking to yourself if you're not careful. 'Here's a great marketing idea!' you say, and no one will agree or disagree with you. 'Great!' you announce, 'We made x per cent profit in the last year!', but you will have no idea how that compares with the marketplace as a whole. 'Anyone else had a problem with recruiting good staff?' you cry, and the answer is silence.

Around 90 per cent of design firms worldwide employ fewer than ten people.[1] Only the largest businesses in the sector, therefore, will have reasonable-sized management teams, parent companies, sister divisions or subsidiaries to discuss commercial matters with. For the rest, it's a case of relying on external advisers such as lawyers and accountants (who will be good in their own skills set but might not be very design-knowledgeable) or just dangerous guesswork.

Before you sob gently into your mug of tea, all is not lost. For annual membership fees which are very modest in comparison with the benefits they offer, you can join a number of professional and trade associations, societies and groups. There's no need to be lonely.

JOINING IN

There are three main sectors whose organisations are worth considering:

- the design sector;
- the business sector;
- and the client sector.

---

1   Design Council Design Industry Survey, 2010

It's not a case of 'either/or'. Within the limits of budgets and common sense, many successful design professionals are members of one or more organisations in each of the different sectors. They will all give you a wide range of benefits, not least the advantage of similarly-minded people to talk to. Even if you're not a natural joiner-in, now might be the time to give it a try.

The design sector

Design sector associations, societies and membership groups further sub-divide into three main types:

- individual (or professional) which is for you and corporate (or trade) which is for your company;
- national and local;
- general and discipline-specific.

Although availability and quality varies from country to country, the overall quantity and quality are improving rapidly. Most are based in the relevant capital cities, which is where the majority of design businesses will be located, and so they tend to focus most of their activities there. However, they will hold regional events if they can marshall sufficient numbers, and they are often open to suggestions.

What will you get for your money with these fee-paying associations, societies and groups? What are the real benefits? Do they outweigh the cost?

The mature and well-established organisations offer a very wide range of benefits. They will have directories of membership, which allow clients to find you and allow you to find potential strategic alliances. They will help with your own and your staff's professional development through their design-specific training courses, webinars, conferences and seminars. They will have a Code of Conduct and encourage you to display the association's logo, which you can use to promote your professional services to your clients. They issue regular magazines, newsletters and blogs which will keep you in touch with general developments in the sector. They provide information and assistance for your business, and are able to put you in touch with expert advisers. They often have online discussion groups where you can join a debate or pose a question to your peers. Some have awards schemes which recognise and acknowledge excellence. Some have favourable deals with providers of business services such as insurance, pensions and travel. And most hold networking events, usually with a topical business issue at their heart.

In the UK, we are very fortunate compared with most other countries. Almost every region has at least one membership network of its own, often several. Nationally, we have the corporate membership opportunities afforded by the Design Business Association (DBA). For individual membership, we have the Chartered Society of Designers (CSD), British Design and Art Direction (D&AD) and the Royal Society for the Encouragement of Arts, Manufactures and Commerce (RSA). There are several discipline-specific membership and promotion organisations such as British Design

Innovation (BDI), which concentrates on industrial, service and innovation design. Interior design seems to be particularly well-served: organisations include British Interior Design Association (BIDA), Interior Design Association (IDA) and Society of British Interior Design (SBID), all representing slightly different facets of the discipline. In architecture, we have Royal Institute of British Architects (RIBA) with 40,500 individual members as well as its Chartered Practice Accreditation scheme. Others exist for other disciplines and new ones appear regularly.

Finally, some countries have government-funded design bodies, which are not open to membership; the UK's Design Council is an example. Their services are usually free at the point of delivery, and they can be an excellent source of information and expertise through their websites, publications and mailings. Attending their workshops and events can provide good networking opportunities as well as knowledge, as can volunteering for one of their task forces or being appointed to a committee. All you need to do to use them is to visit their website and get on to their mailing lists.

The small business sector

Design businesses are small businesses, and the challenges that face you are often the same as those facing other entrepreneurs. Most countries have their share of national and local business organisations; in the UK we have several that design businesses can join, including the Federation of Small Businesses, the Institute of Directors and local Chambers of Commerce.

Each will offer slightly different benefits and, if you happen to specialise in working for small businesses, you can also use these forums to meet potential clients.

The client sector

Some of the larger, national client-sector organisations can be all-embracing, with members from a wide range of markets and skills sets; others are very specific and specialist. If you think about your own client base – or perhaps more importantly your desired client base – you should be able to work out where people are likely to gather. If you're not sure, ask your own clients.

On the assumption that you are eligible for membership – some societies are strict about 'suppliers' joining, and others require relevant professional qualifications – what can you hope to achieve? The main advantages lie in access to the specific market. Membership lists can be of use in your sales activities; networking events, seminars and conferences can provide opportunities for meeting people; and magazines, newsletters, blogs and online discussion forums will keep you in touch with facts, issues and trends.

By immersing yourself in the marketplaces of your clients and prospects, your new business activities and existing client relationships will become easier and more meaningful. No client wants to work with someone who doesn't understand what's going on.

BE A LEADER, NOT A FOLLOWER

If you don't make use of any associations you are a member of, then give them up; there is little point in renewing your subscriptions. But if you do use them, why not engage fully with them? Why not take John F Kennedy's approach of asking – to paraphrase – 'not what your association can do for you, but what you can do for your association'? Get involved. Make suggestions. Write articles for its newsletters. Join a committee or a task force. Become a regional representative. Stand for President.

Once you have become established in your career, there is something enormously rewarding in 'giving back' some of your experience and expertise in order to shape the future of the design industry. In addition, you can cite the position on your CV or profile, and use it in your marketing and promotional materials.

It will take time and effort, and you will need the support of your colleagues, but the value that such involvement brings, if done properly, is priceless.

2.13 The network

Phil Jones

You only get to keep what you give away.
- Anon

THE ULTIMATE PARADOX

To make the most of networking opportunities, it helps to know your strengths. Are you a natural networker? People come in all shapes and sizes, and a good way to find out how to play to your strengths is to understand what they are. There are some good analytical tools on the internet, and they are a great place to start discovering what makes you who you are.

These days, too much emphasis is put on short-term payback in networking. Many people assume that merely being seen at industry events, and offering the odd handshake and cheek brush with the right people before slipping out the door on the way back from the toilets, is all that's required to 'network'. Minimum time and effort expended; job done.

In reality, to get the most from a network it's important to leave more behind than a handshake and a business card. People need to feel valued, including the driver who takes you to an appointment and the receptionist who greets you; time spent in a car speaking to the driver will help you grow your network far better than playing with your iPhone. Word of mouth is still the best PR tool there is and to create a great network it's more important to be interested than interesting.

The election of Barack Obama in 2008 was a triumph of great networking. *Camp Obamas* took place all over the USA, and instead of conventional focus groups or indoctrination events, priority was given to listening to the stories of individuals, to taking a genuine interest in them. It captured the imagination of ordinary people on the election trail, and the rest, as they say, is history.

WHO TO CONNECT WITH?

Success in business is all about making connections with interesting people, and a great network includes your family, your own team and your suppliers. In an ideal world, you need a good sprinkling of people who fit into categories 4 and 5 below. But realistically, to find those precious 4s and 5s, you'll also have to waste a little time with categories 1–3.

1. Those who just don't know what's going on.
2. Those who simply watch what's going on.
3. Those who always criticise what's going on.
4. Those who get involved.
5. Those who make things happen.

Building a network with the right talents and personalities doesn't happen overnight, and you'll have to invest time in order to get the best results. Some design organisations offer great networking opportunities, particularly if you're prepared to give up time and help the organisers, rather than just attending events. In the UK, for example, *The Typographic Circle* was kick-started in the nineties by pulling together a committee full of 4s and 5s who knew how to have fun and make things happen.

There are some interesting and original networking events that are put on by individuals in our industry. Sweden has *Digital Crayfish*; Madrid and London have *Bladdered Again*, a quarterly social drinks event that came out of the old *Bladdered by Fax*; there is a global initiative *Creative Social*, where international Creative Directors can compare notes. In the UK, there is *She Says*, for women in the digital sector, and regional events like *Manchester Digital*, *Bristol Media*, *Wired Sussex* and *Long Lunch* in Scotland. Also in the UK, the Design Council, Design Business Association (DBA) and British Design and Art Direction (D&AD) run excellent talks and events that give the opportunity to meet like-minded people and network.

CREATE YOUR OWN

Rather than relying on existing ones, some individuals choose to create their own networking events. Taking the initiative (and time) to create an event around something you feel especially passionate about is a great way to meet like-minded people, as long as you create a reason for them to attend. New technology and a boom in social networking sites make this much easier to achieve.

An example of an event born out of a need for something different was the *Podge Council Lunch,* created in 1994 after a major recession in the early nineties had ripped through the design industry. Its aim was to allow owners of design businesses to chat informally about how they had fared during the recession, and to offer help to each other. Thirty top designers attended the first lunch, and

Podge is still going strong now with over 160 in regular attendance. Arguably, the success of this particular annual networking lunch is because it has never been called a networking lunch. It is about creating an environment that allows people with similar interests and challenges to get together, to meet their peers and chat informally with absolutely no agenda (but a lot of booze).

Few of the companies which attended that first lunch came out of the recession unscathed, but those that did were happy to share their experiences, and a genuine camaraderie was established. *Digital Podge* was created shortly after the dot.com bubble burst, and has been doing the same for the digital world since.

IF YOU GIVE, YOU'LL GET

Social events like these attract a great cross-section of creatives and naturally provide an excellent networking opportunity. However, the people that make the most from such opportunities are those who go with the flow, and turn up regardless of whether there will be any tangible payback in it for them. These are the people that make themselves available to others.

Giving your time and offering your ear to listen are the greatest gifts you can make. Whether it's to a student looking for advice, or a prospective client, it shouldn't make a difference. Give your time to people and they'll help you to build your network. Networking is essentially about 'paying it forward'. You help someone, asking nothing in return, and one day they will remember your kindness and help you. This is the simplest, purest form of networking.

Whether it is through social media or real-world, face-to-face connections, the magic ingredient for creating a great network is remembering that 'you only get to keep what you give away'.

2.14 The working environment

Shan Preddy

No man is an island entire of itself; every man is a piece of the continent, a part of the main.
- John Donne (1572–1631), lawyer, diplomat, chaplain and metaphysical poet

YOU ARE WHERE YOU WORK

Take a good look around you, as though you were seeing your offices for the first time. Do they reflect your firm's corporate identity? Do they form a visual signpost to your business's culture and personality? The answer – whether you like it or not – is yes, they do. The appearance of your offices, intentional or unintentional, sends out a clear message about how you run the rest of your business.

Your working environment is a key part of your business, and it will either contribute to or hinder your commercial success. If you have invested in a great place to work, with attractive, well-functioning workspaces, you will be much more likely to attract and retain good staff, and to reassure clients and prospects. You will also be more motivated personally. On the other hand, if your workplace is a mess, with brushes and mops in the bathrooms, tatty furniture everywhere, dirty coffee cups piling up in the sink and boxes of unfiled paperwork everywhere, it will do exactly the opposite. Either way, the environment you have created says something about you and your priorities.

CORPORATE OR CREATIVE?

Beyond the obvious basics of common sense, employment legislation and health and safety requirements, there's no right or wrong about how you create your working space. Whether you reflect your clients' offices in style, or have an innovative space which could only belong to a design company, the choice is yours.

There are many excellent examples of creative firms' interiors available for reference in print and online. Some use sleek minimalism to create calm, serene workspaces. Others use funky elements such as slides and fireman's poles instead of stairs, or mud huts and space-age pods instead of meeting rooms. What your working environment should look like depends on your culture, your positioning in the marketplace, your product, your offer and, of course, your needs and resources. Whatever your business stands for, however, it should look the part.

Once you have decided on your overall interior direction, make the time and budget to do it properly. It isn't just a question of decor, although that will obviously act as a powerful motivator or demotivator. You need to think carefully about what you want the space to do, how you want it to work. Here are a few questions you might like to ask yourself:

- Does the space function in line with your working methods and processes?
- Are there enough storage areas, now and for the foreseeable future?
- Where will all of the IT requirements go?
- Could some of the space be flexible, with more than one use?
- How much of your furniture needs to be fixed, and how much needs to be loose to allow different 'break-out' combinations?
- Does everyone need their own permanent area, or can you hot-desk?
- What do you need on and around each desk-space?
- How much latitude will you allow your staff over their own space, and over shared spaces?
- Could you have areas with different styles for different functions, such as one formal meeting room and one with squishy beanbags?
- What is the immediate visual impact on entering the space?
- Where will you display examples of your completed projects?
- Do you need waiting areas for visitors, away from the confidential areas of the studio?
- Can visitors get to the bathroom without passing ongoing confidential work for clients?
- Have you got places where staff can work quietly, and where they can work in teams?
- Are there places to meet, to have discussions, to generate ideas? Places to think? Places to eat, and to chat? Places to have fun, play, relax?
- Is there somewhere to store coats, bags, bikes?
- What functions do you really need in the kitchen area?
- Is there somewhere to pin up notices, information, inspirational items?
- Where will central-resource reference and library items be kept?
- Can you expand the workspace as your business grows?
- Is it secure from potential theft of valuable equipment?

- Is your client work secure and confidential?
- Does the space inspire everyone to do better work?

FROM BUZZER TO BOARDROOM

What is the journey like to your place? Most of us never 'visit' our own workspaces. With the exception of the largest and most professional design firms, the journey often goes something like this. With a downloaded map in hand, realisation dawns on the visitor that it is not to scale or oriented north-south, and that it contains no phone number for directions. Arriving eventually and finding a small sign, he rings the buzzer and a voice on the other end says something incomprehensible due to the traffic noise outside, followed by a loud parp of the door-release. The internal signage is poor and, once at the right door, the visitor finds that he is unexpected. Nobody takes his coat away or offers refreshment. He waits on an uncomfortably low chair, flipping through dog-eared, irrelevant trade journals. Finally, he is greeted and collected, and the meeting finally starts with a very stressed guest and a slightly puzzled host.

Try taking 'the journey' and find out how it works at your place. Even better, ask a friend to make the journey with you. In particular, make sure that your directions and signage work, and that clients, prospects and other important visitors (such as talented potential recruits) are greeted by name and made to feel welcome: it is very rare that they will turn up unexpectedly. It's in your own interest, after all, to hold meetings with people who are relaxed and in a positive frame of mind.

2.15 The neverending story

Shan Preddy

It has taken me all this time to discover which notes to leave out.
- Dizzie Gillespie (1917–1993), jazz trumpet player, bandleader, singer and composer

KAIZEN AND THE ART OF DESIGN MAINTENANCE

It could be argued that if you want to run a successful design business, you'll need to enjoy it and you'll need to make a profit. Not enjoying it, and never will? Give it up and do something else. Life's too short. Not making a profit, and never will? Ah, well then, your decision is shortly going to be made for you.

However, even assuming that you are enjoying it and making a profit, you can't afford to be complacent. Part of the enjoyment of running any business – and part of the profit – comes from making continuous improvements to knowledge, culture, staff motivation, financial performance, client retention, pitch wins, time recovery, office environment and all of the hundreds of different elements, large and small, which go into making a business tick.

This process of continuous improvement, or the art of 'kaizen' as the Japanese call it, is the philosophy and practice of making constant, small advances. It's not a one-off activity; it's a process. We need to ask ourselves – continuously – 'are we getting better and better at doing what we do?'

STANDING STILL ON THE UP ESCALATOR

Here's just one example of continuous improvement in the area of knowledge: keeping abreast of trends and innovations.

The design world, in common with other fast-growing business sectors, is developing rapidly. New technologies are leading to new products and services, which are leading to new market behaviours and new demands from clients. These will, in turn, lead to the arrival of further new products and services and the hunt for new technologies to supply them.

If you don't understand the changes taking place in technology, products and services, market behaviours and client needs, you will still progress by absorbing things through the media, through conversations and through projects. But taking such a passive stance will slow you down. It's like standing still on a flight of up escalators instead of walking up them: you will get to the top eventually, but when you get there you'll find that the market – and your competitors – are already half way up the next escalator.

DANGERS AND SOLUTIONS

Introducing a culture of continuous improvement is not always as easy as it sounds. There are four main pitfalls.

The first is the feeling of gloom that can descend if you decide that absolutely everything needs improving. The second is the failure to improve the right things. The third is not knowing whether your improvements have worked or not. And the fourth is the sense of 'improvement fatigue' that can set in among staff and colleagues.

Let's look at each of these, together with some solutions.

Feeling gloomy

Once you start looking into all of the improvements you could make to your business, it is easy to become disheartened and imagine that you're useless at everything. And this can become contagious, spreading though your firm like an unstoppable force.

Stop right there; beating yourself up isn't going to help anyone, least of all you. Instead, make sure that your culture is one of constructive feedback so that you, your senior management team and all of your employees find the continuous improvement process motivating and are empowered to join in.

Constructive feedback isn't based on 'good...bad', or 'yes...but'. It focuses instead on 'good...better', or on 'yes...and'. A simple but very effective feedback framework is to ask two questions: first 'what do we do well?', and then 'what could we do better?' Give yourself a well-earned pat on the back for the former before you start to fix the latter, and be realistic about goals, resources and timescales.

Improving the right things

Focus on the important things. There's little merit in spending a lot of time on trivial improvements, satisfying though it can be to tick them off the list.

To make sure you fix the right things, it's important to know what's broke and what ain't. One sure way to find out is to conduct a 360° survey, where everyone is asked for their views: your clients, your employees and your suppliers. Asking for constructive feedback from people who know your business well can be enlightening.

If you ask an independent consultant to do the survey for you, and if you make the responses non-attributable, you will get better results than if you do it yourself.

Knowing what's worked

There is an old business saying: 'If you can't measure it, you can't manage it.' You will certainly find a continuous improvement programme easier to operate if you monitor and measure it.

Start by identifying the most important areas for improvement. Financial results? Staff knowledge? Client satisfaction? Internal processes? Benchmark where you are now, and then go on to repeat the reading at a later date to see how you have progressed. This doesn't need to be over-complicated: as long as you are consistent in its application, you can set up your own 'scoring' system.

Some things are easy to measure in figures: financial results, staff resignations, client retention, sales conversion rates, electricity consumption, waste. However, other things in design can't be measured numerically: creativity, for example. Here, you will need to decide how it will be measured. Who will be the judge? In whose opinion has the team's creativity risen or fallen? This is where a good creative director comes in.

Improvement fatigue

Finally, too much change, too often, can be exhausting, and continuous improvement programmes can be frustrating if objectives are not swiftly followed by outcomes.

If you announce brilliant ideas for improvements and then don't execute them, your staff and colleagues will become disappointed and disillusioned. If they offer suggestions themselves, and those suggestions are never acknowledged, they will stop thinking of them. If their suggestions are praised, but never see the light of day, they will lose respect for you. It's difficult to know which is worse: the dullness of never having ideas in the first place, or the frustration of good ideas which go nowhere.

Why not turn improvement fatigue into improvement invigoration? Engage and empower the whole company. Set up a 'suggestions box', physical or digital, and encourage everyone to post their ideas for improvements whenever the thought strikes them. Empty it at regular, fixed intervals and evaluate the ideas with the management team. Present both the ideas and your evaluations to everyone in a group session, indicating which ideas will or will not be carried forward, and why. And make sure that you only announce planned improvements once it's absolutely certain that they will be implemented. As the old proverb says: 'Measure a thousand times, cut once.'

Section Three:
The People

3.1 The management team

Shan Preddy

A man is nothing without his hat.
- Buzz Lightyear, character in 'Toy Story 2', Disney/Pixar

HOW MANY HATS DO YOU WEAR?

Senior people in design businesses tend to wear a lot of different hats, and the smaller the firm, the more the hats that will be on your head. There might be a shareholder's or owner's hat as well as a Company Director's or Partner's hat. There might be a whole wardrobe of workers' hats, such as team leader, practising designer or consultant. Sometimes, there will be a coffee-maker-and-biscuit-buyer hat, or a stationery-orderer hat or a find-a-plumber hat. Anyone reading this who works in one of the larger design companies, by the way, might suddenly be remembering why they don't want to run their own business.

When thinking about the structure and function of a senior management team, you need to understand the different hats and their relative roles, whether you personally wear one of them or all of them. You need to make sure that you are constantly playing to strengths, both yours and your colleagues. You also need to get professional advice from your lawyers to make sure you fully understand the legal implications of all senior appointments.

THE DIFFERENT HATS

Shareholder/owner

Shareholders or business owners might or might not play an active part in the management of the business. Even if their involvement is purely financial, however, it is likely that that they will have an interest in design in general and in your business in particular; they probably wouldn't be investing in it otherwise. In many cases, the main shareholders will also be the management team; they own and run the business. Either way, shareholders should expect to receive a financial return on their investment, whether that initial investment is in money, time, expertise or all three.

Don't forget to record properly how the relationship between shareholders will work. What will happen if an owner – whether a shareholder or a partner – wants to sell or give away the interest they have in a business? Or if a shareholding employee leaves the business? A shareholders' or partners' agreement will provide the proper record, and the process of considering these issues before they are recorded can be illuminating.

Company Director or Partner

Whether you are a Director of a Limited Company or Public Limited Company (plc), or a Partner in a Partnership or Limited Liability Partnership (LLP), the title isn't just a status symbol. It carries duties and responsibilities, legal and otherwise.

According to the UK's Institute of Directors (IOD): 'The Board of Directors of a company is primarily responsible for:

- determining the company's strategic objectives and policies;
- monitoring progress towards achieving those objectives and policies;
- appointing senior management;
- accounting for the company's activities to relevant parties, for example shareholders.'[1]

The same would apply to Partners. In addition to their Board responsibilities, individual Directors or Partners might have specific, specialist functions: finance, marketing, HR, creative and so on.

Directors are responsible for making sure that the company fulfils its statutory duties. Again, the IOD is clear on the subject. 'Many of their duties and obligations are mandated by the Companies Act 2006. Others are governed by the Insolvency Act 1986 and the Company Directors' Disqualification Act 1986'.[2] A Board Director is also expected to ensure the company seeks and gets appropriate professional advice on those matters where there is not sufficient expertise on the Board itself. So the Board has to ensure, for instance, that it is provided with good financial information so as to enable it to properly manage the affairs of the company. If someone is not a Director but tells the Board what to do – for example if someone owns all or a significant part of the company – then the law might consider that

---

1   Institute of Directors Factsheet 2010, *The Duties, Responsibilities and Liabilities of Directors*.

2   Ibid.

person to be a 'shadow director', with the same duties and responsibilities as any other member of the Board.

The Managing Director or Chief Executive is responsible for the performance of the company, as dictated by the Board's overall strategy. He or she reports either to the Chairman, if there is one, or to the Board of Directors. In Partnerships and LLPs, each Partner is responsible for – and liable for – the performance and statutory duties of the company.

It's worth mentioning one thing which sometimes catches people unawares. Many senior roles in design firms have the word 'Director' in their title: Creative Director, Design Director, Account Director, IT Director and so on. However, the people holding these titles might or might not be Directors of the company and it is important that everyone concerned is clear whether the title is only an indication of seniority, or whether it indicates the legal status of Company Director with a place on the Board.

Non-Executive Directors and other influencers

There is an option of appointing non-Executive Directors. Their job is to advise the Board but they do not, as the name implies, have executive powers and may not vote on resolutions. They tend to be experienced people with a good general track record, although they are sometimes very specialist. They are not just consultants: they have statutory duties and, arguably, a moral obligation not to work for competing or conflicting businesses. Occasionally, a non-Executive Chairman will be appointed: this can be particularly helpful in firms whose management teams are relatively young and inexperienced.

WHICH HATS DO YOU NEED FOR YOUR MANAGEMENT TEAM?

The composition of your management team will depend on the size of your business, on its structure, on its legal status and on its areas of operation.

Who might you include? All of the Board Directors, or all of the Partners, of course. You might benefit from appointing a part-time Finance Director, or HR Director: smaller companies need the skills and advice these experts can provide, but not their full-time input. You might consider a regular, retained consultant, or a non-Executive Director or two. A design company which works with clients in the medical sector might, for example, appoint a consultant for business development experience and a non-Executive Director from a pharmaceutical background for specialist knowledge and, possibly, contacts. You might think about a non-Executive Chairman.

For all but the smallest firms, it can be helpful to include a senior representative from each section, or specialist area, of the business on the team: design, client service, production, finance, HR, IT, marketing, administration and so on. These people, who might be 'Heads of xyz', do not have any legal responsibility for the business, other than the obvious requirements of fulfilling their employment contract obligations and behaving within the law. Their purpose on the management team is to share their knowledge and opinions with the top people, and to take information and directions from those top people back to the teams which report to them. They influence and help to drive the current and future performance of the firm, but they don't run it.

Finally, if you have one, an Office Manager or Practice Manager should also sit on the management team and attend management meetings.

WHICH HATS GO TO MANAGEMENT MEETINGS?

All members of the management team should attend regular management meetings, whose purpose is to debate and decide on issues relating to the running of the business. Other issues, such as project work, should be covered in a different meeting.

A few words on management meetings. Hold them at regular, scheduled intervals, at least monthly. Keep them short, start and end them on time, and make them productive. How many meetings have you had which start late and run over time, and where the agenda meanders about between half-year profits, staff birthdays, client gains, upcoming pitches, the quality of the coffee, tax matters and project planning?

The shareholder hat, by the way, should be left firmly on its peg during management team meetings, and only worn when the Directors or the Partners are carrying out their periodic reporting on profitability (or otherwise) and on the dividends which will be paid (or not). If you are both a shareholder and a Director/Partner, try to separate the two functions as much as is sensible, in the same way that you will already separate, say, running a company and running your household. Think like an investor and like a business director, but not necessarily at the same time.

PUTTING ALL THE HATS TOGETHER

Finally, it's important that the management team is just that: a team. It needs to work together properly, not just as a group of people with fancy titles. This can particularly be an issue in the larger design consultancies.

No matter how many people, and which sorts of people – Directors, Partners, senior section representatives or non-Execs – you have on your management team, it must share common goals, and have clearly assigned roles which suit the capabilities of the individual members. Everyone on that team should be involved in your business's vision and values, its strategic direction and its operating policies. Everyone is collectively responsible for monitoring the performance of the business and ensuring that the agreed goals are reached. If your management team isn't working, your business isn't working.

3.2   The creatives

Rod Petrie

Creativity is an expression of self. Therefore, belief in what they're doing is essential for creative people.
- Sir John Hegarty, founder of advertising agency BBH (Bartle Bogle Hegarty)

HOW TO MANAGE CREATIVITY

To achieve the best from design and production, you need the right combination of people, a process that results in great work from beginning to end, clear communication and a spirit of collaboration. Then you need to make sure you have a best-practice policy that keeps you there. One of the key challenges in the creative world is the different skill sets involved in all aspects of the process: from pre-design strategy, through front-end creative design concepts, to back-end production, with project management expertise and systems keeping things on track throughout.

Achieving the best over time relies on four key factors:

- recruiting and keeping exceptional talent;
- building collaboration;
- getting the best results;
- staying on top.

RECRUITING AND KEEPING EXCEPTIONAL TALENT

Talent is a gift, with serious talent in short supply. Ours is a people-first business, so recruiting and retaining the best people is key to competitive advantage and getting it right is never easy. Talent might present itself in an ability to come up with original ideas, approaching problems from left field, putting teams together and getting the best out of others, or an eye for detail that makes for consistently accurate artwork.

The common thread is an exceptional quality standard, usually associated with a love and passion for that activity. To be the best, you need people with the right attitude and the ability to become 'one of us'. You need to know what makes someone exceptional, whatever their skill traits and this is often down to gut feel and personal chemistry. You need to be able to make a connection with that individual so they want to work for you and no one else. Then you need to make sure you keep them.

The approach to recruitment and personal development might need individual strategies for each discipline so you need to think outside the box. Consider bringing in unconventional staff, exploring unusual talent pools, and being flexible in what you offer to persuade someone to join the team. Don't forget the talent pool you already have as this is often the most rewarding way forward and, if you get it right, the most economic.

BUILDING COLLABORATION

True collaboration is a seamless process, from start to finish. It's no easy task, however, when the skill sets involved in the process differ so widely. It's essential to foster mutual respect between individuals with different job roles. One of the most common problems in a design agency is the lack of understanding between disciplines, leading to a culture of 'Them & Us'.

Every part of the process is as important as the last. It's no good having great strategic input to a brief if the designers don't take it on board, or having a great creative idea if it can't be implemented commercially. Also, the best people often have egos to match. Talented creatives, like other brilliant minds, can be notoriously temperamental with strong characters that need creative management, or their undisciplined behaviour will affect team performance and ultimately the quality of the work produced. Handling emotions and strongly held principles is often the biggest challenge of running a successful creative agency.

You need a common vision and goal that is clearly communicated and understood, with each team member knowing their role and value. Just as someone is responsible in the agency to lead and champion a project, it is critical that the creatives are led by someone who knows the difference between right and wrong, someone with talent, skill and a grown-up approach to leadership. They must know when to support and when to challenge, and be able to spot a great idea in a scribble. They should never hog the limelight, but should give credit where credit is due.

GETTING THE BEST RESULTS

The best design will result in creative ideas that exploit a genuine opportunity or address a core problem, that answer a commercial brief, and that make designers proud. The best production is a faithful translation of these ideas, consistently and accurately implemented in collaboration with supplier, manufacturer and client.

You need to focus on getting the best out of each individual and each discipline. When people feel their ideas are valued they contribute more. For design there is a need to recognise a client's real problem, empathise with the target audience, be creative and inspired about potential solutions, and identify those ideas that best meet and stretch the brief.

For production it is about being thorough, having rigorous systems, managing effectively, being accurate and interpreting design solutions across a range of products and media. Exceptional talent and ability is rare, so knowing the emotional pressure points of when to stroke and reassure people and when to boost their confidence is critical.

STAYING ON TOP

Getting to the top is tough. Staying there and remaining there is even tougher without the best people working together. The real trick is consistency of performance. This means being flexible enough to respond to change, and being confident and brave enough to fix something that might not be broken.

Businesses need to be successful in the long term, not necessarily for financial reasons but also to recruit and retain the best talent and to maintain a position at the top. The best people stay ahead by constantly upgrading themselves, by keeping in step with developments, not just in their own area of expertise and industry but in other sectors.

Creativity needs to be kept fresh and alive at all times or it will become a factory-processed, mass-produced commodity item. Creatives need to be constantly breaking new ground in finding ways to fuel their creative fires, as profitable ideas can create profit. Creative leaders need to establish a clear philosophy and a criteria for judging work that inspires risk-taking, and should never be afraid of working with the very best people. Successful companies stay on top by establishing best practice procedures, and continually investing in the foundations for growth – their people, and the goodwill of those people.

3.3 The client facers

Jan Casey

The single biggest problem in communication is the illusion that it has taken place.
- George Bernard Shaw (1856–1950), playwright

WHO LOOKS AFTER THE CLIENTS?

Design businesses have a variety of operating models. Some have account management and strategy as separate functions to the creative process, some designers manage all aspects of a project themselves and in some cases the managing director or creative director has the principal relationship with the client. Whichever model you adopt – and indeed there are many more than these listed – take the time to assess not only whether it is right for your business, but whether it works for your clients. Perhaps it works for most, but not all. Some clients prefer to work with account managers but others, particularly those who come from a design background, prefer to liaise directly with designers. There is a tendency in all businesses to develop systems on the basis of what suits them rather than their customers, but it is vital to remember that your clients are your income and you are there to support them.

Below are seven key points that, if fully incorporated into your practice, will improve your delivery beyond measure.

KNOW YOUR CLIENT

It's essential that you understand your client's business. This includes their audience, products, services, competitive environment and the challenges they face. If you enjoy your work, seeking out this information will become an integrated part of your daily life.

It's also important to understand what the client organisation is trying to achieve. Often we focus on the task in hand rather than the end goal. Be proactive: ask your clients to share their marketing plans so that you have a full appreciation of the organisation's vision. Clients commission design because they want fresh thinking but they know more about their product and organisation than you do, so respect the tacit knowledge of the individuals you work with and consider them as part of the creative process. It's good practice to invest some time conducting internal research or brainstorming for each of your client relationships. This will enable you to go to your client with ideas to take your project and their organisation forward.

UNDERSTAND THE BRIEF

The project brief is a key document. Understanding a client's requirements seems a statement of the obvious, but many clients experience designers saying little in the briefing session and then returning with work that is inappropriate. Interrogate the brief with intelligent questions, challenge where necessary and define what needs to be done. Ask for the brief ahead of the meeting so you can do some fact-finding in advance. If your client hasn't written a brief, do it for them. This will highlight your skills, show that you are proactive and demonstrate your investment in an integrated client/agency team.

SUPPORT YOUR CLIENT

Many clients put chemistry as the key criteria when assessing the success of an agency relationship – even above creativity. They look for a collaborative and trusting partnership where the creative and client teams are aligned. You need to empathise with and support your clients, especially when they are having difficulties. Understand what matters to them and try and feel what they feel. Design can be a step outside of a client's comfort zone and can be a nerve-racking experience, with its accompanying pressures – credibility, money, even their job. So it is important to be sensitive to this, to demystify the design process and support the client on the journey. You should work with your clients to move them forward and give them reflected glory.

We live with design every day and are in the advantageous position of having been involved in many projects before. The client may not. So make use of this fortunate situation and ensure you are always one step ahead across every aspect of your project. This approach will also build the relationship – the client will immediately feel supported and their confidence in you will start to build. Keep the client informed of your progress and look after their budget as though it were yours. Make them feel comfortable and never blind them with technology. Some designers love the big reveal, and understandably: delight can come from creative theatre. Clients, however, fear the nasty surprise. Involving them at interim stages in the process will help ensure approval of your work, as they will take more ownership.

AGREE RELATIONSHIP PRACTICES

At the start of a client relationship share your working methods and agree how best you can collaborate. Explain your tools of communication and at what point they will receive documentation: for example, a Contact Report should be issued no later than 24 hours after a meeting. This not only helps the client understand what, how and when work will be delivered but also sets their expectation so they are not disappointed. But don't impose your process on your clients: make sure you tailor one that works for them.

Agree the contact procedure. At the early stages of the relationship you need to understand who the key stakeholders are and whether there is someone more senior to your client who is really driving the project, so you can address this situation early on. Be available for your client, return their calls and emails at the earliest possible moment, even if it just to acknowledge receipt and confirm when you will supply an answer to their question.

QUALITIES AND CONDUCT

Be attentive: people like to be heard but unfortunately designers not listening is a common experience for clients. A crucial part of your work is understanding your client, so you need to concentrate on what they are saying. Actively listen to them and really focus on the moment. It's not only courteous but you will learn more and be able to ask the right questions.

Be confident: be sufficiently secure to say 'no it's not the right thing to do', if this is what you believe.

Be genuine: pretending to be someone else comes into play when you're out of your depth and feel insecure. If you're good at what you do you can relax into your authenticity.

Be honest: right down to not allowing your colleagues to say you're in a meeting when you're not. At some level the client will pick this up and then question whether you are truthful in other areas.

Be open: your client should have visibility of your fees at the start and throughout the project. Money needs to be discussed openly and confidently, though ensure you choose the right moment so that it doesn't provoke the wrong reaction.

Be accountable: don't over promise, know your limits and don't offer skills or disciplines that you are not able to deliver. Concentrate on what you do, and do it well.

Be appropriate: if you think negatively about a client, somehow it will leak out, even if it's just to your team. Question whether these feelings are more about your inadequacies.

Be knowledgeable: read, listen and learn. This will help you and your clients.

Be clear: check with your colleagues that you are articulate both in the spoken and written word. Also ensure you don't use terminology that may be unfamiliar to clients: this can lead to misunderstandings.

Be skilled: lack of clarity when presenting work is weak and unconvincing. Client-facing individuals need to be competent as well as talented.

DELIVER WHAT YOU ARE PAID TO DO

As a design consultancy you should think strategically as well as tactically, deliver both breadth and depth with the end customer in mind and present ideas that are commercially viable as well as creatively excellent. Make sure you plan. Presentations are often left to the last minute with no time to review, whereas you should be assessing the creative work against the brief on regular basis. Make sure you debrief after each meeting and ask your colleagues not only what you did well, but what you could have done better. It's very helpful to get feedback from your clients and on the whole they enjoy expressing their thoughts. Whether you employ an external consultant or appoint someone internally to instigate a client feedback process, if you want to continue improving you need to know what you are doing well and where you are not performing. Make sure you take constructive criticism in a receptive way.

GO THE EXTRA MILE

A huge amount of energy is put into winning clients through credentials, website, PR and your profile. Make sure you put as much energy into keeping them. Don't settle into a routine but aim for a long-term fulfilling relationship by constantly challenging yourself, being diligent, surprising your client and delivering unwavering commitment.

Go over and above what is asked, and do more than what is simply required. The extra effort is really appreciated and, as a consequence, you will develop long lasting relationships.

3.4 The hunter-gatherers

Blair Enns

The timid man yearns for full value, and demands a tenth. The bold man strikes for double value and compromises on par.
* Mark Twain (1835–1910), writer and humorist

WHO BRINGS IN THE BUSINESS?

No other role in the firm carries such weight of expectation, such belief, that the firm is but one über-human person away from success as the business development magician, the rainmaker. Such large expectations are rarely met.

Consistent business development success requires a compelling positioning, strong business development processes and good personnel. Too often a design firm looks to overcome weaknesses in the first two areas with unrealistic expectations of the third. This is the real reason that rainmakers are as rare as unicorns.

JUST OFF TO RUSTLE UP SOME NEW BUSINESS –

Node DESIGN Inc

THAT MEANS HE'S GOING TO MEET A BUNCH OF COWBOYS, TALK A LOAD OF BULL ABOUT BRANDING AND TRY TO ROPE IN A LETTERHEAD JOB!

CENTRALISED VERSUS DISTRIBUTED BUSINESS DEVELOPMENT MODELS

There are two main strategies for allocating new business responsibility within the firm. One is to centralise the efforts through one person, either an employee or a principal, and the other is to distribute responsibility across many individuals.

The question of centralising or distributing responsibility arises as the firm grows and the principal begins to delegate. To better understand whether to centralise or distribute, let's first explore the various functions of business development.

THE FUNCTIONS OF BUSINESS DEVELOPMENT

There are five main functions within business development, some of which can be delegated and/or distributed, and some of which the principal should retain.
They are:

- planning
- lead generation
- lead conversion
- nurturing opportunities
- closing opportunities.

Planning is the preparatory work that comes after the firm's focus has been chosen and before leads are generated and converted. It includes identifying the target market and determining the criteria that will frame the engagements the firm pursues.

Planning is the domain of principals and partners, with input from others. It must not be delegated.

Lead Generation is the collection of activities that surfaces potential opportunities for the firm, from sales-based unsolicited enquiries, to marketing activities and the PR and publicity-based activities of speaking and writing. Lead generation can be delegated, and is typically the first function to be so. And while the responsibility for seeing that lead generation targets are hit resides with one individual (usually the head of business development), lead generation responsibility can be distributed widely across the firm.

Lead Conversion is the act of following up on leads to determine if they represent any specific near or mid-term opportunities. Lead conversion also includes assigning the next steps in the buy-sell cycle, and all appropriate record keeping. Lead conversion can be delegated, but should be centralised in order to maintain a consistency in their evaluation and the assigning of next steps. So, while firms will ask numerous employees to bring leads to the table, the most efficient approach to following up on and categorising those leads is to centralise the function with one individual. This takes the pressure to sell off of people who have no inclination or training for it.

Nurturing includes the follow-up conversations with viable prospects that have no identifiable opportunity associated with them. This includes follow-up phone calls and emails and distribution of the firm's nurturing tools, typically newsletters and other vehicles of the firm's thought-leadership. Nurturing can be delegated but should be centralised through one person.

Closing describes the final acts, late in the buying cycle, that secure the engagement with the client, culminating with the final meeting with, and typically a presentation to, all the client decision makers. Before clients hire a design firm, they want to meet with and evaluate the brain trust of the organisation. For this reason, closing remains the function of principals and should not be delegated. Others are often enlisted to help, particularly in setting up the closing meeting and in helping to facilitate proper sales process within the meeting, but the principals of the firm must see closing as their domain.

Of the five functions of business development, it is the first and last – planning and closing – that should not be delegated. Thus, when you hire a business development person, you are looking for someone who is skilled at generating leads, who has the probing conversational skills to be able to convert those leads to opportunities where they exist, and who is able to nurture over time those prospects that are furthest from buying. You also want your hire to be able to transition to closing opportunities and possibly help to facilitate the close.

THE SKILLS OF BUSINESS DEVELOPMENT

The business development role requires a combination of sales, marketing, public relations and networking skills. The required balance of these skills will vary from firm to firm, primarily based on how the firm is positioned.

Narrowly-positioned expert firms that are seen to have a deeper expertise than their more generalist counterparts can often get away with less sales and networking skills, as they typically enter into the sales cycle already commanding a differentiated position relative to their competition, and therefore can get by with fewer of the personal interaction skills of selling and networking. Maintaining that expert position is far easier for someone who does not trade on personal rapport.

More broadly-positioned firms that invite much more competition require a higher level of sales and networking skills, as they are more likely to win business based on chemistry and relationships.

VETTING CANDIDATES WITH THE FOUR TOOLS QUESTION

When interviewing candidates for the business development role a good question to pose is the Four Tools Question:

> *Business development is a combination of four skills: sales, marketing, public relations and networking. Consider each of these skills as a tool that is lying on the table in front of you. Playing to your strengths, what tool do you pick up first? What do you select next? And which do you choose third and then last. Why?*

The ideal candidate would select sales as one of the first two tools. This indicates a high competitive drive and an ability to overcome obstacles such as call reluctance. A generalist firm would look for someone who selected networking in the top two as well, while a narrowly specialised firm with well-developed thought-leadership and a broad geographic trading area would look for someone who selects networking as one of the last two tools.

3.5   The farmer-growers

Shan Preddy

There were four people named Everyone, Anyone, No one and Someone Else. There was an important job to be done, and Everyone was responsible for doing it. The trouble was, Everyone thought that Someone Else would be sure to do the work. In the end, however, although Anyone could have done the job, No one actually did it. As a result, Everyone got angry and blamed Someone Else.

• Anon

FARMING THE CLIENTS' BUSINESS

It can take a lot of effort to win business from a new client. The delicate sowing of the seed, the watering and feeding of first growths, the protection from harsh weather and hungry predators. Even in design disciplines with a reasonably rapid turnaround of projects, such as communications and packaging, it can take several months of time, money and energy before a prospective client becomes an active client. In disciplines where projects have longer durations, such as in industrial design and interiors, it can take many years. However, it only takes a very short time indeed – sometimes merely a matter of hours – to go from 'you're hired' to 'you're fired' and to lose a client's business.

The previous chapter, 3.4 *The Hunter-Gatherers*, deals with the rainmakers, the people who bring the business in. Here, we are concerned with whose job it is to satisfy clients and keep their business once it has been won, and then to develop the relationships so that you are given bigger and better projects in the future. The aim is to get to a point when either you are the preferred design consultancy, automatically appointed for relevant projects, or you are retained, with a contract and a regular schedule of payments.

CULTIVATION DANGER POINTS

At different stages in a project's life, it becomes easier or harder for a client to decide to work – or to continue working – with you.

The first danger point comes at the appointment stage. Unless you are the only design business in the world who can do a particular thing, the client holds the balance of power and can choose whether to work with you or not. Once you have been appointed, however, and right through all of the concept and development stages, the balance shifts slightly in your favour; rigorous timelines tend to mean that replacing design firms mid-project isn't something to be undertaken lightly.

The next major danger point arrives when the project reaches its implementation stages. Although few clients would think it desirable to do it, another design firm could be appointed to take the project over at this stage if you are not delivering what the client wants. The final, and toughest, danger point comes at the end of the project, before plans are made for the next. Will you be reappointed automatically? Will you have to pitch? Or will the project go to one of your competitors?

Like most of us, clients aren't always good at complaining. They often don't tell you that they have no intention of ever working with you again, but just slip quietly away into the sunset. Often, the first time you realise that you have lost that client is when you hear that they have just appointed one of your competitors for a project which should, by rights, have come to you.

WHO GETS TO DRIVE THE TRACTOR?

So who is to blame if a project doesn't develop into a relationship, and the client wanders off to seek pastures new? Who should have been ensuring client satisfaction? Who should have been nurturing the relationship and actively cultivating and growing the business? The easy answer, of course, is 'everyone'. Each encounter the client has with your firm – from major project meetings and budget updates to minor phone calls and emails – contributes to the decision whether to continue working with you or not. But one person needs to be responsible and, ultimately, accountable, regardless of the job title that person uses.

There are two main alternative operating structures in design firms: those where an account (or client, or project) director, manager or executive takes the main client-facing role, and those where designers have responsibility for it as well as for creativity. Neither model is better than the other; they are just different. Communications and branding consultancies often use the first model; digital, interior and product consultancies tend to favour the second. This is due, in part, to the in-depth knowledge of design technicalities that the client-facer needs to have in addition to their strategic and project management skills. In each case, the farmer-grower should be the most senior person allocated to each client, whether that is an account person or a designer.

KEY PERFORMANCE INDICATORS (KPIs): HOW DO YOU KNOW THE CULTIVATION IS WORKING?

It's not enough just to 'encourage' the farmer-growers to do this part of their job. Like all other aspects of their work, you should outline the responsibility for both client satisfaction and proactive client development in their job descriptions, set clear, measurable targets and evaluate the person's ability to do it successfully or not in their performance appraisals. This means establishing measurement criteria, or key performance indicators (KPIs).

On top of the absolute baseline of the successful and profitable delivery of projects, specific farmer-grower KPIs might include:

- no loss of clients mid-project;
- evidence of client satisfaction from post-project completion surveys, or client audits;
- growth in income value from existing clients;
- improvement in quality of projects from existing clients;
- appointment to new projects from existing clients without having to pitch competitively;
- referrals and recommendations from existing clients to new clients for new projects.

In some design businesses, farmer-growers are incentivised and financially rewarded on their performance in this area, just as hunter-gatherers often are.

3.6   The strategists

Ann Binnie

'Would you tell me, please, which way I ought to go from here?' 'That depends a good deal on where you want to get to,' said the Cat. 'I don't much care where,' said Alice. 'Then it doesn't much matter which way you go,' said the Cat.
*   Lewis Carroll (1832–98), mathematician, writer and photographer, from 'Alice's Adventures in Wonderland'

PLANNERS, AND WHAT THEY DO

Having invented the role and given it the name, the advertising agency business has spent decades trying to explain planners to outsiders. 'Planning' attempts to describe an activity which is usually about guiding or facilitating a disciplined process of creative development. Knowledge and understanding about the market, its customers and consumers is collected and turned into insights which are then applied to the enhancement of the creative development process. At the core of what the planner does is the need to understand customers and consumers, how they interact with the category, the brand, its competitors and what influences their behaviours and attitudes in the context of the brand.

DETAILED SCIENTIFIC ANALYSIS SUGGESTS THAT THIS COLOUR STIMULATES A POSITIVE PSYCHO/EIDETIC RESPONSE IN POTENTIAL INVESTORS *

* TRANSLATION : "I LIKE RED, ME"

In their natural habitat you might find planners operating in a variety of ways. They might be in research mode, analysing and interpreting data, moderating qualitative focus groups, using online methods to conduct primary research, seeking out published sources on the internet, or conducting studies using the principles of anthropology and observing (even living with in some cases) users of brands in their own environments. This last is known as ethnographic research and can provide tremendous insights, particularly for packaging and ergonomic related design.

They might be operating in the manner of a shop steward of the target audience, making sure the latter's needs are understood and bringing their point of view to every step of the creative development process.

Or they could be in thoughtful strategist mode, developing and guarding the strategy, mining data for insights. You might also find them in creative catalyst role, writing the creative brief, facilitating workshops and brainstorming sessions.

Some planners do all of these and some have clear favourites. Some do all their own research, others wouldn't dream of it. Some like nothing better than burying themselves in excel spreadsheets of quantitative consumer data, others would rather be surfing relevant consumer blogs and making inspired connections; still others would rather spend their time with a few representative consumers and really get under the skin of attitudes and motivations. You can expect all to take on the consumer or customer perspective and to have a strategic role, some looking at the big picture, others loving to get down and dirty with the creative product.

BE CLEAR WHAT YOU NEED FROM THEM

It is useful to work out what you want and be sure that you hire the right flavour. Much will depend on the nature of the project (for external planning resource) or the kind of agency you want to be (for an in-house resource). It also helps to take account of who in your team they're going to work with. Planners at the creative end can work beautifully with their creative counterparts if that's what the creatives are used to; but they can cause a sense of insecurity if perceived as a threat or encroachment upon creative territory. So make it clear to them and to the rest of the team what they're there for.

GET THEM IN THE LOOP EARLY

Let planners in as early as possible in the design process. That way their focus can be on the strategy and early guidance and not on using your precious ideas as cannon fodder in a last minute research shoot out. Tell them everything: let them get close to the client and give them all the inputs they ask for.

Give them room to breathe and space to think: open plan offices are rarely ideal when the planner is in thinking mode. And remember they work with data, experience, models, connections, but they can't magic strategies out of thin air, not ones with any robustness anyway. Listen seriously to their requests for investment in published or proprietary data sources or some focus groups. A little data or input can go a long way in the right hands and are grist to the mill of a happy and productive planner. With the right stimulus (grain of sand) the most valuable interpretations and insights (pearls) can emerge. So do let them loose to their hearts' content.

If they want to research your ideas, trust them. If they know what they're doing they are not looking for respondents to say what they like but rather to understand how your ideas work. If in the process they discover some unintended consequences that render an idea unviable, they will be gentle with you.

And do bear in mind that they're keen on measurement and accountability; they like to set objectives and see if they have been met. They really aren't trying to be difficult, and you will thank them in the end: see outcomes below.

WHAT PLANNERS ADD TO DESIGN OUTCOMES

1. *Clarity.* Early clarity in design direction saves hours of wasted effort. Setting and agreeing clear design objectives, sensitive creative development research and/or communications knowledge gained at an early stage can point everyone in the right direction and thus avoid unnecessary pain.

2. *Objectivity.* An ability to stand back from the everyday preoccupations of the client on the one hand and the glorious fantasies of the creative in flight on the other. Taking an overview of the brand and design issues in its widest context, competitive, business, social and over time. Ensuring objective measurement and accountability against objectives helps embed positive outcomes with clients.

3. *Relevance.* Identifying the correct target audience and understanding what makes them tick; unearthing powerful insights that inspire powerful design solutions.

4. *Discipline.* Planners can create a strategic framework into which to place design which enhances credibility for presenting to clients. The good ones can start a story that the design completes. The discipline of a strategy also helps remove some of the subjectivity demonstrated by clients (and even – whisper it – wayward colleagues).

5. *Inspiration.* Writing creative briefs that challenge, that go outside the received rules for a category in the knowledge that consumers are ready for it or simply revealing possibilities borne of a wider understanding of how the audience ticks and what the market needs.

3.7 **The orgs and ops**

Shan Preddy

I don't have anything to do with the washing up.
- Prince Philip (b1921), Duke of Edinburgh

WHOSE JOB IS IT TO CHANGE THE LIGHT BULBS?

We design professionals can be our own worst enemies. We spend a lot of time and energy doing things which we really don't need to do. We have a 'can-do' and a 'will-do' mindset. When we see a problem – any problem, at work or in real life – we want to find the solution. We know it's there, just waiting to be discovered; we want to find it ourselves, and we want to find it quickly. The result is that we can sometimes be poor delegators and team leaders; fundamentally, we just want to get on and do things.

This urge to find solutions is compounded with our natural human tendency to seek the security of comfort zones. We get huge satisfaction from completing tasks, and so we actively seek those we know we can do well. Equally, we don't like the idea of failure. We postpone decisions and procrastinate tasks, sometimes indefinitely, which are slightly beyond our current skills and which look, well, a bit difficult. Take a moment with a mirror. Are you putting off tough jobs, the ones which no one else can do, and spending valuable time on activities which should be done by someone else? Are you failing to sort out your HR strategy for next year, or to develop a robust future marketing strategy and plan, or to think about the vision and values for your business? Are you enjoying a displacement activity because it's easier and because you know you can do it? 'Sorry, no time to write the business plan, I need to change the light bulbs and then rearrange my markers in Pantone™ reference order'.

Management guru Peter Drucker is reported to have said: 'Management is about doing things right, leadership is about doing the right things.' The former is efficiency; the latter is effectiveness. You constantly need to ask yourself whether you are being effective or merely efficient. If you are spending time and energy on tasks which are preventing you from completing tasks that only you can do, who's running the business? No one.

PLAY TO STRENGTHS, YOURS AND THEIRS

You will, of course, already employ external experts such as accountants and lawyers to help you with specialist tasks for which you're not skilled. But have you got the right infrastructure in place for dealing with the organisational and operational elements in the business, the areas which are essential but which don't relate directly to income-generating client projects? Broadly, these are: legal issues; finance; marketing and business development; HR; IT; and office administration.

If you are running a larger design business, you will have several members of staff under the management of a specific Director or a team leader to cover each area of expertise and responsibility. If you are running a one or two person business you will inevitably have to cover a lot of ground, doing a bit of everything, both business-facing and client-facing. However, you still have the option of bringing in help on an ad-hoc basis, or on a regular part-time basis.

Whether you are CEO of one of the top 10 design companies worldwide, or a single person starting the journey from freelance to business-owner, a simple exercise to make sure that you are not changing too many metaphorical lightbulbs is to carry around, for two working weeks, a big sheet of paper. Jot down all of the business-related things you do in a day. On one side, record the things you – and only you – should be doing in your role in the business. On the other side, note the things other people could do instead of you, either because they could do them just as well or because they have specific skills and expertise to do them better. The second side will help to inform the list of orgs and ops people (among others) you need. You might not be able to appoint them immediately but, having identified them, those future appointments can be included in your forward business planning.

Treat it like a project planning exercise, and do a needs analysis. Work out exactly which orgs and ops resources you need, draw up a checklist and then work out how best to find and afford the people. Do you need someone full or part time, bearing in mind that part time could be as little as a few hours a month? Do you need to line up some external, independent experts for guidance and advice, so that you get top advice whenever you need it without the regular salary?

For example, a 15–20 person business might decide that it needs:

- For legal matters: an external law firm.
- For finance: an external accountant plus a part-time employed book-keeper or financial administrator.
- For marketing and business development: an external consultant, plus a part-time employed business development manager.
- For HR: an external consultant, plus a part-time employed HR administrator.
- For IT: an external consultant.

Different sizes of design businesses will need different mixtures of orgs and ops resources. In a smaller firm, some of these roles, such as financial and HR administration, might be combined.

SECRET WEAPONS

Finally, there are two secret weapons that many successful design businesses have discovered: the PA, or Personal Assistant, and the Office Manager.

A good PA, sometimes known as an Executive Assistant, is not the same as an old-fashioned secretary. They will help you to accomplish more things in less time, and will help you to work both more efficiently and more effectively. Their work frees you up to do the things that only you can do, and they are a strong right-hand support in everything that you do in the business. Not everyone will be able to afford to employ a PA, but remember that they can support more than one person in your firm, or they can work part time. Often, a small part of a really excellent PA is better than no PA at all.

The precise job title of an Office Manager will vary from firm to firm; Practice Manager is sometimes used. The role, however, is to take care of all of the administrative aspects of a business. This will include areas like travel logistics, insurance, security, fire regulations and health and safety. It will almost certainly include dealing with – and negotiating with – suppliers of all of the products and services the office needs, from paper jotter-pads to major building maintenance. In smaller firms, it might also cover finance and HR administration. Whatever the size of the business, it's an ideal appointment for businesses whose owners are wearing far too many hats to be effective.

The only time a PA or an Office Manager should interface with clients is in communicating with them, inbound or outbound. If they get involved in project management, they will end up doing someone else's job and will not be able to do their own properly. And the only time you should step in to do the work that they should be doing is when they are away for any reason.

You know you've got good people in these roles, by the way, when the very thought of either of them going on holiday for two weeks is enough to give you sleepless nights.

3.8   The incoming resource

Madelaine Cooper

First-rate people hire first-rate people; second-rate people hire third-rate people.
- Leo Rosten (1908–97), teacher, academic and humorist

HOW TO EMPLOY PEOPLE

The old nursery rhyme described the genders as being made of either sugar and spice or slugs and snails. A design company is even easier to analyse. It is made of people and their talent. There isn't anything else.

You might change the colour of the walls, the style of the reception desk or the layout of the studio. You might have developed a process, or a unique way of managing your clients' needs. But even if all of the above were missing, a creative and wonderful design studio could still exist and thrive if it had creative and wonderful people working there.

The people you employ define your company. There is no DNA of a design agency, only the DNA of the people who work there. So you will, of course, make every effort to employ only the very best people.

Much is written about the knotty problem of How To Get a Job. Surprisingly little is available about How To Employ People; an issue which can be particularly problematic in the design business since talent is a subjective matter. But there are certain disciplines which will help you to make clearer and better-informed decisions about your most important commodity.

WHO TO EMPLOY

First of all, who do you need to employ? Writing a job description helps a company to clarify what sort of person is needed, and what they will need to bring to the company. This can be a curiously therapeutic process in itself. By reflecting on why you need to employ someone, fundamental questions about the company itself can be raised. Is this employment process a knee-jerk reaction to the departure of someone else or in anticipation of new or increased workloads? Or are you covering bits which might be missing from within the existing team?

If it is a replacement for somebody, are you sure that you want to replicate that person or would it be good to revise your needs as the company evolves, the dynamics of the team change or the market opportunities shift? If the recruitment is to respond to a new client or more work, do you simply want another person who is like the other people who are already working with you? Could this be an opportunity to step out a little and capture ideas, techniques and experiences that are not yet represented within your company? Otherwise, the company will be full of people who are all a bit like you, which is neither healthy nor wise.

DESCRIBING THE POSITION

A recruitment job description might include:

- the job title;
- what the company has done, is doing and where it is going as an organisation;
- where the company is located, with website map links;
- an outline of the general nature and objectives of the role;
- a summary of the principle tasks involved in the role;
- some of the personal qualities which will be needed.

Don't go mad on the last point. You want to employ a human being, not a saint, and there are, of course, legal limitations around this area. Be careful not to indicate preferences or prejudices on the grounds of sex, race, disability, marital status, age, religion or number of dependents.

POSITIVE INTERVIEWING

Another fundamental question is whether you need to employ someone on a permanent basis, or whether it would be more expedient, and perhaps more interesting, to purchase the talents of someone purely for the duration of the project. That way you can afford to experiment with skill sets, personality types and levels of seniority before making a long-term – and hard to back out of – decision.

Once you have a vision about what and who you need, and have written it down, add a profile of your own company. Whatever the market trends as to whether it is a buyer's market or a not, it is helpful to you as a company, to the applicants for the role and to the recruitment consultant if you are using one, to have a profile on the company.

It is often said that ours is a small world. People in design know other people in design, and they like to talk about where they have been, who they have met and what they think about it all. So, as you no doubt say to your clients often enough, it is important that all the brand touch-points give positive messages to your clients and consumers. It is a good idea to use the employment process to send out good vibrations about your company, your company's vision, the way that you behave and the way that you treat people. Make that profile of your company on the job description a positive one; give it structure and enough vision to make candidates feel that this is somewhere that they would really like to work, and to spread that good feeling around amongst their peers.

The next step – and still part of the positive brand messaging about your company – is to prepare yourself for the interview. Don't just roll up to meet the candidate without doing any groundwork. Just as it is considered courteous for the candidates to have done their homework on your company, it is not only courteous but advisable to have taken time to study their CV, look at any work samples they have sent in advance of the meeting and be equipped to ask questions based on what you have found there.

THE ENCOUNTER

Time spent carrying out good interviews will be a worthwhile investment. Don't try to interview more than three or four people each day or you won't have time to do any work before or after each meeting, and all of the candidates will meld into a blur of faces. Be consistent across the interviews, and make sure that if you are going to conduct the interview with somebody else from your company they are available for all the meetings.

Then there are the courtesies which not only make a good impression with the candidate, but make the difference between a company which is poorly run and one which has ambition, shine and class:

- brief other people in the office so that the candidate is expected and dealt with appropriately when they arrive;
- be on time for the interview yourself;
- book a room for the interview to take place in;
- make sure that the room is clear of clutter and dirty cups from previous meetings;
- allocate enough time for the interview and stick to it;
- shake the hand of the candidate when they arrive and make them feel at ease;
- don't take calls during the interview;
- explain the job that you are looking to fill, give something of the background of the company and where the job fits in both now and, if appropriate, in the future;

- at the end of the interview give the candidate a chance to ask questions and if you don't have answers immediately, offer to come back to them with the information;
- close the meeting in a conclusive way by telling them what will happen next and when you hope to be able to make decisions or hold further interviews.

Plan the questions and make sure that there are some worthwhile questions that can provoke more than just a 'Yes' or 'No' answer, something which will engage the candidate to tell you something about their work, themselves and their ambition.

For example:

- 'Looking back at your career so far, is there anything you might have done differently?'
- 'Where do you see yourself in five years time?'
- 'What is the most interesting piece of design work that you have seen recently?'

Create a structure so that there is a continuity across different interviews and a way of making comparisons between people. Take the time to understand both the job role that you are seeking to fill and also the details of the individuals so that you can make an informed decision. Gut instinct is powerful and important, but make sure that you don't get seduced by an engaging personality and find six months down the line that the job in question is not getting done.

AND AFTERWARDS?

After all of that, make some notes both during and immediately after the meeting so that you can remember the individual people you have met.

When you get to the final round of interviews it may well be helpful to ask a neutral, but trusted, outsider to join you in those meetings to help you to decide who to employ. Someone who can stand back from the company and help you to see whether the vision that is there for your company can be fulfilled through this person.

You are asking a lot from everybody that you employ: they are the realisation of the ambitions that you have for the company. If they are any good, they will relish that chance.

3.9 The ongoing resource

Kim Briggs

The two most important things about a company do not appear on its balance sheet: its reputation and its people.
- Henry Ford (1863–1947), automobile manufacturer

SETTLING IN

The induction period is a critical time for any business to secure the talent that it has invested so heavily in recruiting. It is during this period that you establish the roles and relationships that individual will have with the business. An 'induction crisis' where people arrive, do not like it and leave within the year is costly.

Induction allows people to settle into their new role as quickly and easily as possible and to start delivering value to the business. Meetings should be set up with the appropriate people, but be aware that too much information too soon can overwhelm people.

Whilst there are many formal aspects to induction; you should consider fun activities to immerse new people in both the culture and the role they will be taking on. Be creative! You really need to consider interesting ways to get your people 'on brand' and engaged.

PROBATION TIME

The probationary period allows people to understand their role before either they or the business commit to permanent employment. As a business you must establish that the individual is the right cultural fit and has the talent and skill set required. It should be a period of continuous assessment. Regular reviews throughout this period are essential; both parties need opportunities to reflect on progress made and to raise any issues they may have. If at the end of the probationary period, the business is uncertain of the 'fit' then the probation should be extended. Do be aware that people need to know why; do not do it to avoid the difficult task of letting someone go if you know they are not right.

It does take time to fully engage a new person. The nature of the business, the timing and the role are all key factors, and new people will quite naturally feel overwhelmed. It will often take the probationary period and beyond to fully grasp the culture and the role.

JOB DESCRIPTIONS

Many businesses make the mistake of overlooking clear job descriptions but it is at their peril to do so. It is important to have these in place for all roles, not just for the purposes of recruitment and induction but also as an ongoing foundation for the measurement of performance and delivery. Without clearly defined expectations from the outset it is very hard to provide meaningful feedback or tackle issues relating to underperformance.

Roles can never be set in stone, particularly in smaller and creative businesses. Roles are often very diverse and continually evolving and it is important to recognise this. It is a good idea to regularly review roles as part of appraisal process.

PERFORMANCE APPRAISALS

Ultimately people need to know if they are doing a good job, but there are many other reasons for the performance appraisal. People value being listened to and managers benefit from hearing a different perspective. Regular appraisals provide a framework for objective setting and measurement and an opportunity to ensure consistency across the business, and to establish both company culture and expected behaviours. Training needs and potential stars for the future will also flow from appraisals.

The timing and frequency of appraisals will depend on the type of business and client demand; some businesses only require one formal annual review, for others there is a need for more frequent reviews. Remember, it is all about the quality of the dialogue, not the form.

Whatever approach you go for; appraisal meetings should provide people with:

- an in-depth understanding of their role, responsibilities and the what is expected of them;
- feedback on their performance;
- an opportunity to discuss their development and objectives for the future.

People are motivated by feeling they have both the support and the opportunities they need to reach their full potential. Without a regular appraisal or review, it is very hard to achieve this.

An appraisal process should be highly participative and include an element of self-appraisal. Individuals play a key role in their own development and the process should reflect this; development and growth require input and careful consideration from both sides. Appraisal meetings should never be a post-mortem.

It is important to engage the creative minds in your business. Whilst not all people are in exclusively creative positions, those who are need this acknowledged in the way you approach reviews; invite them to bring their work in and talk about it, and avoid being too dry in your approach.

DISCIPLINE AND GRIEVANCE PROCEDURES

The very words 'discipline and grievance' conjure up an image of something very serious and a formality that many design businesses would rather shy away from, but really they are just about the creation of a fair and transparent working environment, one in which people will know what they need to do to meet the expectations of the business or what to do if they are unhappy about something at work.

Discipline

Any disciplinary policies and procedures in place should be designed to help your people achieve and maintain the right level of conduct and performance. It is often possible to resolve issues relating to poor performance informally. When it is not, the business should then take formal disciplinary action, following best practice and the correct procedure. In the UK, the Advisory, Conciliation and Arbitration Service (ACAS) sets out very clear guidelines on the process that needs to be followed.

It is a statutory requirement for all businesses to provide all employees with access to the disciplinary and dismissal procedure. Such policies provide fairness and equity for all, but more importantly help to clarify the relationship between the business and its employees. Having the right things in place will also allow you as a business to show that you have protected people's rights.

Grievance

Grievances are still reasonably rare in businesses, many problems that people have can be resolved informally, but sometimes people do feel that they have a genuine grievance against the business. This can be difficult, but a formal grievance procedure can really help to resolve the conflict fairly. It should however not replace open communication between all parties.

As with handling disciplinary situations, ACAS sets out the required process and procedure. Ensuring adherence to best practice will allow for greater consistency in such areas and ensure that the business has the records in place that make life simpler.

In an ideal world everybody would perform and deliver brilliantly and never have any complaints but, as you will be aware, people can and always will provide the greatest of challenges. By giving clear consideration to the above you will find it a whole lot easier.

STAFF DEVELOPMENT AND TRAINING

Training and development is an important part of the employment offer: you will be far more appealing to talented people if you present a culture that encourages development and progression. People are motivated by training and by businesses that will ultimately contribute to their 'personal portfolio'. Training is an investment that will keep people loyal and improve retention.

Providing training will ensure that people have the skills and knowledge they need to achieve the overall business goals. The more skilled and knowledgeable your people are, the more it will impact on the work they deliver for clients. This will ultimately lead to stronger and more sustainable relationships.

Make sure the money and time dedicated to training and development is both relevant and well spent; decide on where the management wants to focus the business. A lack of clarity will risk the training failing to enhance performance in key areas.

Information on training needs can be gathered from a number of sources, including induction feedback, appraisal and review notes and client feedback.

The business needs to establish gaps by reviewing the levels of competence and expertise required and comparing it with current levels. This will provide the basis for any training undertaken and can be used to inform an annual plan. Attention should be given to which strategies are most appropriate, timeframes, providers (both internal and external) and any cost implications.

It is important to consider evaluation when planning any investment in training. It is through evaluation that the business can ensure that it is addressing the needs identified. It also allows you to assess the quality of the training, the content, the delivery and whether learning has been transferred back into the workplace. Evaluation can take place immediately after training but there is some merit in re-evaluating at a later date. It is only then that a business can measure whether or not training has had an impact on performance.

Training and development is not all about external courses, there are many other ways to develop people. The actual role, client exposure, internal coaching, planned internal projects and experiences will all provide a range of development opportunities. Creative people will benefit from taking in the world around them, reviewing competitors, visiting exhibitions and sharing what they like. Equally, when sourcing a trainer that is right for your business, make sure they understand the creative mind and know how to engage it.

3.10 The outgoing resource

Kim Briggs

If you treat people around you with love and respect, they will never guess that you're trying to get them sacked.
- Ricky Gervais (b1961), comedian, from his television series 'The Office'

DISMISSING STAFF

If you have been unable to recover or improve performance through the disciplinary process, you may have to terminate employment on the grounds of capability. Other reasons for dismissing someone would be:

- conduct
- a legal reason
- some other substantial reason
- redundancy.

Under current UK employment legislation, an employee who has been employed for more than a year has the right not to be unfairly dismissed. If an employee claims to have been dismissed unfairly, the complaint will heard by an employment tribunal. Many claims do not make it to tribunal, but when they do, it can be very costly in terms of time, money and management attention. It is therefore in every business's interest to avoid such claims being made. A tribunal would need to establish whether or not there was adequate reason for the dismissal, and whether the employer acted reasonably in the circumstances.

Dismissals are likely to be considered unfair if you have failed to demonstrate that the dismissal is linked to one of the above reasons. A dismissal can be considered to be 'constructive' if the employee felt, through actions of the employer, that their position was untenable and resigned as a result. A dismissal will also be considered unfair if the business has failed to follow the legally required redundancy procedure, as outlined below.

Following the required disciplinary procedure, where appropriate, will ensure consistency and fairness. It is worth highlighting that even if the dismissal is valid, the business still needs to be regarded as having acted fairly and reasonably at the point of dismissal. Demonstrating this is the responsibility of the employer.

What is a reasonable and fair approach? The individual should be informed of the issue and given a chance to explain, and they should be, or have been, given the chance to improve, unless the dismissal relates to gross misconduct. They must be made aware that failure to improve could result in dismissal. They must also be given the right to appeal. Employers should ensure that they have sufficient evidence to uphold the dismissal and that they have considered any extenuating circumstances. It is all about research, investigation and preparation.

REDUNDANCY

Redundancy is a legally regulated dismissal and, as such, there are very clear procedures that must be followed. Failure to do so as highlighted above will result in the dismissal being deemed unfair. Managing redundancies is a particularly demanding and stressful part of running a business, but the process is very clear and the structure, whilst a little time consuming, does make it reasonably straightforward. Employment law specialists will always be on hand to guide you through this process should you need them to.

The first step is to make sure the process of selection is fair and objective. The redundancy process must begin with consultation. People need to understand:

- the reasons for the potential redundancies;
- the steps the business has taken to avoid redundancy;
- the numbers likely to be affected;
- how redundancy payments will be calculated.

It will be important to outline the process, covering how people will be selected and the likely timescale. The scale of the redundancy will dictate how wide the announcement has to go and how long a consultation period must last. Remember: redundancy should never be presented as a decision already made.

People should be given as much notice as possible about any potential redundancies. The process then falls into the following four stages:

1. Individuals should be invited to an initial formal meeting to inform them their position might be at risk of redundancy.
2. The next meeting will confirm to them that their position is at risk, and that they are now entering into the consultation period. They should be informed of how the decision will be made and shown the objective selection criteria against which they will be measured. Consultation should be genuine and the business should remain open-minded.
3. During this period, both parties should consider ways of avoiding the redundancy. The business must consider and respond to any suggestions made.
4. If no alternative is found the business must then confirm the redundancy and inform the individual of the right to appeal. All employees have the right to

appeal against the decision to dismiss, and all appeals must be considered and responded to in writing.

Whilst consideration must be given to how the business can support those being made redundant, it is essential that attention is given to those who remain. People will naturally feel very vulnerable, as well as emotional, about losing people with whom they have established a working relationship. Follow-up communication must be timely and sensitive, but at the same time motivational and providing energy for the future.

EXIT INTERVIEWS

Turnover in any business is natural. When people are leaving the business of their own volition it is good practice to invite them to an exit interview: people are often at their most candid when they are leaving. The aim of any exit interview is to gain insight into why a person is leaving and to allow you to establish areas of possible dissatisfaction or unhappiness. Exit interviews conducted by an independent external provider will often provide greater insight.

It is important to question skilfully and sensitively to establish which feedback is justified and to decide what can be done about it. A standard template of questions relating to all key areas of employment is advisable.

A FINAL THOUGHT...

People come and people go, but it is the business that must control both ends of the employment relationship. Inevitably, when people want to leave, they will focus on what is best for them. This does not always reflect what is best for the business, so consider how long they should stay for. Risk must be considered, and caution is advisable: those who have left the business emotionally can have a big (and not always good) impact on those who remain. Always do what is right for the business.

3.11   The training

Liz Lydiate

The real voyage of discovery consists not of seeking new landscapes, but in having new eyes.
*   Marcel Proust (1871–1922), novelist, critic and essayist

FROM TO COLLEGE TO WORK

Most people now enter work in the UK design industry through some form of educational qualification, and this is most commonly located in the Higher Education (HE) sector. Since the 1990s there has been a conscious shift of emphasis by the UK Government towards academic rather than specifically vocational education, which has had a strong impact on design educational provision. Vocational education emphasises skills and competences; academic education encourages research-based analytical thinking. The difference lies between a journey following a prescribed route or one hacking a new path through the jungle with a machete. The Higher National Diploma (HND) was a well-regarded qualification which many design industry employers found delivered potential new recruits with a sound skills-based education, but it is now frequently replaced with newly validated BA programmes. Recent years have also seen the introduction of the two-year Foundation Degree.

During the same period, the design of educational programmes has become more formal – some would say rigid – with validated, framework-based curricula and provider institutions subject to a complex infrastructure of quality review. Colleges and universities have worked hard on building active and valuable links between HE and real-world design practice, including the involvement of assessed internship, work-based learning and live projects within many design programme curricula. There has also been a rise in flexible HE provision which has encouraged many mature students to re-enter education, making career development and changes through HE much more accessible.

I'M TRAINED IN DESIGN – IT EQUIPS YOU FOR LIFE IN THE MODERN WORLD

HOW DESIGN EDUCATION LINKS TO EMPLOYED SKILLS

It is the role of HE to be aware of the needs of industry and to mastermind a complex balancing act between preparing students for practice whilst at the same time preserving and encouraging radical academic growth and enquiry. Study of the current UK design industry reveals that while there are still some self-trained practitioners, particularly in the technologically-based areas of creative practice, the predominantly graduate entry of an average company comes from a surprisingly wide spread of subjects.

Designers usually come from practice-based programmes that aim to develop creative thinking, autonomous practice and a broad underpinning of wider general education to support creative work. In the client-facing and management areas of design companies, staff are sourced from very diverse educational backgrounds, reflecting the need for skills profiles to meet the business needs of design consultancy. Examining their education and career trajectory is very interesting. A minority of design business people come in with a fully formed skill set: there is much 'growing into' the work through learning on the job, with or without formal training. HE design management programmes annually provide a small number of graduates with specialised design business knowledge, and contribute to the important business of generating research about how design works.

Design consultancy practice is a team-based activity, and the extent and nature of the linked and complementary skills within any particular company require careful management planning. To what extent do designers interface directly with clients? What is the exact nature of the consultancy on offer, and who contributes what? Doctors and lawyers do not usually need special colleagues to help them interface with their clients; is design actually different in this regard? As this type of questioning increasingly reconsiders the nature of what designers do, it also raises enquiry about appropriate education provision and recruitment profiling for this industry.

CONTINUING PROFESSIONAL DEVELOPMENT (CPD) – WHAT IT IS, WHY IT'S IMPORTANT

Soon after the establishment of the UK's Design Business Association (DBA) in 1986, one of the core business needs addressed was education and training. The founder DBA members reported that the design graduates who comprised their entry-level staff intake required challenging amounts of additional training before they became effective employees. Interestingly, this has not changed and the need for continuing professional development (CPD) has increased.

Building on experience from the 80s recession, steps have been taken to include new elements of personal and professional development (PPD) in the HE design curriculum, addressing what level of professional awareness should be embedded in the education process and to what extent the new design graduate can be expected to hit the ground running.

Educators increasingly subscribe to the view that BA and MA programmes cannot be expected to turn out a 'fully-cooked' design professional, but should ensure that graduates have a real understanding of the role of business knowledge in the provision of design consultancy and an expectation that they will add to their capabilities and understanding through a process of life-long learning.

As a people-based service industry, design stands to gain enormously from investing in developing its greatest asset, the staff. CPD helps companies to develop new skills and to re-tune their offer to meet changing market needs. It rewards valued staff and helps in staff retention. The shared experience of working with peers from other – sometimes competitor – companies in a CPD situation builds stronger ties across the industry sector.

SELF-DIRECTED AND MORE FORMAL TRAINING

CPD is also the responsibility of individuals. A positive attitude towards CPD demonstrates a commitment to growth and career development. It is also an aid to recruitment and staff selection, and as people move around within the design industry for career progression there is an incremental sharing and cross-fertilisation of the CPD investment.

Surveys of design professionals indicate that there has been a major shift in employer attitudes towards appraisal and performance review, with more and more staff reporting that they take part in a formal structure that supports self-reflection, internal discussion and personal development planning. At their best, line management and appraisal relationships can provide a supportive environment for personal development, and an appraisal meeting may be a natural place to discuss CPD. Recent growth in mentoring, professional mutual interest groups and peer support can help individuals to address whether CPD should be playing a role in their professional lives, and can also aid the challenging task of researching and evaluating potential CPD opportunities.

Not all CPD involves attending actual training courses. In its 1992 report *Developing Design Excellence* the Chartered Society of Designers (CSD) identified many additional types of industry-relevant CPD activity, including reading published material, visiting exhibitions and attending seminars and debates. To these can now be added: use of the internet; creation of websites; creation of archives. The important thing is that the activity should be conscious, targeted and planned.

IN-HOUSE, IN-JOB TRAINING

Traditionally, in-job training involved 'sitting by Nelly'. Learning from Nelly represented maintenance of the status quo; today's needs are different because business survival requires an ongoing process of corporate questioning, review, innovation and change. In the complex life of contemporary design companies, making time for in-house training can deliver enormous dividends. Away-days and residential events make time for staff to work together and build shared values and real developmental growth. In *Leadership is an Art,* former Hermann Miller CEO, Max DePree, writes about the power of tribal storytelling. In-house training builds both tribes and stories.

Commitment to in-house training also signals investment in staff and a commitment to participative management. The work of a design consultancy involves being able to deliver on the promises made and expectations created during the client courtship period. Shared standards, goals and values are needed to achieve this, and in-house training is an important tool for the achievement of performance standards. Learning together is valuable for team building and helps with the creation of an environment and work practices conducive to creativity. Commitment by management to in-house training can be a differentiating factor in employee perceptions of the workplace and in building commitment and loyalty to the company.

Bringing training to the staff, rather than vice versa, is also cost-effective and allows for finely calibrated customisation of the learning experience. Small organisations have to watch costs carefully but, with imagination, in-service training experiences can deliver great value for money.

EXTERNAL COURSES AND PROGRAMMES

External training creates dedicated space and time for learning, away from the distractions of the workplace. Designers and design employers are often unsure whether CPD should be industry-specific or sourced from a wider professional pool. Training represents a major financial investment for design companies, so the spectre of making a poor choice of provider is real one. Sometimes there is benefit in sourcing training outside of the home sector, related instead to the needs and specialisms of key client markets. Learning alongside existing and potential clients can be an effective way of building in-depth knowledge of their context.

Universities and colleges have made an important contribution to individual personal development/qualification opportunities through development of part-time courses that can fit alongside employment. MA work, in particular, is generating a new body of committed research and practice development of great benefit to the design industry and its clients. Educational institutions also provide short courses, offering affordable and relevant updating and knowledge extension. Technological developments have brought the benefits of online courses and programmes within the reach of most people, offering a particularly flexible and effective method of learning.

Many of the UK design industry bodies source, promote or signpost training programmes in order to help design companies buy wisely. Their contact details can be found in *The Reference Library* section.

GRANTS AND FUNDING

Training should be seen as an investment and, where possible, factored into the annual operating budget as a regular provision. Taking account of the predominantly small size of design companies it is easy to understand why it is often viewed as a one-off expense to be considered 'only when money permits'.

From time to time, external financial help to pay for training is available to both organisations and individuals. In the UK, a number of different Government grants and schemes have been offered in recent years to meet either all or part of the cost of approved training, as part of economic development initiatives. Information about such schemes can be obtained from the design organisations, from branches of Business Link and other Government-funded support agencies and, for individuals, from any of the major clearing banks. Support may be available for education and retraining connected with unemployment and redundancy, such as schemes applied to part-time university Masters programmes if the student is unemployed or in receipt of benefits.

Universities and colleges sometimes obtain development funding for particular types of training provision which is then offered free of charge or heavily subsidised to the relevant groups of users, and savings can occasionally be made by organising training as a company-wide activity. A level of vigilance is needed to monitor these frequently changing opportunities.

DEVELOPING A LEARNING CULTURE

Traditionally, vocational education and training were thought to occupy a space between school and work, with the results expected to last a lifetime. External changes have now altered work culture, causing a complete change of view, with real recognition of the value and importance of life-long learning. People are no longer pigeon-holed into a single career direction and great creative benefits arise from the migration of staff from one field to another.

Both individuals and organisations have responsibility for their own learning, including its design, development, care and maintenance. A learning culture makes one workplace preferable to another with more dynamic and effective results. Learning can be built in to company life, whether it be lunch-hour yoga or sponsoring an MA opportunity for a valued employee through a period of flexible working hours. Offering time and support for learning is a powerful and appropriate reward for great performance, and the shared celebration of learning achievement is an effective endorsement of company culture.

What simple structures could you put in place to encourage knowledge sharing and knowledge transfer? Could you interrogate your address book to find stimulating speakers for evening events for the shared benefit of staff and clients? What benefits might come from a link with your local design college or university? Could offering internships transform lives and also deliver some valuable input and insights? Might investment in an away-day – with some built-in magic – reward and cement commitment from your key staff members? With a little creative thinking, you can build and maintain an effective learning culture.

3.12 The development

Rod Petrie

I always sum up people's ambition with a simple analogy. Some people like to go to Blackpool on holiday; some just prefer to stay at home and go to the local park. If you take people from my time in Govan they were just happy to get out of the shipyards for two weeks. Some people like to go to Majorca, and then there are those who want to go to the moon.
- Sir Alex Ferguson (b1941), footballer and football manager

UNLEASHING SUCCESS

Successful agencies take control of their people, beyond simply the recruitment process. They invest in their people, sending out a global message of the consistent desire to improve quality, productivity and profitability and that people come first. They turn the workplace into an environment that encourages individuals to be themselves, to have fun, to take risks with confidence. As a result those agencies fuel and unleash creativity. The key to this focuses on five key areas:

- team building and growth
- effective management
- motivation
- coaching
- mentoring.

TEAM BUILDING AND GROWTH

A team is not just a collection of individuals. It's about getting more out of each person because they are part of that team. Together Everyone Achieves More. It is an organic and dynamic thing, so will be constantly changing as individuals change and respond to each other differently.

It is the people, their creativity and the way that they are led and managed that differentiates a successful design business, not the latest gadget or hi spec piece of kit, and this needs to be consistently brilliant, day in and day out.

It is the way a team of people interacts, feels about one another, connects, works together, shares a common purpose which is harder to copy and sets them apart from the competition. If you focus on the team performance you will find the individual performance will improve.

Start with a vision and a goal so you know what type of team you want to create. Make sure you communicate the vision and goals clearly to everyone. Create a checklist for building your team, so that you aren't tempted to pick someone for the wrong reasons. They might tick all your normal recruitment boxes but not be right for this team. In the ideal world build your team around people whom you like and respect, who fit your criteria and who have different views and ideas and start from there. Choose people with complementary skills and personality traits and think of their individual roles within the team, for example, diplomat, energiser, strategist and so on. Once you have selected your people, give them the creative space, inspiration and opportunities to bond and grow as a team.

EFFECTIVE MANAGEMENT

There are many definitions about what is good and effective management. The key is to have a strong and inspirational leader who understands the different styles of management required to achieve the task, who trusts the people, has loads of common sense, is totally dedicated and has the ability to get the very best work from their people. In the creative business there is a need to understand the problems involved in the management of creative people and the creative process. You need to be a creative manager. You are not there to block people being creative, but to inspire and motivate people to be creative. That said, the creative manager needs to make sure that everyone is made responsible and understands the commercial disciplines and deadlines involved and the importance of what they do. It is the responsibility of management to create the right environment for individuals to flourish and produce their best commercial work. A group of individuals needs a structure and a set of rules; people need to know where they stand and what is expected of them. They need direction and a collective vision and goal. Imagine a game of football where the goalkeeper ignores responsibilities to team mates and charges off down the field to take a pop at goal.

Managers need to be chosen for their relationship skills, and not just their technical capabilities, as they are dealing with highly talented people and there can be a clash of cultures. Great managers start with a vision and communicate it clearly and they tend to be 'people people'. They lead by example and they are great role models. As 'man managers' they have empathy with their staff; they know what makes each individual tick and what they want to achieve. They never avoid the people issues, and they inspire total confidence in others.

MOTIVATION

Motivation is what gets you out of bed in the morning. It's all about your intent, your purpose and your ability to put to good use qualities like passion, commitment, fire, heart and energy. It's what empowers you to succeed and makes light of the barriers and roadblocks that cause others to stop and give up.

Motivation is key to success. Look at any successful person or business and you will find motivated individuals who are driven to an end goal. Motivated people have a positive mental attitude that makes things happen. They think differently and creatively along the way to overcome the barriers that can suddenly appear from nowhere. Stress levels are turned into a source of energy that enables them to go on and make those big and decisive decisions.

Understand the individual triggers that work for people, what their learning strategies are and how they process information. Some crave power and prestige, while others look for recognition of a job well done. Focus on the positive; shouting and negativity doesn't generally work in motivating people to reach peak performance. Be consistent. Don't forget the power of small things: a kind touch; a word of encouragement; the simple act of listening; an honest compliment. Help people to create tailor-made challenges: achieving a personal challenge will prove one of the most effective motivators, just like athletes or explorers who push themselves to the limit and beyond. Never stop talking to one another as this can lead to confusion, bad decision-making and a distortion of reality. When the heads in the team start to drop and the captain has stopped talking, the game is up.

COACHING

The context for coaching is creating the space, 'your space,' to create tangible shifts and changes in people's performance and behaviour so they can step up to the next level. In a business context it is an ongoing process designed to help people to gain greater competence and overcome the barriers to improving performance. Coaching requires dedicated time. When it becomes a time-driven activity that pushes people, it becomes 'direct coaching', and the results are less effective. Successful outcomes are achieved by 'holding the space coaching', offering time and a helping hand to pull people forward. This is often easier to do via an external coach than internally.

Because a creative services business is about people, it is by coaching those people that you will get the most out of them. When you are looking at why people aren't fulfilling their potential, it doesn't matter what job they do or who they work for, it's how those things make them feel that is important. It should be an ongoing process that helps employees gain competence and overcome barriers, particularly in situations where an individual clearly has ability and knowledge but hasn't reached peak performance. Coaching is a powerful business tool that creates differentiation and a competitive advantage for an agency. Make it part of the business culture and not a one-off activity. Focus on people within the context of your business and give everyone the opportunity to benefit from it, in whatever way best suits them. Imagine having someone in the business that was there solely to help you to succeed.

MENTORING

We all remember the names of our favourite teachers at school and, if you're like me, they were probably your first mentors without you realising it. Mentoring is an advanced level of coaching. It is more relational in that it provides both personal and professional help, both within the context of the business and outside it. Most top athletes and businessmen have mentors, not on how to play the game or run the business, but on how to control their frame of mind, especially in very challenging situations when not playing well or unable to cope with high-powered negotiations.

At its best it is a one-to-one relationship that allows the younger partner to confide in someone who understands something of wider life. Traditionally it involves the younger, less experienced person learning from the success and non-success of someone older and, perhaps, wiser. In the most successful agencies everyone is important and they will be nurturing every single individual. Think of it as another 'benefit' like healthcare/pension.

People need to feel that the mentor understands their issues and is truly there to help them succeed. There must be mutual respect, liking and a real connection, and potentially things in common beyond the business itself. Focus on the whole person, not just their performance in the context of the business. A good mentor gets the right balance between inspiring creative work and commercial success, tells it as it is and doesn't play politics. It is all about helping people to embrace change, to be courageous, to create a vision, and to have a more trusting and open dialogue with one another, so that everyone can be even more successful.

3.13 The rewards

Mandy Merron

Treat your staff in the same way you would like them to treat your best customer.
- Stephen Covey (b1932), author and trainer

WHAT ARE YOU SEEKING TO ACHIEVE?

Getting the balance right for rewards is a difficult trick to pull off. You want to contain employment costs in line with income levels but also to pay enough to attract and keep the right talent.

It is important to understand the underlying reasons for wanting to motivate and reward key employees. Is the aim to provide an incentive to work towards a common corporate goal, or to 'lock in' key people? A number of options are available. The key is to find the most appropriate incentive for each employee.

TARGETING THE INCENTIVE TO THE EMPLOYEE

Understand your employees

The first step is to understand each employee's value to the business and their individual motivation. Figure 3.13.1 suggests how employees can be segmented by their motivation and loyalty.

Select the right incentive

The most suitable incentives for each of the key employee groups are usually:

- Core Team and Transfer List Employees: salary and possibly simple discretionary bonus.
- Nomads: performance-related bonuses or a profit-sharing scheme.
- Superstars: potential shareholders.

Nomads often require an incentive, whereas Superstars are more motivated by recognition and reward.

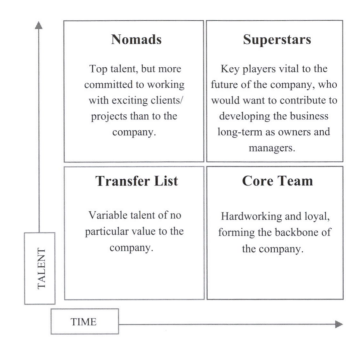

Figure 3.13.1   Employee segmentation by motivation and loyalty

Source: Kingston Smith W1 ©

DIFFERENT TYPES OF REMUNERATION

Salaries

Salaries are a function of market rate. In the UK, an invaluable tool for assessing what different members of staff should be paid is the Design Business Association's (DBA) annual confidential salary and charge-out rate survey.

Simple bonuses

For the Core Team, a market rate salary is often sufficient. Care is needed before embarking on a firm-wide bonus scheme: regular bonuses not linked to specific performance measures can soon be taken for granted. When this happens they no longer make staff feel rewarded but in the year they are not paid staff feel hard done by. A lose-lose outcome!

Bonuses are often linked to company performance, and sometimes to multiples of salary. The most important thing is to ensure that both the performance measures and their likely monetary outcomes are well understood. Complicated bonus schemes too often leave staff confused, so they discount this element of their reward.

Benefits

The provision of staff benefits is an area where designers can, and should, get creative. In a survey commissioned by Kingston Smith W1,[1] over 90 per cent of respondents offered benefits to staff over and above basic salary and holiday entitlement. Of this number, 73 per cent provided a fixed suite of benefits, while 27 per cent provided some form of flexible benefit package.

Creative businesses offer a selection of 'well-being' benefits such as health club membership, sabbaticals and company outings as well as 'insured benefits' such as life and health insurance and pensions. The key is to ask employees what they themselves would value.

Profit-sharing scheme

The top contributors in our Nomad category are not wedded to the company, but enjoy working on challenging work (or are salesmen) and should usually be rewarded by a more sophisticated form of performance-related bonus scheme. Often these are referred to as Long-Term Incentive Plans (LTIP). The scheme is often linked to individual, team or company performance, and involving the individual in target setting is important. Normally LTIPs are structured so they serve as an incentive to stay, by paying the bonus in instalments in the future.

Equity incentives

Superstar employees are really the only ones who will find equity incentives truly motivating. The main ways to provide equity incentives are:

- phantom shares;
- employee offered chance to buy shares;
- unapproved share options;
- Enterprise Management Incentive (EMI);
- Share Incentive Plans (SIPs);
- Employee Benefit Trust (EBT).

These fall into two main categories: those approved by HM Revenue and Customs (HMRC) and those which are not. The fact that certain schemes are not approved does not in any way mean that HMRC dislikes them, it just means that they do not meet the specific criteria that enable them to be eligible for special tax reliefs.

---

1 Kingston Smith W1 *Employee Benefits Survey*, 2009

HMRC UNAPPROVED EQUITY SCHEMES

Phantom share schemes

Phantom shares are effectively future bonuses, based on the value of the company but which are presented as shares. These allow staff to share in the growth in value of your company, without giving them real shares. Any proceeds will be taxed as remuneration, but corporation tax relief will be available for the expense. Phantom shares can be a drain on resources if the phantom share price is high when the employees cash them in.

Employee offered the chance to buy shares

This is the simplest way to offer key employees the opportunity to acquire shares, but it should not be done lightly. Shares can have a significant value, and should only be made available to those few individuals who can make a real difference to the business.

How the share price is set can vary depending on what level of reward is offered, but employees should always pay something. Any purchase of shares at below market value can result in employees having a significant tax bill.

It is important to plan for what happens should an employee shareholder leave and the company rules should be written so the company can get these shares back at a reasonable cost.

Unapproved share options

In order to avoid the immediate income tax charge that can arise with the direct issue of shares at a discount, the company can grant options for the issue of shares at a future date.

When employees exercise the options and obtain real shares, they will have an income tax liability based on the then market value of the shares less any amounts paid for the shares. There may also be a National Insurance liability. After exercise of the option, further growth in the value of the share will be subject to capital gains tax.

An unapproved share option scheme is very flexible because, unlike an approved scheme, there are no restrictions such as size of company or value of options that can be granted. For this reason they are popular despite the fact they are less tax effective.

HMRC APPROVED EQUITY SCHEMES

Enterprise Management Incentives (EMI)

This scheme is popular and relatively easy to implement. It is specifically designed for growing businesses wanting to give options over shares to a small number of key employees. The main features are:

- The company must carry on a qualifying trade with gross assets of less than £30m.
- Each employee may hold up to £100,000 of options.
- The total value of options that may be granted under the scheme is £3m.
- There will be no income tax or National Insurance arising on the grant or exercise of the option (provided market value is used for the option price).
- Conditions may be applied to the right to exercise the options.
- The shares must be ordinary shares but can have restricted rights.

Share Incentive Plans (SIPs)

Unlike EMI, SIPs must be open to all employees and not just a select few. Consequently, these are rare in practice. The main features are:

- Employees can buy up to £1,500 worth of shares each per annum out of gross pay.
- The employer can provide up to two free 'matching shares' for each share that they buy.
- The employer can also provide up to £3,000 of performance-related shares.
- The shares are held in a trust on behalf of the employees for a period of five years, at which time the employee can take the shares free of income tax and National Insurance.

Employee Benefit Trusts (EBT)

An EBT may be established by a company as a means of rewarding employees. Most commonly this will involve the trust acting as a 'warehouse' for employee shares, so that it initially purchases shares from the company and then issues them to employees, perhaps under some form of share option scheme.

This is a simpler process than if a company repurchases its own shares, and it ensures that other shareholders' proportionate holdings do not change every time that shares are issued or repurchased.

The EBT may also be used to provide other employee incentives and rewards such as cash bonuses.

TO SUM UP

A scheme to motivate and reward key members of the company is something that no design business can afford to ignore. Whilst a scheme should provide the company with significant long-term benefits, a poorly implemented scheme can demotivate employees and leave them with unexpected tax and National Insurance liabilities.

When implementing any incentive scheme, whether share based or otherwise, careful planning and consideration is vital.

- Define the objectives of the company; is it reward, retention or succession that you are trying to encourage?
- Consider the key motivational drivers of the individuals concerned.
- Choose the most appropriate method of incentive based on the type of people.
- Where applicable discuss with employees before implementation.
- Ensure the scheme is effectively communicated.
- Do not overcomplicate it.
- Regularly review whether incentive schemes are achieving the aims.

The information given about remuneration schemes in this chapter is based on the UK situation, and applied at the time of writing. Make sure you get advice from your own professional advisers before implementing any schemes.

3.14 The cavalry

Madelaine Cooper

Knowledge speaks, but wisdom listens.
- Jimi Hendrix (1942–70), musician

CALLING FOR THE EXPERTS

Imagine that you are alone in your home and there is an ongoing monotonous buzz coming from your electrical appliances followed by an almighty explosion and a blackout. Would you:

a)   Set about sorting out the fault by yourself?
b)   Call for the best electrician you could find?
c)   Sit in the dark?

If you value your personal safety as well as the integrity of your electrical appliances, you will hopefully opt for (b) and get the best person possible in to sort it out for you. It is too important and tricky to mess about with yourself.

Yet in a business context, most owners and managers of creative agencies have to turn their hands to a pretty daunting range of tasks. They regularly tackle everything from having the vision about the company as a whole, managing the client relationships, running the projects, being creative, innovative and impressive, having an understanding of finance, employment, business, law and people management as well as the paperclip-ordering aspects of running a company. It is asking a great deal of anybody, and particularly someone whose only management training has been 'on the job' training at the feet of others, and who are essentially making it up as they go along. To continue the analogy, it would be like trying to fix that big electrical problem based on knowledge that you have picked up from someone who has no training as an electrician but who has changed the fuses a couple of times.

Wouldn't it be wonderful to be able to talk to people who are really good at some of the things that you aren't so good at? People who have done these things before and who have real knowledge and practical experience. People who are acknowledged experts in their field, who are independent and impartial, and who aren't part of the ongoing politics of the company and can bring a bigger view from outside the company. Experts who aren't there all the time, and therefore become affordable, and who can be asked to go away when not needed.

There are three main categories of outside expert: the Non-Executive Director (NEDs), the Consultant and the Mentor. All have subtle, yet discrete, differences in their offer.

NON-EXECS

Funnily enough, there is no categorical job description in company statute for Non–Executive Directors. They tend to be independent, part time, self-employed, hands-off from the day-to-day running of the business, and valued for their external perspective.

Prospective NEDs should note that company law assigns equal responsibility to all Directors whether they be 'executive' or not. NEDs share the same legal duties and responsibilities as Executive Directors, whereas a consultant does not. If the company trades whilst insolvent or operates outside the law in any way, the NED is as responsible for those actions as the other Directors. The role should not be viewed as a way of popping into the company every once in a while to pick up a cheque and slap a few backs. Despite broadcaster Michael Grade's view that 'A non-exec is like a bidet: no one knows what he does but he adds a bit of class,' the position carries real responsibility.

Unless they are able to bring real strategic thinking to the company, and unless that company will allow that strategic thinking to be actively implemented, the role really has no value at all.

CONSULTANTS

Equally, there is no written brief for the use of a consultant. The reasons and the situations for using an expert consultant are as varied as the consultants themselves.

It might be that your company is going through a period of change, or moving towards a particular business issue such as succession, sale, merger, downturn, growth, change of management or change of culture. The insights and knowledge of someone who has been there and done it, who can view it from the outside looking in, or who can offer guidance and support through challenging times would be hugely reassuring.

Or it could be that the company is pitching in a particular business sector or geographic region which needs expertise from someone who knows the area. Or perhaps the company has simply run out of ideas and lacks context and perspective on a particular project. Instinctively, you know that you need something extra that you don't have within the company, and how could any company have all of the expertise that is needed all of the time for every project and every business situation?

By inviting a consultant to work with you, you aren't losing control of the process. Consultants are able to add something extra, but ultimately the decisions rest with you and the other Directors.

MENTORS

A mentor has a different role; they are there as personal confidantes to one particular Director or member of the senior management team. Being an entrepreneur can put you in a very isolated position, and often it is important to be able to talk through decisions and situations with someone who can bring judgement and wisdom without being judgemental. All conversations with a mentor will remain confidential; they are not intended to be shared by the company as a whole but to support the mentoree. There must be complete understanding and trust in this relationship and the range of topics covered may extend beyond the purely professional and into aspects of personal development for the mentoree.

Because it is generally accepted that the biggest barrier to growth within the Small and Medium Enterprise (SME) business sector is the capacity and capabilities of the management team itself, it is easy to see how NEDs, expert consultants and mentors can bring immense value to a company which is smart enough to use their knowledge.

Bringing on board some extra, expert help is not a signal of management weakness but of sound judgement. It means that you don't have to sit in the dark and figure it all out for yourself.

3.15 The self-incentive

Kevin Duncan

If a problem is hard, think, think, then think again. It will hurt at first but you'll get used to it.
• Barbara Castle, Baroness Castle of Blackburn (1910–2002), politician

WHAT GETS YOU OUT OF BED IN THE MORNING?

This section is all about staying sane and relentlessly enthusiastic. Here are five ideas that should help:

1. You're the boss. So what?
2. You are the company culture.
3. Take the issues seriously, but not yourself.
4. Thinking is free, so do it more often.
5. Heed your own counsel.

Apply one of these ideas a week, and you will never lose the incentive to run a successful business.

YOU'RE THE BOSS. SO WHAT?

Try asking yourself some of these rather irritating questions:

• You're in charge. So what?
• You have lots of people reporting to you. So what?
• You have a large office. So what?
• You have your name on the door. So what?
• You are your own boss. So what?
• You earn more money than before. So what?
• Your sales are up this year. So what?
• Your profit is up on last year. So what?

The knack is not to give any particular answer, but to know *why* you have given that answer. If you do know why, and are happy with that response, then excellent. If you are not happy with any particular answer, then work out why and change something.

YOU ARE THE COMPANY CULTURE

You need to confront the fact that, as the owner of the company, you are the company culture. You need to behave as you would like others to behave. What does that mean? Well, disregarding personal style for a moment, there are some basic principles of good conduct to which you should adhere. Being polite and realistic, returning calls when you say you will, and paying your bills diligently are all important.

You can create your own list of this type based on your personal preferences. Over time, you will undoubtedly receive back as much good behaviour as you dish out. You will gain a reputation for high standards, integrity and honesty. Repeat business will follow.

Over-deliver if you wish, but never under-deliver, and should you choose the former, then make sure you charge for it. Pursuing perfection rather than progress has killed many an agency.

Pay close attention to the effect that your personal behaviour has on your staff. If you are small-minded, then you will in turn attract those who are small-minded and unreliable. Map out what you believe to be the important parts of how to conduct your business, and use that as a blueprint to determine how you should conduct yourself, and in turn what you expect and desire of others. This will stand you in good stead if you have to confront a dilemma about whether to release a member of staff or decline some business, or if you have to take the harsh decision to inform an existing customer that you will no longer work with them. Making such a fundamental decision on the spot often comes across as impetuousness or impatience, but if you have thought through your principles carefully, you can state calmly and clearly that their way of doing things does not tally with yours.

TAKE THE ISSUES SERIOUSLY, BUT NOT YOURSELF

This is a maxim that really, really works. Customers want their issues taken seriously, but this doesn't mean that you have to do things in a boring way. Earnest subject matter does not mean that the people dealing with it have to be in a permanent state of melancholy. So relax and don't take it all so seriously.

Humour and lightness of touch are great ways of staying calm and sane. A good laugh can really take the pressure off. On the other hand, being downhearted too frequently makes you annoyed with yourself, and you can be sure that it's no barrel of laughs for those around you either. This is not to suggest that you wear a revolving bow tie and clown suit to your next meeting. But do try to lighten up the working day. You and your staff will benefit hugely. Make things fun and good things will follow.

THINKING IS FREE, SO DO IT MORE OFTEN

'I haven't had time to think.' How many times have we heard that said? Millions of people say it every day in all walks of life, let alone in business. What does it actually mean? If you analyse the phrase carefully, it is complete nonsense. Every sentient being spends the entire day thinking, absorbing circumstances, and reacting to them. Of course, the phrase is not literal. What it really means is: 'I haven't had time to pause and think about the things that really matter, because lots of irrelevant stuff has got in the way.'

Aha. That's more accurate, and because businesses usually generate vast amounts of irrelevant stuff, businesspeople are very prone to the problem of not having enough thinking time. This is a tragedy, and it is your job to create the appropriate time to rectify the position. Why is this so important? Because, although you may claim that you are too busy to create the time, if you haven't worked out whether what you are doing is the right thing, then you may only be busy pursuing all the wrong things.

So now is the time to get thinking. It is a free activity. All you have to do is set aside the time and create the appropriate conditions. Some people like total peace and seclusion, others like something to shake them up. Work out your style and develop different ways of creating thinking time.

HEED YOUR OWN COUNSEL

Respect yourself by paying close attention to your instinctive reactions. When you are confronted with a tricky problem, ask yourself:

- What do I personally think of this issue?
- If it's a bad thing, do I know how to fix it?
- Is there something I can learn from it?
- What is my immediate thought about what to do next?
- If I don't have a strong view, shall I ask a respected colleague?

Trust your instincts and start making some decisions. If an idea is unsuccessful, then ditch it, or refine it as you go along. Indecisiveness has killed many a business, so go for imperfect action rather than perfect inertia.

Section Four:
The Income

4.1   The marketing strategy

Shan Preddy

It is a truth universally acknowledged, that a client in possession of a good budget, must be in want of a design consultant.
- Shan Preddy, with thanks to Jane Austen (1775–1817), 'Pride and Prejudice'

SO WHAT IS MARKETING ALL ABOUT?

The purpose of marketing is to generate income from new and existing customers, or clients. It is not the same as sales, which comes later on in the process, nor as negotiation which is the skill used to close the deal. Nor can it ensure profit from the income it brings; that's the job of business and project management. Marketing is what we use to attract buyers to our services in the first place and then, in conjunction with client relationship management processes, continue to attract them.

The consultant and writer, Peter Drucker, defined it like this: 'The aim of marketing is to make selling superfluous.' If you get your marketing right, design buyers will come to you. They will be 'purchase-ready', knowing what you do, how you do it and who you do it for. All that remains is for you to reassure them that you can do it for them.

On the whole, designers understand marketing. Around 60 per cent of all design firms work in the branding and communications arena[1] with clients in marketing roles. Designers working in other disciplines are also regularly exposed to the theory and practice of marketing, and anyone living in the Western world is all too aware of the effect that consumer marketing has on us and our behaviour.

---

1   Design Council *Design Industry Survey*, 2010

So why is it that when design firms launch their own marketing initiatives, they start in the wrong place? Why do they rush to produce websites, brochures and mailshots without first developing an intelligently constructed marketing strategy? Is it 'because they can', falling into the comfort zone of producing marketing outputs? Without a good marketing strategy, they might as well take a fistful of money and throw it in the air in a gale-force wind for all the good it will do; it feels like action, but it's pointless.

Putting the strategy together

It's not difficult to create inspirational, robust strategies, but it does depend on starting in the right place; that is at the beginning, with a clear vision and a robust business strategy. Once you have the proper focus, you can develop your marketing strategy, then your marketing plan, and then the accompanying marketing aids and outputs. In that order.

There are three main elements in any marketing strategy:

- your positioning in the marketplace;
- your target markets;
- your propositions.

A simple way to work on these is to ask three questions; the answers will inform every marketing activity you undertake:

- What are you?
- Who wants you?
- Why should they bother appointing you?

POSITIONING: WHAT ARE YOU?

If you have a business, you have a brand, and that brand will have values. Strong or weak, intentional or accidental, they will be there.

The market positioning of your brand will depend on your product and its quality and it will be relative to your chosen target market's needs, your competitors' products and what is happening in the marketplace as a whole. In turn, your positioning will influence your pricing policy, your geographical location and your employment strategy. In marketing, your activities should be based around your desired positioning, which might be different from your current positioning.

As a simple non-design example, let's take a look at positioning in practice with five brands of tea. One might position itself as a no-frills, cheap-and-cheerful product; a second as a reliable, good-value family drink; a third as a high-fashion luxury treat; a fourth as a working man's tea; a fifth as a low-calorie, decaffeinated drink for young women. None of these positions is inherently better than the others:

they are just different. Their product formulations, prices, promotional campaigns and places of distribution (the so-called 'Four Ps' of the traditional marketing mix) will be determined as a result of the decision on positioning, not before. The same thing applies to design firms: positioning first, and the rest will follow.

Let's go further. The five tea brands will not necessarily be differentiated by target market demographics: one customer might well buy all of them, seeing them as a range of options for use at different times and under different circumstances. In the same way, design-buying clients will have a number of differently positioned design companies on their radar.

Now let's dig a little deeper. There is another important 'P' in the cocktail: personality. Two budget – or mid-range, or premium – teas might have exactly the same product at exactly the same price, but the buying and drinking experience will 'feel' different in each case owing to their brand personalities. In the design sector, two firms might offer the same capabilities and the same levels of project delivery, but they will 'feel' different.

Finally, it is possible for one tea to be positioned in different ways to more than one target market; a healthy drink in one country and a luxury in another, or a breakfast drink for men and an evening drink for women. The product formulation will be similar, and often identical, in each case. But the positioning differs, and this will dictate different prices, promotions and personalities. In the design world, a firm might position itself differently in a mature marketplace and in emerging markets: 'Food and drink branding' in the UK, for example, and 'packaging' elsewhere. Sole designers might decide to present themselves to direct clients as 'independent design consultants', and to design groups as 'freelancers'. In both of these cases, the products remain the same, although the pricing will probably be different. The promotions certainly will.

How clear is your positioning?

Having decided on your desired positioning, you will need to articulate it in everything you do in marketing from sales calls and meetings to websites. If you can't describe clearly and simply what you are and what you do, how can other people understand it? And if prospective clients don't understand it, how can they be expected to buy your services?

Many design firms find it difficult to describe their market positioning, and it is often because they haven't worked it out properly themselves. Try this simple test. Ask every member of your company to describe what you are in one short written sentence; apart from some inevitable variances in wording, they should all contain the same content.

A website can be a useful window into a business's clarity of thinking. Take a look at the sites of as many design firms as you can. Look at them as though you were a client. How many of them state on the homepage exactly what they are and what they do? How many make blind assumptions that because they know, everyone knows? Next, ask a few friends who don't work in design to browse your own website for no more than 60 seconds, and then write down from memory what they think you are. If they can't do it accurately, your website needs some adjustments.

Working on your positioning

Here are ten questions to ask when working on your own positioning:

1. What exactly do you do?
2. Who do you do it for?
3. How do you do it?
4. What are your current strengths and weaknesses compared with the market as a whole?
5. How many design firms offer much the same as you do?
6. Which firms are your direct competitors?
7. What are their strengths and weaknesses compared with yours?
8. What are the trends in the design sector?
9. What are the trends in business and in market behaviour in general?
10. What are clients likely to want from design firms in, say, five years' time?

Design is an over-crowded, over-supplied sector worldwide. But how many direct competitors do you really have? Once you have mapped out your competitive set, you might discover that there aren't as many as you had feared. Even within one narrow design discipline, companies are not always as competitive as they might at first seem. For example, an interior design company specialising in boardrooms and office suites for directors might not be directly competitive with one working on large-scale office interiors. A branding design firm working on food might not be directly competitive with one working on wine and beer. Although both might describe themselves as 'office interior designers', or 'brand designers', their positioning is different.

Specialisation

The more mature and crowded your marketplace is, the greater need for specialising. The more you position yourself as an expert, the fewer competitors you will have and the easier your marketing and selling will be. In design, there are several tried-and-tested methods of doing this (see Table 4.1.1).

A specialisation can be developed by combining wide or narrow capabilities with wide or narrow markets and functions. You can offer a wide range of capabilities to a narrow client market or job function: 'Branding and communication, on and offline, for financial services'; 'Industrial and product design for medical equipment manufacturers'. You can offer a narrow, but deep, capability to a wide client base: 'Websites for businesses'; 'Packaging for manufacturers and retailers'. If you offer a narrow capability to a narrow client base, you are working in a niche market:

Table 4.1.1 Expert specialisations

Specialisation	Example
By capability	Branding Communications Packaging Product Interiors Digital
By market	Medical Leisure Food Retail Education Public Sector Museums Automotive
By function	HR Marketing R&D Finance IT

'Interior design of museum shops'; 'Internal communications for HR professionals in public sector bodies'. The combination to avoid is a wide capability offer to a wide client market or function; you will be seen as a 'jack-of-all-trades' but master of none.

By joining forces with other, differently skilled firms – design or otherwise – a more complete service for specific client sectors can be developed. For example: 'Branding, packaging, communications, ecommerce, interiors and point-of-purchase for retailers', or 'Design, PR and advertising for the property market'.

Health warnings

There are two main danger areas.

Firstly, if you have discovered a gap in the market, check that there is also a market in the gap. There might be a very good reason why no one else is offering that particular specialisation.

Secondly, some clients worry about design firms working for other clients in the same market, and they might ask for a non-competitive agreement as well as the usual confidentiality and non-disclosure clauses. The problem comes when you work with only two competitors; once you work with three or more, it makes you a specialist and your expertise will usually outweigh other considerations. At worst, you might need to exclude one or two of a client's closest competitors from your portfolio for the duration of the relationship. If you decide to limit your potential income by agreeing to requirements of this kind, negotiate a compensation payment.

TARGET MARKETS: WHO WANTS IT?

Once you have decided on your positioning, you can move on to target markets. Filtering down from the big picture to detail, the process goes like this:

1. The geographical area you will cover.
2. The market sectors you intend to focus on, both direct clients and middlemen.
3. The likely demographic and psychographic profiles of the relevant design buyers in those companies.

Geography

If you receive incoming approaches from clients, there is nothing to stop you working anywhere in the world provided that you can do it profitably. For outgoing sales approaches, however, the geographical area you can realistically cover will relate to the size of your business. The smaller your firm, the more local your outgoing target market will need to be; you can't afford the time, let alone the expense, of travelling the length of the country to go to sales meetings. The exception would be if you have a very narrow specialisation; in this case you might need to travel some distance.

Market sectors and components

Not only do you need to identify the sectors which best fit your chosen positioning, you also need to check that those sectors have appropriate budgets, and that they are likely to continue having them for the foreseeable future. Then think about the companies or organisations which operate in those sectors. It's worth putting together a 'wish-list' of those that interest you and that you want to work for, as well as those you would rather avoid. If you heart isn't in it, there's not much point in chasing after that business.

As well as targeting direct clients, it is worth marketing your services to 'third parties', or middlemen, who will either recommend you to their clients or commission you directly as part of a larger project. In either case, you will need to negotiate appropriate financial arrangements and, possibly, reciprocal agreements. Interior designers could consider forming relationships with architectural practices which don't have their own interior studios. Creators of large-scale environmental graphics could promote their services to brand, identity and service design firms as well as to advertising agencies. Packaging design companies could team up with product and industrial designers who can help with structural design; ecommerce specialists might link with retail designers.

This kind of work, although usually of lower financial value than working directly for clients, can be very profitable. It can also provide a good entry-point into new markets if you are diversifying or repositioning your business. Make sure you have written contracts with the other people, and insist on contact with the client. The relationship should be positioned as an alliance, not a sub-contracted arrangement.

Demographics and psychographics

After you have identified the country, sector and company names, you need to focus on the individual, budget-holding design buyers and think about more than just the job title. At the moment, you don't need their names; you are simply putting together a portrait of representatives.

First the demographic profile, which will affect the choice, tone and content of your marketing materials. What are the most probable design-buying job roles or titles? How much annual design spend might be under their control? What age and gender are they likely to be? What nationality are they?

Next, the psychographic profile, or what makes them tick. How much knowledge and experience might they have of buying design? What is their attitude to design likely to be: at the heart of what they do, or only a part? What status do they enjoy in their own organisations, and how might they behave as a result? Will their age, gender or national culture influence their buying behaviour?

Demographic targeting is like knowing which pond to fish in; psychographic targeting is knowing which bait to use.

PROPOSITIONS: WHY SHOULD THEY BOTHER?

Why should anyone read your brochure or take your phone calls? Why would they want to meet you? What benefits can you bring to them and to their company or organisation? Why should they appoint you instead of one of your competitors, or instead of doing it themselves in-house? Should you have a Unique Selling Proposition (USP)?

This three letter acronym (TLA) has a lot to answer for. It was developed in the early 1940s by the American agency, Ted Bates, for advertising campaigns, but the hunt for a business USP has now become something of a Holy Grail for design firms. If you have been searching, stop it right now: you will make yourself unhappy in the attempt. Not only is it is very unlikely that any of the propositions, or sales benefits, that you put to prospective clients will be genuinely unique, it is also unnecessary. If you really can't live without a snappy TLA, call it an MSP instead. A Meaningful Sales Proposition. You need to be good at what you do, not the only one to do it.

To work, propositions must be expressed as benefits, not features. That you are expert digital designers – or brand identity specialists, or award-winning interior designers, or innovative product designers – is a feature. That your expertise results in commercial effectiveness for your clients is a benefit.

Propositions come in two types:

- Universal, which will apply to any client or client-to-be. These will appear on your website and any other promotional materials.
- Specific, which will apply to a particular individual prospect at a particular time and in a particular set of circumstances.

Universal propositions will remain relatively static over time, changing only as you change your vision and business strategy or when market forces dictate. Specific propositions are always dynamic, changing with each sales situation. It is the combination of the two which wins clients but it is universal propositions which you need to concentrate on for marketing strategies. Specific propositions come into play later within the sales process.

FROM STRATEGY TO PLAN

Once you have developed your marketing strategy, complete with positioning, target markets and universal propositions, you can then – and only then – draw up a practical marketing plan. Don't waste time and effort by trying to do things in the wrong order.

4.2   The marketing plan

Shan Preddy

To achieve great things, two things are needed: a plan, and not quite enough time.
- Leonard Bernstein (1918–1990), conductor, composer and pianist

GETTING TO KNOW YOU

Marketing, when it's done properly, is a mainstream business activity, just like finance and HR management. It should be a continuous, controlled, planned process, not an irregular, ad-hoc, activity undertaken whenever incoming business is looking a bit slow and you have a few spare moments. If you drive your search for income in fits and starts, you shouldn't be too surprised if your workflow pattern follows peaks and troughs.

Let's assume that you've developed your marketing strategy by establishing what you are (your positioning in the marketplace), who wants you (your target markets) and why they should bother appointing you (your sales propositions). In case you skipped it, all of this is outlined in the previous chapter. Now, and only now, is the time to work on your implementation plan.

Just as with the marketing strategy, there are a couple of questions you can ask:

- How will they find out about you?
- How will they remember you?

Brands, both corporate and consumer, need to become visible and relevant, and then retain that visibility and relevance. A few brands fail because they don't satisfy needs, but many more simply fade away, either because people don't know they exist or because their otherwise perfectly satisfied customers forget all about them.

Once you've achieved visibility and relevance for your own brand, therefore, your aim is to keep it. At the precise moment a need for design occurs in your targets' minds, your business's name should pop up as the solution.

OUTGOING APPROACHES

The best marketing plans deploy a combination of initial 'active approaches' (AA) and follow-up reminders, or 'keeping in touch' (KIT).[1] Once you have made contact with AAs, you need to follow up with regular KITs; this is relationship marketing, and it's where proper planning and good database management come in.

The frequency at which you KIT will depend on the design discipline you offer and on your prospective clients' buying patterns. The cycle for product and interior design, or for major corporate identity campaigns, is much longer than it is for some areas of communication design. You don't, however, want to make contact too often, Not only is it wasteful, it is counter-productive; over-frequent communications just become irritating. As a rule-of-thumb, you should aim to get your brand and its key messages in front of each prospective client at least four times a year, excluding seasonal greetings cards.

Don't forget, by the way, to KIT all of the people present in any credentials meetings and pitches you have, not just the main contact. Even if they didn't want to take the relationship any further at that point, they might in the future.

MEDIA CHOICES

Good marketing uses a mixture of direct ('bullseye') and indirect ('broadshot') media.[2] Used together in a planned programme, they can be very powerful.

Bullseye media are those which are targeted at a named individual. They include:

- telephone;
- mailings (print or digital) such as letters, emails, mailshots, newsletters;
- invitations to seminars and events, yours or others;
- personal contact (face-to-face or remote) such as networking, social media;
- stalking: tracking down a specific person at an event or conference.

Broadshot media are those which reach a focused group of like-minded people, but not named individuals. Options include:

- websites;
- brochures (print and digital);
- PR through the media;
- advertising in any medium;

---

1   *How to Market Design Consultancy Services* by Shan Preddy (Gower ISBN 0-566-08594-1) contains more information on AA and KIT: these terms are specific to this way of thinking, although the principles they represent are universal.

2   *How to Market Design Consultancy Services* by Shan Preddy (Gower ISBN 0-566-08594-1) contains more information on bullseye and broadshot media. Like AA and KIT, these terms are specific to this way of thinking; the principles they represent, however, are universal.

- pay-per-click online schemes;
- registers and membership lists;
- directories;
- exhibitions and trade shows;
- awards;
- sponsorship;
- speaking at conferences, workshops, seminars.

It's not a question of scale; the difference between bullseye and broadshot is whether you are addressing a known person or not. Even if they involve thousands of people, mass mailings and social media are still bullseye activities; they go to individuals, although all you know about them might be their email addresses. The best relationship-based bullseye campaigns know a lot more than that, of course.

How can you get the names and contact details of these bullseye individuals? The best way to develop high-quality lists is to build your own, using the target market criteria you have identified in your marketing strategy. However, you can also buy or rent lists from commercial providers. If you do this, make sure that you clean and validate them before use: they are often out-of-date and inaccurate.

Broadshot activities will keep your brand visible, relevant and memorable, and the more multi-channel you make them the better. They support bullseye approaches by attracting incoming enquiries and by creating fertile ground for outgoing AA and KIT approaches. When busy prospective clients receive mailings or phone calls from design firms they have never heard of, and which they know nothing about, they are much less likely to look and listen.

When selecting which broadshot media to use, choose those which provide the best match to your defined target market, with as little waste as possible. For example, to reach prospective clients who work as marketing directors in food manufacturing, you might be better concentrating on media which has food production as its main focus rather than on the more general marketing media, which will reach a lot of other, irrelevant (to you) marketers.

With paid-for media, such as advertising and exhibition space, don't base your financial calculations on the absolute cost but on the 'cost-per-thousand'. This is the amount it will take to reach 1,000 of your prospective clients, and it will allow you to compare one media option with another. Something which costs £5,000 and potentially reaches 10,000 of your prospects provides better cost-per-thousand value (50p) than something which costs £1,000 but only potentially reaches 10 (£100).

DISPLAY YOUR EXPERTISE

Press articles, thought-leadership pieces and speaking at conferences will demonstrate your expertise and attract potential clients; these are broadshot media. However, you can also use bullseye options. What about running your own, invitation-only events and seminars? Or client workshops on design management? Or dinner debates? To be most effective as a business development tool, include both current and prospective clients.

And what about writing guides – or even books – and offering them free to clients and prospects? If they contain usable advice, they will stick around for years, and will be passed from person to person. How to develop a website? How to manage design? An A–Z of digital? Or print? Top tips for rapid prototyping? Using retail design for best effect? Make sure they are properly branded, with full contact details including your website address, but don't be tempted to turn them into brochures masquerading as thought-pieces, or you will lose the reader. And if you publish them as downloads from your website or send them to people in digital form, make sure you give them a file title which has both your brand name and the name of the publication and not an internal system name which will be meaningless to anyone else.

FIND THEIR SPACES

Occupy the spaces your current and prospective clients occupy, both physical and virtual. Find out where they go for professional information, advice, inspiration, challenges and 'go' there too, using the spaces as shop windows for your services. Why not start discussion forums on the appropriate sections of online networks, and engage with the letters pages of their trade publications? Are there any membership bodies, or trade organisations, or professional groups which you could partner? Could you advertise on their websites, or sponsor their events, or run workshops alongside their annual conferences? Go where your target markets go. If you have third-party sectors, or middlemen, in your marketing strategy, remember to occupy their spaces as well.

VIRAL BUZZ

Word of mouth (or mouse) is one of the cheapest marketing channels available, and one of the most powerful. It is also the most difficult to control as you can't dictate what other people will say about you. As businesses, and smallish businesses at that, design firms aren't the ideal candidates for concerted viral campaigns, unlike, say, a new album or soft drink aimed at teenagers. However, on top of the references and testimonials you will already be discussing with them, it's worth asking your current clients for referrals and introductions to others, especially those in their own organisations. You can also proactively ask third parties to spread the good word; make it easy for them by providing information in a way that they can pass on.

RESOURCES

You will need to cut your marketing cloth to suit your means. What resources have you got: budgets, time, personnel, skills? Is your business big enough to employ a dedicated marketing and sales person or team, or will you have to supply the muscle in other ways, such as outsourcing all or part of the work? Are there any aspects of your plan that need specialist skills, such as cold-calling? Do you need someone for simple database cleaning? If you intend doing it all yourself from existing internal resources, make sure you release sufficient time and budget to do it properly and invest in appropriate training and coaching.

Setting marketing budgets falls into the 'more art than science' category, and even the largest organisations in the world struggle to get it right. Looking at data from 2005 to 2009 in its twice-yearly Marketing Trends Survey, the Chartered Institute of Marketing (CIM) reports that, in general, UK marketers are working to an annual budget of just over 8 per cent of turnover, excluding salaries.[3] Anecdotal evidence suggests that some design businesses are working to 10 per cent of fee income, excluding staff costs.

For you, the important thing is to decide how much you want to achieve in what period of time, and then work out how much you can afford to spend. For example, if you are aiming to raise awareness of your business to a high level over a short timescale, you will need to do much more marketing than if your objective is to maintain that awareness over time; your budget will therefore have to be larger.

Different design firms include different elements in their budgeting. Some account for bought-in items alone; some cover bought-ins plus outsourced resources; some add in staff time as well. Only you and your accountant will know what's right for your business.

The good news is that marketing implementation isn't particularly difficult, and it needn't cost a lot of money. It will, however, take time and effort to do it properly, as with all aspects of running a business.

DON'T JUST THINK IT, INK IT

Once you have decided which weapons in the media armoury will work best for you, and how frequently you will deploy them in AA and KIT approaches, and which resources you can afford, you need to bring them all together into The Written Plan. There's no point imagining that you can manage the process if everything remains in your head or on a dozen or more different pages.

Marketing plans are dynamic, not static, and should be developed on a rolling monthly basis; as each month finishes, add another to the end of the plan. You can work to the conventional 12-month pattern, but 13 months are preferable. Why

---

3   UK Chartered Institute of Marketing (CIM) *Marketing Trends Survey*, conducted by IPSOS MORI. This data: Autumn 2009

the extra month in the calendar? If your plan starts in June, ending it in June the following year, not May, allows you to cut-and-paste and view annual events such as press features, exhibitions and conferences without having to look them up each time.

What goes into the plan? Three main things. First, your financial targets for future fee income, month by month and accumulated for your financial year; secondly, your planned marketing activities with item details, dates, and who's responsible for doing it; thirdly, your budgeted costs, month by month and accumulated. Update it at least monthly, recording actual income, activities, expenditure and results as well as making changes ahead as circumstances change or as opportunities present themselves. By being able to look backwards as well as forwards, you can evaluate future ideas against past performance.

Finally, what does it look like? Every plan from every firm is as different as the firms themselves. If spreadsheets are your style, use them. Some people use project management software, others simple tables or spreadsheets. It really doesn't matter. The only important thing is to do it.

4.3　The geography

Christine Losecaat

We all live under the same sky, but we don't all have the same horizon.
• Konrad Adenauer (1876–1967), statesman

WHY WORK INTERNATIONALLY?

Working internationally, or exporting, can increase turnover, keep you and your staff motivated and generally improve overall business performance. If you operate in an industry sector that moves geographically, for example the manufacturing shift to the Far East, it can be imperative.

Whatever the reason you are looking to work internationally, it should be stimulating, inspiring and fun. What it isn't, is a solution to an already weak business. Exporting gives you a whole new set of challenges to grapple with, and if your business is wobbly for operational reasons in your domestic market, working overseas is not the answer. It costs time and money and it will take you out of the office for extended periods of time.

WHERE DO YOU BEGIN?

The first thing is not to feel overwhelmed. Working internationally is not that different from working at home: you still need to find customers and have a compelling proposition for them to buy from you. The sensible route is to make your international marketing strategy an extension of your UK strategy.

That still means having to identify potential markets, and there are two ways of doing that. You can choose a geographic market: this could be because an existing domestic customer has a branch office there and might find your services useful, or because you might have cultural or family links to a particular country or region. Alternatively, you can choose a specific industry or sector specialism: for example, you may have a speciality in the automotive sector, or food and drink.

Whichever route you decide on, you need to undertake market research to identify if there is a demand for your services and, if so, who your customers might be. It will also help you identify potential competitors and partners. Your research will help you understand how best to promote yourself to your target market, and whether there are any regulatory issues or specific procurement practices you should be aware of. It should also tell you early on, before you have invested too heavily, if you have chosen a market that is inappropriate for your capabilities.

Researching your market is easier than you think: the internet has made all our lives simpler. If you have chosen to look at a sectoral route, identify the major international trade fairs and conferences for that sector. Most will list speakers, who will be leaders in the field, as well as listing exhibitors. You may find that key international events in a given sector take place in your domestic market, or close by, so you can easily attend. If you have chosen a geographic focus, don't forget that most countries have special Chambers of Commerce or Trade Development Councils you can join where you can network with domestic representatives of relevant international businesses. You can also look at countries close to home. Many regions have trading blocks which have simplified cross-border regulations and accounting practices, for example the European Union or North American Free Trade Agreement (NAFTA). Another source of invaluable information is other design companies who are already working internationally. Many are willing to share information, especially if you find someone in a different discipline to yours.

Whichever countries you choose, visit them as part of your research. Make sure you plan your visit properly. You will get much more out of it if you time it to coincide with a relevant industry event, such as sectoral exhibition (for example, a furniture fair or motor show) or a design specific event (Tokyo Designers Week, Shanghai Creative Week) and if you have a full itinerary of relevant meetings.

Lastly, don't forget to check that your insurance policy covers you for international work.

ON YOUR OWN OR FIND AN AGENT?

There is no single answer to this question. You are the best person to sell your own proposition, and most clients want to buy from the owner or senior partner in a design company. Having said that, it can be useful to have a representative or an agent to help with business development, especially where there are language and wider cultural barriers. A representative may also become imperative for project delivery.

Agents usually work on a non-exclusive basis, and largely on commission. Representatives work for you, or perhaps one or two others, on an exclusive basis and would expect a contribution to their salary plus all relevant expenses paid. This makes a representative more expensive, but you have better control. The best way of finding someone is by word of mouth and keeping your eyes and ears open when doing your initial market research.

DO YOU NEED TO SET UP AN OFFICE?

Setting up an office in another country demonstrates commitment to the market and will stand you in good stead when pitching potential customers. It is a big investment, however, and one that you should only consider doing on the back of considerable existing business in a given country. When you decide to do it, send your best senior executive– who must be willing to relocate – to set it up. This obviously has implications on your business at home.

CULTURE AND LANGUAGE

There will be cultural differences no matter where you go. In most countries, you just need to look at the difference between north and south to give you an idea! Don't worry. On your first few visits, any cultural faux-pas will be politely forgiven, and you will soon pick things up. Culture becomes a bit more challenging when trying to design for a particular market. For example, you may be asked to design a specific product or service for India: if you have never lived there, restrict your offer to design strategy and process and get a local partner to help you with the implementation.

When it comes to language, people prefer buying in their own language. However, we live in a globalised world and most business people are used to conversing in different languages and working through interpreters. If you are looking for repeat business from an overseas client, consider employing a designer or client services manager who can speak that language. And, if you are a graphic designer, think twice before looking for work in a country with a different alphabet if you don't speak the language.

CONTRACTS AND GETTING PAID

In some countries, a contract is a moveable feast. Where it is not worth much, your personal relationship with the client's key executives is what underlines any agreement: this is why it can take two to three years to win any business in some Asian countries. Also, your first commission is likely to be a 'test' commission. This means that you will be asked to deliver a project that is considerably smaller in scale to what you are used to working on. This is simply risk management from the client. If you accept it, and deliver it well, it should lead to more significant business.

Key contractual learning points are not unlike domestic ones. Clarify ownership of copyright or any licensing issues, in writing. Follow up any agreed points from telephone conversations or meetings promptly, also in writing. If you feel an issue arising at any point, deal with it openly and quickly; if you have spent time building a relationship with a customer, this should be easy. Often, issues result from simple misunderstandings and airing concerns early should lead to quick resolutions.

Internationally, payments terms vary hugely. In many countries it can take several months to get paid, which can play havoc with your cashflow. It is not unusual to ask for stage payments in a contract and, where possible, load your costs into the upfront payment. In some countries you may never get your last payment, or get it up to a year later, so allow for that.

Experienced lawyers can help with contract negotiations. They can be based in your home country, or you can ask a Chamber of Commerce, or get a word of mouth recommendation from other designers.

WHAT PRICE?

Do not compete on price, compete on value. You will undoubtedly be more expensive than a local agency, sometimes as much as 50 per cent more. It is much easier for clients to work with local agencies, and they need proof of your value to their organisation.

Remember, too, that you will have invested time and money in a given market. You are a running a business, and one of key reasons you are working internationally is to expand it. You can always reduce prices, but it's impossible to negotiate fees upwards once you have set a precedent.

Pricing in a local currency is mandatory in some countries and, where it isn't, it can make you more competitive. However, it means your business takes the exchange rate risk. Your bank will advise you on how to reduce that risk.

Finally, look into the local tax regulations. Many countries insist on a 'withholding tax', which can easily wipe out any profit if you have not allowed it.

4.4   The reputation

Julia James

The purest treasure mortal times afford is spotless reputation;
That away, men are but gilded loam or painted clay.
- William Shakespeare (1564–1616), poet and playwright, from 'Richard II'

REPUTATION MANAGEMENT

The reputation game has seen huge change recently. It's probably changed more in the last three years than over the last 30 years put together, and design businesses need to think seriously about how they are managing their profile if they want to stay ahead. This chapter will give you some practical help, whether you want to start some simple PR for the first time or revitalise your communications using blogs and opinion pieces to build thought-leadership.

Let's start by thinking about what reputation is. Only then can we begin to manage it.

Whether you're an organisation or an individual, your reputation is determined by three main factors: what you say, what you do and what others say about you. Reputation is not based on the image you project, but on the personal experiences others have with you and your company. It grows slowly over time. Your reputation is based on how people experience the design products and services you offer, how they interact with the people in your company, and how well you fulfil your promise to deliver what you say you will.

Everyone's experience of you affects your reputation. Not just your clients and the media but your staff too. Your reputation among your colleagues and employees is just as important, both in terms of recruiting good quality candidates and influencing potential clients. And if you think you can keep your clients, peers and the media away from your people then social media, the blogosphere and the local pub should have put paid to that idea.

A SOLID REPUTATION IS WORTH ITS WEIGHT IN GOLD

Everyone who interacts with your company falls into one of two categories: apostle or terrorist. The apostles will help strengthen and build your reputation; the terrorists (often unwittingly) will destroy it.

A word of mouth referral is much more likely to bring success than other forms of selection. If your reputation is strong, your credibility among clients and potential clients is strengthened too. And the smart design company knows that the upside of delivering beyond a client's expectations is that their reputation will grow as a result.

BUILDING REPUTATION

There are four principal audiences your reputation matters to; the industry you operate in, the industry your clients operate in, your colleagues and the media.

To start building reputation, you need to define your goals. Ask yourself, 'Where do I want my business to be in five or ten years' time?', then draw up a list of related questions.

- What do you want to be known for?
- Who would you like to work with?
- What sectors do you want to work in?
- What will be your expertise or specialism?
- What kind of business will it be?
- Do you have the skills sets to deliver?
- Are you commercially minded, strategically led, creatively led or a combination of all three?
- Does your name reflect the playing field that you wish to be in?

By focusing on the answers to these questions you have something on which you can start to build your reputation.

AIM HIGH

When it comes to influencing clients or prospective clients, aim as high as you can. Try and build a rapport with the chairman, CEO and other Board members of the company, regardless of whether they operate at a national or international level. They are the ones who pull the underwater cables, and it's often the Board directors who place most emphasis on the 'reputation' of people they're looking to work with.

THE PR CHALLENGE

Now it's time to think about your reputation in the press. People think PR is many things. Anthony Davis, author of *Everything You Should Know About Public Relations* defines it like this: 'The communication by an organisation, with people who matter to it, in order to gain their attention in ways that are advantageous to it.'

This is a good start. At its most simple, PR can be just providing a source of material for the media. With journalism in decline and more media outlets than ever before, there are some really good opportunities to take advantage of PR. If you can assist a time-strapped journalist to do their job by becoming a trusted source for news, information and opinion, it will help immensely.

TAKE A 360-DEGREE VIEW

PR is not just about getting your story and your name into the press and having a dog-eared clippings book on reception. PR is about the relationship you have with all of the various publics or audiences you wish to engage with. It's about how you speak to the world at large, whether it's through a great content-driven website (your shop window), speaking at conferences, working a room full of potential clients, entering awards, producing newsletters or e-bulletins, creating thought-leadership pieces, book inclusions, running your own events, or getting involved with your industry bodies. These don't necessarily cost a great deal in financial outlay, but they do need dedication of time, effort and focus.

Every business must take every opportunity to make itself known in order to attract clients, and small companies and start-ups can grow quickly by adopting a PR strategy early on. But PR takes time to deliver worthwhile results. Done well, and at a sustained level, it will go a long way to building your reputation and attracting clients, quality job applicants and the media to your door.

DO IT YOURSELF OR HIRE A PRO?

Undertaking a simple PR programme offers you a low-cost option of building your profile. As a start-up or small business, you could certainly consider doing it yourself. There are comprehensive 'how to' courses and books available for beginners and the Chartered Institute of Public Relations in London, or its equivalent body outside the UK, can help here.

The other option is engaging an external person or agency to run your PR programme for you. As your company grows, you might consider employing a professional as an internal resource, although this will only be cost effective if your company is fairly large.

PROFILE RAISING

Times are changing. The old media and PR rules no longer apply, and the advent of the web has presented a huge opportunity. If you really want to stand out from the crowd nowadays, you have to be seen to have valued opinions, to be engaged with debates, to demonstrate your expertise. For those that really want to stay ahead, you need to think like a media company.

Profile raising is not just about speaking through the print and broadcast media any more, even though it remains an important component. You really do need to think about becoming your own publisher and harnessing the power of the web to tell your story or stories.

LAUNCH/RELAUNCH YOUR BLOG WITH VALUABLE OPINION PIECES

Draw up a communications plan that takes into account all types of media, but make sure you are self-publishing high-quality ideas. An excellent way is starting or revitalising your blog, generating useful content related to your expertise, and linking it with other sites, blogs and social media streams.

In terms of content, you have your news stories to get out, but you also have your professional expertise and the ability to solve problems for your clients. Think about developing ideas for opinion pieces on a topic that is relevant to the audience you are trying to reach. Post them on a blog, direct other bloggers that operate in your sector (they can be extremely influential) to your blog, contact a journalist or publication and share your idea. As long as it is relevant to the target audience and you have understood and researched the topic, it might prove to be successful. In the case of journals and publications, it could well be turned into a feature.

NEWS AND VIEWS

You need to have an informed voice, to get your news out regularly, and you can do this yourself or through your PR person. For news stories there are really simple syndication (RSS) feeds, newswire services and of course regularly sending news and views to your target media titles. Journalists and freelance writers will often subscribe to keywords for RSS feeds, and as long as you have embedded these keywords into your release, they will alert journalists worldwide who might well come to you for input and opinion.

Thinking like a publisher on the web is not about hype and spin and messages. It is about delivering relevant content when and where it is needed and, in the process, branding you or your company as a leader.

CONCLUSION

There is an enormous opportunity right now for design companies to take control of their own reputation, with all its benefits. Conducting a focused PR and communication programme that aims to position you as thought-leaders, engaging and delivering professionally across all media touch points, is easier and more effective than ever before.

4.5 The media

Lynda Relph-Knight

Journalism is printing what someone else does not want printing. Everything else is public relations.
* George Orwell (1903–50), novelist and journalist

ENGAGING WITH THE MEDIA

There was a time when, just as a brand's success was gauged purely by sales, the effectiveness of media relations was measured solely in column inches. The more coverage you, your product or service achieved the better, with little account taken of what was said or where the coverage appeared.

Things are different now. Just as brand owners seek 'engagement' with their customers – encouraging interaction online, gaining points through association with events and initiatives they sponsor and creating 'customer experiences' – so dealing with the media has become more about building relationships.

Journalists are constantly on the lookout for interesting things to share with their audience. They appreciate fresh angles, genuinely new projects and, with project stories, stunning visuals. They are also seeking to build contacts with experts, whose views they can trust, to provide a reliable source of information and opinion.

Designers and design groups are meanwhile seeking to engage with that audience, be it their peers, potential clients or City backers. The medium you choose and the message you seek to put across depends on the audience you are courting.

MEDIA RELATIONS

So how do you build relationships with the media? You start quite simply by making contact with the most appropriate person on the editorial team of your chosen medium. Who on your team makes that contact, and who it's with, will vary according to the publication and the nature of any potential interest it might have with you. If, for example, you have a story relating to design in the financial sector, it is pointless approaching the political editor of a national newspaper.

For the sake of argument, let's say the media – be it print, online, TV or radio – separates into three main areas: design and related media; business-to-business; and consumer.

If you are published in design and related media, you are reaching your peers and involving yourself in the creative industries. Coverage of your work or your business helps to build profile, which is invaluable in attracting the best staff. You will also reach: committed and serial clients, who are looking to buy design and keep abreast of the consultancies out there; potential backers active in the sector; and other media, which use specialist publications as a source.

When you contact the design press, it is best to deal direct with the journalists. They speak the same language as you and can give you a snap decision about whether or not your story is interesting. You can probably get direct access to the editor, which is a great starting point, but if you have a news lead you might be better approaching the news editor. A bigger idea might suit the features editor better.

It is also worth getting to know freelance design journalists. They make their living out of selling stories and have inroads into the key titles, so foster them. Check out their by-lines in your chosen media, discover where their particular interests lie and get to know them. Specialist freelances can be a useful link to the national media, as they often ply their trade there too.

Business-to-business titles may be harder to crack and, if your resources extend to it, it might be worth bringing in a public relations consultant who knows the field you are targeting. But they too are interested in stories that are slightly beyond the norm for them, and that might spark bigger ideas for features.

If, for example, you have created branding for a garden product, or interiors for a garden centre, or designed a garden chair, it is worth contacting the gardening media or gardening correspondents on the nationals. If your work is engaging enough and relevant, you may attract new clients from the sector and eventually be recognised as an authority on design in the sector who can be called upon for comment or appear on conference platforms.

SENDING MATERIAL

What you submit for publication depends on what the publication wants. In most instances, journalists are looking for brand new projects – just won, or just about to complete – and stories about people and business moves. They also have seasonal specials or publish a 'features list' of topics they are planning to cover that offer you the opportunity to pitch in ideas or projects they might pick up.

Whatever you put forward has to be interesting and relevant and not, for example, just another brochure win, unless it is in some way quirky, or the process behind it is innovative, or the client is particularly important.

If there is an image, send a high-resolution version with a brief written outline of the story, preferably by email. You might like to call the publication first to see who is best to deal with and to get their email address, but never pester, particularly not by phone, something public relations consultants are apt to do. If the story is of interest, the journalist will get back to you, but remember that stories date quickly and attention spans are short in most media.

BEYOND PRESS RELEASES

Editors are also looking for opinion and for people prepared to raise the debate. Never be afraid to raise your voice on issues affecting your industry or the client sectors you work in. If you are heard, you can enhance your own standing and that of your consultancy, and be called upon for further comment as coverage is rolled out.

Letters for publication or comments to online stories and blogs are particularly welcome to most media as they stimulate debate. These should be pithy and pertinent and never self-promotional, unless your experience of a particular issue genuinely adds to the discussion.

But there are other potential outlets for your thoughts, whether it is as an invited respondent to a voxpop-style question or as someone choosing or commenting on a piece of branding or design. Some titles or blogs run regular columns, contributed externally, and the key here is to attract the attention of the editor, and to have something meaningful to say. The personal approach is always best, even if someone else – a public relations consultant, colleague or assistant – helps you to pen the words.

There is a difference between print and online media, even within the same title. What editors choose to put online is often very different in terms of type of story from what they publish in print, and audiences vary so that, too, needs checking out. Timing is crucial here, as online stories can be released immediately, while the print title will have an obvious delay.

RULES OF ENGAGEMENT

You need to observe certain etiquettes when dealing with the media, most of which are based on common sense. The most fundamental of these is that if you are talking to a journalist it is their job to gather information from reputable sources, and even the most chance remark at a social event could be quoted. You need to make the terms of engagement clear at the start of any interchange, and build a relationship of mutual respect and trust at every opportunity.

If something is 'off the record' then say so at the outset. A statement cannot be retracted later and, if faithfully reported, is fair game. You might wish to share something that you don't want published to put a potential story in context, and a professional journalist will respect this. If you're in a social situation you might agree to discuss the story 'on the record' later, when you are both in a position to have a proper dialogue.

You may wish your comments to be 'non-attributable', particularly if talking about a pitch or a potential client, in which case your sentiments may be reported as coming from an industry source. Again, make it clear at the outset if this is the case and your request will be honoured. Don't overuse this privilege though, as named sources carry more weight with journalists and their audiences.

Never expect to be shown the copy before it is published. No reputable title will ever do this and you must trust the professionalism of its journalists.

A final word needs to be said about advertising. The only way to control what appears about you in the media is to advertise, but advertising in a publication doesn't guarantee editorial coverage so don't ask.

AND FINALLY...

Journalists are generally looking for exclusive stories, and blanket press releases don't have much merit, particularly to the specialist media. It is important to work out where you'd prefer to see coverage and then negotiate with the journalist concerned. This is where relationships come into their own in that mutual trust invariably means better coverage for both parties and more likelihood that you are mentioned in the piece, something that is rarely guaranteed outside the design media.

Remember that the media isn't scary. Publication is a fundamental part of any industry, providing opportunities for you to promote yourself, but also to keep readers and visitors informed, enlightened and entertained. Engage with the media and you could reap huge benefits.

4.6 The social media

Gemma Went

Communication leads to community, that is, to understanding, intimacy and mutual valuing.
- Rollo May (1909–94), psychologist

TALK WITH YOUR AUDIENCES, NOT AT THEM

Traditionally, the tools for keeping your brand front-of-mind included advertising, press coverage, tradeshows, networking and so on. These days, the toolbox is much larger, with a raft of digital additions. The introduction of social media has given us a compelling way to engage with clients and stakeholders. It has changed the way we communicate which, in turn, has brought about a massive step change in marketing strategy. In the past, activities followed the broadcast method of talking at your audience: these days it's all about talking with your community; listening, communicating, engaging and collaborating. This is powerful stuff. Where else do you get the chance to listen to your audiences' conversations, learn from them, monitor trends, spot potential opportunities and act on them there and then?

But what is it? Social media as a term can be confusing. In basic terms it's a range of digital platforms that allow us to find, communicate and with a range of people online. These platforms allow us to make our businesses social and include networking sites, micro blogging sites, blogs, bookmarking sites, forums, video and photosharing sites and such like.

What does this mean to you? It allows you to build relationships, position yourself as a thought-leader, earn trust, build community and encourage brand loyalty amongst clients, prospects and industry leaders. This, in turn, facilitates word-of-mouth activity, one of the most useful tools in your marketing armoury.

By standing out, sharing knowledge and opinion, helping and engaging with your community, you give them a reason to talk about you positively.

You should not ditch traditional marketing activities altogether; far from it. Not all of your clients will be active in the digital space but studies have shown that many are and this audience is growing, which means you need to be there, engaging with them. So integrate digital tools with your existing strategy to get the most out of them. For example, social media activity can bolster email campaigns and newsletter sign-up.

If you think social media is a viable activity to add to your marketing strategy, first consider whether you have the time and resource to give to it. Once you open the door to social media activity, you can't shut it if you find suddenly that you don't have the time. You've invited people to connect with you and, once they do, you need to continue to engage with them; so think about who could be responsible for the activity. Much of the time it's someone who is already active on social media, someone who knows and understands your business, your values, your objectives and someone you feel comfortable with speaking on behalf of the company.

SETTING OBJECTIVES, MEASURING RESULTS

Before you jump into the social media pool, you need a strategy. Think about the objectives. What do you want social media to achieve for you? Do you want to raise brand awareness? Establish credibility in a specialist area? Drive traffic to a website? Reposition your brand? Launch a new service? Then think about the tactics that will help you to achieve these objectives, which social media activities to use and how you use them. Once you have your tactics mapped out, these will drive your content, resources and what you'll need to measure to ensure Return On Investment (ROI). For ideas on what some of these key strategic elements could look like, see Table 4.6.1.

Of course never forget the Holy Grail: sales! Keep track of any leads gained through social media and if or when they convert to get an idea of how this is working for you.

There is so much that could be written about the various activities themselves, far too much to fit into this chapter. Instead, here are two key areas that will give you a taster.

BLOGS

A company blog is a great way to raise your profile, establish credibility and engage. Get it right, and you can become an authority and opinion-former in your industry. Content is king when it comes to blogging, so keep to your specialist area. Don't use it as a vehicle to 'sell your wares' as you would on a website. Readers will lose interest, and you'll lose subscribers. Think about your

Table 4.6.1   Measuring social media return on investment

Objective	Tactics	Measurement
Raise brand awareness	Grow a relevant, engaged Twitter audience	Relevant followers Number of @ replies Number of Retweets Increase in brand mentions across the web
Establish thought-leadership	Launch a blog to showcase your knowledge in your niche area	Blog subscriptions Number of comments Number of links to the blog How much is this content being shared and bookmarked? Increase in approaches to contribute in speaking and writing opportunities
Drive traffic to the website	Create an eco-system of social media activity, driving traffic to relevant pages of the site	Number of links to the site Increase in traffic to the relevant pages Unique versus return traffic Bounce rate (you might be driving them there, but how relevant are you to them when they get there?)
Launch a new service	Create a campaign of activity across various social media sites showcasing your abilities in this new service	Traffic to the service page on the website Mentions of the new service across the web Emails or phone calls enquiring about the new service

social media strategy and what you want the blog to achieve, then think about what the people you want to read your blog are interested in. This should help to form your content strategy.

Make the most of your internal talent pool, and seek out any budding writers. Management of a blog becomes much easier when you share the load. Create an editorial calendar by listing the topics that interest readers. This can include practical advice on the stuff you're great at, opinion on the latest industry trends, reviews on events or books, how you solved a particular problem. Then work out who can write about it. Once you've done that, be clear about how it should be written. A blog is very different from other forms of business writing. It is much less formal. Readers want to get a sense of the writer, so the rule of thumb is to write how you speak. Finally, put together your calendar with deadlines. The frequency of new posts is dependent on how much time you have available. If you can manage at least one a week, so much the better. However a successful blog is reliant on regular posts, so be strict with your scheduling.

Time should be set aside for this, so give it to someone to manage. The blog won't become a success overnight: be prepared for readership to build slowly. You will need to establish a reputation for regular, relevant, quality content.

If you don't have the budget to build your blog as part your website, there are plenty of blogging platforms you can use; these allow you to brand the blog so it fits with your identity. They are well optimised, which will help with search engine optimisation (SEO) activity, and integrate easily with other platforms. Link your blog with other online activity to ensure full integration and be sure to send out links to new posts through social networking sites.

SOCIAL NETWORKING

There is a range of platforms available including, at time of writing, Twitter, Facebook and LinkedIn. By the time you read this the landscape could be somewhat different, with the addition of new platforms. But these are just the tools: the way we communicate through social networks is here to stay.

Before you start, do some research; work out where the people you want to connect with are, and set up profiles on those platforms. There are some niche communities on the web that you can get involved in, outside of the bigger networks. Don't be fooled into thinking you just need to connect with potential clients either; widen your pool to include industry peers, industry leaders, journalists and others. Opportunities can come from less obvious places and getting different viewpoints can provide great insight. The main thing to remember here is that it's a place to listen, connect and engage.

Content is important and your social media strategy should drive the messaging to fit with your objectives. But be flexible with this and allow the conversation to flow. As with the blog, write as you speak, it's not a place for 'business speak'.

Those that get the most from social networking sites are flexible. They don't broadcast sales messages; instead they share useful advice they know their audience is genuinely interested in. They help people and share links to useful advice. They listen and respond to questions and conversations they can participate in. All of this will help to establish credibility, raise awareness and build your community.

Although you don't need to be present on social networks 24 hours a day, allow yourself time to check in a few times a day to listen and respond.

4.7   The sales process

Shan Preddy

T'ain't what you do, it's the way that you do it, that's what gets results.
- Melvin Oliver (1910–88) and James Young (1912–84), songwriters, first recorded 1939 by Ella Fitzgerald (1917–96) and by many more since

FROM CONTACT TO CONTRACT

It takes anywhere between a few days and several years for prospective clients to become active clients. The sales process contains a series of encounters and there are opportunities for failure at each stage along the way. While you might have every intention of reaching the journey's destination, the clients-to-be can leave it at any point.

The main opt-out moments are:

- first impression;
- receipt of information about your services;
- credentials, or chemistry, meetings;
- pitches, proposals and tenders;
- the legal contract.

Along the way, you will need good marketing, sales and negotiation skills, and they come into play at different times in the process.

MAKE EACH ENCOUNTER COUNT

First impressions count. It is surprisingly easy to give the wrong idea about what you do, whether you are contacting people with outgoing marketing activities such as phone and mail, or whether they read an article about you in the press. Your 'elevator pitch' might not be great: this is a brief summary of what you do and, either by overt statement or by implication, what you could do for them. A claim for accurate project delivery might be undermined by spelling mistakes in written work, or elements of content, style and tone might simply put them off. Many prospective clients will opt-out at this earliest encounter.

Assuming they are interested enough to continue, the next departure point is when they look more closely at your firm. They might visit your website, read a brochure, make enquiries among their colleagues or speak to your recent clients. If they don't like what they see and hear at this stage, they are not going to go any further.

Up to this point, you've needed marketing skills, seasoned with some good interpersonal skills. So far so good? Now they will want a credentials, or chemistry, meeting, whether that meeting is held face-to-face or in a conference call. The result of this meeting – the 'first date' – will dictate whether the relationship goes any further. Here, you're going to need presentation and sales skills.

Then the hurdles get higher. If you succeed at the chemistry stage, the next opt-out point is the pitch or tender process, almost always competitive. Here, you will continue to need presentation skills – written as well as spoken – and sales skills. But you'll now also need to negotiate professionally, not only with the main contact but also, possibly, with procurement experts.

Are you then clear? No more opt-out points? Regrettably not. It sometimes happens that either you or the prospective client can't agree to the terms and conditions of engagement, whether they are outlined in a legal contract or specified in a simple phone call. Even at this last stage, one or both of you can decide to call the whole thing off, and the journey you have embarked on will stop short of its destination.

SALES MEETINGS

Credentials meetings and pitches are sales meetings; they are about the prospective clients' needs and what the design firm can do to fulfil them. And they are meetings, not presentations. Although it is likely that a presentation will be involved at some point, if you spend 90 per cent of the meeting talking about yourself and your work in loving detail, you will fail.

It takes a lot of time, effort and money to get to the point of the credentials meeting, and then a lot more again to get to the pitch. Make the most of them. Here are ten tips:

1. The meetings are just a part of the whole sales process and its encounters. Make sure that your messages are relevant to the prospective client, and that they are consistent throughout in their messaging and their style. If your website, your brochure, your newsletters, your presentations and your documentation don't all resonate visually and verbally, you will weaken your case; they will appear to come from a number of different sources.
2. Meetings start before meetings start. Investigate the prospects' companies or organisations, their customers and their marketplaces, and use your expertise to interrogate their briefs. Ask which other design firms they are talking to, and work out why they should appoint you instead. Find out how many people

will be at the meeting, and who; think about their expectations so that you can deliver against them.

3. Don't just react, pre-act. In advance of the meeting, build as much rapport as you can with the main contact and with any 'gatekeepers' such as support staff. If appropriate, build rapport with the other people who will be at the meeting as well. Without hassling them, phone and write: the objective is to make communication between you as easy and as fulfilling as it will be when you are actually working together.

4. Remember that these meetings are sales meetings, so use sales skills. Know your own product, and those of the prospects and your competitors, inside out, upside down and backwards. Then use that knowledge in the meetings to inform the content; it will also allow you to ask penetrating questions which will demonstrate your expertise. Uncover the prospective client's real needs, and then match your propositions, or benefits, to those needs. There's no point in rambling on about your skills in identity creation if the prospects are looking for an interactive website; not only is it a waste of time, but it might be counter-productive. Answer any voiced objections, and take a judgement on tackling any which are unvoiced but probably there, such as 'you are too small/big/inexperienced/expensive'. Finally, make it as easy as possible for them to buy your services by reassuring them about your capabilities, clearly identifying the next steps in the process and creating a real desire to work with you.

5. Understand what they are looking for; it will be the same as all prospective clients look for, plus the specifics of their own situation. The bottom line is that they want to know that you have the right skills, capabilities, processes and talents to do the job. They want to see evidence of your creativity, of course, but also of your strategic ability. A survey carried out by *Design Week* indicates that just over a half of the design buyers interviewed (53 per cent) unsurprisingly cited 'visual work' as 'the key role of design in your business in three years' time'. But almost a third (31 per cent) cited 'strategic advice on brands or products' as the key role, and nearly three-quarters (73 per cent) rated 'business skills such as strategy and working with you to spot new opportunities for your company' as 'important' or 'very important'.[1] Increasingly, prospective clients want to hear about the value you bring through design effectiveness. They want to experience flawless service: if you can't get it right at the sales stage, it doesn't look good for the future. They want to be reassured that you have a good client list, with relevant sector experience, and that you have processes in place for successful project delivery. They want to know that you are the appropriate size for the project and in an appropriate location. And finally, they want to believe that you will be good to work with; these sessions haven't earned the nickname 'chemistry meetings' for nothing.

6. You're the one who has to do the convincing, so make your case clearly. Discuss their specific needs, and only use casework which demonstrates your suitability

---

1   *Design Week* survey. Fieldwork carried out by YouGov in September 2008 among 199 commissioners of design

to fulfil them. A robust three-part method of framing case studies is to identify the problem or opportunity that you addressed, then show the work, then state the results of your intervention. For example, can you demonstrate that your work resulted in increased sales, or entries to new markets, or improved staff knowledge and skills? Were there identifiable improvements in production processes, or employee morale, or brand perception, or user compliance? Can you show reductions in manufacturing costs, or time to market, or complaints, or waste? If you have quantitative data, so much the better, but qualitative information is important as well. Testimonials from existing clients will help, as will an offer to provide contact details for references.

7. Make sure they remember your work, and that they are impressed by it. It is often hard for prospects to tell one firm from another. Sales presentations from design firms are often no more than a set of slides which talk at length about the business's history and development from its conception, followed by an endless portfolio of casework. Fascinating to them; very dull to the prospects.

8. Get your paperwork right; good leave-behind documentation will go on making the case for you once you've left the room. It is likely to be distributed to people who were not present in the meeting, so the content needs to be comprehensive. In the case of tenders, it needs to stand alone entirely. What should it contain? A summary of your business and its appropriateness for the work in question; visual and verbal references to the casework shown; a client list; an outline of your delivery processes; photographs and brief descriptions of the people from your firm who were present at the sales meeting; full contact details. For pitches, the documentation will also include: your understanding of the brief; the work to be carried out, phase by phase; fee proposals; timelines; proposed delivery team, with relevant details; the rationale for appointing you; terms and conditions. Obviously, sales documentation must be well-written and accurate as well as persuasive.

9. Meetings don't end when meetings end. Get in touch with the main contact to follow up; if you let anxieties about being a nuisance stop you, it will be interpreted as a lack of interest. Even if you lose a pitch, you were successful in being shortlisted, so make sure you keep in touch afterwards with everyone you met in the sales meetings, both immediately and in the longer term. You never know when they might want to talk to you again and, in a mobile market, they might need you if they change jobs.

10. After each successful encounter, make an opportunity to find out what they liked about you; it will help you with the next stage. If they opt-out, try to find out why; it will help you in future meetings with other prospects. Ask an external consultant to help if you think you might not be told the real reasons. It's easy for prospects to tell you that you were too expensive or that you didn't have the right capabilities; it's very much harder for them to tell you that they had no confidence in you personally.

FREE PITCHING

Try this. Log the unrecovered time and bought-in costs of the pitches you took part in over the last year. The amount is what it has cost you to market your company to that small handful of potential clients. What else could you do have done with that budget? Hired a PR consultant? Developed a new website? Employed a business development manager? Run a major marketing campaign?

No pitches are fully paid, and most are completely unpaid. It makes no sense to work for nothing except when it's for charity, and yet design firms of all shapes and sizes freely donate their work in unpaid pitches. Is it because 'everyone else does it'? Or simply because they are bad at business?

Free pitching is not necessary. You will need to have sales meetings, of course, and prepare proposals. You might need to negotiate with procurement professionals, and complete lengthy pre-qualification questionnaires. You might need to work hard to get onto rosters. But you do not ever need to free pitch.

Clients don't ask for pitches, free or otherwise, because they lack budgets; they ask because they lack the confidence to appoint you without seeing proof of your ability. It's your job to help them. How? Firstly, through your marketing activities and your specialisation; prospects need to understand what you offer and believe that you can deliver that offer better than your competitors. If you get this right, clients will come to you rather than responding to your approaches, and you will have less to prove. Secondly, through what you communicate in sales meetings; by focusing on your expertise, your processes and the proven effectiveness of your work you will remove doubts about your capabilities. That's the proof they need, not visuals created in the absence of a proper working relationship.

There is a well-known negotiating strategy called 'sprats and mackerels'. The idea is that instead of eating small fish (sprats), you sacrifice them as bait to attract bigger fish (mackerels); by going hungry now, you hope for feasts to come. It is based on risk assessment, and in markets when the sprat is tiny and the mackerel huge, it can work. In design, however, our sprats are enormous, and the mackerels are puny. If we give away the early development and creation stages of a project in a pitch, we use mackerel as bait instead of sprats. Worse, we also send the message that we don't value sprats at all; how can we ever hope to charge full price for mackerels in the future?

There is a significant disconnect between attitude and behaviour in the design world; firms complain vociferously about free pitching, then go out and do it anyway. Any business model which has at its heart the notion of donating its core skills – not just creativity, but also analysis and strategic thinking – is flawed, and if design firms continue to give away their main product, they will fail. No design business will survive if it's not profitable, and no design industry will survive without successful design businesses.

Where does the remedy lie? With the design industry. Over the years, we have trained clients to see free pitching as normal and, therefore, as expected. It is now our responsibility, not the clients', to change it. Act now. Just say no.

4.8 The pitch

Jonathan Kirk

You're such a lovely audience, we'd like to take you home with us, we'd love to take you home.
- John Lennon (1940–80) and Paul McCartney (b1942) from 'Sgt Pepper's Lonely Hearts Club Band'

WHY YOU NEED TO PITCH

Whether we like it or not, clients are now locked into pitching as the accepted, 'due diligence' way of selecting agencies. Realistically, pitching is here to stay.

However, the nature of pitching is changing. The best pitches are now 'entertainment' pieces. This doesn't mean they are frivolous or lightweight. It means they are akin to a well-crafted documentary, a complete story with a beginning, middle and end. As Diane Thompson, Chief Executive of Camelot, is quoted as saying, 'There is no excuse for a boring presentation nowadays.'

Alongside the 'entertainment' comes an increasingly hard edge. Clients are interested in return on investment as never before. In clients' eyes, appointing a design agency is always something of an intangible, a 'leap of faith'. In this respect, the marriage of strategy and creativity has become vital. Agencies that construct a seamless rationale and give convincing business reasons for their recommendations will succeed.

Pitch decision-making is also changing. The rise of procurement has reduced the role of personal chemistry whilst the number of major decision-making points is reducing. More brands are now owned by fewer companies so brand decisions are tending to be taken higher up for more markets. This represents a challenge for the mass of small/medium-sized agencies who can struggle to gain access to these levels.

So how can agencies succeed in this environment? Here are five pointers that may help:

1. persuade clients to buy into your argument;
2. ignore the brief;
3. simplify, don't confuse;

4. make sure you 'get it';
5. bring it to life.

PERSUADE CLIENTS TO BUY INTO YOUR ARGUMENT

At a recent big pitch in India, it soon became apparent that the Chairman of the Board never looked at the screen. He was concentrating on the presenter, to know if he was someone he could do business with. It was a salutary reminder not to over rely on the slide presentation.

So, let's get out of the 'presentation' mindset. What's your argument? Clients want to know what the agency thinks, and they want to know this very early in the proceedings, so state your big thought right at the outset. The rest of the pitch is an argument to prove that assertion. Don't meander in. People tend to remember introductions and conclusions more strongly than what is said in the middle. Spending the first third of the pitch talking about the agency, regurgitating the brief and telling the client what they already know is doomed to failure.

Many agencies are guilty of asking the client to choose the picture they like rather than buy into their argument. A useful test is whether the client would be able to sell on your recommended concept to their boss without you being there. Does it have a real business context and rationale? Alternatively, imagine the client came in three days before the pitch and said, 'Tell me in a couple of minutes what you're going to tell me in three days time.' If you can do that, then you might have a good argument, not just a presentation.

IGNORE THE BRIEF

My advice is to ignore the brief. Alright, that's an exaggeration to make a point. However, over 70 per cent of 'lost pitch' interviews undertaken with clients reveal that the winning agency went against the brief.[1]

In some way, large or small, the winner rejected a direct requirement of the brief, showed a better approach and made the client think, 'We hadn't thought of that.' Many agencies are understandably eager to please at the pitch stage, sometimes a little too eager. This can easily result in simply giving the client what they want to hear. In fact, clients rarely know exactly what they want. That's why they called you. You're the experts.

SIMPLIFY, DON'T CONFUSE

Beware of leaving the client more confused than when you came in. It's fine to raise lots of questions and issues, but remember that this is a pitch not a client project.

---

1   Lost pitch research: interviews with clients conducted by 2Fruition, 2006–2009

The point of this exercise is to win the business. At pitch stage most clients are looking for clarity from complexity, crystal clear advice and straightforward next steps. Are you making it easy for them to buy? If you are one of three agencies, possibly all pitching on the same day, you need to be memorable. When the client discusses the three pitches, they need to be able to remember the main thrust of your argument: 'They were the ones that said…'

Therefore, keeping it simple is a vital factor in winning pitches. Remember that there is no such thing as several big points. They simply become several little ones. To put it another way, it is generally agreed that you can only make two major points in 20 minutes, three in 30 minutes and four in 45 minutes.

There is a famous Mark Twain quote: 'I didn't have time to write a short letter so I wrote a long one instead.' In other words, it takes time and effort to produce something sharp and concise. For every thousand presentations that go on too long, only one or two will be too short.

MAKE SURE YOU 'GET IT'

A typical client comment about the losing agency is that they didn't really 'get it'. This often comes down to a fundamental misunderstanding. For example, the agency presented creative work that the client believed was 'too radical' or conversely 'too cautious and didn't go far enough'. This can be a difficult nut to crack. After all, one man's 'evo' can be another's 'revo'. Partly, the answer lies in a really good interrogation of the brief and client, as well as a thorough understanding of the target market.

Some agencies, however, are going further. As well as the usual pre-pitch questioning, they are using imagery to help clarify what clients mean. It is almost a client-agency workshop approach to understanding the brief. The main currency of our industry is visual so why not use visuals early on in order to align expectations and reach better mutual understanding?

BRING IT TO LIFE

We often talk about the need to add 'theatre' to the pitch. But what is 'theatre'? Firstly, it is a mistake to confuse 'theatre' with wackiness. Simply setting out to shock, surprise or amuse for the sake of it is not pitch 'theatre'. Nobody wants to buy something important from a clown. 'Theatre' is about how to capture and maintain the client's full interest and engagement throughout the pitch.

With this in mind, mixing the media is a good idea; showing slide after slide is a sure way to lose the audience's attention. Analogies with other brands/markets will show that you understand the bigger picture and can be an interesting but relevant 'break out' from the project in hand. Similarly, relevant personal anecdotes about your experiences of the brand in question can help make pitch content real and less abstract. They can help win the support of your audience by revealing more of your personality, the 'real you' not just the business persona.

Many clients tend not to fully appreciate the thought processes behind visual concepts that can often appear 'finished'. Sketches and drawings are rarely seen in design agency pitches but can be very powerful. Most clients (and some designers!) cannot draw and are impressed by such overt creativity. The veil can suddenly be lifted with the realisation that images do not just magically churn out of a computer. Another way to 'lift' the presentation is to show a route that you explored and rejected. Explaining why you rejected it shows the effort you put in, demonstrates your understanding and can serve to strengthen the appeal of your recommended concept.

Unfortunately, the 'about us' and credentials part of the pitch can all too often be the most tedious part for clients. An introduction to the agency can usually be done in two or three minutes. Don't make the mistake of turning it into a ten minute speech. You wouldn't be there if the client wasn't already reasonably convinced of your credentials.

As for case studies, clients are interested in direct analogies with their situation, useful insights and what you really did for the client. In other words, how you helped that client's business. Most clients are less interested in the merits of the particular teal blue that you used.

WHICH PITCH?

Finally, it almost goes without saying that an agency must choose its pitches carefully. It is important to recognise pitches that you are never going to win and not get sucked in. You may be too small for the project/client, you may be the incumbent agency and it is obvious that the client wants change, you may not have enough relevant experience or you may not have the international network the client is looking for. Without being defeatist, it is important to know when to pull out and put your effort into pitches where you have the highest chance of success. After all, the agency must have a return on its investment, not just the client.

4.9   The no pitch

Blair Enns

Whenever you find yourself on the side of the majority, it's time to pause and reflect.
• Mark Twain (1835–1910), writer and humorist

THE FOUR PHASES OF ENGAGEMENT

A pitch is any defined selection process that pits design firms against each other and invites them to give their thinking away without appropriate compensation. This free or underpaid thinking is not limited to designs, but includes also the phases in the engagement that precede design.

Let's begin by looking at the four phases in any client engagement.

In this order, the design firm:

• diagnoses the challenge;
• prescribes a strategy;
• translates the strategy to design direction;
• applies and reapplies the design across various tools and tactics.

Many firms with a policy of not pitching will routinely diagnose and prescribe for free. But it is success in these first two phases that predict a firm's ability to do the third at a consistently high quality. The value a design firm brings to its clients therefore, and the profit margin it is able to command as a result, is highest in the first phases and diminishes as the engagement progresses.

This frontloading of high-margin opportunities means that diagnosing and prescribing for free is a costly way to win new business, even when no designs are included.

THE TWO REASONS WHY THE CLIENT ASKS

There are two primary reasons why clients ask you to free pitch. The first is that they can, and the second is that they are afraid.

The over-supply reason

The first reason clients ask you to part with your thinking is because they have the power to do so. Their power comes not from their money but from their choice – their legitimate alternatives to hiring your firm. In any market with a large number of undifferentiated sellers, the power rests with the buyer. The buyer can use that power to get a lower price and to dictate the buying process. If any undifferentiated seller chooses not to participate in the arduous, expensive selection process, the buyer simply substitutes a seller who will participate.

The way to gain power back in these market conditions is through differentiation, but most design firms fail on this front. The only meaningful differentiator of design firms is the depth of the firm's expertise, and the only practical means to deepening a firm's expertise is to narrow its focus. Therefore it is the specialised firms that are most able to win without pitching.

Power in the buy-sell relationship is had through positioning. The goal of positioning is to reduce or eliminate competition. By drastically reducing the viable alternatives to hiring your firm you begin to take back power and then use it to win without pitching.

The fear reason

The second reason clients ask you to free pitch is because they are afraid of making a mistake. They want to be certain that yours is the right firm for the job, so they ask you to begin to solve their problem as proof of your ability to solve that problem.

To fully appreciate this, we need to understand how clients' motivation change as they progress through the buying cycle. They begin by seeking information to educate themselves on their challenges. Once informed, clients then move to seeking inspiration to help them form the intent to take action. And then, once intent is formed, a change in brain chemistry takes place that triggers a sense of elation over the decision just made. When the elation subsides however it gives way to doubt, commonly referred to as 'buyers' remorse'.

Your job as salesperson changes as clients progress through the buying cycle, matching their need for information first, inspiration second and reassurance third. Closing the sale is all about managing this doubt and delivering reassurance late in the buying cycle.

The first step to winning without pitching is to properly position the firm to have few real direct competitors. This has been covered in Chapter 4.1.

The second step is to offer alternative forms of reassurance. Positioning gets you the power to make the client consider your alternative way forward.

RAISE OBJECTIONS

As soon as the client asks you to pitch, respond with the objection that it is your policy that you do not part with your thinking for free. When clients mention that they are about to send you a tender, raise the objection that you do not typically respond to tenders. Raising objections early is the most effective way to gauge how much power you actually have. By raising these objections you need not be saying 'no, absolutely not'. You're just saying 'we don't typically do that'. And then you're waiting to see what the clients do next. Do they try to convince you to participate? Do they say they are willing to work with you? Or do they immediately turn to leave, unbothered by the idea of you not participating?

You reserve the right to remove any objection you raise, but you will not get a sense of how much power you have to affect the buying process unless you raise them and see how the client responds.

You can then follow up your objections by telling the clients that you understand their motivation and that you're willing to work with them to help them get the reassurance they need.

ALTERNATIVE FORMS OF REASSURANCE

Three of the more powerful alternative forms of reassurance are defined processes, phased engagements and money-back guarantees. They may be used individually, but are most powerful when used together.

Defined processes

Repetitive problem-solving inevitably leads to a standardisation of the problem-solving process. If you can prove to the clients that you follow the same 'diagnose – prescribe – translate – apply' process, they will draw a very important inference. They will understand that little variability in process equals little variability in outcome. This is vital, because late in the buying cycle the clients' doubt is not rooted in your ability to do good work, but rather the likelihood that you will do good work. Every firm the clients consider can show them an inspirational portfolio of beautiful outcomes. But now they are grappling with odds. They're wondering, 'How do I know that I will get a beautiful outcome?' The most reassuring thing you can do is to prove that you follow a defined process.

Talking about your process isn't enough: every design firm claims to follow a process. You must prove it. Take your traditional before-and-after case studies, break them up and reassemble them to reflect the process you claim to use. These process-framed case studies become the content of your pitches. Where others are pitching free ideas, you are saying, 'We won't begin to solve your problem without being financially engaged, but we will show you how we've helped other companies like yours solve problems like this. And we'll show you how we work, so if you do hire us, you'll know what it's like to work with us.'

Get the focus off the ideas and onto the power of your process. Again, your process is only meaningful if you prove that you follow it, and you won't prove it by showing one case study. Reassurance comes when clients see two or three case studies and sees for themselves that you do in fact follow a defined process. From there they can extrapolate a likelihood of outcome.

Phased engagement

If the client is experiencing doubt around a 100k investment, do you think they would experience more or less doubt with a 20k first phase?

Once you've walked through your case studies, point to the most relevant one and propose to the client that they proceed with you to the initial design concepts. Suggest that they hire you, begin at the beginning with a proper diagnosis and strategy, and then, once the strategy is agreed upon, you will present design direction. At that point they can agree to proceed with the rest of the engagement, or they can end it right there and resume their selection process.

Money-back guarantee

Once you've walked through your process-framed case studies and proposed a phased engagement you can now add in a money-back guarantee. Tell the client that if at the end of the design direction phase they feel like they have made a mistake in hiring you, you'll refund their money.

If you do follow a defined process and the client does let you lead the engagement, then you should have no problem guaranteeing their satisfaction to this point. Do not guarantee anything after design direction: there's too much out of your control.

Some people have a hard time with the idea of giving money back, but the financial risk in doing so in this manner is far less than it is in a pitch. Using the methods laid out here the client is committed and working with you. Usually the worst that happens is the design direction goes back for some tweaking. When both parties are invested it's easier to make some fixes than to start over.

Each of these alternative methods can work, but they work best when strung together, and they work best of all in the hands of a well-positioned firm that has done the hard work of eliminating much of its competition.

4.10 The record

Shan Preddy

Insanity is doing the same thing while expecting a different result.
• Albert Einstein (1879–1955), theoretical physicist and philosopher

THE BROKEN RECORD

There's a guilty and rather shocking secret in the design world. A lot of design businesses spend time, effort and hard-earned money – and often a great deal of all three – on marketing without ever properly recording what they've done, who they've approached and how much they have spent, nor analysing the results.

There are, it's true, some things in creative businesses which can't easily be recorded or measured. Fortunately, marketing isn't one of them. There are three main areas to consider:

• marketing databases;
• marketing metrics;
• client performance analysis.

MARKETING DATABASES

A database is only a way of keeping information records in one place so that multiple users can create, retrieve, amend or remove them. You can use scraps of paper and a shoebox if you want, but you'll find it very much easier if you use proper relational database software; this will allow you to 'interrogate' the data in the most flexible way possible.

Would you like the details of all of your medical sector prospects who are female and based in Edinburgh? Or of past clients who have not given you work for six months, who came to a recent seminar you ran, but who have not yet opted in to your blog? No problem, provided you have entered the appropriate data in the first place. The more your database relies on tick-box categories or alternative 'buttons', the easier it will be for you to interrogate it for different purposes.

Records should be organised by individuals, not by their employers, although a relational database will, of course, allow you to search on companies or organisations and call off lists of everyone you know there if you want them.

What should you record?

All databases are different. For yours, what you record will be whatever you think you'll need. Here are a few suggestions.

1. Demographic data (name, gender, job title or function, full contact details, geographical location and market sector) for:
    *   current, active clients; you might like to indicate the type of work you're doing for them, and their levels of expenditure;
    *   recent clients; as above, plus project dates so you can tell how recent or otherwise they are;
    *   prospective clients, with their current status within the sales process: 'hot prospect', 'pitch shortlist', and so on;
    *   past clients you never want to work for again; it's galling if new members of staff accidentally contact someone who turns out to be a former client you sued five years ago;
    *   media contacts;
    *   people from any strategic alliances you might have;
    *   opinion-formers, such as consultants and network contacts, who might act as channels for your business.
2. Information about each person. Where have they worked previously, for example? How might they relate to your other contacts? The names of their partners, children, dogs and cats, perhaps, and their interests outside of work: there's no point inviting them to a football match if they hate it, or to a steak supper if they are a life-long vegetarian. How far you go with this personal content is up to you.
3. Information about their organisation and its activities. Who do they own? Who are they owned by? What are the main issues facing them?
4. For prospective clients:
    *   an ongoing, chronological narrative of the dates and details of your marketing approaches;
    *   all responses and conversations;
    *   next actions to be taken: what should be done, how, when, and who by. Many database programmes have automatic reminder systems built in.
5. For all others, anything and everything you think you'll need to inform your conversations with them and fuel the relationship.

Who's in charge?

Someone needs to be put in charge of creating the database and updating it continually so that it is accurate, or 'cleaned and validated'.

You'll also need to decide who will have access to it, in full or in part, and who will be authorised to enter, change or remove data, again in full or in part.

Make sure you're legal

Finally, it's important that you comply with the law on keeping personal records on computers and registering, if necessary, with the appropriate authorities. In the UK, it's the Data Protection Act and the Information Commissioner's Office.

MARKETING METRICS

With simple records and a consistent approach to measuring and monitoring, you can tell which elements of your marketing activities are working, and which are not.

The main things to look at are planned versus actual expenditure, and at the results of your activities. However, there are also other areas which lend themselves to measurement, such as certain media choices. You should also be measuring your conversion rates.

Planned versus actual expenditure

Your planned marketing expenditure for the year ahead won't be set in stone. Your strategic and implementation thinking might change, resulting in altered budgets, and media opportunities which are too good to ignore sometimes come up.

You should already be recording your overall planned and actual marketing expenditure in your business accounts, monthly and annually. But if you want to know what has worked, you will need to be able to collect information in more detail, activity by activity, and then analyse it against the results. If you know what has worked, you can replicate it.

Results of activities

Good marketing is always multi-channel. It also uses a mixture of bullseye media, to a named individual, and broadshot, to a focused but unnamed group. In case you skipped Chapter 4.2 *The Marketing Plan*, you'll find details there.

This multi-channel, multimedia approach can sometimes make it difficult to isolate exactly what has worked and what has not. You will need to take a view on which marketing activity was the main purchasing influencer, and which was simply a trigger for action: both are important. Suppose you have been mailing a prospective client six times a year for three years, and they suddenly phone you with a request for a meeting after seeing an article about you in the press. Although the press coverage has triggered the contact, it is the long-term mailing campaign which has done the real work for you; without it, the prospect wouldn't even have noticed the article.

One interesting exercise is to draw up a list of your clients over the last few years. Where did the initial introductions come from? Which led to easy conversions? Which led to profitable projects? The results can be surprising. If you discover that the majority of your clients got to know you through an activity which is, on the face of it, financially unprofitable – unpaid work with their trade organisations, for example – keep doing it.

Media metrics

Certain media activities are easy to measure quantitatively; you can track usage patterns for websites and other digital media, for example, or see the effect of online advertising and pay-per-click campaigns. High unique visitor figures or click-through rates won't bring in business on their own any more than column inches, regardless of their content, in press-based PR campaigns. But at least tracking tools give you the information to ensure your digital media is working as well as it should.

Conversion rates

How many cold approaches do you need to make in order to gain a client? How many credentials meetings? Proposals? Pitches? Regrettably, there is no set formula: it will depend on your target markets, on how competitive the marketplace is and on how specialist you are. However, by logging and analysing the numbers, you will be able to construct a model which works for you. If you discover over time that your conversion ratios for credentials-to-pitches or proposals-to-client are falling, you can address the problem by finding out why and by investing in training and advice.

CLIENT PERFORMANCE ANALYSIS

Having clients is good; having profitable clients is much better. Most of your marketing measurements will be against your plan, but it's also worth checking from time to time that your strategy is valid.

Which are your most profitable client companies? In which market sector, geographical region, country? Among individual design buyers, which job function tends to return the most profit? Do certain types of clients tend to repeat purchase more than others? What is the most profitable kind of work that you do? By analysing where you make your profit, you will improve your future marketing and business strategies.

INTEGRATION OR SEPARATION?

Finally, some design firms integrate their marketing database and activity records with their overall business management software systems. It makes a lot of sense to have everything in one place, from timesheets and invoices to employee and supplier records, but if this doesn't work within your current system, and you have no ambition to upgrade it, use what you've got. The single addition should be relational database software if you don't already have it. Otherwise, start now. Record, measure, analyse, act. And then record again.

4.11 The procurement

Tina Fegent

As I hurtled through space, one thought kept crossing my mind. Every part of this capsule was supplied by the lowest bidder.
- John Glenn (b1921), astronaut and US Senator

SORRY, WE'VE DECIDED TO REUSE LAST YEAR'S GRAPHICS!

DESIGN AND PROCUREMENT

Procurement has existed for as long as man could buy or barter for goods and services. However, getting procurement formally involved in the area of design is relatively new, starting just 10–15 years or so ago at companies such as Cellnet (now O2), Guinness (now Diageo), BA and NatWest. Today, it is on the increase.

To say that procurement is not a design firm's favourite subject would be an understatement. To illustrate this, here are a few opinions:

I cannot remember a time, in the 30 or so years I have been in the industry, when clients have been so focused on cost. Given overcapacity, low inflation and lack of pricing power, and high management turnover, that is perhaps understandable. However, the question remains whether the procurement process can successfully purchase creative services in the way door handles or widgets are bought. The emphasis on procurement seemed to start in the pharmaceutical industry and then moved elsewhere. It may work in media buying, where there are clearly economies of scale, but not necessarily in media planning or other creative or intuitive areas.
- Sir Martin Sorrell, CEO, WPP, 2007 Annual Report

We've lost our confidence in the face of procurement, preview, prevarication and process. But fight back we must; it's that or a slow and painful death.
- Simon Sherwood, CEO, BBH Worldwide, July 2009

If you had a trained monkey, what would you make it do? Talk to some procurement people.
- Frances Royle, Head of TV, BBH, September 2009

You would think that after seeing these quotes, procurement professionals would lick their wounds and retire gracefully from digging into costs in the world of marketing and design.

'Why do they have to get involved?' is a lament heard very often in the corridors of design agencies. 'They know the value of nothing and the cost of everything.' This is an outdated and incorrect view. Many agencies in all areas of marketing are finding that procurement can, and does, add value to their commercial relationships with clients.

THE ROLE OF PROCUREMENT

Strategic purchasing, as procurement is also known, is defined by Chartered Institute of Purchasing and Supply (CIPS), the official body for procurement, as: 'Satisfying business needs from markets via the proactive and planned analysis of supply markets and the selection of suppliers, with the objective of delivering solutions to meet pre-determined and agreed business needs.' Procurement should work strategically and not in a tactical or reactive way. It is simply good practice.

Procurement contributes to the overall profitability of an organisation. The tougher the economic climate, the greater the scrutiny on external expenditure, with clients cutting budgets or seeing if they can make them go further. The role of procurement is to manage the organisation's external resources (suppliers) in order to minimise risk and maximise value.

Risk is defined as impact (what is the impact of failure on the company's operation?) and supply (what sort of market is it, how many suppliers are there, and what is the cost of switching?).

Value is defined as size (how much does the company spend?) and impact (what is the impact on the company's cost base?).

Many would regard buying as being as important as selling. A £1 saving in expenditure will benefit the bottom line immediately, whereas a £1 increase in revenue will, depending on margins, benefit the bottom line by as little as 35p after the reduction of the cost of sales. Good procurement has helped bring companies back into profitability.

Procurement departments are responsible for:

- managing costs that are acceptable to the business and that represent good value;
- ensuring that quality and delivery are not compromised;
- developing and implementing sourcing strategies for external expenditure;
- ensuring corporate and departmental governance principles are applied;

- instilling good project management skills, working collaboratively with internal and external departments;
- ensuring that appropriate contracts are implemented and managed.

WHAT'S IN A NAME?

You may hear different titles used to describe this role: they are effectively all the same thing (see Table 4.11.1).

Table 4.11.1   Procurement roles and titles

Purchasing	The original name of the role.
Procurement	The name preferred by CIPS.
Category Management	External expenditure is divided into 'categories' (eg design, media, market research) with a buyer per category. It can be done at a local, UK, European or global level.
Buyer Senior Buyer Category Manager Purchasing Manager	The person responsible for that category of spend.

PROCUREMENT DEPARTMENTS

Client organisations vary in the way they structure their departments, but a typical Marketing Procurement team might look like Figure 4.11.2.

Figure 4.11.2   Procurement departments

PROCUREMENT TERMINOLOGY AND ACRONYMS

As in all areas of business, procurement uses specific language to describe aspects of its work. Here are some of the more commonly used terms, along with their acronyms (see Table 4.11.3).

Table 4.11.3   Procurement abbreviations

RFI	Request for Information	A document asking for your company credentials, main clients, key staff and areas of expertise.
RFQ RFP ITT	Request for Quotation Request for Proposal Invitation to Tender	A document asking for a proposal from suppliers, which would typically cover the creative solution, methodology, timing and fees.
KPIs	Key Performance Indicators	Measures of performance, used to define, monitor and evaluate the outcome.
SLA	Service Level Agreement	A contract, where the details of the service are defined.
PRF PBR	Performance-Related Fee Performance-Based Results	Payment in arrears, based on performance, or results.

HOW DOES THE PROCESS WORK?

There are seven steps that a traditional procurement team will follow.

1. Identifying opportunities

This is the stage where challenges are made to the requirement. Does the company need to buy this product and service, now or in the future? Does the purchase meet the business goals? All parties take part in these discussions, especially the key stakeholders.

2. Research and analysis

The historical demand for the requirement is profiled, together with the expenditure and volume of orders placed for that particular item or service, the number of current suppliers, and the number of products. The specification is identified and confirmed, and future demand and requirements are estimated. Industry data is analysed, and a shortlist of potential suppliers for tender is drawn up.

3. Developing the strategy

A sourcing strategy will include:

- evaluation of the opportunity;
- supplier evaluation;
- research of sources, and identification of possible risks;
- product or service specification;
- draft SLAs;
- volume of product required;
- number of suppliers to contract with;
- type of supplier relationship;
- contract term;
- main features of the negotiation method (for example, eAuctions or standard);
- overall sourcing approach.

4. Request for proposal

It is vital that the most important evaluation criteria have been selected before the tender is issued. The RFP includes a draft copy of terms and conditions. Cost data from the suppliers is collected, analysed and verified. Suppliers' capabilities, as defined under the non-financial criteria, are evaluated and a scoring system is confirmed.

5. Negotiation

The points from each proposal which require discussion are identified. 'Must haves', 'nice to haves' and 'giveaways' are clarified. A negotiation pack is produced to support meetings and summarise the strengths and weaknesses of the supplier's tender response. Discussion points are highlighted, and data provided to support the summary. Payment terms are confirmed, and the agreement is signed.

6. Implementation of agreement

The agreement is communicated to the relevant stakeholders: all parties who will be working within the agreement need to be fully aware of the agreement and its contents.

7. Management and development of suppliers

This is often missed by procurement, but it is critical that clear responsibilities are agreed to manage supplier performance effectively.

TOP PROCUREMENT TIPS

When dealing with procurement

- accept and respect their role;
- appoint an opposite number as their point of contact;
- be transparent in your dealings;
- push back if you feel bullied;
- try to see the procurement person and the commissioning client at the same meetings;
- educate them about what you do and how you work;
- ask for their help in improving client/agency processes;
- talk about measurement and effectiveness;
- provide regular financial reconciliations on fees and costs;
- invest in relationship management, using a formal feedback process such as a questionnaire or an independent third-party survey.

When replying to a tender

- follow the instructions;
- answer all the questions in the correct sequence;
- make your reply interesting and readable;
- don't provide flippant answers;
- sell yourself, but not too egotistically;
- always prof red the docment;
- take the initiative, and provide extra information as an appendix;
- ask questions throughout the tender process;
- provide alternative choices (for example, a discount for a 3-year contract, or different bonus schemes);
- be honest, open and transparent.

WHY YOU NEED TO WORK WITH CLIENTS' PROCUREMENT PROCESSES

Procurement teams can be involved in:

- roster creation;
- market analysis (they may use intermediaries);
- pitch process management;
- scoping the work;
- contract and fee negotiations;
- suggesting PRF/Bonus plans;
- drafting SLAs;

- reviewing your own supplier arrangements, or decoupling them;
- generating rate cards;
- quarterly or annual reconciliation of fees versus scope of work;
- annual performance reviews, and fee or contract renegotiation.

Although procurement has its foundation in the traditional areas of manufacturing, it now performs a key role in the majority of clients' organisations, and is becoming firmly embedded into marketing teams. Design firms need to learn to work successfully with procurement departments to get the best outcome for all: to generate great ideas that create profit for both the client and the agency.

4.12 The prequal

Simon May

The term 'client'? I hate it. If I go to see the doctor, technically, I'm his client. I'm paying him, after all. But that doesn't mean I'm in charge. Not if I know what is good for me.
- Peter Phillips, designer and author, from 'Creating the Perfect Design Brief'

WHY THE PRE-QUALIFICATION QUESTIONNAIRE (PQQ)?

As more and more agencies understand the tendering and bidding processes, the more clients will be obliged to reduce the number of responses to a manageable number.

Traditionally, this screening process meant assessing a large amount of information about agencies and their approaches and technical responses to briefs or tenders. The process of ensuring a complete audit trail, as well as managing communication with unsuccessful applicants, added to both the complication and the time taken to set up a project.

Increasingly, the use of a Pre-Qualification Questionnaire (or PQQ), especially in public sector tendering, has been introduced to help manage the early stages of procurement. More often than not this is now the first stage in the process, and it is what is likely to be sent out when an agency registers its interest in taking part in the tender.

The PQQ document is a screening tool, a way of getting the number of agencies the procurement team will need to work with down to a manageable number. It is designed to make sure that all the agencies invited to the next stage are capable of carrying out the work required, and that they can deliver from a business perspective. The procurement team also wants to be satisfied from the responses given that the agency is financially sound, and that it has systems and procedures in place to cope with the demands of that particular client.

Although it is an extra stage, using a PQQ as the first stage in the process makes the selection process easier for the client. It helps reduce the amount of time that elapses between the first and second contact with an agency, and it helps reduce the cost of the process, especially in higher-value projects, where more time will be spent ensuring the best selection of agencies are put forward to pitch.

The feedback process is made easier, as the first screening is more business-orientated, and therefore less subjective, according to a 'pass' or 'fail' for each criteria. This may not be what the agency wants to hear at this stage, but it is how clients reduce risk.

It is likely that this system will be used elsewhere in the business, so the purchasing of design services will be brought into line with other purchasing projects, as well as complying with and satisfying purchasing standards.

WHAT IS THE CLIENT ASKING FOR AND WHY?

The clients are asking for information about the business and the way it is managed, its performance to date, and some background on the management team and their experience in delivering similar projects for similar clients. They are assessing whether the agencies selected to go forward to the next stage are capable of carrying out the work proposed, and that they are financially stable. They want to ensure that they don't waste time engaging a business that is unable to deliver: at this point in the process, it is unlikely that a full brief has been issued.

The PQQ therefore satisfies two requirements: it reduces the amount of agencies they will need to communicate with at the next stage, and it provides a level of risk reduction early on in the process.

TYPICAL CONTENTS OF A PQQ

PQQs vary in length depending on the number of questions and the level of detail required. However, they will usually cover five sections:

- Initial overview, or background
- Financial status
- Business probity
- Technical response
- Additional information.

1. *The initial overview, or background section* will introduce the PQQ and indicate its purpose in terms of project, roster or framework agreement. It will specify the terms under which the PQQ is being operated. Most importantly, it may cover the guidance notes for suppliers. This section will tell you how they would like the agency response made, and by when. It will give instructions on completing the document, whether there is a need to complete it online, and information about how to supply your response to pricing and fees.
2. *The financial status section* will usually ask for your last two to three years turnover and your ability to supply a set of audited accounts. It might ask for a statement of turnover, profit and loss and cash flow for the most recent year of trading, as well as a letter from your bank on your current cash and credit position if you cannot supply audited accounts. You might also be asked to answer questions in areas such as loan agreements and obligations to creditors and staff.

3. *The business probity section* will ask for information about the agency, contact details for the person handling the PQQ, date of registration, type of company and ownership. You might be asked to confirm the main activities of the business and provide up to three references that reflect the type of work you will be asked to deliver under the final contract. Some PQQs might ask for information about your business structure, key personnel and reporting methods as well as sub-contracting and risk management policies.

4. *The technical response section* will ask questions about the contract and the lots, or projects, you would like to be considered for. Case studies might be the required format for responses, illustrating your ability to deliver the requirements of the chosen lot or lots.

5. Finally, *the additional information section* can cover a host of questions. Typically, it might include insurance, quality assurance, health and safety, equal opportunities and environmental management, as well as professional or business standing where questions are asked about the owners or Directors of the agency in relation to previous bankruptcy, insolvency or other misconduct, including criminal proceedings.

COMPLETION RULES

Do exactly as the PQQ requests. In most cases, if you fail to follow or comply with basic completion guidelines, it will be treated as a way of screening out responses. Answer all of the questions where possible and, if in doubt, check to see what the required action is. If you don't know the answer, or it is not applicable, leaving empty spaces or blanks will be seen as failure to respond and, again, you will be screened out. If you don't understand the question or the reason for the question being asked, there is usually a contact number or email address for queries. Make sure that every attachment asked for is submitted at the same time as main documents, especially in an electronic response. It is unlikely that you will ever be asked to submit these separately, if you have failed to submit them initially.

DECIDING TO ATTEMPT A PQQ

Most agencies will not have the resources available to complete every PQQ that they see. From the technical perspective, it is likely that you will be able to supply the service requested and will have a suitable case study to support the application. However, it is worth looking for certain clauses and requests before deciding to start the response process.

Key areas to look out for are the way the client wishes to deal with the Freedom of Information Act, the type of guarantees required and how they will be evaluating the responses. A big part of the response will be the way you are asked to detail fees and costs. They will ask for your fees against job descriptions in the format requested, but may also start to identify your approach to volume discounts and, in some cases, payment settlement discounts. They will look to see how you deal with ancillary costs or bought-in items, and how flexible you are on these.

The decision to respond or not will usually depend on your approach and feel for some of these questions, rather than on your ability to deliver the service required, and there may be questions that you feel uncomfortable with or unable to respond to. These are the areas that will need some sort of debate, usually with your accountant or financial advisor, to explore the financial implications of providing what you have been asked for in order to stand a reasonable chance of getting through this first round.

The rest of the response is usually quite straightforward. You either have the experience and can demonstrate it, or not; you are either able to answer all the questions positively, or not.

BEING PQQ READY

Recording your responses to previous requests will build a bank of information that will allow faster decisions on whether to respond to PQQs. Having that information to hand electronically will, over time, reduce the time spent filling in basic questions about the agency and the ancillary data required. Collecting case studies in a typical response format will also help reduce preparation time. Once your PQQ process has been established, it will leave only the key technical response sections to be confirmed.

With an established process which includes feedback from previous responses, both successful and unsuccessful, you will have the benefit of being able to respond to more requests, more rapidly, and with an improved chance of success.

4.13 The roster

Simon May

The moment clients realise that revisions are not an all-you-can-eat buffet, suddenly, they realise that they are not so hungry.
- Soonduk Krebs, Principal, SK Designworks, design firm

WHY ROSTERS?

The subject of rosters (or 'framework agreements' in the public sector) occupies nearly as much discussion time as that of free pitching but – good, bad or indifferent – they are here to stay. Rosters are similar in process to Pre Qualifying Questionnaires (PQQs) in that they provide a way of pre-selecting and screening agencies for working with a client over a period of time instead of just a single project.

Typically, rosters are a management tool for companies with geographically dispersed design buyers, or a large design spend that needs to be controlled, or where there is no real design control and the onus for brand and identity management falls on the selected agencies. The roster represents the smallest group of people the company will need to communicate with in order to ensure design consistency through the use of published guidelines, whilst keeping reporting lines simple.

The additional benefits to a client are the ability to negotiate specific contractual agreements based on the length of the proposed term; these might include fee structures, performance targets or guarantees, and impact or effectiveness measures. For most however, it will be the time and cost saving of being able to select agencies from a list without the need to repeat the entire selection process. There will always be requests for project-specific fee estimates or written proposals: these are part of the normal process. It is accepted, however, rostered agencies will still occasionally be asked to pitch competitively.

Clients might also use existing rosters as a way of managing requests by agencies for credential meetings (see 'The Agency Approach' overleaf).

THE ROSTER PROCESS

A typical roster process will have about six stages:

1. understanding

2. long list
3. shortlist
4. pitch/evaluation
5. communication
6. contract start.

Understanding covers the work done prior to an invitation, or an advertisement, for inclusion on the roster being sent out. It will comprise a review of the current performance levels in design, any incumbent providers, the future needs of the business and a plan for the process. It will involve meetings between those responsible for procurement and those who need the design services. The biggest issues usually faced at this point are trying to decide what the selection criteria are, and how many agencies need to be selected.

The long list represents those agencies who have responded to the invitation to take part. A filtering process gets the list down to a manageable size for the next stage. This will be carried out following the instructions for responding set out in the invitation. At this point, it is critical that agencies answer all the questions, where applicable, and carry out all instructions: these may be used as a way to reject agencies for non-compliance. Successful agencies will be invited through to the next stage. For unsuccessful agencies, feedback should be available but this will be dependent on the number of agencies applying.

The shortlist stage aims to get the list down to the target size. Agencies will be issued with a second set of instructions, and a date for a credentials pitch to the selection team. The number of meetings required will depend on the organisation of the roster and the way the service provision, or specialisms, are split up. There will always be exceptions to having this stage, from just notifying the agencies that have made it (or not) to selecting all of the agencies seen at the pitch level.

The communication stage is where all agencies taking part in the shortlist stage are spoken or written to. As there is now a shorter list, a higher level of communication is possible, with feedback for the successful and unsuccessful. This stage will also cover the contractual negotiations required by the procurement team with the successful agencies. This is key, as the contract term is likely to be for up to three years. Understanding the likely implications is vital on both sides.

The final stage is the *contract start*, and this will vary from organisation to organisation. In some cases, design users will just be made aware of the roster and the agencies on the list; in others, they are told who they should use, and who to contact for information. Occasionally, rostered agencies will be brought in and taken through the client's thinking, strategy and requirements. This also allows the design guidelines to be presented and understood before the first project is commissioned.

THE AGENCY APPROACH

Roster applications typically ask for the same information, albeit in different formats. When first responding to an invitation, collect all the information required in one place so that future applications don't need the same amount of time spent on them. It is also useful to keep track of what works and what doesn't, to increase your chances of a positive outcome. Always ask for feedback, good and bad.

When applying, look at the outgoing roster or the agencies the client has used in the past. This will indicate the level of design they are used to, and who else is likely to be responding.

If an approach is made to a potential client and they already have a roster in place, ask when the roster is due for review and who is likely to be doing it. Make a note, and re-contact a month or two before the date to see what the position is.

Once you are on a roster, find out how the clients intend to communicate with the selected agencies. If they have asked for information about your agency, ask how they will be using it and who will get it.

Finally, on a new roster, don't just expect work to appear. Agencies that are proactive about letting people know who they are and what they do by marketing themselves internally are far more likely to get the first projects under the new contract, and therefore be used again at the exclusion of other, quieter agencies.

4.14   The client journey

Shan Preddy

Because you understand 'one', you think you understand 'two', because one and one makes two. But you must also understand 'and'.

- Sufi proverb

A SCENT, ASSENT, ASCENT

Working for new clients in new markets keeps the grey cells ticking over, providing opportunities for fresh thinking and shiny new creativity. Hunting after new clients can also be very exciting: the potential dangers and the hoped-for rewards make the adrenalin-loaded thrill of the chase dramatic, if slightly scary.

But the best design solutions come from within deep working relationships, where the client and the consultant act as a team, each bringing a different set of skills and knowledge to the project. This is why world-class design solutions often come from in-house design teams working with their in-house clients, and it is why, for consultancies, the most profitable design work is almost always done for existing clients. There are fewer steep and wasteful learning curves.

Marketing's role is to generate income, and it involves two separate, but linked, areas of activity. The first is new business development (NBD), the search for commissions from client companies and organisations which you have not worked with previously. The second is client relationship management (CRM), the satisfaction, retention and proactive development of existing clients. When used together in integrated strategies and plans, they provide powerful income-generators. In addition, good CRM will result in increased profit.

In newly launched design firms, NBD will naturally take precedence, as it will in businesses which are undergoing a dramatic repositioning exercise or which are tackling the danger of relying on too small a handful of clients. Among established and stable design businesses, however, CRM should outweigh NBD, with as much as 80 per cent of marketing time, effort and expenditure put behind client relationship programmes.

The Chartered Institute of Marketing (CIM)'s Marketing Trends Survey,[1] explores what marketers think and how they are deploying their budgets. Respondents stated

---

1   UK Chartered Institute of Marketing (CIM) twice-yearly *Marketing Trends Survey*, conducted by IPSOS MORI. This data: Autumn 2009

that 10 per cent of their overall marketing resources is spent on CRM; this is just behind the highest proportion of 10.8 per cent on PR. However, when asked 'Which one of these activities do you believe delivers the best return on investment?' CRM was cited by 21 per cent of respondents. All other marketing vehicles used – including PR, advertising, email campaigns, telephone, direct mail – come in at a rather less impressive 12 per cent or less. The conclusion? CRM works.

CLIENT CATEGORIES

Despite what you might list on your website, your clients are the individual design buyers, not the companies. There are four basic categories:

1. Prospective: people who you would like to become clients.
2. Current: those whose projects you are actively working on at the moment.
3. Dormant: those who you have worked with recently or in the past, including when they were at other companies, and who you would want to work with again.
4. Ex: people you do not want to work with again.

You might have several hundred fully databased prospective clients, and a dozen or so current clients. You will have very few genuinely ex-clients, possibly none; these are people you never want to work with again (or vice versa) for any reason, including legal disputes.

Unless you are in a launch phase, your dormant clients will form a large group, and they are often ignored by design firms in the rush to approach prospects and the drive to satisfy current clients. They are, however, the easiest and most productive targets for your marketing activities: they know who you are, they know what you offer, they know your strengths and your weaknesses. In turn, you know their structures, their systems, the way they set their design budgets and when they set them. And, unlike prospects, dormant clients will always take your calls. They are slumbering, and all you need to do is to wake them up. How loudly you'll need to shout will depend on whether they are having a little nap between projects or deeply hibernating.

WHY IS GOOD CLIENT RELATIONSHIP MANAGEMENT (CRM) SO IMPORTANT?

You can look at sales options by putting four elements into a simple grid. The first axis relates to your clients: 'prospective' and 'current-and-dormant' (there's no point including ex). The second axis comprises your products and services: 'existing', which is everything you are doing at the moment, and 'new', which is anything you might introduce in the future (see Figure 4.14.1).

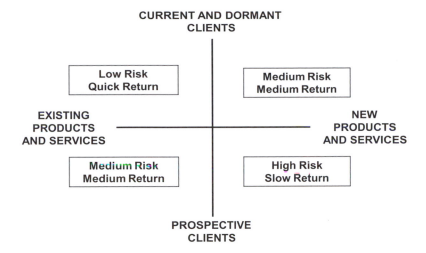

Figure 4.14.1   Sales options and relative risks

Source: © PREDDY&CO

By looking at the options and their associated risks, you will see that selling existing products and services to current and dormant clients will give you the quickest return at the lowest risk. Joint second are the promotion of existing services to prospects and the promotion of new services to current and dormant clients. Unsurprisingly, the option with the worst conversion potential is always selling new services to prospects; they have no reason to trust you.

MOVING DEEPER

Not only do you have to satisfy your current clients, but you need to deepen the relationship so that you can proactively develop it.

You might like to assess and monitor on a regular basis the relationship you have with each of your individual clients. Your own checklists will need to suit your own business, but here are a few suggestions.

Your clients' areas of operation

Are you thoroughly familiar with all of your clients' companies or organisations, their products and brands, the market(s) they operate in, their strengths and weaknesses compared with their competitors, their challenges and opportunities? Do you understand their consumers, or users, or audiences? Are you familiar with their promotional activities?

Your individual clients

Do you understand their design needs, now and in the future? Do you know the total budgets they have under their control? Do you know which of your competitors they also work with? What are their professional needs: career status and ambitions? Do you know anything about their interests and personal life?

The current relationship

Is it one of trust and friendliness? Can you easily discuss design needs and finances? Are you able to resolve problems?

Your communications

Are you communicating the status of projects as often as they want it, daily if necessary? Are you clear what all of the current issues are? Having bigger picture conversations? Post-project reviews? Are you keeping in touch in the periods between projects?

Your initiative taking

Are you actively suggesting new design projects? And regularly sending items which might be of interest to them, such as market and competitive information?

Your promotion of your company

Are you making opportunities to talk to them about your firm's services, skills, people? And keeping them constantly updated with recent news?

Deepening the relationship you have with each individual client will allow you to become the automatic choice for design work, and will give you opportunities to 'cross-sell' and 'up-sell' your services without ever having to 'hard-sell'. If you want to promote an aspect of your business that you think they might not be aware of, it's very easy to drop a comment into a normal conversation, such as: 'We've just completed a fantastic new xyz project for one of our other clients; would you like to see it?'

Strong relationships will also help you to qualify for, and remain on, rosters or approved suppliers' lists and it will make it easier for you to negotiate retainers, where you are paid regular fees for ongoing consultancy, not just project-by-project.

GOING WIDER

As well as deepening a relationship, you can widen it. This means looking for opportunities from your clients' sister departments, divisions, companies and organisations. If your ambitions lie in international work, it means looking worldwide.

To investigate where the possibilities might lie, draw up an organisational chart for each client company based on what you know already, and what you can find out. Your clients are good sources of information, as are published sources such as annual reports. Identify potential sources of design work, moving 'up and out' from people you know, to people who work in the same department and sit in the same open-plan office, to people who are in quite separate organisations on the other side of the world. Then work out how you can best reach them. You can ask your clients for introductions or, as a minimum, for permission to mention their names in your initial approaches. Instead of cold calling, use the warm connections you already have.

FROM FIRST DATE TO LONG-LASTING MARRIAGE?

In design, we tend to expect clients to remain for a project, then hope they'll come back for more. In other business sectors, such as PR and advertising, there is an assumption of an ongoing relationship and a contractual, paid-for commitment. Their expectation is that clients will be kept until lost. They sell relationships: we sell projects. They enjoy 'marriage until divorce': we're 'just dating'.

The journey that clients embark on with you does not have one, big, final destination; it is ongoing. It takes them from being prospects to current clients, and from current to dormant. Then, if you are doing your job properly, it takes them back to being current again, whether they are still in their original role or have moved during the dormant period to another job, another employer or even another country.

For design firms which get it right, client relationships – both with individuals and with the companies and organisations they work for – can last for decades. But it takes effort. The duration and the direction of the journey is largely controlled by you, not them, and it relates to your skills or otherwise in client satisfaction and retention and in CRM.

The design market is very competitive, and clients are becoming increasingly mobile. It's worth remembering that their loyalty, like their respect, is not yours by right. You need to earn it.

4.15   The client experience

Shan Preddy

You ponce in here expecting to be waited on hand and foot. Well, I'm trying to run a hotel here. Have you any idea of how much there is to do? Do you ever think of that? Of course not. You're too busy sticking your noses into every corner, poking around for things to complain about.

- Basil Fawlty, owner and manager of Fawlty Towers, aka John Cleese (b1939), actor, comedian, writer, film director

CLIENTS? WHO NEEDS 'EM?

Without clients, there would be no design consultants, no one working for in-house design units, no freelancers, no design teachers or students. Quite simply, there would be no design industry.

The relationship you have with your clients – that's each individual person, not the companies you list on your website and in casework – is one of your greatest assets. However, given the competitive nature of the design sector, and the inevitable stresses that time-urgent projects can cause, it is also one of the most fragile; you need to actively manage their experience of working with you.

Finding and winning business takes a lot of time and effort. It can often take years of approaches, meetings, proposals and pitches before a prospective client becomes an active client. Losing that client, however, can take no time at all. And, unfortunately, you sometimes won't even know that you've lost a client until you see that they have taken their next projects to one of your competitors. Most of the time, clients don't make a point of firing you; they just slip quietly away when you're not concentrating.

WHAT DO CLIENTS WANT?

There was a time when the design industry could get away with less than perfect delivery. Experienced design-buyers would build in contingencies both for time and budgets, and they would take on the burden of micro-managing projects in ways that they would never have considered in other areas of their business. Some anxious clients still do this.

As an industry, we have now put some shiny new markers in the ground. We rightly charge good fees for the expert work that we do, and we refuse to be treated as suppliers, asking instead to be considered partners or consultants. But are we living up to this desired positioning? What do clients really want from us?

At appointment stage, prospective clients are looking for assurance that you can do the work to the desired quality, at the right price and within the right timeframe. Once you are in a working relationship, the hurdles get higher, not lower. In order to stay in that relationship, what clients want – consistently – is no less than perfection in project delivery, in value and in service. None of these is an optional extra.

Project delivery

The baseline in delivering projects is that every aspect of your work needs to be 100 per cent accurate, on brief, on budget and on time. But are you succeeding in delivering more than that baseline? Do you provide expert strategic thinking alongside appropriate creativity? Is your implementation faultless? Is your communication seamless? Do you achieve hands-free (for the client, that is) project management? And are you remembering to celebrate project completion with the client as well as with your team?

Value

The baseline on value is that you deliver what you have promised at the quality you have promised, and that your budgets are in line with those of your competitors. It's not simply a question of how much you charge. In life in general, some things which are extremely cheap represent poor value, and some things which cost a lot of money can be great value if they deliver the right results. Are you demonstrating proven commercial effectiveness? Are you delivering more than the anticipated results?

Service

The baseline with service is to provide a rapid reaction to whatever is being asked. Clients certainly aren't always right, but they need a swift and positive response before, if necessary, you recommend an alternative course of action. Increasingly, however, you need to be proactive in the service you offer, not just reactive. Are you regularly giving your clients that little bit extra? Are you making suggestions, rather than waiting for instructions? Are you benefiting their businesses in unexpected ways? Are you keeping in touch with them between projects, or are you like insurance companies which only ever contact their customers when they have a new product to sell or at renewal time?

GUARANTEEING SATISFACTION

Satisfaction and dissatisfaction are never about absolute quality (or the lack of it) on its own, but about delivery against an expectation of that quality.

If our expectations are met, we are satisfied. When we get better than we expect, we are very satisfied, and sometimes delighted. When our expectations are not met, we are dissatisfied.

But it gets more complicated than that. Human beings are a grumbly lot. When we are disappointed or angry, we tell other people – sometimes a lot of other people – about our dissatisfaction; in fact, we are much more likely to moan to others than to complain to the person or organisation concerned. We do this spontaneously, without being prompted. Conversely, we tend to keep satisfaction – and even delight – to ourselves, unless something prompts us to share it with others, such as someone asking us for a recommendation. Bad news always spreads more quickly than good.

Let's look at a simple analogy of having a cup of coffee in three different cafés on three separate occasions.

- In the first, a high-street chain, the coffee, price, service and surroundings are all fine, just as you thought they would be from the look of the place. Your expectations are met, and you are satisfied. You will go there again next time you want a coffee in that area, and if someone asked you, you might or might not think about recommending it.
- In the second, an expensive, fashionable café at which you had to book a table in advance for a special occasion. The place looks great, the coffee is excellent and the staff are attentive; the price, although expensive, is understandable. However, there is a dirty mark on one of the teaspoons and they add an outrageous 25 per cent service charge to your bill without asking. Your expectations, which were high, are not met and so you are dissatisfied. You won't go there again and, over the next week or so, you tell nine friends about your dissatisfaction.
- In the third, a cheap-and-cheerful roadside café, the coffee is good and the service is wonderful: all much better than the low expectations you had of the place. They also gave you a free chocolate biscuit, and there were fresh flowers in the bathroom. You are very satisfied, perhaps delighted, and you will make a point of going there again, even if you have to go out of your way. The next day, you post an enthusiastic comment on your blog about the experience.

All successful relationships, business or personal, rely on good expectation management, and it is only by managing your clients' expectations properly that you will keep them in a state of continual delight.

RELATIONSHIP MANAGEMENT

As satisfaction and delight are based on the management of expectations, it follows that we need to be careful not to make overclaims to our clients about our capabilities. In their eagerness to secure the business, design firms are sometimes guilty of making exaggerated claims in their marketing materials and over-promising at pitches. Inevitably, if those claims and promises aren't fulfilled at project delivery stage, the result will be disappointment and dissatisfaction.

Your task, therefore, is to make sure that you establish your clients' expectations properly right at the start of the relationship, and then strive to meet and slightly exceed them consistently. Why 'slightly exceed' and not 'massively exceed'? Because once something has been achieved it becomes standard practice, and it will be expected again. If you did it last time, you can do it this time, and the next time. Don't hold back from delivering excellent service, but do hold back from performing minor miracles; they can be very bad for your health.

Ask yourself these questions. Do you know what your clients' expectations are now, and what they are likely to be in the future? And, if you do know, are you fulfilling them? The only way to find out accurately is to ask them, through regular post-project reviews and through more formal client surveys.

Your clients' expectations won't only be set by yourself, by the way, but by your competitors, by the design industry as a whole and by other related industries. And, in growing and developing industries like the design sector, the baseline almost always moves in an upward direction. The hurdles get higher and higher.

DEALING WITH DISSATISFACTION

Clients who complain are not difficult clients; they are just people who are in a difficult situation. At times, that difficulty will have been caused by you. If you know something isn't working, you can fix it, or at least have the conversation about fixing it even if you eventually conclude that it's unfixable. As computer giants, Dell, said in one of their advertising campaigns: 'To all of our nit-picky, over-demanding, ask-awkward-questions customers; thank you and keep up the good work.'

Treat all client dissatisfaction seriously, whether it comes as a prompted response in reviews or surveys or as an unprompted complaint; never ignore it in the hope that it will go away. Investigate the cause and address the problem. Then tell the client you've fixed it (or that you can't fix it), and thank them for pointing it out.

A good relationship will survive any number of small problems if they are acknowledged and treated properly, but one small dissatisfaction can signal the end of a beautiful friendship if it is allowed to fester.

WHEN (AND HOW) TO FIRE CLIENTS

There will be times when the dissatisfaction is on your side, and you will sometimes need to fire a client. Examples would include clients whose projects are not profitable and never will be; clients who break their contracts with consistent late payments without compensation; clients whose business conflicts with a larger, more profitable client and needy clients who are just more trouble than they are worth. There will also be clients whose business no longer fits your desired market positioning. In all of these cases, the relationship can't continue.

You will need to handle the split professionally. The time to fire clients is between projects, and the way to do it is to help them to find another consultancy by offering to advise them on the selection process, charging an appropriate project fee if they want you to be very hands-on in the search. Although you don't want to work with them anymore, you should aim to part company on the best possible terms. Clients move jobs, and they talk to other clients; you are, after all, only as good as your reputation.

FROM PROJECT TO RELATIONSHIP

Regular clients, working within long-term relationships, not only make the design process much more enjoyable, but they will also save you time, effort and money both in project delivery and in marketing activities.

With projects, you will not have to spend so long researching marketplaces and investigating consumer behaviour. You will understand their business goals and processes, and you will be able to arrive at design recommendations much more quickly. Communication will be easier, and you will be more likely to get swift approval of design strategies and concepts. And, if you are running a sizeable business, you will be able to match the right team members to each client, and avoid the risk of personality clashes which would hinder project progress.

With marketing activities, regular clients will automatically come back to you with more work, reducing the number of sales meetings you would otherwise need to have. They will make sure you are on the shortlist for major pitches and tenders. They are more likely to agree to a retainer-based way of working. They will remain clients when they move to a new job. And they will recommend you to other potential clients both in their own organisations and elsewhere, becoming roving ambassadors for your business.

If the relationship you have with them is good, your clients will do half of your work for you, but only if they are satisfied to the point of delight.

Finally, it's worth remembering that your clients will be under surveillance from your direct competitors, who will constantly attempt to seduce them away from you. Whether your clients stop to listen to – or even notice – their tempting approaches will depend entirely on the condition of the relationship you have with them.

You are running a business. Make sure that it is successful business, both now and in the future. Aim to work within relationships, not just on projects, and make sure that you consistently satisfy – and delight – your clients.

Section Five:
The Work

5.1   The terms

Barry Morris

A verbal contract isn't worth the paper it's written on.
- Samuel Goldwyn (c. 1879–1974), film producer

Ts AND Cs: YOUR TERMS, YOUR CONDITIONS

Stop! Don't flick past this chapter because it looks 'legal' and boring. It isn't boring, and it is important.

In all your dealings with clients, a contractual relationship binds you whether you realise it or not. It can be expressed in a letter, or a written contract, or an acceptance of terms of business. Communicating clearly about these issues will show that you are professional about your work and it will help to avoid misunderstandings. As a last resort, it will stand you in good stead if there is a future argument.

Set out below are some guidelines and comments about quotes and proposals, terms of business for clients, and terms of business for suppliers. We also take a look at delivering the work against contract.

QUOTES AND PROPOSALS

There are many ways of setting out your ideas before you win a piece of work. More often than not this will include some form of quotation, estimate, proposal or simply a letter or email.

There is a difference between a quotation and an estimate. Quite simply, a quotation is a fixed price for an agreed piece of work or a project. An estimate, on the other hand, is your best guess at how much the work will cost. It is difficult to quote for a job until you really understand the scope and scale of the work so, if you have to talk money, try using a range of prices ('Stage 1 prices will be between x and y') or quote a similar recent piece of work ('We cannot give firm prices without knowing xyz, but a similar piece of work for an existing client cost x').

The key points in any proposal, estimate or quote are:

- *Introduction/background*: the definition of the job and your understanding of the work required.
- *How*: your method of working.
- *Who*: your team, with details of who is doing what, and the client's team if you know it.
- *What*: the deliverables.
- *When*: the timetable.
- *Fees and other costs*.
- *Terms*: Intellectual Property Rights (IPR) and when you get paid.

If in doubt about what is worth putting in a proposal ask yourself: 'What would I want if I were the client?' Put yourself in the client's shoes.

Assuming you win the work, the proposal also serves as the basis for the contract, which is another incentive to make it clear. If you set out what you think you have been asked to do, you have a 'paper trail' and can say 'that will cost extra' if the client changes their mind later.

It is worth bearing in mind that many buyers of design do not understand the design process. Don't make assumptions. Set out the stages of the work and explain – without jargon – what happens at each stage, and why it's important. Explain the basis of your costs ('We have allowed for three roughs of the first stage design'; 'We have assumed no more than 10 changes of copy'). The more clients understand about what you do and why you do it, the more likely they are to accept your price and the less likely they are to argue later.

So, the proposal has gone in, the client has said 'yes' – what next? If you attached your terms of business to your proposal, they are the 'rules' for this project. If you didn't, now is the time to do it.

Terms of business for clients will be different from those you use with suppliers, but in both cases they are a statement of how you are going to do business. Often, you don't need to refer to them at all, but they can be crucially important. They can help to make relationships with clients and suppliers smoother and more professional.

TERMS OF BUSINESS WITH CLIENTS

Any job you undertake for a client needs to have a written agreement. In practice, this ranges from an exchange of letters or emails, to an acceptance of a proposal with terms and conditions attached, right through to a full-blown legal contract argued over by respective sets of lawyers.

If you submit a proposal with terms of business to a client, and the client accepts, then your terms are what govern that relationship and will be looked at in the event of any disagreement. Project-specific contracts often crop up in bigger pieces of work, or if you are working for large national and international clients. However, the principles also apply to smaller jobs and smaller clients.

Whatever sort of contract you have, write down the main points and agree them with your client. The golden rule? Write it down. Make it clear.

The starting point is to know who is producing the contract. Many clients want their own: others expect you to do it. This sends some consultancies rushing to their lawyers, but there are a number of common sense things you can sort out and get right before getting legal advice. If in doubt, draft as much as possible yourself, then get a lawyer to look at it.

There is no 'one size fits all' here, but set out below are some headings which you can use as a checklist.

Parties: who the contract is between. Check if you are dealing with a subsidiary company or the parent: whoever the contract is with is ultimately responsible for paying your bill.

Recitals: what has already happened, or the background information. Often the full contract comes after you have started the work, or at least after your proposal has been accepted.

Interpretation: this defines specific words used in the contract.

Performance/Engagement: This section could contain approval procedures or payment terms or timings or definition of deliverables – or some combination of all of those.

Approval procedures: details of who is authorised to approve your work and sign invoices for payment.

Payment: should simply state agreed payment terms.

Timing: the overall timing plan.

Deliverables: what you will give the client.

Term of contract: how long does the contract last? Check against restrictions on termination.

Disputes: how any disagreement will be resolved, preferably by negotiation between you and the client. It's often useful to have an escalation chain. If your account manager or designer falls out with (say) a client marketing manager, the contract might say the disagreement should be resolved by your respective managing directors. It is difficult to resolve disputes about creative work as subjective opinion can be involved, so it's far better to involve clients during the design process. If you get sign-off at each stage or sub-stage, there will be no surprises for the client, and no disputes.

Termination: who can end the agreement, and how.

Assignment of IPR: if possible, don't pass over IPR until you have been paid: one of your main weapons in terms of payment or disputes will be lost.

Design credits: for use after completion of the work. It is entirely reasonable that you should be allowed to use your work in your own marketing materials. Unless you reserve that right through the contract, however, you run the risk of the client subsequently refusing permission, and there will be little you can do about it.

Warranties and indemnities: what you are warranting (guaranteeing) to the client, and any indemnity you are giving them, or they are giving you. Expect to see something about you guaranteeing that you own the copyright in all that is produced. This provides no problem if all the design work has been done by your staff, but remember freelancers' contracts, and any limited copyright you have bought on specific items such as music for the project. Some clients will seek indemnity so that, if they are accused of breach of copyright, you, the consultancy, will pay any costs. This may be acceptable if it is proved that you have breached copyright, but is unreasonable if the client tries to get you to indemnify them against claims of breach alone. Under those circumstances, all the costs of defending that action would fall to you, however unreasonable the claim might be.

Confidentiality: what you are assuring the client in terms of information security.

Restrictions: consider a clause which prevents clients poaching your staff. If clients seek exclusivity, restricting you from working with other companies in their field, read the section carefully and only accept it if you are happy.

Assignment: larger companies might want the right to assign (that is, pass on) the contract to a subsidiary, and at the same time restrict you from assigning the contract to another design company. Neither should cause a problem.

Additional work/variations to contract: what is additional to the contract, and who can authorise changes. Clearly, if the contract is to produce 1,500 brochures and the client changes his mind and says 2,000, an exchange of emails should cover it. But beware of subtle changes to the brief: they can cause a lot of extra work, but are often not regarded as much by the client.

Law/jurisdiction: which country's law any legal action will follow: in Canada or the USA, for example, it is expensive. In the UK, English or Scottish law should prevail.

TERMS OF BUSINESS WITH SUPPLIERS

You don't need a breakdown with one of your suppliers. How do you avoid that? As with terms of business with clients: be clear, write it down.

Most consultancies will use purchase orders to cover everything from buying copier paper to commissioning freelancers. Your purchase order should contain your terms and conditions of business, often printed on the back.

What you are buying will dictate how relaxed you can be about it. You should be:

* relatively relaxed about buying items like stationery, or coffee;
* slightly less relaxed about, for example, employing temporary staff; or renting mobile phones and photocopiers; or booking studios you might hire for a shoot, with potential overtime rates and cancellation charges;

- very unrelaxed about freelance staff, and anything you buy that will be used as part of your work for a client, for example, music, stock, images.

The relaxed category is unlikely to cause problems. It won't matter whether your purchase order or the supplier's terms of business prevails.

In the less relaxed category, you will be asked to sign a contract, drawn up by the supplier and their lawyers. They will usually be big companies, and unwilling to negotiate on standard terms. Check out the important points and make sure you have understood them. If you struggle to find information in the small print, ask the supplier to put it in writing. If you negotiate something different from the standard terms, exchange emails. If you have an argument later, you'll have a written understanding of what should have happened.

Be very careful about the final category, unrelaxed. This is where IPR comes in. Read Chapter 2.9 *The Intellectual Property* for more details, and involve your lawyer if necessary.

For freelancers, the contract (which is your terms of business) should set out clearly the usual information on duration of contract, fees and confidentiality, but it should also give you, the company, IPR in the work. Without it, you cannot pass it on to your client. You might also include restrictions to prevent freelancers pinching your client when the project finishes.

Be particularly careful when buying copyright. For example, if you buy for a particular project the right to use music on UK television channels, or the right to use an image in a UK catalogue, you can only pass on to your client exactly the same rights. If your client uses the music in Europe, or publishes the catalogue in Asia, you are heading for an expensive settlement and, at worst, a court case. Make sure you know exactly what you are buying, and make sure your client understands any limitations.

DELIVERING THE WORK AGAINST CONTRACT

The creatives are working away on the project; account handlers, too, if you have them. Who is looking after the non-creative bit?

There are links between project management and conforming with the contract. There are no hard and fast rules, but somebody needs to make sure that the right hand knows what the left hand is doing. It needs to be seamless for the client, but important areas, often invisible to clients, must be covered.

Make sure responsibility is agreed in-house for:

- monitoring deadlines;
- watching hours spent;
- knowing what to recharge and what not;
- stage billing;
- approvals procedures;

- monitoring changes to brief;
- writing to clients about cost and timing implications of changes;
- producing contact reports.

In summary? Write it down. Make it clear.

5.2 The knowledge

Liz Lydiate

An investment in knowledge pays the best interest.
* Benjamin Franklin (1705–90), politician, statesman and polymath

FROM EDUCATION INTO DESIGN PRACTICE

What does a practising design consultant need to know? It is generally accepted that the business of design is creativity, but very many additional and related skills are needed to put the wheels on the ideas and to deliver practical, workable design solutions, on time, to budget and hitting the precise targets defined in the brief in a way which can be monitored and evaluated.

Since the 1980s design consultancy has changed radically, repositioning itself away from a purely creative service (as it used to say on the back of the Design Council's envelopes '...*not something you stick on afterwards...*') and increasingly maturing towards a true business management consultancy service. As a very necessary part of this process, during the 1990s and to the present there has been much enquiry and debate about the review and development of the Higher Education (HE) design curriculum, including heavyweight Government intervention such as the Cox Report.[1]

UK practice-based design programmes have a strong and distinguished reputation for the encouragement and development of creativity, but sometimes have not caught up with the radical change in the nature of the design industry. As design works hard to establish itself as a true business consultancy service, this orientation is not yet fully reflected in the HE design curriculum. Is there still a place for the

---

1   *The Cox Review of Creativity In Business*, Design Council/ HM Treasury, 2005

highly creative designer who does not have an integral knowledge of the business needs that clients seek to satisfy through design? Are the HE design programme directors who worry that inclusion of more business education in design courses will damage the core business of developing creativity correct? What are the real knowledge-based needs of the UK design industry, now and for the future?

There are also important unresolved issues about whether design management practice is about running design companies or something else altogether. Design management programmes provide a very important source of business and academic knowledge, and are of great benefit to the design industry, but study of the UK HE sector reveals that the delivery of design management courses at undergraduate and postgraduate levels has been complex and often problematic. Many courses have had only a relatively short life before being redesigned or closed, reflecting external confusion about the changing nature and professional competences of design consultancy. It is not the role of design management education to act as a Band-Aid™ to make up for other skills deficits in the design industry, particularly among designers.

It has become apparent that even if the HE curriculum changes and develops in the manner discussed, it will never be possible within the parameters of an undergraduate design programme to produce 'oven ready' graduates, fully versed in all aspects of professional practice. Instead, the aim should be to produce young designers with a realistic understanding of design practice, aware of the many different branches and sectors of the design industry and associated possible career paths and expecting to undertake further Continuing Professional Development (CPD) as an integral part of their career development.

The necessary skill and knowledge base for successful contemporary design consultancy is both broad and deep and needs constant refreshing and updating. Not all things will be found in all people, and a successful consultancy will look at the interconnection of collective complementary skills within its team as whole. Because design consultancy is a service industry, it is vital to understand the business needs and objectives of the client. The subsequent development of design solutions is a partnership process, where the efficient and effective execution of the project is of paramount importance.

CREATIVE SKILLS, DESIGN AND CRAFT SKILLS

If the studio – the hub of creative activity, generation and execution – is the centre of a design consultancy, it can also be visualised as the essence of the organisation, surrounded and supported by a large number of essential and interconnected activities that together make up the consultancy's ability to deliver. Sourcing and attracting good designers, whether employed or hired as freelancers, is the life blood of the design organisation. It is well recognised that good companies attract the best staff, and that company reputation plays a key role in the recruitment process

The hiring activity alone is not sufficient. Care must also be taken to harness the true value of the staffing investment through nurture, refreshment and extension of the designers' knowledge base and capability. In his introduction to a predecessor to this book, *Professional Practice in Design Consultancy,*[2] Sir John Sorrell comments that design is a business area where the key capital assets walk out of the door at the end of each working day. Management has to attend to making sure that they want to come back in the morning, that they will have a working environment conducive to creativity, and work practices which enable them to interact effectively and enjoyably. Training and active staff development make a major contribution to staff effectiveness, profitability and retention.

Meredith Belbin's work[3] on team roles can be applied to design consultancy to interrogate and understand the different roles and skill sets within the organisation. Knowledge of the company's market positioning, specialisms and core offer should pro-actively influence the blending and mixing of creative, craft and design skills, rather than the other way around, where a company attempts to reactively adapt its market offer to suit existing design competence and preferences.

INITIATIVE AND RESOURCES

There are some magic ingredients which are hard to define, difficult to source or order up, but essential to creative success.

Research skills are seldom specified on design industry job descriptions, but deliver enormous competitive benefit at many different stages of the design process. Can team members get the best out of the internet, use libraries, source reports and statistics and use these things to enhance the robustness of design consultancy work? Will appropriate primary research – surveys, focus groups, interviews, visual research – be implemented to enhance and extend the range of the creative solutions? Can observation and deliberate strategies for maintaining an open mind help in the initial interrogation of the brief and the development of better and more accurate interpretations of the situation and the requirements?

Similarly, the recruitment process is unlikely to explore the mechanics of a candidates' thinking processes, but these are central to what they will contribute. Design is built upon effective thinking, but this can be enhanced by knowledge of different tools and techniques that complement and extend the creative process. Most organisations will use versions of brainstorming, but a 'thinking tool kit' can contain many wider possibilities. Shared understanding of thinking – and thinking techniques – will help a team to function more effectively, as will knowledge of different team roles and personality. Deliberate activities which facilitate sharing of individual knowledge are helpful and can be built into company and team working styles.

'Blue sky thinking' and 'thinking outside of the box' can be nurtured by company behaviour. Are wild ideas encouraged or shot down? Can the company deliberately

2   *Professional Practice in Design Consultancy*, ed. Liz Lydiate, Design Council, 1992

3   *Team Roles at Work*, R Meredith Belbin, Butterworth Heinemann, 1993

undertake challenging and stimulating experiences as part of a central commitment to shared creative growth? And what resources are available to support this?

STRATEGIC PLANNING AND PROJECT MANAGEMENT SKILLS

Design is about making new things happen, and making ideas into working reality. A successful design company actively reviews actions and possibilities all the time, in response to external drivers and stimuli. An inward looking company, pre-occupied with internal concerns, will not be as in tune with the external environment as one which constantly looks outside. This data and intelligence informs the strategic planning process that should be an integral part of the activity of well-run company.

Learning about strategic planning can be tackled in different ways, but the first step is to recognise its critical role. Some companies work with external consultants, some hire staff with specialist qualifications, and some work on their strategic planning skills incrementally. At the same time, design consultancy work is going to link in to the strategic planning of clients, and this requires understanding and insight arising from theoretical knowledge.

In order to execute and deliver the work required by the client, there is a need for excellent project management skills, linking in to the overall requirement that standard of service is at all times equivalent to the standard of creative work produced. Good project management practice enables a design consultancy to manage concurrent projects, over an extended period of time where it will often be essential to accommodate change and revision. Like so many things in this section, this activity is driven by shared knowledge and shared standards, understood and practised by all. Although there will be staff with dedicated project management skills and responsibility, success can only be guaranteed by the performance of the team.

BUSINESS CONSULTANCY SKILLS

During the late 1980s design business consultant Paul Southgate developed a model of the buying climate for design, showing how design expenditure related to corporate spending on advertising and management consultancy. Design formed the lowest tranche of expenditure, commissioned by less senior staff, followed by significantly greater investment in advertising, commissioned by different, more senior people, and then finally by high-level expenditure on management consultancy commissioned from the top. In subsequent years, design and advertising expenditure has become more integrated, but the great challenge of repositioning design as a form of management consultancy has been achieved by only a very small number of companies.

Clients buy design as part of marketing, but is marketing recognised as an essential part of the knowledge base of a designer, or even as part of the core knowledge base of the consultancy overall? Can HE design programmes justify a curriculum which does not include marketing knowledge an integral part of design activity? Recognition of the importance of marketing and business consultancy skills is not only essential to the successful delivery of the present design offer but also key to releasing the industry's greater potential in a world driven by visual communication. By resolving and recognising its inalienable link to marketing, design can take its rightful place as a high-value consultancy service.

Another skill set resides in the management of the consultancy relationship. Neither empirical research into the movement of clients between agencies, nor an interrogation of the reasons for this has been conducted. Finding and winning clients is hard work and keeping them by making reality meet (or exceed) expectations is a very sensible idea. This can only happen with incorporation of high-level business consultancy skills as an essential component of the design offer.

COMMUNICATION: VISUAL AND VERBAL, WRITTEN AND SPOKEN

In order for the consultancy partnership process to flourish, excellent communication is essential. From the outset of the client relationship, communication skills will influence future progress. The way in which the telephone is answered in response to the very first enquiry should be compatible with the company's overall values and image, and this should follow through in all subsequent activity: meetings, presentations, emails, proposals, reports and events. All of these interactions define the company and express personality and attitude, whether or not this has been intended and planned. The aim should be to proactively direct and manage this activity to say the right things in the right way, but this is not going to happen by magic. It needs a positive decision, and acceptance by everyone involved that good communication skills are critical to success and require a programme of sustained action.

How does the company communicate? What does it say, when and why, and to whom? And through what means? Every single member of the company is involved in this activity so everyone needs to know the answers to these questions. The overall aims of company communication should be to uphold and endorse company values, to make life as easy and efficient as possible for clients, suppliers and associates and above all to achieve clarity and accuracy.

Design has its own language, practices and technical terminology. Good consultancy involves making sure that appropriate language is used in all circumstances, with sensitivity to differing levels of client knowledge. Any creative process taking place over a period of time generates many opportunities for misunderstanding and mistakes. Clear communication and good communication discipline can overcome this, and needs to be part of the ongoing skills audit of every member of the team, with appropriate training action taken.

TIME MANAGEMENT AND SELF-ORGANISATION

The large number of books available on time management skills and self-organisation techniques might suggest that these are skill needs which can be speedily resolved, and reflect the many different routes and approaches to success. Design is a creative industry, made up of creative people, who constantly struggle with the need to balance perfectionism and profitability. As discussed in the *Team Leadership and People Management* section below, design company staff make a transition from individual performance to shared responsibility because of the team nature of the work undertaken. They also contribute to the delivery of corporate values and standards rather than undertaking virtuoso individual performance. This does not sit readily or naturally within the stereotypical 'creative' role.

Foundations for personal organisation and good time management can often be learned by example and by the implementation of good shared practices within the company. Mentoring and 'buddying' can make a strong internal contribution to the development of individuals, and this can be supplemented by provision of external input through courses. Delegates attending industry-specific training discuss matters such as identifying effectiveness among people they know and dealing with over-demanding clients, before exchanging techniques and solutions. This type of focused learning experience is particularly valuable in adjusting self-expectations and goals, enabling individuals to enhance their performance.

One of the most demanding time management issues is resolving the displacement of scheduled and planned activity by unplanned things which through being left have become urgent and demanding. Through discussion, trainees examine the feasibility of assessing tasks according to priority, carrying out careful scheduling and then resisting being pushed off course by urgent and noisy distractions.

There are no quick fixes in this area of learning, but real progress can be made with a focused approach and sustained commitment over a period of time.

TEAM LEADERSHIP AND PEOPLE MANAGEMENT

As a people-based business, design has particular needs for team leadership and people management skills. Research has established that most design consultancies are small; they are therefore unlikely to have dedicated Human Resources (HR) staff. Personnel management issues are often handled by someone who also fulfils other roles. In learning about staff management and HR activity, there has traditionally been a gap between theory and practice, with staff in design consultancies finding it hard to identify their work practices within the more corporate theory on offer.

This is now changing as more study is made of the creative industries and management practice in small organisations. Twenty years ago very few design consultancy employees would report having formal review and appraisal procedures in their company, but appraisal has now become widespread. This makes it much easier to identify useful learning activity in this area and to identify a body of knowledge which will sit comfortably across the whole sector.

The same change is reflected in the growth of flatter management structures and democratic working practices, with employees having much more direct control over consultancy planning and activity. Many design businesses now organise 'awaydays' and team-building activity which feeds back into enhanced collective performance.

When staff take part in team leadership and people management training, it creates valuable possibilities for opening up discussion on return to work. Design as a sector benefits from very high calibre staff with strong motivation but has sometimes suffered from lack of opportunity for team members to raise problems or to suggest new ways of working. Growing activity in training in this area and recognition of the relevance of sections of the great body of theoretical HR and knowledge of human behaviour will help with progress.

CLIENT INTERFACE SKILLS, INCLUDING NEGOTIATION AND SALES SKILLS

Because design consultancy is a service and a partnership undertaking, with a long gap between the buying decision and the eventual realisation of completed work, client interface skills are the oil that makes all the wheels go around smoothly. There are several different stages to the client relationship, and these require a whole range of skills and expertise. Initially there is good market intelligence, driven by the company's strategic plan and supported by excellent research skills and marketing knowledge. This same knowledge informs the preparation of well-targeted and appropriate marketing material and new business initiatives, and then underpins the preparation of strong credentials presentations and business proposals.

The significance of research skills continues. The UK Design Council's 'double diamond' model (see Figure 5.2.1), divides the design process into four distinct phases.

It maps the divergent and convergent stages of the design process, showing the different modes of thinking that designers use. Through its use, it is possible to understand the crucial significance of the unpacking and questioning of the initial brief or design opportunity identified by the client. This leads to providing true consultancy through development of a more detailed and more extensively researched set of objectives.

Alongside this activity runs the need for deep understanding of negotiation and sales skills, together with keen awareness of the activity of competitors. Forming and managing client expectations during the initial business enquiry

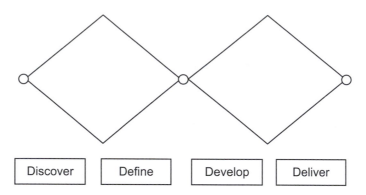

Figure 5.2.1   The 'Double Diamond' design process model
Source: © Design Council 2005

and development stages demands strong interpersonal skills, sensitivity and keen business awareness.

Different approaches can be taken about who then manages the client relationship, but the quality of client care skills applied will have as strong an effect on client satisfaction and retention as the eventual quality of the work. There are also no rules about how to source client care skills – excellent client services managers come from a wide range of backgrounds – but it is important that the skills and knowledge needed in this activity area are fully recognised and actively incorporated into recruitment and HR activity.

5.3   The brief

Kate Blandford

Give me the freedom of a tight briefing.
- David Ogilvy (1911–99), advertising executive

SO, WHAT IS A DESIGN BRIEF AND WHY DO YOU NEED ONE?

Whether you call it a brief, a design brief, a creative brief or any other label is unimportant. What is important is what's in it and, crucially, the response it elicits.

You may have heard a brief referred to as the roadmap, or compass, for your impending project. Others think of the brief as a bridge. Those analogies are fair. The brief is essentially the bridge between what has hitherto been an intellectual exercise and a live design project. More importantly, perhaps, it is the bridge between the challenge and your creative team. Your brief, like a bridge, needs to be robust, well-built and easy to cross, and it needs to ensure you arrive in the right place on the opposite side, whilst also allowing you to cross backwards and forwards to check progress and understanding with those on both sides. Elegance and an ability to raise a smile help too.

A more contemporary and appropriate analogy is perhaps a SatNav. Like a brief, it is at its heart a tool to get you where you need to be. But it also talks to you in a language you understand, shows you the journey and breaks it down into milestones, is fully customisable, and can talk to you in a voice that appeals. But, most of all, it's flexible. When you take a wrong turn it brings you back onto the right road.

Like a SatNav, a brief needs to be setup correctly from the start. It's essential to create the right document for your purpose; one that it is clear and focused, and that everyone who needs to use it understands.

A brief usually still takes the form of a physical document, even in this digital age, but often with verbal, visual (static and moving) or even audio appendices. It is good to have the brief in physical form so that everybody is clear on the final, approved version, but never let this paper-based document limit your creativity in making the brief come to life.

Whatever your favoured name and format, every project in the commercial world has to start by outlining three things:

1. Where you are now: your start point.
2. Where you want to be: what you need to achieve; your objective.
3. How you are going to achieve it: the strategy.

The role the brief plays is to bring all of this to life for those with the huge task of coming up with the creative magic. And that is the key. Although it is vital that your client understands, agrees with and is excited by the brief, the primary audience is your creative team. Think about how best to motivate and inspire them to turn those blank sheets of paper or screens into award-winning, commercially effective design solutions.

THE QUALITY OF A BRIEF IS DIRECTLY RELATED TO THE QUALITY OF THE OUTPUT

Without wanting to flog the SatNav analogy too hard, you will not get to your destination unless your SatNav is fully charged, has the right lead and has the correct maps loaded. In the same way, neither will you solve a complex commercial brand or consumer issue with an ill-considered, woolly design brief.

This hypothetical letter really brings this to life: it is widely available in various forms on the internet although it seems that details of the original source have been lost.

Dear Mr Architect

Please design and build me a house. I am not quite sure of what I need, so you should use your discretion. My house should have somewhere between two and 45 bedrooms. When you bring the blueprints to me, I will make the final decision of what I want. Also, bring me the cost breakdown for each configuration so that I can arbitrarily pick one.

Please don't bother me with small details right now. Your job is to develop the overall plans for the house: get the big picture. At this time, for example, it is not appropriate to be choosing the colour of the carpet. However, keep in mind that my wife likes blue.

While you are designing this house specifically for me, keep in mind that sooner or later, I will have to sell it to someone else. It therefore should have appeal to a wide variety of potential buyers.

PS: Perhaps what I need is not a house at all, but a travel trailer. Please advise me as soon as possible if this is the case.

A high-quality, concise, well-considered brief will draw the same from your design team. A broad, confusing or conflicted brief may well lead to great design work, but you have no way of knowing if it is the right answer to your ill-formed question. Don't expect the design process to solve strategic questions that you have not resolved in the brief.

If you get the brief right, you will also stimulate creative ideas that can be executed in every place, format and channel that the clients' customers touch, not just those you are addressing in the immediate brief.

WHAT SHOULD – AND SHOULDN'T – A BRIEF CONTAIN?

The problem. Start with a clear articulation of the problem to be solved: what is the business issue? Then describe, succinctly, which part of this business issue design can resolve.

The offer. Articulate the brand's, product's or service's vision and strategy, and what this project aims to make consumers think, feel and, crucially, do differently as a result of the (re)design?

The USP. Define the unique selling point. Why will the customer pick out this brand, product or service from all the others on offer? What are the reasons to believe that the USP is true?

The customer. Provide a clear articulation of who the brand, product or service is aimed at. This should be less about standard demographics (although these can have their place) and more about their lives, how they use or interact with the brand, product or service, and ideally, genuine insights that could drive new creative direction.

The application. Describe clearly where the design will need to work; in which media, in what channels or formats.

The success factors. The brief should also contain a really good idea of what success actually looks like: a physical or metaphorical picture of your destination, and how you'll know when you've got there. These could be customer, commercial or brand measures and you will need to be clear on how evidence of success will be gathered. It is invaluable when judging creative output along the way, as it keeps the whole team on track and acts as a counter to subjective feedback.

The practical stuff. You will also need things that will affect the design, such as sacred cows ('thou shalt not touch the logo') and mandatories ('there must be the following icons on the front of pack' or 'this is the variant colour coding convention') and those that will drive the project such as overall project timings and key meetings.

A few watch-outs too:

- Try to avoid long lists of do's and don'ts, personal likes and dislikes, and wish lists that could simply act as creative fog.
- Avoid reams of numerical data. Derive insights from them and present that in your brief rather than leaving it open to individual interpretation.
- Sense-check your brief thoroughly when you've written it, making sure that the story is clear and concise without conflicting information. And watch out for meaningless jargon words that are so often used like 'accessible', 'premium' and 'classic'. They are so generic as to be useless for the creative team; a few, carefully chosen words are much more powerful.

HOW DO YOU KNOW WHEN YOU'VE GOT IT RIGHT?

Can you answer all these questions in the affirmative?

- Is it brief?
- Does it focus on one key message?
- Are you telling a simple, inspiring story?
- Does it lead the designer from the key message, through the insight, to the reason to believe, with each building on the other?
- Is it clear on genuine sacred cows and mandatories?
- Is it jargon-free? Will everyone understand it?
- Does it have your designers reaching excitedly for their pencil or mouse before you've finished presenting it?

HOW TO HELP CLIENTS DEFINE THEIR BRIEFS

As an agency, it is well worth your while assisting your client so that they can clearly define their brief. The relationship is yours, so you will understand the best way to approach this, but the first job is to illustrate to clients where more clarity is required and why. Use all your creative skills to do this, by using examples already in your portfolio, or in the wider marketplace. You may need to use imagery in order to bring your point to life, or to magnify the differences between alternative design directions.

Bringing things to life is really the key here, and a client workshop that brings all key team members together can be invaluable. Break down the brief with them, and build it back up again. Illustrate points of conflict, and generate consensus. Identify gaps, and agree how they will be filled. This agreement will be invaluable later in the project when you need the whole team to be galvanised around the same creative execution.

It can also be illuminating to ask customers themselves at this point, to understand more about their views on the brand, product or service and its place in their lives or – more deeply – to generate insights that allow you to innovate. More often than not it is preferable to generate customer insight upfront rather than to subject design concepts to a 'beauty parade'-style consumer research programme later in the project. Often this will create a list of things that customers do and don't like without any clarity: this can lead to an endless round of design iteration and subjective judgement. Avoid that at all cost.

THE BENEFITS OF GETTING IT RIGHT UPFRONT

Clients often don't want to spend money on the brief, especially during belt-tightening times, as they feel it to be something they ought to be able to do alone. They may even hand you a brief and simply not understand why you can't start straight away. This is where all your best verbal and visual persuasive talents come in. Add value for them; help them understand the benefits for time, cost, morale and quality of the end results of pulling that brief apart, reconstructing it and ensuring that it is focused on its one key audience – not their directors, not the end consumer, but your creative team. The creative solution is for their customers: the brief is for your designers. This is also where you should bring all your design effectiveness evidence into play. Talk to them about the benefits to their return on design investment of getting it right first time.

DON'T CONFUSE THE BRIEF AND THE BRIEFING

A last word. The brief may be a paper document, but you should also think about how to inspire your team through the briefing. Take the team to the front line, where the product or service or brand lives, face-to-face with its customers. Bring the whole experience – the current issues and the vision for the future – alive for them and you will generate infinitely greater understanding and emotional connection than leaving them with a document to read or talking it through around a boardroom table.

5.4   **The projects**

Lorna Dallas-Conte

Tell me and I'll forget, show me and I may remember, involve me and I'll understand.
* Chinese proverb

WHY YOU NEED GOOD PROJECT MANAGEMENT SKILLS

A key element in a successful consultancy is control over the type and quality of client projects. Robust project management skills and systems are vital to maximise the potential of the selected projects and to secure future relationships and further business. This chapter describes the stages of a project, links aspects of the design process to these stages, and highlights areas to improve the cost efficient delivery of creative business solutions. It also explores the use of your project management process as a powerful marketing tool.

KEY SUCCESS FACTORS

Projects and their management start long before the brief is confirmed and end long after the solution has been delivered.
    A successful project relies on:

* a shared, common purpose;
* identified resources and timescale;
* appropriate skills and experience of key personnel;
* a positive attitude towards team working;
* an effective project management process.

THE SKILLS AND QUALITIES

Project management skills are often learnt through handling client projects, rather than through the study of a professional qualification in the subject. The basic skills and qualities – such as communication, information-gathering, relationship development, common sense – are usually inherent within an individual. They may be further developed through a consultancy culture that encourages and supports the transfer of skills through good team working and professional practice training.

The client perspective

Clients will assume that your consultancy will be competent in project management as part of your professional and business service offer, and that this is backed up by robust systems and processes which ensure your ability to deliver.

Reassuring the client by keeping them involved and informed in a controlled way through a professional approach to project management helps to build positive relationships, keeps the unexpected to a minimum and ensures a good outcome for all parties, including a better understanding of each other's businesses.

The consultancy perspective

Client projects are the soul food of a design business: they offer opportunities for creative challenge and staff motivation as well as business rewards. An additional, and sometimes undervalued, element of a project is the transfer of design and business knowledge between consultancy and client. This is often difficult to measure, but the development of a common understanding and language can be pivotal in achieving an outcome that is considered successful by all parties. Internal projects are equally important. Often running alongside client work, they provide enhancement of business processes, changes to the working environment and diversification into new areas of the market place.

THE FIVE STAGES OF PROJECT MANAGEMENT

The management of a project within a design consultancy will take account of the specialist design processes employed.

In theory, a project can be divided into five stages. In reality, a project is rarely as clear cut and – depending on the complexity of the range and variety of design skills required, the type of solution and scale of the project – it is possible for elements of a project to be spread across more than one stage at any one time.

However, an awareness of this simple five-stage model helps to identify opportunities and issues that support efficient project management:

1. Initiate
2. Plan
3. Execute
4. Control
5. Close.

STAGE 1: INITIATE

The start of a project is influenced by the expectations and assumptions of both the consultancy and the client. The business problem is articulated, the extent of the opportunities for finding a solution is explored and a particular type of output may be discussed. The extent to which these discussions are formalised and exchanged in writing will depend on a number of factors, including the complexity of the need, the previous client-consultancy relationship and the level of risk that both parties are prepared to accept. This is the start of the opportunity to build client confidence, and it plays an important role in the continuous marketing and delivery of your own 'brand behaviour'.

Client expectations

A client will be influenced by both their knowledge of a consultancy and their expectations of the commercial benefits of design, long before the decision to place a piece of work is made. These expectations will be informed by the extent and success of a consultancy's marketing activity, by previous design project experience with the consultancy or by word of mouth recommendations. They may or may not be in line with the consultancy's business offer. It is valuable, therefore, to re-establish what these expectations are, and also the level of design experience the client brings at the start of the relationship.

Consultancy expectations

Understanding how a project fits into your own business strategy is also important. A clear knowledge of the type of projects that are within your available resources, competency range and expertise – as well as having the potential to generate the right level of profit – will help to inform initial discussions and lead you to accept or refuse a piece of work. Understanding and taking control of the relationship between the three main 'project drivers' of time, quality and resource is vital to supporting this decision (see Figure 5.4.1).

Accepting a project that is low in budget (resource), tight on deadlines (time) and demands a high level of attention to detail (quality) is a familiar scenario for many consultancies. Identifying from the start how the design solution is going to balance these resources will improve planning and allow the subsequent execution of the project to take place within the constraints.

The more complex a project is, the wider the range of activities and processes, the greater the resources employed, the more global the reach, and the longer the timescale. When combined with a reduced certainty about the outcome, it becomes more difficult to control the project drivers, and problems with budgets, late-running and issues around quality will result. Lack of control will make complex projects more likely to be high risk, and will have an impact on the likely success for all parties concerned.

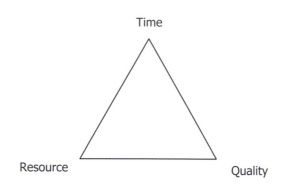

Figure 5.4.1   Project drivers

Getting started

As a result of initial conversations, possibly a pitch and/or a brief, important information about the project is captured and exchanged between the parties. A business proposal is then generated as a firm quotation or an estimate by the design consultancy. This proposal articulates the stages and costs of the consultancy's services, as well as its terms and conditions.

It is good practice to be as clear as possible in this initial stage so that all parties share a common understanding of the extent of the project. However, it is in the nature of a design-led project that within this certainty there needs to be room for flexibility and creative solutions: the extent will vary between clients, consultancies and projects. The degree to which the brief and the estimate are formalised depends on the processes of the design consultancy, the degree of complexity of the project and the familiarity of relationship between the consultancy and the client.

STAGE 2: PLAN

Transforming the brief into a plan of action involves both the client and the consultancy. The purpose of the plan is to articulate the key stages of the project and the design processes that will be used. It should identify the resources required, including team members and responsibilities. Finally, a timescale and the order of the main activities, expressed as 'milestones', should be identified to ensure a critical path through the project. Plans may be developed using software, whether simple spreadsheets, commercially available project management systems or customised software developed for your own particular needs.

Depending on the way that your design consultancy is organised and the complexity of the project, there may be a range of people (staff, freelancers and suppliers) who will all need to be in contact with the client, crossing offices, geographies, time zones and cultures. Each of these members of the team needs to be aware of the project and have sufficient information to be able to manage their own teams of staff. This formalising of the programme of activity allows you to start monitoring and controlling the process, and will help to identify any concerns or unforeseen issues such as time considerations, conflicting business activities or suppliers' needs.

Client considerations

Clients will feel reassured by the sharing and agreeing of the plan, the milestones for delivery, the introduction to the key staff from the design consultancy and the identification of an effective mechanism for communication between all the parties.

At this stage, it is vital to identify within the client organisation the personnel, locations and key systems or processes that need to be considered. Continuing to monitor this information over the lifespan of the project will help to prevent problems and hold-ups. It is also useful to gain an insight into the levels of key personnel and their commitment to the project. This will help you to develop effective relationships, and can be instrumental in anticipating potential barriers to success.

Consultancy considerations

The opportunity to formalise the project plan will enable you to involve and select the appropriate staff and other resources for the delivery the project, as well as plan the project into the present workload of the individual teams. To protect your long-term business goals, it is important to take care not to overload your personnel or suppliers. Agreeing communication channels, planning meetings and scheduling the timings of client-facing activities will allow members of your team to prepare properly, and will maximise your ability to maintain the client's involvement in the developing project.

It is good practice to include the creative team as early as possible in the planning process to ensure that an appropriate amount of time has been allowed to get the most from their skills.

Contingency

Within the proposal there will be a calculation for a contingency to allow for the risks associated with each particular project. It is important that, in planning the key milestones of the project, this contingency is taken into account. Transparency between clients and consultancies regarding contingencies varies. Best practice encourages an open and trusting relationship, where deadlines are respected and the impact of slippage on milestones is understood both commercially and practically by all parties.

STAGE 3: EXECUTE

The complexity of the project and the number of different design disciplines that are to be employed will influence this stage of the project management process. The project manager has to balance a difficult combination of leadership and management skills during this time. Leadership skills will ensure overall ownership and responsibility for the project, and will protect the business and design integrity of the project for both parties. Management skills will enable a flexible approach towards the project team and will build trust. They will also encourage information sharing, vital to the success of the project.

Design process

Different design disciplines use different components of the design process. Following the briefing and planning stages – which will take account of these differences – all design projects will share the three activities of research, initial concept ideas and presentation.

Depending on the response of the client to the concepts, there will be a development stage which will produce a test design solution. This may be two or three dimensional, be physically presented or be shown in a digital format. Again, depending on the complexity of the project, these initial design solutions may need to be tested with the target users to enable further design refinements and presentations to be made and, eventually, a final design solution to be worked up.

Where other suppliers are to be used to execute the final design solution it will be appropriate for a specification to be developed. Some form of tendering or selection process will need to be undertaken to clarify further costings and to arrange for the final stages of the project. The client and appropriate design consultancy staff need to be involved at the relevant times, according to the original plan which identified their roles and responsibilities.

The final steps within this stage of project management will be the implementation of the design solution. From the initiation stage, the intention of all the parties has been to ensure that this happens on time and to budget. 'Capturing' the successful delivery of the project in casework is good practice, and can be useful for further marketing for both the client and the consultancy.

STAGE 4: CONTROL

The role of the project manager is to take control of the project from the start, identify key milestones, check with the project team to make sure that the project is following the plan, and report back. The plan will have identified the aspects of the project that require control, and will have identified the methods and measurements that will be used to monitor progress. This monitoring and control process may be captured in a range of different ways from formal to informal, according to the design consultancy. It may be supported through commercial or customised computer software, or paper systems, or a combination of the two.

Client needs

Clients need to be reassured that the project is developing to plan. By involving them in a timely manner, information can be shared and risks identified and ameliorated. Budgets can be checked and, if necessary, the project can be revised to take account of the most recent knowledge about the design solution and the evolving business needs and success criteria.

Consultancy needs

There can be tension within a design consultancy between the creative and the commercial aspects of the business. It is important to be clear about the relationship between time, resources and quality for a particularly project, and about its placing within the creative and business strategy of the consultancy. There can then be a conscious decision about whether more time can be found to work on a design solution from within the budget for the project, or whether there needs to be a further discussion with the client to review and revise any milestones.

A consultancy also needs to take control over other costs associated with the project, such as expenses or orders made to other suppliers. Creating control systems – such as an order book – and allocating responsibility for placing the orders will ensure that checks can be made.

Job management systems

Information about each design job or project is usually captured through a timesheet and then entered into a job file. The job file, or 'job bag', is a collation of all the individual contributions that make up the development of the design solution from different members of the design team and others. This system may be digital or physical, but either method relies on the integrity of the data collection: this, in turn, is influenced by how useful the data collected is to the design consultancy. Management information can be extracted from the collected data, and may be used to improve the efficiency of the studio and support your costings, as well improving the delivery of future jobs.

IT systems and software

Design consultancies use a range of software programmes, both commercial and customised, to support the design and project management processes. Some still rely on a mixture of software and paper systems which sometimes overlap and duplicate each other. You will need to understand which information needs to be captured and used most effectively in order to balance the cost of the capture. Where a design consultancy opts to use software to support the collection of data, it is important that the programme integrates with other backroom systems and back-up processes.

STAGE 5: CLOSE

At the closure of a project it is good practice for the client and consultancy to review and evaluate the progress and delivery of the project. This review will capture useful information, and can be used to develop further work for the consultancy as well as to develop marketing material for both parties. It is an opportunity for the client to reflect on the business value of the project and its outputs and outcomes, and for the consultancy to maintain and develop its systems and processes, to ensure continual learning, and to enhance business development. It is also important to create a backed-up archive of material from the project which might be reusable, and which can easily be retrieved.

Supplier relationships may be reviewed, and any outstanding accounts need to be settled. The client's ability to settle invoices should be noted, so that costings for any future work can take account of poor or slow payers.

A discussion between the in-house members of the team involved in the project will identify any necessary future improvements, and follow-up activities or projects can be passed to team leader or the account manager for further discussion and development with the client.

CONCLUSION

Good project management can help a design consultancy to develop both the business and the brand. The use of simple stage models – tailored for your own design discipline and company – will allow you to position your project management processes in a relationship with your design processes. It encourages the development of good relationships between client and consultancy throughout the project. Finally, it can be used as a powerful marketing tool.

Although project management skills are often developed through in-house experience, it is worth noting that it is a profession in its own right with a global institute and a UK association overseeing the discipline, offering qualifications and promoting the subject across sectors.

5.5   The research

Don Preddy

Predicting the future is easy. It's trying to figure out what's going on now that's hard.
- Fritz Dressler, photographer, designer, academic

FIGURING WHAT'S GOING ON

There are a number of situations when design businesses might encounter market research. These include clients' own data about their brand and their market, perhaps provided as part of the briefing process. If they don't offer to provide this, it is important to ask for it to help you understand the market in which their product or service operates, and doing so shows willingness to engage with the client's business.

Clients may then want to carry out research into the work you do for them, either during the development stages or after it has been exposed to the market. Rather than resenting this as an intrusion into the creative process, why not embrace it and use it to inform your own future work?

You could do some research of your own, to help you get under the skin of the consumers in the market you are working in, and to understand how they interact with the product or service you are interested in. Many design business already do this as part of the discovery or exploration phase of a project, and it needn't be complex or difficult, or expensive.

You may also want to commission some research amongst your clients, or prospects, to get a sound and objective view on how you are perceived and how you could improve the service you offer.

Let's look briefly at the broad types of research you might encounter. There are many research techniques, but they can be grouped broadly into quantitative, qualitative and desk research.

QUANTITATIVE RESEARCH

A design consultancy is perhaps most likely to encounter quantitative research in the background information provided by a client in connection with a brief, or when carrying out desk research into background information on a market.

Quantitative research aims to provide robust data with statistical reliability. It provides information such as what percentage of people in a certain category think one thing rather than another, or prefer one brand of a product to another, and to some extent can explore why. It uses relatively large samples of people, or 'respondents' (typically in the hundreds), chosen at random from the relevant 'universe' as a whole (for example, the universe of car owners, or chocolate eaters). By using a sample which is representative of the universe of interest, in terms of demographics, product usage and so on, inferences can be made about the opinions of that whole universe, and of sub-groups, with a statistically measurable degree of confidence.

To achieve this robustness, the questions have to be asked in exactly the same way with every participant in the research. You can ask different questions of different people according to their answers to previous questions, but the way this is done has to be exactly the same for everyone. Interviewers can't say 'That's an interesting point, tell me more about that', unless the questionnaire instructs them to do so and it is done every time.

Questionnaires can be administered by trained interviewers, or designed for self-completion. Interviews can take place by phone or face-to-face, the latter especially being used where respondents need to be shown something such as a pack or a design for an interior, or where a product needs to be tested, or tasted. Whether face-to-face or on the phone, quantitative research frequently uses computerised interviews, with the interviewer guiding the respondent through a questionnaire on a computer and entering the responses. This facilitates accurate questionnaire delivery and fast analysis of results. Self-completion questionnaires can be provided online, but that depends on the whole sample having internet access; you shouldn't use one method of data capture with some respondents and another with others in the same study.

Writing a quantitative questionnaire is a skilled task, to make sure that questions are clear, in the right order and avoid the trap of leading the respondent towards a particular answer. Interpretation of the results also requires expertise and familiarity with the use of statistics, as it can be easy to draw wrong conclusions.

QUALITATIVE RESEARCH

Qualitative research approaches things differently. Here, the aim is to achieve more in-depth understanding of the beliefs, feelings and perceptions of the target audience, rather than statistically robust figures. The researcher not only can, but must, follow up answers to questions with further enquiries and probing.

A quantitative interviewer does not need a thorough understanding of the subject of the research (although the questionnaire designer does), but a qualitative researcher needs to be comprehensively briefed and in many cases have an existing in-depth understanding of the market being studied, as well as empathy, understanding and curiosity.

Qualitative research uses a topic guide rather than a structured questionnaire, as an aide-memoire for the researcher, who will depart from it as each session requires, just making sure that all relevant points are covered. It uses small samples, typically in the tens. This is partly because of cost, but mainly because even the analysis of a large sample would not enable statistically robust comparisons to be made, as every interview will be different. The aim is to dig deep and reach real understanding.

Typical techniques are focus groups and individual interviews, although there are many variations on these. Focus groups typically consist of six to eight respondents, meeting together under the guidance of a researcher or 'moderator'. They have the advantage that the views and feelings of individual respondents help spark off those of others, who may agree or disagree, and this can lead to a greater depth of understanding than may be obtained from individual interviews.

Individual 'depth' interviews are preferred in some situations, for example where a specialist sample of respondents from a small universe is required and they are geographically spread, or where they may be reluctant to come to a group venue; examples would include medical consultants and senior business people. They are also useful where the topic is sensitive, perhaps because of commercial confidentiality, or where it is personal in nature. Depth interviews are often conducted face-to-face, but where the subject matter is not too complex and can be covered in no more than, say, 30 minutes, telephone works well.

You may see the results of qualitative research in the background material a client provides as a part of a brief. A design business is also likely to encounter this type of research when it is commissioned by a client to assess consumer reactions to your work, at various stages in its development.

If the research includes focus groups, go and watch if you can. Focus groups often take place in viewing facilities, with a one-way mirror allowing clients to observe the proceedings first hand; ask if you can go and join them. It may give you a closer insight than reading the report or attending the presentation of results. You should still go to the debrief as decisions based on research findings are often made then and there, and it is better if you are there and have the chance to influence those decisions.

Another qualitative approach involves observational studies, or ethnographical research, where the researcher spends time in the relevant environment (for example, a supermarket, museum or other public space) watching how people behave, and perhaps asking them about it. It may be worth doing some of this yourself; go out and watch how people interact with the product or service you are working on. If you are working on a public space go and experience similar places for yourself, putting yourself in the position of a consumer. How child-friendly are they? How accessible for disabled people? Some ethnographical studies go to great lengths, spending prolonged periods with small groups of people, but there is no need for you to go this far; an afternoon spent in fieldwork can be very informative.

DESK RESEARCH

Finally, desk research, as the name implies, is done without actually going out and talking to people. It looks into published and other available data on a market, product or universe of people, to gain background information. It can range from a large-scale structured piece of work conducted by a specialist, down to half an hour on Google™. The internet has, of course, made it much easier, and the move towards making more and more data available, and the development of applications to combine datasets to explore new kinds of information, means that the possibilities are growing.

Again, you are likely to encounter it in background information provided by clients, but you can easily do some yourself to increase your knowledge and awareness of the market you have been asked to work in.

CHOOSING IT, USING IT

Quantitative, qualitative and desk research are fundamental parts of good business practice. Time spent in learning how best to use research, how to commission it and how to read and understand it correctly will inform and improve your design outputs. It will also enhance the professional relationship you have with your clients. Embrace it, and make it an integral part of your working practices.

5.6 The meetings

Sean Blair

9 out of 10 people daydream in meetings.
- Donald Wetmore, time management and personal productivity expert

MEETINGS: THE CURRENCY OF BUSINESS

Meetings are where business happens. They are the time and space where people work together to plan, create and deliver projects. Yet below the surface appearance of people sitting in a room working together live vital factors that determine organisational energy and vibrancy.

Critically, meetings are where organisational and project leadership lives (or not), culture thrives (or not), mutual respect grows (or not) and meaningful progress occurs (or not). Meetings are also where fragile new ideas live or die.

You could say that meetings are the barometer of organisational vitality: ten minutes spent in an average meeting will indicate the health of an organisation's leadership and culture. Dr Donald Wetmore, founder of the Productivity Institute, reports that nine out of ten people daydream in meetings. Additionally his research shows that 60 per cent of meeting attendees take notes to appear as if they are listening, and that managers spend over ten hours a week in meetings, with the majority saying more than half that time is wasted.

While many of us can identify with these findings, it shows that poor meeting cultures that waste valuable time, create confusion, breed disrespect and demotivate previously enthusiastic team members are all too prevalent.

WHY ARE SO MANY MEETINGS DREADFUL?

So many meetings stink. This is hardly a new insight, but what is a better way of working together?

Most people have never received any formal training on how to conduct a meeting. Instead, they simply adopt the dysfunctional, hierarchical habits created many, many generations ago in less democratic times. It's time for a fresh look at how we can work better together.

Although there are hundreds of kinds of meetings, from two people taking five minutes at the water fountain to hundreds of people in a multi-day strategy workshop, research has shown that the same principles, if used skilfully and sensitively, apply to almost every type of meeting.

FIVE PRINCIPLES OF THE MEETING EXCELLENCE MODEL

Let's begin this brief overview by looking at the five principles of the Meeting Excellence model. This is based on theoretical and practical research, and some of the source material can be found in Section 9, *The Reference Library*.

Excellent meetings:

- *Are participative*: they include the right people, with full intellectual, emotional and energetic engagement.
- *Are purposeful*: they motivate people with a compelling, over-arching purpose, and have specific and clear objectives, not agendas.
- *Have a process*: they are designed to achieve the meeting objectives, maximising energy and diversity.
- *Use visibility*: they align the energy in the room creating visible collective wisdom and clear actions and learning.
- *Are healthy*: they build authentic respect for each other and deliver real learning, both individually and collectively. This in turn creates an energetic, vibrant culture.

DECEPTIVELY SIMPLE AND ALL TOO RARE

These principles sound simple, yet the prevailing meeting orthodoxy does not usually welcome full participation and is often limited by positional power and the vagaries of ego. What academics call the 'action strategies' of traditional meeting 'chairmen' are often due to not wanting to look silly or lose face. These largely unconscious strategies seek to control contributions, and can dramatically limit real participation.

The ubiquitous list of 'agenda items' almost guarantees a disconnection with motivation and, by default, delivers a bland meeting process that is based on taking turns to talk. It creates fertile ground for ego, and ensures that the diversity that is so vital for creativity remains unexpressed. Instead, why not break into small groups or pairs and work concurrently?

By looking at bad meetings it is clear that energy is all too often unaligned, and that actions and learning are far from clear. If people spend as much time after the meeting as they spent in the meeting, trying to make sense of what was said or licking wounds, it's clear these principles are not in operation.

WHAT EACH PRINCIPLE MEANS IN ACTION

Participative

This is the core principle: it is a fundamental attitude and belief. The most powerful way of using it is to want participation, to want the joyful experience of working together, thinking together and creating together. Put simply, it is respect for other people's presence, perspective and outlook.

'Participative' means:

- meetings led with a state of mind that wants participation;
- welcoming intellectual, emotional and energetic engagement, especially from those with diverse views;
- participants who own the meeting's objectives and process.

Purposeful

Know what a meeting is for. Most organisations have an over-arching purpose that in some way serves the better parts of humanity. In really great meetings, people know, believe and want to achieve that over-arching purpose, and they understand how it connects to a clear set of meeting objectives.

'Purposeful' means:

- a compelling, over-arching intention;
- clear, specific meeting objectives, not an agenda;
- staying focused to achieve the common objectives.

Process

Why sit round a table and talk (or not) when there are so many better ways to work together? Meetings cover huge terrains of information, tricky decisions, differing views and perspectives, and apparently contradictory positions; having a process means planning time for all the right things to happen in a logical order, and in a way that allows all to contribute.

'Process' means:

- designing a set of steps to allow everybody to participate in achieving the objectives and getting results;
- designing steps to maximise energy;
- harnessing diversity of views.

Visible

Using large wallcharts will make the meeting process visible. It will help people's energy levels if they are focused at the same time on the same part of the journey. It will also reassure people that 'the thing I want to cover will be covered at the right point'. Progress, or lack of it, will become obvious, and it will help to keep the collective brain awake: everyone will be seeing the same data at the same time.

'Visible' means:

- aligning the meeting participants' focus on the same thing at the same time;
- creating a map, or wallchart, of the 'collective wisdom' as the meeting progresses;
- creating clear actions and clear learning points.

Healthy

Our effectiveness is directly related to the culture we work in. Healthy cultures are good, and dysfunction in meetings often equals dysfunction in what follows those meetings.

'Healthy' means:

- getting the best from each other through deep and authentic respect;
- using every meeting as the way of constant and ever deeper learning;
- using meetings to create energy for action;
- listening, and respecting the fact that everybody has a piece of the truth.

HOW TO RUN GREAT MEETINGS

These five principles operate best inside the four phases of a meeting:

1. *Establish Clear Objectives*
   Ensure your meetings are serving your organisation's goals by defining and agreeing clear objectives for the meeting. Before your meeting write, in very clear language, a statement of what the objectives of the meeting are. An objective is best written with a clear active verb: 'To agree... 'To create...' and so on. Begin

the meeting by reviewing the objectives with all of the participants and, if the objectives are not right, be prepared to modify them. During the meeting, review the objectives periodically, especially if the meeting goes off-track.

2. *Have a Clear Process*
   Make sure that meeting time is well spent by following a process designed to allow the meeting objectives to be fulfilled. Before the meeting, plan a process to allow the intended objective to be achieved and be prepared during the meeting to change it if the objective changes, or the process is not working. Give meeting participants clear steps by which they know the meeting objective can be achieved, allowing their full contribution.

3. *Clarify Actions*
   Clarify the real actions that people want and need to take because they own the action and the responsibility. Make time in the meeting for participants to write down and share the actions they would like to take because they are passionate about them. Explore where the energy for action is, and align actions with people's passions.

4. *Learn*
   Grow the culture of your organisation by using every meeting as the central time and place that learning occurs. Conclude meetings by reflecting on learning about:
   • Me (what have you learnt about yourself in the last hour).
   • It (what have you learnt about the subject at hand).
   • Us (what have you learnt about the team in the room).

It only needs one sentence for each, written on a Post–It™ note. It takes a couple of minutes and, when done properly, it is powerful stuff for growing team effectiveness and vitality.

5.7   The feedback

Shan Preddy

O wad some power the giftie gi' us
To see oursel's as ithers see us
- Robert Burns (1759–96), poet

LOOK WITHIN

We know we are doing well when our clients come back for more, and we know we aren't doing so well when we lose a client. But around those polar extremes, the rest can be a dangerous mixture of guesswork and wishful thinking. We all need to know what our clients think about us and our abilities, and it's all too easy to make assumptions.

There are two main ways to find out exactly what they think. The first is to focus on project delivery and client satisfaction; if you're not already doing it, you should be carrying out regular post-project reviews. The second is to look at the bigger picture by conducting formal surveys into the relationships you have with your clients. They are not mutually exclusive, and both have an important part to play.

Most clients are very willing to share their opinions of how your work, your value and your service match up with their expectations. They see post-project reviews as good housekeeping, an essential part of basic working practices. They see client surveys, on the other hand, as part of advanced business management, and they will be impressed that you have taken the trouble to invest in them.

POST-PROJECT REVIEWS

You might already have internal 'wash-up' meetings after a project has been completed. You might even be asking your clients what they thought. But are you doing it in such a way that you can record the results, and compare them with the results from projects for other clients? Or over time for that same client?

You don't need to over-complicate the exercise, nor do you need statistically significant quantitative data. All you need is regular, comparable findings. Here's how:

1. Decide on your Key Performance Indicators (KPIs), or measurement criteria, for external, client-facing areas. You might want to know how your clients thought your business performed on quality, creativity, strategic thinking, scheduling and delivery, budget control, responsiveness, technical knowledge. You might also want to know what they thought about individual team members. These KPIs will differ from business to business; the important thing is to get them right for you.
2. Decide on your KPIs for internal use; again, they will depend on your own business. You could consider overall project profitability, or actual time spent against billed time, or final bought-in costs against budget.
3. Create a simple template which allows you to rate each project against both the internal and external KPIs. If you decide to work with a numerical system, such as 1–10 scores, make sure you also include room for comments and thoughts.
4. Although you won't be able to access much information at this point, you might also want to start recording the initial impact of your design intervention for use in promotional casework and design effectiveness awards entries. This is often a good time to ask clients for testimonials.
5. Carry out the post-project review with the client, looking at your external KPIs. This is best done face-to-face or on the telephone by a senior member of staff, preferably one who has not been directly involved in the project. However, if you tend to work on a very large number of small, low-budget projects – especially if each individual client gives you a lot of work – simple self-completion questionnaires might be the answer.
6. Next, look at the internal KPIs.
7. Log the results and benchmark them against previous reports for that client individual, for that client company and for all of your clients together.
8. Act on the findings, maintaining and reinforcing what you are doing well, and fixing any less-than-perfect areas.
9. Ask the team members for suggestions on general improvements to internal processes, policies and practices.
10. Finally, remember to tell your clients that you are acting on the results of their feedback, so that you 'close the loop'.

CLIENT SURVEYS

In addition to a review of every project you work on, it is good to carry out a more formal survey among your clients from time to time to look at the bigger picture.

What might you ask them about? On top of questions about your product, your service and your value for money, how about why they chose to appoint you instead of anyone else? And where they would position you in the market, according to your strengths and weaknesses? Or which other design firms they are working with, or have worked with recently, and how you compare? Wouldn't it be good to know what they think they will be looking for from design firms in the future? And what their selection processes are likely to be?

Client surveys are best conducted qualitatively so that the interviewer can probe responses and ask the client to clarify or expand the information given. In-depth telephone interviews usually get the best level of client compliance: it's easier to agree to a 15-minute telephone conversation than to commit to a face-to-face meeting or a focus group, or to complete a lengthy questionnaire. However, short self-completion questionnaires will still provide enough material to work on, especially if they are properly designed and are user-friendly.

Some companies include their hot prospects in their surveys, and people who they have presented or pitched to but failed to convince. Some take it even further and extend it into a 360° perception audit by including staff, suppliers, strategic partners and relevant opinion-formers such as the press.

If you have very limited budgets, you can carry out client surveys yourself. However, you will get better results if you ask an external consultant to do them. Not only are you unlikely to have professional skills in-house for interviewing, analysing and getting constructive feedback, but a badly conducted survey can be damaging to the relationship. It's hard for clients to comment on your failures to your face, for example, and it can be just as hard for you not to react with counter-criticism. But if you give the job to the right, suitably skilled consultant, you might find that your clients will say things that they wouldn't dream of telling you, including that they think you're wonderful. Now, wouldn't that be worth knowing?

5.8   The proof

Deborah Dawton

Don't accept your dog's admiration as conclusive evidence that you are wonderful.
- Ann Landers (1918–2002), advice columnist

DESIGN EFFECTIVENESS

Proving that design can add value to business has been the Holy Grail for many a designer over the last few decades.

Effectiveness is not the antithesis of creativity, however. If you were to offer designers the option of marketing themselves on an effectiveness ticket or a creative ticket, most would give it some serious thought. There's attraction in both, and the trick is to use both: they are not mutually exclusive. Prowess in creativity and prowess in effectiveness act as magnets, but to very different audiences.

Creative awards are an important way to benchmark yourself against the industry. They are an indicator of what your peers – who are normally the judges – think of your work in the creative context. They gain trade press coverage and are a magnet to the next generation of creative talent coming out of our universities. They are also the means by which creative teams can be rewarded for great output although, in the most part, that output is not linked to commercial result.

Being able to prove the effectiveness of your work, on the other hand, is a magnet to prospective clients. As one winner of a design effectiveness award put it: 'The award put us on the map. It acts as a beacon for clients.' When a consultancy can lay claim to an idea that has achieved impressive levels of effectiveness, it opens doors to other clients. It's a very different way of talking about design work, but one that a left-brained budget-holder will engage with instantly.

The discipline of forcing yourself to think about your work in tangible, measurable terms is exactly that: a discipline. Some designers aren't created with this as a default setting. However, given the nature of the competitive markets design businesses operate in, you need to leverage as much as possible those things that make you stand out. A market positioning based on effectiveness will never let you down.

NOT A BLACK ART

Design effectiveness is not a substitute for the creative process, but a way of working. Measuring the impact of any piece of work or thinking requires you to know your starting position, to have set very clear objectives, and to stick around long enough to evaluate the outcome. Then you apply the lessons learnt to the next piece of work, and the next.

Measuring the effectiveness of your design interventions is the means by which you can help your clients to make informed decisions about the future of their brands: for them, the battle is never over. As Jack Welch, Chairman and CEO of the American company, General Electric, once put it: 'Change before you have to.' As long as your clients' competitors are out there, your clients will need change, and they will need you. As your knowledge of their sector increases along with your knowledge of what works and doesn't, the more valuable you become. Importantly, for the very same reason, you also become much harder to replace.

ONLY FOR BIG AGENCIES?

Larger agencies have greater resources to put behind measuring the effectiveness of their design outcomes, and bigger projects to supply the evidence. In practice, however, it is often easier for small firms with smaller design projects to prove the effectiveness of their work. The challenge in large-scale projects can be to isolate and determine the specific impact of design, as opposed to that of PR, marketing and advertising, all of which usually accompany big launches.

Smaller agencies also have the benefit of servicing smaller clients for whom design is the only option: they simply don't have a budget for anything else. The impact of design on a small client business can be monumental.

DELIVERING CORPORATE OBJECTIVES

Measuring design effectiveness is not always about measuring sales or financial data: it's about measuring the impact of your design interventions against all of your clients' corporate objectives. What might these objectives be? There is a huge range. To reach a new market, perhaps. To reposition a brand into the quality sector. To aid expansion into new territories. To secure listings with all the big retailers. To increase a brand's share of its market. To increase sales value while reducing manufacturing costs. To increase a museum's footfall and drive its shop sales. To change the behaviour of a hard-to-reach group in society. To enable patients to inject higher doses of insulin painlessly. To get people to their destination on time.

No reputable designer should start work without a clear understanding of what needs to be achieved, and this requires you to check that the outcome you've been asked for is actually the right one. It's a bit like going to the doctor, having decided yourself what's wrong, and asking for the prescription you want. All self-respecting doctors will carry out their own diagnoses and prescribe the appropriate remedies. As a designer, you have an obligation to make sure that any self-diagnosed client has got it right, and that's before you prescribe your remedy. Not only is it your job as a design professional to do this, it also ensures that the control in the relationship resides with you. Given that you're the expert with the demonstrable track record, you need to be driving the process.

The clients that commission you can be several steps removed from their Board of Directors, and their interpretation of corporate objectives can, frankly, sometimes be dodgy. To produce effective design, you need to avoid that all-too-familiar meeting when you sit there on the receiving end of information that, had it been available at the start of the process, would have sent you down a completely different route. Question their intent, and encourage them to focus on the project's outcomes (the results) and not on the outputs (the items you have designed). Using your experience and expertise, recommend the best route to take and don't be afraid to offer them only one. How many times have GPs offered you a variety of drugs to cure your problem? If they did, might that not undermine your view of them as experts? Experts solve problems. Become your client's corporate problem slayer!

DRIVING MORE BUDGET YOUR WAY

Think about this. Your client commissions you to do something for her. The results are great. She uses that to justify her spend to her boss. Her boss is impressed with the return on their investment in design. In the next round of budget discussions, her budget is increased. She commissions more work… and so on. Simple. Get your clients involved in talking about design effectiveness internally. It makes them look good, they become valuable within their own businesses, and the value of design to that business is profiled. If you do this time and time again, you will change corporate attitudes to design.

BRINGING INEXPERIENCED CLIENTS WITH YOU

Most people base their decisions on the experience they've had to date: it's the only frame of reference they've got. Designers, on the other hand, leapfrog into the unknown, often leaving their inexperienced clients behind. It's no wonder they won't run with the idea that you 'just know' is going to change their lives. Take smaller leaps. Consider what the objectives are, and plan very carefully how to get them there. Growing clients' interest in design effectiveness will lead to better briefs and to their involvement in all the right places. It will also lead to their gratitude each time you deliver.

TACKLE IT OR KICK IT INTO TOUCH?

The big question: do you embark on the discipline of design effectiveness or not? In truth, you can't avoid it. Your competitors are mastering the discipline. Your clients are expecting it. And, led by the UK's Design Business Association (DBA) and Design Council and the US's Design Management Institute (DMI), the major design bodies worldwide are becoming more and more vocal on the design industry's ability to change the fortunes of those who commission effective design. The aim is make design effectiveness the default setting for every client, and for every designer.

5.9   The recognition

Stef Brown

You can never be guaranteed good roles because of an award, but I think your profile and net worth as a performer has to do with awards, unfortunately.
- Minnie Driver (b. 1970), actress

CHOOSING YOUR RED CARPET

Utter the words 'what about entering awards this year' in any agency and you've unleashed a can of worms. Which schemes should we enter? Which work? How much will it cost? How much time will it take? Can we measure the return on investment? Does anyone really care if we win awards?

The design industry is awash with hundreds of creative awards schemes, not to mention business impact and client sector specific awards. Awards make good business sense for the awards bodies themselves, but do they make good sense for agencies?

It's difficult to know if awards translate directly into increased revenue, but they can be an important profile-raising and marketing channel. People might spot you've won an award. That might push them to your website. Then they might call you.

ONE IS OVERWHELMED BY THE SHEER OPAQUE REPRESENTATION OF SPECIFIC AND SIGNIFICANT CONTRADICTORY FUNCTIONS WITHIN THE RHETORIC...

There are pros and cons to entering awards. On the plus side, awards can raise your profile. You can use them to promote yourself to clients and prospects. They are good for staff morale, and a bit of silverware can act as a spur to creativity. They cement your client relationship, and can help you attract talent. But entering awards is expensive, they take up a lot of non-billable time and, if you don't win, you risk disappointing your clients.

When planned carefully, with a strict eye on budgets and on maximising your exposure post-win, awards can be an exceptional route to supporting your positioning and building your agency's reputation. The most important thing to remember when tackling them is to be practical and realistic, or you risk spending all your non-billable time and cash in just this one activity.

CHOOSING THE RIGHT AWARDS

The starting point should be your positioning. Are you aiming to be the most creative agency? The most effective? If you are single-mindedly determined to build a creative positioning, only enter creative awards. Your bulging trophy case will be testament to its position.

Next, you need to align your awards strategy to your business strategy, your key audiences and what they want. Do you need to attract talent to your agency? Then creative awards might be right. Trying to attract new clients? Then business impact awards could help. Trying to get work in a particular sector or new geography? Then look into client sector or foreign awards schemes.

Once you know what you're trying to accomplish, it's time to do the research and plan your year. Choose your awards schemes, then apportion an annual budget for entry fees, production costs, copywriters and ceremony attendance with your clients if you win. Many deadlines are around the same time of year, so create a timeline of activities. You might want to make someone responsible for managing the awards process and budget.

HOW TO SUBMIT ENTRIES AND WIN

Every award scheme has different entry rules and criteria, but there are some things to consider to increase your chances of winning:

- Be ruthless when deciding what work to enter; it's better to focus on fabulous entries for two or three outstanding pieces of work than a dozen good pieces.
- Review the previous years' winners to give you a feel for the type of work the scheme recognises.
- Research the judges and the type of work they do to understand their judgement approaches.
- Select categories which attract fewer entries to increase your chances of winning.
- Don't use agency branding on your entries so judges won't pre-judge based on preconceptions about your agency.
- Get your senior people on judging panels to better understand how winning entries are selected. It's also a good profile-raising exercise.

- Understand and follow the entry criteria and rules. By all means stretch the boundaries and be creative with your entry, but make sure the nuts and bolts are covered or risk disqualification.

Creative awards

No matter the category, try to show your work in the context for which it was created. Above all, be visually impactful. In some creative awards schemes judges will look at hundreds of entries in one sitting, so make sure your work grabs them. You should also consider including short captions on any imagery.

As to the writing bit, be succinct: judges have little reading time. The judges see your work in front of them so don't spend time on flowery descriptions of the design solution; focus on the background and the design challenge. Creative awards increasingly ask for evidence of success, so try to include some business impact data.

Finally, many agencies spend a lot of time and money 'packaging' their entries into beautiful boxes so the judges have a spectacular reveal of the work. Don't bother. The judges will only see the contents.

Business impact awards

Business impact awards are all about proving that your design is effective, that it helped your clients achieve their business objectives.

You need to set out the business objectives, and then prove how your design has positively impacted each of those objectives. You also need to explain why your design achieved success over and above any other marketing activities. Try to set things in context: a large sales uplift in a rising market is less impactful than a smaller sales uplift in a declining market. Don't spend too much time describing the design solution as this is about proving the effectiveness of the design. And make sure that all your data has a source and date, even if the source is the client's internal data.

In acknowledgment that clients market their brands in an integrated manner, there are increasing numbers of awards schemes for multi-channel recognition. You may want to consider working with your client and all its agencies on a cross-agency entry.

It does take time to source all the information and write the entry and you will need the full support of your client, but the resulting entry can be used for your agency's business development activities whether you win an award or not.

MARKETING YOUR WINNING ENTRIES

Winning an award is great, but it's only as good as the people who know about it, and you have to assume that most of your target audience won't. The effort you put in post-win can be as important as the entry itself.

Press relations activity: news release

Most awards schemes issue a news release about all winners to the key design and marketing publications, so avoid those: journalists don't need to receive the same story from multiple sources. Consider regional press, client sector trade press, foreign press and blogs, and ask your client to issue a release about the win. Make sure you send out your release within one or two days of the awards ceremony or it's old news. And remember to get your client's sign-off on the release before you send it out.

Thought-leadership

Why not think about leveraging your learnings by writing an opinion piece? It's always better to try to get the piece published as a third party endorsement, but if this isn't possible, self–publish on your website or blog. Wherever possible, articles should have a practical take-away, things the reader can act on.

Business development activities

Some things to consider:

- Post the press release and any actual coverage to your website, and direct people to the link. Make sure you get permission from publications, or you risk contravening copyright.
- Is the case study already on your website? Or in your credentials and capabilities presentations? Revise it to include information on the award win, and include the awards scheme's logo as an endorsement.
- Do you already have a printed case study or brochure and can't afford reprint costs? Create a sticker to merchandise the win.
- Get a testimonial from your client. Draft something for them to edit and sign off, to capture the right messaging. Use it on your website, case studies and credentials.
- 'Dress' your reception area and meeting rooms with details of the win.
- Add a sentence to all email footers, along with a link to the case study on your website.
- Add 10–15 minutes at the end of a meeting to take your existing clients through the award-winning story.

Direct marketing

You've got a fantastic story to tell. Send it to your clients, prospects, suppliers and referrers. Remember that brand owners are inundated with information from agencies, and getting cut-through is all-important. They want relevant and insightful communication that focuses on their needs, so always state the business case. Ultimately, prospects respond positively to beautiful design that works.

Your people

Finally, does everyone know the award-winning story? Why not have the core team and your client present the story to them over lunch? What about investing in a branded cake? Or rewarding the core team with a team-building activity? Celebrate your win, and don't forget to tell everyone how you plan to market it externally.

5.10 The planet

Sophie Thomas

Tomorrow is our permanent address.
- Marshall McLuhan (1911–80), educator and media theorist

DESIGN AND SUSTAINABILITY

Sustainable design is not about hair shirts, unbleached paper, products made from someone else's waste or some other clichéd response. Sustainable design, just like any other design, has to be good design.

Design is the process that lays the foundations for the creation of every man-made object or system. It has to be aesthetically pleasing, catch the attention, have purpose and be a well-resolved solution to a problem that needs material expression. There is too much bad design in the world: rule number one is to deliver high-quality design, which resonates with the user, creates a reaction, is seen as adding value and has a lasting quality.

But sustainable design is much more than this. It must deliver good design whilst also addressing the big issues of our time: climate change, resource depletion, accessibility, pollution, waste, ethical issues like fair trade and child labour. To do this, designers have to recognise that, as creators of things both physical and virtual, they have a huge impact on the way people consume. The design community can have a very significant influence on the environmental footprint of consumers, and can help clients understand how they can do more with less.

The issues that face us will throw up very different challenges to the ones we are used to dealing with. New disciplines such as ethical design, which promote positive change by working with social communities, are becoming more and more evident. In the past, companies who dismissed this lobby paid dearly for their avoidance, and have had to work hard to repair their reputation. Other issues such as resource depletion – the increased scarcity of the raw materials we need to produce our work – now require designs that make 'more with less'. As citizens, we are confronted every day with big challenges that demand change in our habits, and design must change too. We find it all too easy to deposit our concerns on the doorstep of our studios and not return to them until we leave to go home but, in order to affect real change, sustainability must become part of the DNA of the design process and take its place as a continuous, research-led tool.

THERE IS NO GREATER ISSUE NOW THAN CLIMATE CHANGE

Most of us are concerned about climate change. The loss of the planet's resources and the accumulation of waste worry us. Although there has yet to be a calculation of designers' contribution to the global carbon footprint, it is probably much larger than we dare imagine. Our creations shape our society and sell lifestyles. They dress, feed and shelter us. They move us from A to B. The environmental trade-off for all this will be considerable, and we have a duty, therefore, to use our skills to change the way we create. The design sector should lead the way, or at least keep up with best practice of other industries and government initiatives. It can no longer blame the client for not requesting it, or fall back on the myths of expensive production and inferior results as reasons for continuing with unsustainable design practices.

The following environmental statistics illustrate the awful truth:

- At the current rate of global warming, a quarter of the world's species will be extinct by 2050, and 70 per cent of the people alive now will be around to watch it happen.[1]
- The harvesting of tropical and sub-tropical rain forest timber specifically for papermaking is projected to increase by 70 per cent by the end of the decade.[2]
- The estimated remaining official oil reserves represent 40 years of global use.[3]
- There are projected to be around 150 million climate refugees by 2050.[4]
- We are only a couple of generations from losing access to key elements, like copper, nickel, zinc and indium, which is used in LCD screens and is essential for the production of solar voltaic panels.[5]
- Decisions made during the design stage profoundly influence the entire life of a product and determine 80–90 per cent of its total lifecycle costs.[6]

---

1   Adapted from study first published in *Nature Journal*, January 2004. Lead author Chris Thomas, Professor of Conservation Biology, University of Leeds

2   Natural Resources Defense Council (NRDC)

3   Society of Petroleum Engineers (SPE)

4   International Panel for Climate Change (IPCC)

5   Mike Pitts, Chemistry Innovation Knowledge Transfer Network (KTN)

6   *AT&T report*, December 1995

Statistics such as these must influence us and our decisions. The design industry sits between raw materials and producers, companies and consumers, ideas and landscape. We visualise and specify, designing with purpose to create better lifestyles through new products and services.

The International Panel for Climate Change (IPCC) has called for a global cut of 80 per cent in greenhouse gases by 2050. Our contribution as designers must be in the adoption of integrated sustainable design practices. It is insufficient to give a passing nod to the 'green' lobby by way of a token effort. It requires a reappraisal of every aspect of our work from concept development to the processes, the materials and the final outcome. The fundamental beliefs and principles of the studio and its designers should be reassessed so that a change in practice ideology becomes the way of thinking and working. This involves tracing every step of design practice and evaluating each one in terms of its sustainable accountability.

Design teams working within companies have less room to adopt or introduce sustainable practice, but this does not mean that it is impossible. Companies now recognise the kudos of having good sustainable credentials and the general public, their customer base, is better acquainted with – and knowledgeable about – the dangers of unsustainable practices. They are becoming more aware of what constitutes 'dirty' and wasteful manufacturing. Based on thorough research, an argument for a sustainable basis for design products can be put forward. Ethical principles are now frequently being followed when working for certain product manufacturers, such as tobacco companies, and embracing eco-morality can expand and deepen our own design expertise.

WHAT CAN YOU DO?

There are a number of levels on which designers can positively address these big challenges:

- You can seek to influence and educate your clients by challenging briefs so that positive social, environmental and economic outcomes are achieved.
- You can rethink an approach to a client's brief in a way that delivers the same or enhanced outcomes in a different way.
- You can use your skills and understanding of materials to choose better resources for your work.
- You can support sustainable procurement by selecting suppliers who have environmental and ethical management systems, or by only using sustainably certified products such as Forest Stewardship Council (FSC) timber, or by working with suppliers who are actively investing and innovating in green products and systems.
- You can change your own working practices to ensure you minimise your own environmental footprint, and you can help the wider design community to

think about how they can address the sustainability agenda in practical and positive ways.

One lone designer can make big waves. Through open-source networks, like-minded contacts can be made. Use these to give support, advice and a wealth of knowledge that can bolster your convictions (see Figure 5.10.1). There is a greater influence in a well-informed peer group than in trying to change the world's bad habits on your own.

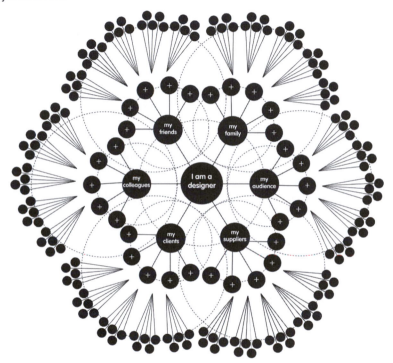

Figure 5.10.1   Links and influences

THE PROCESS

The design process starts with considering how to get from brief to product. Historically, this was a linear process. The brief was handed in, the contract signed with the designer intermittently going back to the client with progress reports and for stage approval. The signed-off product would then go to the manufacturer, who would then create the designed product for the client and the consumer.

Sustainable design thinking, however, should be a closed loop or 'cradle-to-cradle' process. This means that when the product is no longer needed by the user or consumer it can be disassembled and recycled back into useful raw material with minimum effect on the environment. This can only be done if the designer has built this legacy into the design. When considering all the stages of the design of a product, there is a need to understand where the raw materials come from (its 'chain of custody') and also where they will end up, or how they can go back to being useful again. This knowledge forms the foundation of sustainable design (see Figure 5.10.2).

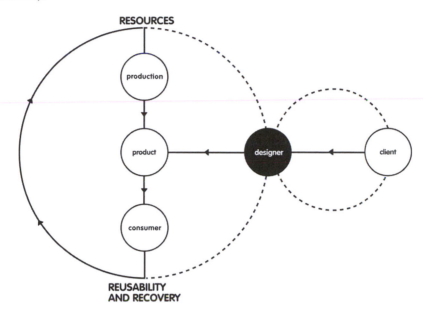

Figure 5.10.2   The chain of custody

INFORMATION AND MISINFORMATION

The more we know, the better we are able to argue against bad practice and misinformation. Sustainable technology is developing at a rapid pace and we need to keep up with the industry's innovations. Finding out who has expertise in processes and materials is important as is discovering trustworthy sources of knowledge through networks and different global media. We need to be able to spot the wolf in green clothing, the sham of 'greenwash', a practice of promoting an environmental fact that has no relevance or is out of scale. We need to be able to search for and recognise true green materials by establishing their credentials. This requires setting up a good relationship with suppliers so that you can demand sustainable alternatives and start an updatable sustainable materials library.

Your clients will ask questions. Is it an affordable solution? Will I like it? Will the consumer like it? Will it promote my product/sell my service? We have to be ready with the answers, together with some questions of our own. Has the client's carbon footprint been reduced? Does this design have good environmental credentials?

The key to turning a design studio or team into a sustainable one lies in acquiring and sharing information which can inform your response to the client and which may result in a rethinking of the brief. The result, if done well, will do 'more with less' and will demonstrate your knowledge of materials and environmental indicators. You will be able to embrace systems such as 'cradle-to-cradle', to look at eliminating waste and reducing the toxicity of the design through the careful choice of materials. And giving feedback to clients, through external footprinting, or impact tools that can measure performance, is a useful means of validating your processes.

Systemic sustainability has to become a normal habit. It should be there at the earliest concept, and should be a reference for all stages of design right through to production and beyond. Clients are beginning to ask for evidence of improved sustainable performance and, as stricter legislation comes into play, business integrity will start to appear on agendas. Sustainability and environmental responsibility must be considered in both the design and the making: as designers, we must keep thinking, researching, persuading and talking about them.

In the end you need to be able to ask yourself 'have I created more with less?' and 'does my design have real value and true quality?' With good sustainable design, the answer for both will be a resounding 'yes'.

HOW TO CLEAN UP YOUR STUDIO

Waste management

- monitor waste and set targets;
- consider how all waste (including hazardous waste) is dealt with through legal and responsible means;
- sort all waste, and research local recycling services;
- replace small waste bins with communal recycling bins.

Energy use and efficiency

- implement a 'switch off' campaign for electrics, with people being responsible for turning off their own computer and screen;
- change to energy-saving light bulbs and install a smart meter to see exactly where your energy goes;
- replace water coolers with water filter tap or plain tap water;
- change your energy tariff to a green supplier;
- look into alternative energy web-hosting sites and energy-efficient server computer systems.

Transport

- use public transport and bikes whenever possible when travelling to meetings;
- use bicycle or motorcycle couriers when practical and set up a green-accredited taxi account;

- set up a company loan scheme for purchasing bikes to encourage employees to ride to work: look into the availability of green transport tax-incentive schemes.

Studio stationery and materials

- use double-sided printing and reuse envelopes;
- use electronic formats when possible;
- consider studio purchases such as stationery, toilet paper, cleaning products.

General

- write and display a studio environmental policy, and keep it up to date;
- create a 'green officer' who can help implement systems and enforce them;
- make sure the environmental agenda is included in meetings.

Section Six:
The Designers

The designers

The following stories from 20 different companies, all listed in the UK *Design Week* 2009 or 2010 Top 100 Surveys, demonstrate how to run a successful design business in practice. They represent most of the major design disciplines, and they range from small to large and from single-focus to multi-disciplinary. They were asked to reveal the secrets of their success, responding to the simple question: 'How did you do it?'

What do these companies have in common? Talent and a driving will to succeed, for sure. But they have also taken a number of brave decisions along the way, streamlining and focusing their offers and investing in help from external advisors. Some of them learned the hard way, encountering setbacks and hardships, but they picked themselves up and went on to become leading firms.

The design market is constantly changing, with arrivals, departures, mergers and acquisitions. By the time you read this, some of these companies might well have changed along with it. However, as a spotlight on what it takes to make it in the design consultancy arena, these stories are both enlightening and inspirational.

300MILLION
Nigel Davies
Managing Director and Founding Partner
www.300million.com

We started for all the usual reasons; greater control of our creative output, lack of opportunity to go further in our existing agency, the desire to do it our way. It may be a bit soon to say we've 'run a successful business' or tell you 'how we did it', but we're happy to share the main factors that underpin our progress to date: people, planning and place.

First, people. The three founding partners came from creative backgrounds, working at leading UK design agencies and spending evenings in the pubs of Clerkenwell (drinking, watching football, planning world-domination – that sort of thing). Most agencies start like this. But for us, the final impetus came from a more unusual source. We formed an electro-rock band. Five tracks and one gig into our glittering career, we realised we were never going to headline at Glastonbury. But we were excited and inspired by creating music, and by the mutual trust involved in performing. We quickly came to the conclusion that we would be better applying our complementary skills and qualities to something we were really good at … running a brand design consultancy.

We have always planned. From initial scraps of paper and Post-It™ notes on the kitchen table to the advisers we regularly consult with, we are aware of the need to work on our own brand. Define the vision, develop the culture, set financial goals. It's the hardest part of the job, and it will never be finished. But we know we need to be our own toughest client to ensure our business constantly evolves in a clearly defined direction.

Our final priority when we started (other than the small matter of finding a few clients) was place. We took a lease on a 1,200 square ft floor in a converted warehouse, a bold statement that we were serious and intended to grow. In the early days, the space definitely played a part in helping us win clients. Location is important, too: the many delights of Exmouth Market help to make clients' visits to us even more of a pleasure.

Maybe when we truly feel that 300million is 'successful' we'll stop developing as people, let planning take care of itself, and never again bother to give the old place a lick of paint. But I don't think we'll ever say, 'This is it. And that's how we did it.' In fact, it's about as likely as a reunion tour for the band.

Disciplines	Brand strategy Brand definition Naming Brand design Print implementation Digital implementation
Company description	300million is a brand design consultancy. We position ourselves as 'pragmatic dreamers'. We aim to improve our clients' businesses by delivering brilliant answers to their most important brand questions – the ones that will make or break their businesses.
Office locations	London
Year established	2003

999 DESIGN GROUP
Richard Bissland
Founding Director
www.999design.com

999 Design Group Limited was established in 1982, after my business partner and I bought a small design business out of the Rex Stewart Group portfolio in Scotland, and renamed it. Looking back, the fact we called it 'Design Group' from day one probably displayed a confidence we had no way of validating. However, having

your livelihood on the line, not to mention the mortgages and welfare of your people, is a wonderful stimulant to perform to your best.

Our early success came from securing contracts with major local businesses and persuading them to pay us quickly: cashflow is king in every young business. We worked all hours, often doing 60–70 hour weeks, and delivered high-quality work. This got us noticed by national accounts, and after a relatively short time we had growing UK brands like Reebok, Co-operative group and BT on our books.

The management style of the agency was: work hard; grow and consolidate 'step at a time'; hire the best creative people we could find; and leave profits in the business. This built a strong balance sheet for rainy days. In business, it always rains at some point.

It duly poured. In late 2001, Orange, who had been a major client for six years, was bought by French Telecom and changed marketing direction. We lost around £1.3m of annual turnover in a month. It was that quick: we had way too many eggs in one basket. However, our balance sheet and resolve were strong enough to see us recover after a year. Trimming the workforce was an extremely stressful task, and some good people lost their jobs. You find out a lot about yourself, and other people, going through this process.

Our success and longevity is based on a genuine interest in seeing our clients prosper. Many have remained with us for years: that takes commitment on both sides to work through the good times and the not so good. Today, our client spread is broader and the business is much less susceptible to the loss of a major client. In retrospect, I wish we'd fully embraced the development of digital communications a few years before we did. Inexplicably, we were too cautious. If I were doing it all over again, knowing what I know now... I wouldn't. My business would be manufacturing and product-led but with a high design philosophy, offering a much greater return than a people-based, service business.

Disciplines	Branding Marketing Literature Digital e-commerce Packaging Events
Company description	Established since 1982. Independent UK-wide digital and brand-based communications business. Blue chip public and private sector client list. Three UK Design Effectiveness Award wins.
Office locations	London, Glasgow, Manchester
Year established	1982

BLUE MARLIN
Andrew Eyles
CEO and Group Managing Director
David Hodgson
Global Human Resources Director
www.bluemarlinbd.com

We met in our mid-twenties, a special time because we felt the invincibility of youth and we were just starting to dream. We recognised a shared ambition and entrepreneurial spirit. We were lucky: that special connection doesn't happen often. Working at an agency in London, we had reached the limit of what we could achieve there, so Blue Marlin was born out of dissatisfaction with the old place and a lot of scotch.

In the small hours of a cold April morning in 1993 we had a big idea: to create a world-class, independent, international design consultancy. To cement our bond we exchanged a sock, the pair of which still graces a wall in one of the offices. Backed by capital from family members, we started work off Andrew's kitchen table. We quickly won three clients (and 16 years on, they are still our clients) and a few months later we opened our first office.

In the early days we relied to a very large extent on gut feel, and it got us places very quickly. We were – and still are – instinctive, decisive and entrepreneurial. Conventional wisdom dictated that when we expanded from our base in Bath it should've been to go to London, the heart of the design industry. We opened up in Australia instead. The decision was based on client business, personal lifestyle aspirations and economic nous. Australia provided the springboard into Asia and the success of those businesses funded further international expansion, and the growth of our business to London.

We may be unconventional, but we are rigorous. We do our homework, we keep a close eye on cashflow and we are always in it for the long term. We've never borrowed from the bank and we invest profits back into the business.

The real secret to our success is our people. Without them we would not be in this book now. We've managed to articulate our vision and ambitions, and have attracted people who like the entrepreneurial environment and want to come along for the ride. The strength of our partnership plays a very important role too. Again, this is about people.

Culture is important to us. From that first sock swap we have been a family, and 'family' remains one of our core values. We are all in this together and we have a very no-nonsense attitude, where everyone gets stuck in.

Disciplines	Brand strategy
	Brand innovation
	Structural design
	Brand identity and graphic design
	Brand environments
	Realisation

Company description	Blue Marlin is the home of landing big ideas, which are at the heart of everything we do. We pride ourselves on delivering relevant, unique and consistent experiences across brand touch points worldwide. Blue Marlin is an independent integrated brand design consultancy with an international network.
Office locations	London, Bath, New York, Sydney, Bangkok
Year established	1993

BOXER
Julian Glyn-Owen
New Business Director
www.boxercreative.co.uk

The now not-so-secret successful habits at Boxer.

We have grown from a small regional agency into a global brand design agency with offices in the UK and US in the space of 12 years. The team believes that there are three habits that have contributed to our success over the past decade.

Firstly, the creative and client-side teams have grown to become a cohesive and well-matched creative collective, the core of which has been working together for over a decade. Ideas, as we all know, don't care where they come from, so our ability to honestly challenge one another throughout the creative process has become the norm. At the end of the day, it comes down to an underlying trust and belief in the collective experience of our combined individual expertise.

Secondly, the team works extremely hard to understand the market challenges to our clients' brands. A good example is McDonald's, with whom Boxer has had a relationship for over eight years, answering increasingly larger and more influential briefs. The most significant result for our business was winning the last global quality packaging project in 2007, designing the look of all McDonald's packaging worldwide. This project was won in a competitive pitch against 20 other agencies, some of whom were amongst the world's biggest brand design agencies. The winning of this business remains a powerful demonstration of an agency understanding the challenges faced by a client's brand. Our creative response simply answered those challenges better than others, and this was possible because the team understood the brand.

Thirdly, we've made an active effort to capitalise on our global brand experiences through our own initiative called 'Soak It Up'. The teams who head out to markets around the world are actively encouraged to sketch, photograph or drag home design that catches the eye. The studios then share these designs between them as a resource for ongoing work, making the creative process more inspiring and fun and allowing the teams to soak up the inspiration, colour and experiences of global travel. Over the years the team has built its own valuable, personal and highly stimulating pool of materials that subsequently provides more powerful creative stimulus for ongoing work. This has the obvious added benefit of bringing very happy memories to the studio environment as we print up a lot of these images into huge montages and use them to decorate the studio.

Disciplines	Brand design
Company description	Medium-sized brand design agency specialising in global brand design and management, working primarily on high street brands in the food, beverage and personal care sectors.
Office locations	Birmingham, Chicago
Year established	1996

CHECKLAND KINDLEYSIDES
Jeff Kindleysides
Co-Founder
www.checklandkindleysides.com

David Checkland and I started our business in 1979, and at that time we had no real plan of what we felt we might achieve. Naively, we set about creating our own version of what we believed a design partnership to be. The important things to me were craft, art and the aesthetics of design. David was the pragmatic one who played out his design on a work bench and who believed in a robust and analytical approach to business, even though at the time there were only two of us.

From the outset there was just something very right about what we were doing, and although we did what came naturally to us, it proved to be unique. Using our combined talents in unconventional ways, having no fear, and advocating that to create in 2D was the same as creating in 3D, we believed that designers needed to have minds to embrace both. Not only that, we felt it was impossible for us to be fully creative without having our own workshop to develop our ideas. One thing fuelled the other, and our thoughts were often demonstrated to our clients with a full sized mock-up.

We believed in tutoring talent – the younger the better – and we invented our own ways of doing things. Through this, a culture developed that had craft, practicality and responsibility running through the veins of each and every person in the company, irrespective of position or job role. This in turn created a solid commercial foundation and, as we began to grow and our ambitions became greater, we were able to confidently create and realise beautiful things in the knowledge that they would be financially viable.

Importantly, we invested in equal measures in our creative ability as well as our business operations. We invented our own accounting systems that gave us the ability to monitor every project and, in turn, the performance of the business week on week. This gave us the freedom to make intuitive decisions about the future of our client relationships and our company.

We have always sought to win clients not projects and, without a doubt, this is the single most important driver in our success. It's important to understand that our culture demands that we do what's right every time without fail, whatever it takes, because it not only carries our reputation, but that of our clients too.

Disciplines	Interiors and retail Branding and graphics Consumer engagement Research and forecasting
Company description	Checkland Kindleysides is an independent design company specialising in consumer-facing design and research. The company has a craft-based culture working in both 2D and 3D disciplines, and is also recognised for its expertise in sustainable retail design.
Office locations	Leicester and London
Year established	1979

DALZIEL AND POW DESIGN CONSULTANTS
David Dalziel
Creative Director
www.dalziel-pow.co.uk

Dalziel and Pow was formed in 1983, after John Pow and I had worked together at McColls on a variety of retail and leisure briefs. We had a desire to be independent, exploiting our skills, knowledge and methods in a more direct and personal way.

The business was formed on a sound financial footing with work lined up from the outset, mostly interior design for bars, pubs and clubs around London. We began to attract attention from retailers interested in how we might help them improve their offer, and our first major retail client was Chelsea Girl and Concept Man, a business that would be rebranded and reinvented as River Island in 1987. This transformation took the high street by storm, creating a lot of interest from the market, and we began to develop a strong portfolio of retail clients.

An ability to maintain the commitment of key clients – over two decades and more in some cases – helped us grow from a team of four in 1986 to over 80 in 2009. The growth has been steady and gradual, built on live projects with guaranteed income. This frugal approach has helped the company trade through various market conditions, both boom and bust, avoiding the pitfalls experienced by many of our competitors.

With John's retirement in 1999, we restructured the company and created a broader, more inclusive management team to take the business on to the next phase of growth. Ros Scott stepped up from Operations Director to Managing Director and continued to develop the company with the pragmatic, considered approach that had served us well up to that point.

Since 2000, we have worked internationally across Europe, China, India, USA and the Middle East. Global work is easier to win: you are respected and welcomed. There is less emphasis on the pitch process and more on your track record in delivering creative services that bring profit. This has been a revelation. Now, up to 40 per cent of our commissions come from outside the UK. We are seen as the experts, a position gained through honing our skills in our highly competitive local market. We now employ as many as 15 nationalities on our staff and opened our first international office, in Shanghai, in 2008.

The key to our success is the work. We build relationships by providing solutions which are rewarding: our design works. We are looking forward to the future with as much enthusiasm as we had in 1983, but now also with authority and experience.

Disciplines	Brand definition Brand environments Brand communications
Company description	A leading international consultancy, focused on design which connects clients with consumers. We have many examples in our portfolio where our work has delivered a 20 per cent to 70 per cent uplift in sales. Our client coverage extends around the globe and we have built projects worldwide.
Office locations	London, Shanghai
Year established	1983

DESIGN BRIDGE
Sir William Goodenough
Executive Chairman
www.designbridge.com

Design Bridge was launched in 1986 after the takeover of Allied International Designers by Addison prompted a breakaway team. Unusually, there were five founders, who spent the early years travelling around Europe at least two days a week building the business, mainly in Holland, Germany and Scandinavia and, to a lesser extent, France, Italy, Spain and South-East Asia.

There were very few companies actively doing this in the late 1980s and it is still unusual today, especially for privately-owned design businesses. That culture is now embedded: nearly 24 years later, with offices in London, Amsterdam and Singapore, we work in 35 different countries, and employ 21 different nationalities.

The Amsterdam office started in 1996 when it became difficult to develop the business on a weekly-trip basis. Having lived in Singapore in the early 1980s, I had contacts in Asia – many of whom are still working with us today – so it was natural to open an office there in 2004 to have a base in the fastest growing region of the world. Both offices were developed by individuals who had been working in Design Bridge for a number of years, and the Board backed them in these ventures.

There are other factors that have determined our success. The financial structuring of the business was based around a number of individuals, rather than one or two people, which was unusual in the design industry. From the outset, there was always the ethos that Design Bridge was more important than the individual. This is still the case today.

If you go down this track, you have to learn how to manage the complex issues that inevitably arise. We set high standards across all the areas that go to make up the business and how they inter-relate from a management perspective. Design is a craft industry, and for most of us a vocation. We do our best to offer everyone a career, by developing a clear line-management system, and a great number of our staff have been with us for more than ten years. Success is a people issue; we employ the best people in the industry, and then back and encourage them in their careers.

Our values remain the same but we have evolved yearly, developing new offers to match our clients' needs. Fundamental to our success is our very real passion for design, and a clear understanding of the role which creativity plays in the success of our clients' businesses and brands.

Disciplines	Branding
Company description	International branding agency, working across a wide range of consumer touchpoints.
Office locations	London, Amsterdam, Singapore
Year established	1986

DRAGON ROUGE
Ian Farnfield
Chief Executive
www.dragonrouge.com

Starting a new London business at the height of the recession in the early 1990s may seem like madness, but to us it was a chance to prove that there was a better way to realise the power and influence of creativity and strategy. We set out with strong beliefs for an agency that worked with clients in a more insightful, forward-thinking way, and whose people enjoyed high levels of involvement and empowerment.

Our approach then, as it is today, was to help clients perform, compete and lead. This requires understanding and insights, not just into people, markets and businesses as they exist today, but also into the opportunities and challenges facing clients in the future. We have never been constrained by the norms of the design industry, and have led the way in matching high levels of strategy with creativity, in developing a rigorous approach to innovation alongside design, and in integrating consumer and corporate perspectives. As brands became more global, we evolved our informal network into a true international partnership with a common spirit, culture and way of working. Developed organically, we are now one of the world's leading brand agencies.

While our commitment has been to deliver the best possible results for our clients, we have always tried to be smart commercially, investing properly in developing our people, expertise and influence. We are more entrepreneurial than other groups and have the flexibility to do what is best for our clients. Our independent ownership structure, with all the shareholders working in the business, has enabled us to take a long-term view, rather than pursuing short-term financial targets. We've always funded ourselves and have a thriving, well-resourced business where we control our own destiny.

Agencies need to be flexible and prepared to change, but getting the timing right is important. For example, clients are often slower than we would imagine in investing in new opportunities and challenges. In areas such as trend-forecasting, sustainability, cause-related marketing, employee engagement and digital communications, we were offering expertise long before clients really valued it. For some time, we've been educating rather than consulting.

We knew what we wanted to stand for, and what was important to us. We delivered what clients needed, not just what was easy to sell them, and we put great work and staff motivation first in our priorities. This is the best route to commercial success in both the short and long term.

Disciplines	Brand identity Brand style Digital communications Packaging design Product design and innovation Printed literature Retail environments
Company description	Dragon Rouge has in-depth knowledge and proven expertise in brand strategy, design and innovation. With us you will find a unique fusion of strategy and creativity, smarter insights and brilliant ideas focused on helping products, services and corporations to be the best they can be.
Office locations	Dubai, Hamburg, Hong Kong, London, New York, Paris and Warsaw
Year established	1991

ELMWOOD
Jonathan Sands
Chairman
www.elmwood.com

Looking back at the defining moments in our success, it is true that we have enjoyed lots of luck. This said, there is no doubt that the harder we have tried the luckier we have become. And herein lies what makes Elmwood, Elmwood: 'restlessness'. It seems that no matter what successes come our way, we are never satisfied. We want to win everything. The tenor of any business is governed by the persona of the boss and it is perhaps no surprise that I have been described by a client as 'a competitive little sh**'! This will to win, or rather a fear of failure, has been a significant driving force in our development and forms one of Elmwood's many mantras in our phrase *There is no finish line™*. It is a fundamental truth that all businesses are taking part in a race that nobody can ever win. Success is only ever in the moment, whether it be a bountiful awards night, a significant client win or a record profits year. You can never sit back and think 'we have made it': you always have to have your eyes on the next prize. The status quo does not exist, and standing still is the quickest way to go backwards.

Being competitive and never being satisfied is one thing but being true to a set of values is another. Success is not about growth for growth's sake. To move forward, you often have to take one step back. Your values are like the roots of a tree rather than the branches that you see. If you mess with the roots you die, but sometimes a good pruning of the branches can lead to better growth next year. On several occasions now we have turned down work when we have disagreed with the strategic intent of a project, only to then win the work back further down the line when our point of view turned out to be right. Being true is hard, especially when the dollar signs are big, but the only thing you have to sell as a consultant is your integrity. In my experience doing the right thing has always led to bigger bucks in the end.

My final words of advice are to be good-humoured and to give back to the industry, but be humble in doing so. It pays tangible dividends beyond altruism. You really do reap what you sow.

Disciplines	Brand consultancy Brand owners (*Make Mine a Builder's* tea and *Good Cheer Beer*)
Company description	On the back of winning more DBA Effectiveness Awards than anybody else ever, we describe ourselves as 'The World's Most Effective Brand Consultancy'.
Office locations	Chicago, Edinburgh, Leeds, London, Melbourne and New York
Year established	1989

JKR
Andy Knowles
CEO
www.jkr.co.uk

There are three phases that have characterised our development, one step at a time.

We started jkr in 1990, just as the remarkable multi-disciplinary, multi-national design empires built by pioneers like Rodney Fitch and Michael Peters were crashing with the bursting of the economic bubble of the 1980s. The end of a boom isn't the obvious time to launch another design business but, by specialising in packaging, we felt we had a chance to excel. With value for money high on every client's agenda, perhaps it was time to take a risk.

We got lucky, landing some high-profile projects early on and set out our stall with design that got noticed. The telephone started to ring and things went quickly from there, pretty much by word of mouth. Inside a year or so we'd moved to bigger offices and almost 20 staff.

That first phase was exhilarating and exhausting. An 'all hands to the pump' mentality bound us like brothers-in-arms, but many of our relationships outside work were suffering and we saw we had to spread the load. This was the beginning of the second phase. Instead of making us slow and expensive, as we initially feared, supporting designers with professional project and technical managers was a catalyst for growth. Specialisation gave us the ability to win new clients and to develop enduring partnerships, which is what most major clients actually want.

Despite great team spirit and some brilliant, dedicated people, we plateaued at around 50 or 60 people until we realised we would only grow by getting organised. We initially attempted to improve our way of working using consultants. Unfortunately, when we introduced their recommendations they made us slow and inflexible. So we put a cross-functional team of our own people together and they came up with a simpler system that continues to this day. By delivering consistent quality and improved productivity we became better, faster and cheaper and no longer fell back exhausted, whenever we'd experienced a surge in workload.

We've taken delegation and teamwork to a higher level in our third phase. Teamwork hasn't replaced the need for individual effort, of course, but in a deadline-driven business, sharing the pressure produces a productive calm that is attractive to talented colleagues and clients alike. It's hard to understand what took us so long, but then everything looks easy with hindsight.

Disciplines	Branding and packaging
Company description	Design that gets noticed and chosen.
Office locations	London
Year established	1990

LIVING GROUP
Duncan Shaw
Group Creative Director
www.living-group.com

Vision, vision, vision... the three most important considerations to run a successful agency. Vision to understand how your business can develop in the future, vision to know that in tough times, there will be better times around the corner and finally, vision to keep an eye on all aspects of your business.

The Living story originally started on 18 October 1972, but let's fast-forward 32 years to June 2004, when my wife and I purchased the business from her parents and relaunched it in London. Kate had previously been a trader at UBS, a global investment bank and I had been Creative Director at Springboard. We were both looking for a new challenge. With just the two of us sitting across a desk from one another, we started out life as a design agency doing all things for all people. Our overriding objective was simple; to do a really good job for our clients.

From the outset we have always taken advice from industry experts and in 2006, we followed the recommendation to specialise in what we really knew best – providing brand and communications to the financial and professional services sector. This seemed like a brave decision at the time, and we were nervous about losing clients who did not fit into that category. However, as time passed, we grew in confidence and new clients warmed to our carefully crafted proposition.

Specialisation, aligned with our creativity, the commitment and dedication of our team and our strong financial acumen has attributed to our growth. We doubled in size year after year, growing to a team of 25 today. We foster a culture of openness and honesty with our clients and have an acute attention to detail, with a reputation of getting things right first time. In 2009 we moved to a group structure expanding our external offering across four key disciplines: Living Designs, Living Digital, Living PR and Living Reporting. We call it joined-up communications.

If we were to do it again tomorrow, we'd probably have the courage to specialise earlier and not give jobs to the first people who walk through the door. Finally, if we had one piece of advice for anyone thinking of starting a creative business... be prepared to put every ounce of your heart and soul into it if you want to be a success. And don't forget to have vision!

Disciplines	Branding and identity
	Literature
	Digital
	PR
	Reporting
Company description	Living specialises in joined-up communications for the financial and professional sector. Our clients, based globally, benefit from our team's inherent knowledge and understanding, which delivers outstanding brands and communications.
Office locations	London, Hong Kong
Year established	2004

MEDIA SQUARE: INCLUDES LLOYD NORTHOVER, HOLMES & MARCHANT, ARKEN, 490
David Worthington
Chairman
Lloyd Northover Group
www.mediasquare.co.uk

There are no right or wrong ways to grow a design business: there is only the way that is right for you. This means doing what you do well, and getting someone else to do the rest. This is my story.

I set up a business, Worthington, in 1980 simply because I always thought I would. I had no strategy; I just left work one day and started the day after in my spare room. I slowly built a list of clients and, 16 years on, we had 35 people, produced good work, won awards and made a profit every year.

Come 1996, I was looking for a new challenge. We sold to the people who owned (but did not understand) Conran Design Group. Our strategy was simple: merge our businesses, put Conran Design Group back on the map, enhance the value for the owners, take a slice for ourselves.

This took four years, and it was the most exciting period of my working life. We travelled the world, worked on great projects, won awards and made remarkable profits. Ten years on, there's 200 or so alumni who still talk well of those times. However, once the earn-out concluded, the market got tougher, my own incentive reduced (plcs don't understand post earn-out motivation) and performance declined. We persevered, but one by one I made trusted people redundant until it was my turn. Not pleasant, but an experience.

Today, I chair Lloyd Northover and Holmes & Marchant, part of the marketing services group Media Square plc. They are both great brands which, like Conran Design Group, have previously been bigger: the cycle starts again. Slowly but surely, with good managers and people, we are swinging in the right direction. That we will succeed is undoubted and, when we do, it will be down to the same sentiment that drove Worthington and Conran Design Group before: people and purpose, together with the sense that we are doing something worthwhile and it's fun.

Disciplines	Branding Packaging Retail design
Company description	Media Square is the fifth largest UK-based quoted marketing communications group. We are experts in advertising, design, marketing, public relations and research. We work to make our clients' brands more valuable through the implementation of creative ideas.
Office locations	UK, Barcelona, Dubai, Singapore, Hong Kong, Shanghai
Year established	1975

What is my advice? Be clear about what you want: independence, money, better work, a nice office, fame. Imagine what the business will look like when it's delivering those goals: size, clients, recognition, people and culture. Draw a route-map, and refer to it frequently. Employ people who are far better than you, and identify what they will get from the adventure: if they succeed, you will too. And follow your instinct. It's all you have.

RUFUS LEONARD
Neil Svensen
CEO
www.rufusleonard.com

We launched Rufus Leonard back in 1989. At the age of 26 I had the overwhelming urge to do something for myself. Working with my friend and co-designer Darrel Worthington, we began with a couple of clients and some shared workspace. Quite quickly we started to get work by word of mouth. We were driven by delivering high quality and real stand-out value. We always knew we wanted to do something of note, and over time, this has evolved into a desire to create and develop connected brands.

Our heritage lies in pure brand and design. We've always had stable foundations and regular referrals and, over time, this has grown into the solid roster of key clients we have today. The launch of our digital offer in the mid-1990s was a key moment for us. We developed a model that worked and was still viable after the first great boom. Since then we've evolved a distinctive brand and digital proposition that we believe has real uniqueness. As a result, we have a far more integrated and holistic client offer today... not to mention almost 100 people in London and Dubai.

We put our clients first and care about what we do. I can remember many sleepless nights thinking about the finer detail of a project, and I wasn't the only one. We created a contagious culture in our early growth years and we've always been pretty good at finding and keeping great people.

The internet boom was a time of massive growth. Around 1996 we developed some initial digital capability. Then the boom arrived and, without exception, our main clients turned their attention to the web space. We spent considerable sums getting to grips with it, and within about six months revenues from digital projects were over 50 per cent of our total. We had a few near misses, one involving a digital infrastructure project for a major financial organisation. But without enduring the highs and lows of this period, we wouldn't have our own unique perspective on the digital channel – or our highly developed offer.

You never always know what's round the corner, so we've learned how to use share options as a way of attracting and incentivising key talent – whilst staying in control. Because our seniors are still all active practitioners, we're learning to celebrate and champion the art of delegation.

Disciplines	Brand Digital
Company description	Rufus Leonard is a highly innovative brand and communications business, specialising in digital. Offering a full service mix, we're experts in bringing brands to life and managing consumer interaction on and offline. We are an award-winning, independently-owned agency working across financial services, telecoms, professional services, utilities and the public sector.
Office locations	UK, Dubai
Year established	1989

SEYMOURPOWELL, A LOEWY GROUP COMPANY
Dick Powell
Founder and Director
www.seymourpowell.com

Seymourpowell was formed osmotically rather than built to a pre-conceived business plan. The two of us, Richard Seymour and I, had both been through the break-up of our former businesses and found ourselves sharing a common workspace in Fulham. Me, a committed product designer, Rich on the run from advertising. Within a few months it was very clear that we had complementary abilities and we increasingly worked together, or at least Rich found himself dragged into my projects. Rather than operate as two solus traders, we created the umbrella company Seymourpowell, moved into adjacent premises recently vacated by the graphics company from whom we rented, and continued to trade as freelancers... but with the image, ambition and shared staff of a slightly bigger business. Two years later, having established the relationship worked and we were winning interesting work, we officially pooled our resources and became a single company. That was in 1984.

Against an industry background that was somewhat dry and striving for professional acceptance, we felt a bit dangerous and different – less 'good design' as the profession understood it, but more creative, fun and adventurous, But it was not just a question of style because innovation was our mantra then... just as it is now.

From the start, we got involved building a brand: working with industry bodies, speaking at events, writing articles and ultimately taking design onto prime-time TV. We really wanted Seymourpowell to be famous and worked hard at it.

There are two key factors in our success. First, it took a major setback before we realised that, if we were to grow, our senior people needed to operate more autonomously, winning and doing the work and owning the client relationship. And second, from the very beginning of Seymourpowell, we focused on the upstream part of the process (the product strategy, user research, brand, market context and rationale) rather than on the downstream delivery of finished products. We never wanted to be labelled as a production design and engineering company and could see our competitors embracing that. As a result, we are quite a diversified design and innovation business doing everything from trains and digital futures, to FMCG products and packaging.

We look back on our mistakes and setbacks and, while it was tough at those moments, we wouldn't change their outcome. Ultimately, they helped create what we are today.

Disciplines	Innovation Strategy Brand User research Product and transportation design Structural and branded packaging
Company description	A design and innovation company with all the disciplines necessary to deliver successful innovative products (durable and FMCG) to market.
Office locations	London
Year established	1984

SMALL BACK ROOM
Callum Lumsden
Creative Director
www.smallbackroom.co.uk

Lumsden Design Partnership joined forces with Small Back Room in November 2008. This was not a merger, or an acquisition; it was a strategic decision by both agencies to expand their individual offer into new business sectors and to create an important adjunct to their core propositions.

Founder and Joint MD John Rushton started Small Back Room, a graphic design agency, in 1977. John and his business partner Ian Tasney have succeeded in building the business into a *Design Week* Top 50 agency, providing brand creativity aligned with strategic consultancy to clients on a global basis. The core offer of Small Back Room has historically been based around the property sector, and focuses particularly on branding and strategic consultancy for clients from Crown Estates for Regent Street through to Northumberland Tourism.

I founded Lumsden Design Partnership in 1995. We're best known for our retail design work for clients such as Lakeland, Habitat, Gap and M&S, and are well regarded for work in the cultural sector for clients such as Tate Modern, London Transport Museum and British Museum.

Fundamental to this whole approach has been the enablement of a crossover of talent, creativity and process allowing both companies to learn from each other, as well as to offer current and prospective clients a far more compelling offer. In simple terms, the process and strategic talents of Small Back Room have enhanced the creativity of Lumsden, and vice versa.

An important and contributing factor to the success of this initiative has been the decision to maintain the high-profile name of Lumsden and to create a separate, but integrated, brand within the agency named 'Lumsden at Small Back Room'. This has enabled us to introduce some of the other core skills from the agency, such as brand engagement and on-screen technology, creating a different offer which a specialist would find difficult to achieve. Having this ability to plug into other teams has also enabled me to win clients who are looking for a wider selection of skills. The benefit to Small Back Room has been the creation of a wider client base, a significant increase in revenue and an introduction to new business sectors not previously available.

In essence, the pairing of the two agencies has allowed us to integrate our individual specialisms, tailored according to project demands, and enables us to market an integrated offer to existing and potential clients around the world.

Disciplines	Brand identity Brand communications Internal communications Environments Exhibitions Retail interiors Interactive media
Company description	An integrated design consultancy delivering outstanding service, strategy and creativity.
Office locations	London
Year established	1977

START
Darren Whittingham
Co-founder
www.startcreative.com

Mike Curtis and I founded Start in 1996 as a new brand and digital agency, with a single-minded plan to put ideas at the heart of our work. With only limited practical experience in managing a company, we found a base in Covent Garden and set out to limit risk and avoid debt by not paying ourselves for the first year. We surrounded ourselves with talented people – creatives, lawyers, accountants – and built strong relationships with clients. We kept our heads down and worked hard and by 2001, with an average year-on-year growth of 79 per cent over five years, we ranked 73 in *The Sunday Times* Fast Track 100.

With 50 people and a turnover of £5m, we moved to larger premises in Holborn. Our work became increasingly multi-disciplinary, and our services expanded. We entered the top 10 in design, marketing and digital leagues, and our rapidly increasing workload took us to around 100 people. Producing streams of award-winning work, we began exploring international markets and searching for complementary acquisitions. To sustain growth, we restructured the company into a holding company and trading company. In 2004, we moved to our spiritual home, Soho, and have now expanded internationally, with clients across the globe and offices in Dubai and Hong Kong.

It's a tough marketplace, getting tougher. We continue to work hard at attracting the most talented people, and have surrounded ourselves with highly regarded non-executives, advisors and industry gurus. We focus on rigorous creative and financial management, and relentless relationship-building. We are investing in next-generation management, in young and hungry digital creative talent and in other skill sets such as brand environments, artist representation and event management. The alignment of brand and digital services is irreversible, and we have evolved to include digital marketing, brand experiences and brand environments to provide 360° creative communication solutions. Creating and promoting clarity and differentiation around our offer is more important than ever.

Start is not built on a traditional model; we are a dynamic creative ideas business that sets its own agenda. We remain independent, not overly swayed by competitors, and adaptable to market needs. Our simple proposition of 'Ideas made well' continues to guide what we do: great creativity from great people with a passion for what they do. We are outperforming the market, and are determined to champion our industry across the globe while staying true to what we set out to achieve. We still feel we are at the beginning: The Start. It's an incredibly exciting place to be.

Disciplines	Brand Digital Retail communications
Company description	An ideas-led integrated approach for brands in online, retail environments and communications. Start: ideas made well.
Office locations	London, Dubai, Hong Kong
Year established	1996

TAYBURN
Simon Farrell
Managing Director
www.tayburn.co.uk

In March 2009, Tayburn celebrated its 30th birthday. This was quite a milestone for the agency; indeed, quite a milestone for any creative agency. Yet, despite a huge sense of pride and achievement, there were no lavish parties or showy celebrations. Why? Because we knew that the couple of thousand pounds spent on such festivities could mean the difference between us making a profit for the year or making a loss.

Now this might not seem like a great insight into how to run an agency but I thought there were some telling pointers behind this seemingly simple anecdote.

Firstly, we knew what our likely profit would be at the end of the year. It may not seem like rocket science, but most agency costs are fixed and we operate in an industry typified by its 'project-by-project' nature. It's vital that you are on top of forecast income as much as possible. We're lucky to have a few large clients that provide us with a steady income of work. But there are no guarantees, so we make sure every team within the agency understands their expected contribution and reviews progress regularly.

Secondly, we knew that the profit would be marginal. Again, that doesn't sound like a ringing endorsement of a well-run agency, but the backdrop to that performance is the worst recession since 1929 and a dramatic loss of income from clients hit really hard by the downturn. Our response was to accommodate their new requirements (rather than letting them find a solution elsewhere) and focus new business activity on a small number of sectors where we thought we could claim a competitive advantage. So far it seems to be working, fingers crossed.

And finally, it matters that we don't make a loss. Tayburn has always been managed with the long run in mind. That means thoughtful planning, prudent investment and ideas on succession. It may not seem that exciting yet despite the caution or, more accurately, because of it, we have made a profit for 30 consecutive years. It's not always been that big, but it's been there. And if we can keep that track record intact in this very difficult year, then we can live without the big party.

Hopefully, things will be rosier when we're 50. We'll have a big knees up then.

Disciplines	Corporate identity Brand packaging Corporate reporting Digital
Company description	A brand and design consultancy dedicated to effective ideas.
Office locations	Edinburgh, Manchester, Istanbul
Year established	1979

THE ALLOY
Gus Desbarats
Chairman
www.thealloy.com

The Alloy was launched in 1999. We had an exciting, turbulent birth when the owners of my previous company refused my offer of a management buyout and implemented what can only be described as a fundamental business re-engineering exercise. The outcome left us all jobless, some more temporarily than others. The Alloy was 'plan B'. I offered the eight best people the opportunity to join a new business opening soon in prestigious new offices being set up in my living room. To my surprise, everyone accepted and we have never looked back.

Our success since then is due to the contributions of many talented people pulling in a common direction, and so it is probably worth focusing on the core elements of this direction.

One of The Alloy's founding strategic ambitions was to build a brand with clear innovation values that would outlast both myself and my co-founding partner, Nick Vessey. From our experience together at BIB in the 1980s neither of us wanted the company to lose momentum when the time came for us to step back.

The brand ambition is followed through by the way we put design (and designers) at both the heart and head of the business. Our culture reflects my belief that industrial designers should think and act like leaders.

This belief is also reflected in our ownership model. The Alloy's second founding ambition was to become employee-owned, a bit along the lines of John Lewis. Design is a people business and doesn't need huge amounts of working capital, so we saw this route as the best answer to many of the barriers to second generation businesses that we believed were holding back our profession and industry.

In addition to setting up a more organic succession, the other aim of the employee ownership structure was to encourage loyalty. To deliver a unique offer in a people business, one needs to train. To avoid training the competition, it helps if people want to stay. To make this more likely, we have always tried to offer career paths in the business. Not everyone has stayed but, mostly, the right people have. Some have actually left and come back.

The outcome of this is a challenging environment, 100 per cent focused on understanding, evolving and delivering best practice in what we do. Clients seem to like the pitch, and tend to come back as well, so we must be doing something right!

Disciplines	Product design Interaction design Innovation strategy
Company description	The Alloy is a team of consultants which helps organisations of all kinds achieve more effective innovation through better connections between people and technology.
Office locations	Farnham, Surrey, UK
Year established	1999

THE TEAM, A LOEWY GROUP COMPANY
Julian Grice
CEO
www.theteam.co.uk

In 1984, a small band of people assembled in a former church in Putney to start work. We had aspirations to do great work and create a stage for diverse creative talent to perform. We believed we could make a difference by helping the public use the government services that will change their lives. We thought we could create communications that could change public attitudes, raise awareness of things they were entitled to and result in people improving the quality of their lives.

We established a reputation as a creative player with an innovative edge that rarely declined an opportunity because we enjoyed learning. Today, that handful of creative people has swelled to 130 as the largest business in one of the world's leading creative services groups, The Team. Some of the faces have changed and the offer has broadened, but the same belief persists: that effective communication can change lives.

In the Nineties we embraced branding, and attracted blue chip clients. We did everything a rapidly growing business did: competed against anyone, embraced digital media, completed a succession plan where original founders left the business and a new management team was created. We focused on what we enjoyed doing most – public services.

In the Noughties we relocated our expanding team of 50 from the suburbs to London Bridge, a hub of real-life where our audiences were all around us. We attracted rainmakers, directors who wanted to work in public services. As a result we sustained 20 per cent growth from 2002–06, building a credible specialist complementary design and communication offer and a reputation for effectiveness.

In 2007, the next opportunity presented itself. We became a wholly-owned subsidiary of the Loewy Group, ranked as the second largest design consultancy group, number four in the Marketing Design League table and number one for creativity and effectiveness. The Team remains an autonomous business, in control of day-to-day decisions but able to access specialist insight from other design leaders including Williams Murray Hamm and Seymour Powell, invaluable to sustaining and growing our offer.

There are four principles that have driven our success: sticking to our core beliefs; deciding on a goal and going for it; knowing that the most important decisions are the people you hire; continuously reappraising services to meet market demand. As we approach the end of the decade we are at the top of our game. The key thing we've learnt is to listen to advice, follow our instincts and take decisions fast.

Disciplines	Integrated brand Marketing Internal communications Digital communications
Company description	We're an integrated creative communications agency driven by effectiveness. We bring together brand, marketing, digital and internal communications in one place. We change behaviours by engaging minds. Helping clients succeed is what matters most.
Office locations	London
Year established	1984

UNIFORM
Nick Howe
Managing Director
www.uniform.net

Uniform was established over a beer in the summer of 1998 a week after finishing university. Pete Thomas, Nick Bentley and I set up the business as there was no-one in the city who we wanted to work for. By the summer of 1999 we were in *Design Week's* 'Rising Stars' feature, and had a few decent projects under our belt.

From our initial meanderings as a multi-disciplinary agency, designing award-winning interiors to furniture and lighting exhibited at 100% Design, we soon realised the need to focus and consider our strategy for success. We built our CGI animation and film team with key corporate clients and began to grow. Our creative edge set us apart, and we soon won major international contracts.

When it came to planning, we were organised, detailed and thorough. There was a good natural balance between the three of us: Pete pushing us creatively, Nick managing production and me focusing on the vision and finances.

In 2006, we won a place on the DBA's 'Small/Medium/Large' programme, and this was a turning point for us as a business. It helped us focus on strategy and planning, and this has been critical to our success: for us, design was about problem-solving, and we felt we could work across any sector or discipline. We cemented our position as a Top 100 agency and built our design team alongside our digital team.

The last three years have seen us achieve many of our goals. We have grown in size but not at the expense of fee income and profit per head, the two key financial indicators of a successful agency. We have upped our creative standing in awards programmes from *Design Week* to the Roses, and in 2009 won 'Design Team of the Year' twice, at the How-Do and Roses Awards. We've also diversified into new sectors and moved higher up the food chain, delivering strategic-led projects nationally.

If I were to dish out advice – not something I'm used to, I might add – I would say: stay true to your roots; keep doing what you believe in; never settle for anything less than producing the best work. Spend as much time as possible designing the perfect business, and work on your own brand. You might think it's dull, but write the business plan, and then design it, just like a client project. Typeset it beautifully. If nothing else, the bank manager will love it.

Disciplines	Branding and identity Graphic design Exhibition design CGI, film and animation
Company description	Uniform is a leading brand, design and digital agency. We help our clients position themselves in their market, raise their profile and achieve their commercial objectives.
Office locations	Liverpool
Year established	1998

Section Seven:
The Clients

The clients

What is it like to be a client? Consultant and psychotherapist Jan Casey asked them. The results of her interviews with 20 experienced design buyers from a wide range of companies and organisations show that it's not always as easy as it looks.

Jan asked them what was good about working with design businesses, and what could be improved. She also explored what, ideally, they look for when they are appointing a design resource. What are design firms good at? Fresh, creative thinking; good consumer understanding and insights; interrogating briefs and thinking differently; being fun to work with. What are they not so good at? Commercial acuity; listening to the brief; swift delivery and proper scheduling; communication and presentation skills. And what are these design buyers looking for, over and above the basics? They would like design businesses to extend their strategic thinking and understanding, to see the bigger picture.

Some of the people Jan interviewed are designers by training, and have roles which are completely focused on design; several of them run in-house design units as well as commissioning creative services from external sources. Others have much broader marketing and management roles; for them, design activities are only a part of their remit. All of them are clear, however, in their views about working with designers.

MUSGRAVE RETAIL PARTNERS GB
Jemima Bird
Marketing Director
www.musgrave.ie

I find generally that design consultancies, more than advertising agencies, really understand what I want from brand building and development. Designers understand the essence of a brand and how to visually architect it in a meaningful way. They have an intrinsic understanding of how great design resonates with the consumer and how it can engage with employees.

That said, one of the utmost frustrations is that design consultancies can become navel-gazing purists, hanging on to a design to the detriment of commercial viability. Although ad agencies all too often throw the baby out with the bathwater to 'flog the product', design consultancies could learn a little from them and, to carry on the analogy, let the water out but leave the baby in, thereby delivering a brilliant creative solution that is also commercially effective.

In my experience there is a more considered and methodical approach to client management from the design side; I find briefs are delivered to a microscopic level of detail, with clear pricing for each stage and timings for delivery. It is rare that I am surprised by hidden costs or additional fees.

There is, however, a tendency for design consultancies to be become obsessive with 'brand guidelines', challenging work produced by other agencies. Given different mechanics and media are at play across my range of brand deliverables, it can become wearing to say the least to manage real-life expectations.

The approach to relationship engagement by design consultancies is second to none, with often even small pieces of work given the same passion and energy as larger projects. They tend to approach a relationship as a lifetime affair rather than a short- to mid-term partnership. There is a real sharing of cultural brand DNA between designers and clients in a way I have not experienced with ad agencies who, whilst caring passionately, always seem mindful that the account may shift to another agency at any time.

Other than the 'negative' points that I've listed, I tend to find that design consultancies have a real desire for partnership and to this end are my favoured part of the agency mix.

> Musgrave Group (a €5 billion business) partners entrepreneurial food retailers and food service professionals in Ireland, UK and Spain. In Great Britain, it partners 2,000 Budgens and Londis retailers.

LAND SECURITIES GROUP PLC
Anna Chapman
Head of Marketing, London Portfolio,
www.landsecurities.com

I have found when commissioning work for Land Securities that most designers are good at interrogating and understanding our briefs, but some are anxious, sometimes too anxious to ask questions. Consequently these designers can leave not having fully understood our requirements and can spend time exploring routes that may not answer the brief. However, there is another breed of designer who will argue until they are blue in the face that we have got the brief wrong. Both styles present their own challenges!

Designers can be very nervous when presenting their work. It seems that they don't have enough faith in their concepts, which is a shame, because they put their heart and soul into ideas that are usually excellent. My team and I accept this behaviour because we can see beyond it, but our corporate colleagues find it very weak and unconvincing. Designers must be confident and slick as well as talented. They need to demonstrate that they are in control and be aware that they will be compared with consultants who work for other areas of our business, and who present in a far more accomplished and confident way.

Brilliant design work takes time but speed of delivery is, I am afraid, the reality of our corporate lives. I am very aware that designers are conscientious, work hard and are earnest about delivering the right result but it can take a long time. I think that the quality/speed equation will always be the hardest nut to crack. Although I can usually schedule their time requirements, it is difficult for others to understand why a design concept can take six weeks, then the detailing another month again.

The relationship aspect of a project is fundamental and designers do this well, yet, as with their behaviour in presentations, when they are confronted with a room full of people they don't know, especially confident consultants from the property world, they can become uneasy and awkward.

I have been fortunate to have worked with some of the best designers around and design remains the most fun part of my job. It always has been and always will be.

> Land Securities is the UK's largest Real Estate Investment Trust. Its London portfolio includes famous sites, such as the Piccadilly Lights, and mixed-use developments in the West End, City and Victoria.

HM REVENUE & CUSTOMS
Julia Coulson
Head of Design, Marketing Communications
www.hmrc.gov.uk

Working with design agencies can be a positive experience. They are able to start a brief without preconceived ideas and have the potential to bring greater scope to projects. Fresh thinking away from civil service processes is always welcome and very often agencies will go the extra mile to solve problems.

The provision of status reports and account management is particularly valuable. We are almost always asked to disclose how much a campaign has cost. There has to be transparency and accurate records of how taxpayers' money is spent. When fees are involved, record keeping helps us get our internal clients to focus on rounds of amends.

But there are times when working with design agencies causes frustration, and they can fall short of expectation. For example, over-promising at the presentation and not admitting to lack of skills in a particular area; or meeting the 'big guns' at the start of a project but then only seeing lesser-skilled staff thereafter. For me, relationship chemistry with the agency is vital, yet often I need to make a special request to include the creative team in meetings. We need to be able to trust each other as well as establish how we are going to work together.

It seems there can be a lack of appreciation of the client's specialist knowledge. The Government sector has an abundance of people who really know their stuff and this can be overlooked. Some colleagues have said at times they feel agencies look down their noses at them and are dismissive of any input. Others have found that designers don't always listen to the brief. It is good to be challenged, but fundamentally if the brief has not been answered it is a waste of time.

We understand that creative ideas will be recycled. However, it is embarrassing for both parties to be shown presentations of rehashed work that still includes a previous client's name. This has happened on more than one occasion.

Finally it is perhaps worth emphasising the benefit of honest feedback – for both the client and the agency – to allow the relationship to grow.

> HM Revenue & Customs is a Government department that makes sure money is available to fund the UK's public services. It also helps families and individuals with targeted financial support.

VIRGIN ATLANTIC AIRWAYS
Joe Ferry
Head of Design
www.virgin-atlantic.com

Virgin Atlantic has witnessed genuine return on its investment in design. Unlike most airlines, I actively employ agencies that are naïve to the constraints of aircraft design in order to push the boundaries and maintain product differentiation. I then rely on my in-house team's expertise to focus on mitigating any risk. Some agencies have little appreciation of the skills and amount of work entrusted to in-house designers, which ultimately results in the design becoming a reality with minimum compromise to the design ambition. When an agency leaves the arena, the in-house team have to field any arising issues and protect the design ambition right through to implementation.

Designers need to be themselves and not pretend to be someone else. It's important for me to know what an agency is good at and where their limits are. If they specialise in interiors they should not aspire to also do graphics if they are not experts in that field: where areas of a project are not their discipline, they should partner with a specialist.

It's also imperative for a design agency to be honest. For example, if they are not happy with their work or there is an issue, they must let the client know, and as soon as possible. Visibility of costs and timings are important at the start and throughout a job. It can be difficult to be explicit sometimes, and it is the responsibility of the client to have an appreciation of what is involved, but it is important for me not to have any unpleasant surprises along the way.

Having a strategic understanding of how design fits into the big picture is also important. This is a gap that I have experienced with many agencies. If designers just focus on their project, it may not work within the wider scheme.

When I see someone with talent I ask the question, 'Can I work with you?' The relationship with an agency is key. It's like employing anyone. Someone could have the best talent in the world, but if we don't gel then it won't work.

> Award-winning Virgin Atlantic, launched in 1984, is one of the world's leading long-haul carriers. With bases at London's Heathrow and Gatwick Airports, it flies six million passengers every year to 30 destinations around the world.

INNOCENT
Dan Germain
Head of Creative
www.innocentdrinks.co.uk

We design lots of things in-house: packaging, web, ads, books and more. In 1999 we started off with one designer but these days there are seven of us in the in-house creative team. It's good to have options though. We like having the flexibility to do stuff ourselves or to work with agencies. Doing everything in-house would be too insular: although we're smart, we only generate a finite number of ideas on any given day. So we relish the chance to work with other smart people.

When we start working with a new agency a period of indoctrination is important, so they can really understand the context of what we do. Agencies might have five or 55 other clients so we can't expect them to know all about us. So we like to collaborate, by going off to work with agency creatives at their place, or getting them to come to ours.

Ultimately, we'll do whatever is necessary to get to the best piece of work. Collaboration (as mentioned above) is crucial, but we don't want to mollycoddle or get in the way, and our underlying entrepreneurial streak can sometimes encourage mild chaos. So we definitely need processes to keep things moving. We have someone who manages the workflow in-house and we want our agencies to be extremely organised at their end too. In terms of what this means in practice, I like meetings that don't take too long (after one hour I'm done). It's also good not to have too many people in the room: clear decision-making is better served by being focused. And I like to talk to the person who is doing the job, not someone who has to relay the information to someone else.

We are lucky that we've been around long enough to know some good agencies that we have worked with for a while. It's good to know that they have an understanding of our history and our DNA so that we can jump straight into the issue of the day.

> Innocent was founded in 1999. It makes smoothies and other healthy food and drink.

CISCO SYSTEMS
Clive Grinyer
Director of Customer Experience for Internet Business Solutions Group
www.cisco.com

As a consultant to Cisco's major clients I sometimes commission, but mainly broker, design, introducing the concept to a wide range of Cisco clients at senior management level.

I need agencies that cross the gulf between pragmatic, cost-effective delivery – which most achieve – and big thinking, the ability to extend understanding in a way that can be digested. It's this latter quality that opens the eyes and minds of my clients at Cisco. Agencies need to have both breadth and depth: maturity, the ability to communicate, to present ideas in the context of the end customer and bring to life the possibilities that design can deliver. Not enough design companies think 'big enough', not just at the designer level, but at design management level too. There have been times when I have chosen an agency where the designers think bigger than their leaders.

Design is an unfamiliar field to some clients and is sometimes seen as a commoditised machine. Recently a public sector client needed an agency which knew about web design but, more than this, they needed to understand how to demonstrate the total experience of the end-user, to explain value and purpose. Design agencies can be so focused on their specialised area that they don't see it in the context of a wider field. They need the ability to zoom from detail to strategy in a microsecond.

A classic problem can be the cultural differences between clients and agencies. I can explain to my clients why designers don't dress like accountants and that they need to embrace these visual beings often missing from business, but designers then need to deliver inspired thinking and with rigour. They can be so focused on their bit that they forget to listen to the parameters or restrictions.

The opportunity for design is enormous right now, but designers must grasp and intellectually understand that the tools they have can be applied to solving fundamental issues in business and the public sector.

Cisco Systems is the world's leading manufacturer of technology systems that power the internet. Based in California, it creates the platform for the 'human network' of communication, entertainment and transactions with innovative products.

BRITISH LIBRARY
Penny Hamilton
Head of Public and Regional Marketing
www.bl.uk

I have commissioned design both in my present role and also when working at the Natural History Museum and Tate. Although at the British Library we have an in-house studio, we do commission external design agencies for exhibitions, 3D design and graphics.

My goal is to achieve synergy between the look and feel of an exhibition and the way it's marketed, but it can be a struggle. It's difficult to know which creative discipline is the driver. Graphic designers are very brand aware but can't translate this into exhibition design, and exhibition designers think they can do the marketing creative but are steeped in the detail of their exhibition. When promoting an exhibition it is essential to grab attention immediately, but what works graphically within an exhibition won't always do the job on a poster. When I appoint two agencies which are expert in their different disciplines, tensions can arise and the solution is not always seamless.

What I like about working with external designers is their breadth of creative expression and free thinking. What I find frustrating is that they don't always read the brief. I have experienced designers returning after a briefing with concepts that don't fulfil our requirements. I explain which elements don't work, and yet they return with the same elements still included. It can sometimes be like pulling teeth!

I prefer working with designers who are not precious, respond to criticism and are prepared to talk about their design. I like to meet with the people actually doing the design work rather than an intermediary. When an account manager is involved, I'm never quite sure what is being fed back and I imagine that designers would prefer to hear comments directly from the client. Then they have the opportunity of explaining why they think the idea works.

One of the joys of the job is to work on interesting projects with creative people, and I love that 'light bulb' moment when I see a piece of really great design and know it's going to stand out in the crowd.

> The British Library is one of the great libraries of the world, containing both the memory of the nation and the DNA of civilisation. Its exhibitions and events create compelling stories and new ways of looking at ideas.

EUROSTAR
Richard Hill
Creative Direction
www.eurostar.com

We have just been through a series of design agency chemistry sessions and the companies that resonated with me are those who not only presented a good creative portfolio, but also used their time with us to really understand our specific requirements, then took the trouble to reiterate the brief back to us. The strongest contenders ended up being those that showed understanding and a genuine interest in finding solutions to our business challenges.

I often find that it's smaller agencies, that have broken away from bigger ones, that are better at listening. The structures for client handling in bigger organisations can end up creating Chinese whispers which removes the creatives from the realities of the coal face – they are much more effective when they are at it. That said, I definitely think there are some big agencies that have successfully adapted the small agency model to good effect.

On the account handling side, the most talented I have worked with are those that manage the relationship between the client and the agency but don't act as the 'front men' for the creatives. They get them in front of you to take the brief, and to take the feedback, and I think this improves both the speed and the quality of work that is presented.

However, agencies should be wary of how frustrating it can become when tempted to use a scattergun approach to creative development, generating ideas with no consideration to the budget or other constraints. I understand that the creative process can be part of refining the brief, and it is good to be challenged back by agencies, but work often comes back that is just too far from the mark.

That said, our creative industries are something to be genuinely proud of and I have been fortunate to work with some fantastically talented people. What they have in common is real creative flair, a passion to do things differently and a well-trained ear!

Eurostar is the high-speed passenger train service linking the UK with mainland Europe. The company celebrated its 100 millionth traveller in August 2009.

WAITROSE
Maggie Hodgetts
Head of Graphic Design
www.waitrose.com

I regularly commission packaging design and believe clients should do their homework, choosing a design company that does what they need, who understands the client-agency relationship and the way the organisation works. I know the work will be good when a designer gets excited and shows real enthusiasm for the project.

Occasionally a brief can seem dull, so I relish a designer who can think beyond it and present further than what is required: good design companies seek insight to validate the brief. Not many design agencies have planners. Introducing them into the process is a slow movement, but it's a wise investment as it really does inspire designers to produce highly creative work.

It helps me when designers reflect the brief before they proceed to the creative detailing. Some produce a stripped-down blueprint and visualise the scale and construction of the information hierarchy: the branding, the title, subtext and so on. Doing this helps colleagues who are less visually literate. It can also show up weaknesses in the briefing, which can be corrected before proceeding to concept design and colour visuals. Having a creative background, I am in the fortunate position of being able to see beyond a visual but this is not possible for everyone.

I prefer, and have had the most success with, design companies who are design principal-led, although account managers have grown in my esteem and good ones can really make a difference. However, to add value they need to understand the creative process and its execution. The best combination is where I get both the creative person and an attuned account manager.

Design companies need to be realistic with scheduling. It's important to respect the approval process and to allow for this in their timelines, but if asked for something that is impossible they should be brave and speak out.

Some projects don't have a huge value (you have to sell a lot of potatoes to cover some design budgets), so it's important for design companies to be realistic with their fees and see the value of a long-term relationship with us.

> Waitrose, the food retailer of the John Lewis Partnership, has 215 shops throughout the UK and a reputation for high-quality, good value food, and excellent service.

TRANSPORT FOR LONDON
Jon Hunter
Head of Design
www.tfl.gov.uk

It's key for design agencies to take the time to understand their clients. What we are effectively selling is all forms of public transport in London – be it on the Underground, Bus, DLR, Overground or even on foot – so it's important that designers engage with the network and have an intrinsic interest in our products. A lot of designers don't connect deeply enough to really understand us. They may be good at branding, typography and have great ideas but if the work they present doesn't resonate with me, it won't with anyone else in the organisation nor, most importantly, our customers.

Often, design agencies don't take the time to gain a full understanding of a brand. They seem to have a preconceived conception that all brands are the same, just with a different logo. They don't take time to understand core values or heritage but rather seek reinvention of the wheel. As an organisation, we have been around for 100 years and seen every idea done many times before. The reason why we still have a roundel and defined tube colours is because, although at times restrictive, in the simplest of terms they work.

For me it's important that I'm not presented with layers of people to deal with. I am happy to brief the account handler and designer, but from then onwards I like to liaise directly with the creative team. Dealing with account handlers distances my team and me from what we are trying to achieve, takes longer and information can get lost in translation. Going directly to the designer means there is no misunderstanding.

Getting absolute clarity from the brief is essential. Too many times I have briefed agencies who nod in agreement and then come back to me with a solution that is off brief. An example of this is a design solution that should cover London (the 'donut effect' as we call it) using only inner London icons such as the Gherkin and London Eye. This is, of course, avoidable if the brief is fully understood.

I also like to catch up with work in progress during all stages of a project. It's useful to touch base and make sure the design work is on track.

> Transport for London (TfL) is responsible for implementing the Mayor's transport strategy and managing transport services across the capital, for which the Mayor has responsibility. Some 10 million passengers use the bus, Tube and DLR network daily.

ROYAL MAIL
Marcus James
Head of Design and Editorial
www.royalmail.com/stamps

The creative process of designing stamps demands a lot from the designer: intelligence, sensitivity, creativity, and, above all, attention to detail. The topics can range from Charles Darwin through to Classic Album Covers; diverse, huge subjects that have to be distilled down into six or eight immediate, yet enticing pieces of design. During my time at Royal Mail a number of key criteria stand out as imperative in establishing valuable long-term working relationships that continue to deliver at the highest level over many years. Continuity in contact throughout a project can be a real issue, as all too often a project is relegated to a more junior designer once a commission begins; this can also be true of account managers, who can create an additional layer of interpretation between client and designer.

The digital world we inhabit today is a great tool for designers, but it can inhibit creativity. There seems to be this overwhelming temptation to jump straight on to the computer and produce visuals that look like finished products, rather than developing ideas through the exploration of the brief, subject and audience. Clever styling and graphic tricks will not cover up the absence of a strong creative solution. It is also essential to have the ability to integrate typography into design as a creative consideration rather than seeing it as something to add at the end.

On such a small canvas as a stamp every element has to earn its space. What the design agencies that we work with demonstrate so well is the ability to respond creatively in a fresh and inspired way rather than utilising a house style. This, coupled with an awareness of how other creative disciplines such as illustration, photography and fine art can be incorporated into their work, results in great design solutions.

It is testament to the tremendous skill of the designers and image-makers who design stamps that they creatively translate great and complicated stories onto a miniature canvas that acts as an ambassador for UK culture, heritage and design excellence.

> Royal Mail's Philatelic team produces stamps that are seen by millions of people and provide a snapshot of the nation's character through creative stamp design.

BRITISH HEART FOUNDATION
Louise Kyme
Design Manager
www.bhf.org.uk

When we have invited design consultancies to present their credentials, it's usually the designer's thought process that has impressed us the most – how they have understood a problem and why they did something a certain way – rather than any creative ideas they present. It makes us feel at ease knowing that a designer has thought about the nature of a problem. To me, problem-solving is what design is all about.

The most effective agencies are the ones that consider the client as part of the creative process. Clients are the direct link to the project's audience; after all they work with them on a daily basis. By working closely together, understanding the specific needs of the audience, the end design should help people, rather than be design for design's sake. This is even more the case working for a charity. It's easy to feel sensitive about design work that is rejected but it's important to understand your client's feedback in an objective way. If your client can't describe what is wrong, then you need to ask intelligent questions to help the client and ultimately the project.

In an ideal world, designers would also take more responsibility for the brand rather than concentrate on their individual design projects. It sometimes feels like designers see the brand as a restriction rather than understanding its positive intention. But once a designer has got a handle on these issues, then they can really start pushing the creative possibilities.

Generally I prefer working directly with designers rather than working through an account manager but this assumes, of course, that they have a clear and organised system in place. Certainly having to chase an agency on basic project processes is frustrating, no matter how creative the design work is.

The best client/agency relationship is when both parties know and appreciate each other. The agency should be investing in understanding the organisation's strategic goals, and the client should be investing in the designer's way of working and thinking. Then the relationship becomes a two-way process, with successful creative work as a result.

> The British Heart Foundation is the nation's heart charity, saving lives through pioneering research, patient care and vital information.

CHIVAS BROTHERS LIMITED
Neil Macdonald
Brand Director
www.chivasbrothers.com

I work with a number of design agencies and really value long-term relationships. I choose each agency according to their skill and craft. For whisky-blended products

I will use an agency where their focus is aesthetics; for malted whisky I look for one that can work effectively with layers of information.

We need to incorporate strict and practical considerations regarding packaging structure and so the best agencies are those who have expertise in both 3D and graphics, and who are able to build good relationships with our internal product design department. I prefer smaller agencies with a creative principal or, when dealing with large agencies, I make sure I seek out the creative leader; these individuals adopt ownership of our brand.

Some agencies are precious about minimum changes to their ideas, and then there are others that will just roll over and do whatever is requested. I look for people who argue for what they believe in but who counter this with commercial acumen. I always appreciate it when a designer speaks from the heart.

Some agencies focus purely on design; others offer strategic advice, but it doesn't work if it's just a 'bolt on' service. I have had experience where agencies offer strategy as an extra service but it can be superficial, rather like a coat of paint. Others, however, provide in-depth analysis, such as semiotics or a DNA brand breakdown, This really enhances the brief and can positively disrupt it, which is very welcome.

We are a complex, decentralised company, involved in a range of markets, and we are not dictatorial, which means that the brief is subject to change. I therefore need my agencies to be flexible and collaborative. Good results come from symbiotic relationships. We use a design roster system and welcome feedback on our performance from our agencies as well us feeding back our experience. This exercise creates promotes an open relationship, where we can each make changes and improve.

> Chivas Brothers is the Scotch whisky and premium gin business of Pernod Ricard – the world's co-leader in wine and spirits.

NHS INSTITUTE FOR INNOVATION AND IMPROVEMENT
Dr Lynne Maher
Director for Innovation
www.institute.nhs.uk

We commission service design predominantly, though we also commission product, graphic and brand design. Designers are fantastic at the initial stage of a project, looking at a situation and identifying the core problem. NHS staff often move quickly to the implementation phase without really understanding the problem; designers demonstrate to us the value of discovery. For example, we needed to create a dynamic poster to encourage health staff to wash their hands. Working with a design consultancy at the initial stage, we identified key errors in the system such as hand gel containers which were not labelled, or not visible, or empty. This significantly impacted on the recommended solution.

Designers are good at taking constructive criticism. When I've said of a presentation 'it's completely off the mark' or 'I hate it!' they have taken the feedback and moved forward in a positive way. However, they can be naïve about the complexity of health organisations. They add a lot of value by challenging the way we do things, but they should do this from a position of knowledge otherwise the value falls flat. For instance, they don't always understand our standard ethical conduct relating to patients and staff, and we have found that reference photos have been whizzed around the world without gaining written consent from the person photographed.

Sometimes designers are too idealistic – they will see a marvellous solution which will enhance the quality of care for the patient but they do not take into account the whole NHS context. We are facing massive financial challenges, and any design solutions must achieve improvements in both cost and quality.

Clarity of language and articulation of findings are areas in need of improvement, as well as writing skills. Recently a design consultancy presented their work which answered the brief perfectly and was high quality, but they presented their insights in a random way. When I contextualised their work the NHS audience loved it, but I had to make the links for them.

Design has a lot to offer the NHS and there are a number of fantastic examples that could be used to demonstrate this. I just wish they were widely published for NHS staff to see.

> The NHS Institute for Innovation and Improvement supports the UK's health service to transform healthcare for patients and the public.

BT
David Mercer
Head of Design
www.bt.com

I lead design and brand identity across BT, and commission design and creative projects in almost every design sphere from graphics and online through to products and usability. In all this there is one common factor: good design unquestionably results from good relationships, the chemistry between me, the client, and the creative designer. Many agencies don't seem to understand this dynamic, and think it's all about designing in isolation against a set brief.

Arriving at the right design solution is a truly interactive and iterative process between client and designer, with no barriers and an intuitive understanding between them. I work mainly with creative individuals – that's what delivers the difference – but I also understand and appreciate the value of agency account people to support and manage the delivery process. I sense such people are generally under-valued by the companies they work for, but not by me. I recall a number of instances where a really excellent project director has won the job for the agency or ensured a project's enhanced success.

A high standard of account and project management is critical in nurturing relationships between clients and agencies, or ensuring the smooth running of a project to time and on budget. This said, many design agencies are, in my experience, not well organised and rather unprofessional in the way they interact with clients. This must change if design wants to be more highly rated and taken seriously in the business world. Agencies need to become more receptive, reactive and rigorous in their everyday client dealings and delivery of work. It's worth remembering these three 'Rs'.

What I'm always looking for from a designer is something more than what I thought I wanted; a spark between the ears that cannot be pre-determined by training, planning or process; a piece of magic that has the power to change everything. This is what I believe makes design so different and so special from anything else I come across in the business world. My role is quite simply to facilitate and elicit that spark, that creative insight, that piece of magic. If we get it, then I know I've done my job.

> BT is one of the world's leading providers of communications solutions and services operating in 170 countries. It consists principally of four lines of business: BT Global Services, Openreach, BT Retail and BT Wholesale.

SCIENCE MUSEUM
Tim Molloy
Creative Director
www.sciencemuseum.org.uk

I've just worked out why some of the agencies that I don't want to work with seem to get masses of work. It comes down to the client/designer contract. A client needs a designer to do something they can't do themselves; they need a professional expert opinion. As that expert, designers must have the confidence to practice their trade, applying their experience and expertise, intelligence and energy. This does not necessarily mean they will please their client during the various stages of the job in hand. I don't work with designers that are ultimately trying to give me what they think I want. I work with designers that will challenge and cajole, for the ultimate good of the project. Many clients find these designers 'difficult', too hard to work with, but these are the individuals I seek. The grit that they add to the creative process exposes something glorious.

Science can be a very opaque activity to interpret: how would you explain chaos theory, black holes or nanotech? At the Science Museum we can marshal up to 15 different sorts of creative activity for a large, permanent exhibition, ranging from traditional notions of exhibition design to software development, creative writing, film, interactive media, poetry, sculpture, comedy, theatre, lighting and sound. The orchestration of these disciplines needs to be focused and cohesive, not just a battleground of activity, so a determined enthusiasm among designers to collaborate is an absolute essential.

How people respond to a brief is key for me. I react very badly to clichés and woolly thinking, the trademarks of an ill-thought-out quest for a quick solution.

I look everywhere and anywhere for intelligent conceptual thinking. The kind of thinking that can surprise me with a big idea will withstand being whipped, pressured and generally beaten up, yet remain strong, effective and memorable.

> The Science Museum aims to make sense of the science that shapes all our lives. Telling stories of science, engineering and medicine, enterprise and creativity, covering issues that matter to everyone now and in the future, it has an international reputation for promoting the value of innovative, collaborative design.

UKTV, LONDON
Matt Scarff
Head of Creative
www.uktv.co.uk

As Head of Creative, I lead the creative output for all ten of UKTV's new-look thematic channels both on and off air, from on-screen identity and promo campaigns, through to online and off air print and posters. The ten channels have very different personalities and I need my agency to have a clear understanding of the network and individual brands. This applies to all of those working on the account, from Production Coordinator and Creative through to Account Manager and Planner.

Having worked previously within an agency, and now as a client, I can vouch that clear communication and project management are vital on both sides of the fence. Good project directors are key to the success of the ongoing relationship, and it's essential they understand the television production process. Timelines are often quick, and spend levels can vary from the more traditional advertising approach. They need to fully grasp the creative process, so that they can set realistic timelines and filter my communication back to the agency creative heads of each channel, so that I can have one meeting rather than several and keep costs to the minimum. It's a skill on the part of an agency Creative Director or Account Manager to make the client feel they are as much involved in the project as the agency, and able to feel that they are making a positive contribution to the creative process.

Budgets are an important factor for any business, but my advice is to avoid these conversations when immersed in creative presentations and pitches. It tends to close down the creative discussion and can provoke the wrong reaction or even terminate an idea. Costs do need to be discussed, but make sure the client loves the idea and couldn't live without it before you start to talk money. That said, it is important not to sell in an idea which can't be produced within an agreed budget, but do remember that a client will always want to be part of the next big thing. Be brave and make them – and you – famous!

> UKTV is an independent commercial joint venture between BBC Worldwide and Virgin Media. Attracting 36.5 million viewers each month, the network consists of ten distinctive channel brands: Watch, GOLD, Dave, Alibi, Yesterday, Blighty, Eden, Home, Really and Good Food.

HABITAT
Theo Williams
Creative Director
www.habitat.co.uk

I commission design at several different levels: renowned individuals who have specific 'creative handwriting' such as Matthew Hilton and Nigel Coates; established studios who have been in the industry for years; right through to new talent which I find through student shows or competitions.

When I commission an established designer or studio, I am interested in creatives who have a specialist knowledge of their design or area they work in. Someone designing a light, for instance, must have the ability to not only work with shape and form but also have an intricate understanding of the technical capabilities of the materials, industry standards, light emissions and so on.

I really enjoy working with young talent for the absence of experience they have which adds a freshness to their ideas, yet I often find that they lack the rudimentary knowledge of product materials, for example the limitations and requirements needed for mass production. To overcome this, if a young designer shows promise I will bring them into the Habitat creative studio to work with us for a while, so we can guide and mentor them. It shows them the process that a design is one element of many to deliver a product to the shop floor and not the only thing.

In general there is definitely a lack of manufacturing knowledge and experience in the design world. I come across designers not understanding that the production of an item requires a completely different approach to a limited edition piece or assuming that if a design can be rendered it can be made.

I also find that young designers have a lack of understanding regarding business matters. Many designers don't have full appreciation of the costs involved in producing and delivering a product, for instance the difference between the wholesale cost and its retail-selling price, the effect of a discount, and the packaging and shipping costs. This lack of understanding will have a direct impact on whether the designs they are producing will be sufficiently commercial, so I ensure that I choose designers not only for their creative ability but also for their business acumen.

> Habitat is an international brand selling inspirational yet affordable furniture and home accessories for everyday living, creating collections which give people the confidence to express themselves in their homes.

FORD MOTOR COMPANY
David Woodhouse
Chief Designer/Design Executive, Strategic Concepts Group
www.ford.co.uk

In times past we commissioned design research in order to gauge differences in trends and approach from the work being executed internally, to get alternative design proposals. Today, when we commission externally it's less about being provided with alternative design proposals and more to do with philosophy, rationale, trending and ideas. Generally we brainstorm a project internally and then work with an external agency or creative who might be a product designer or firm, but equally they could be from the spheres of architecture, graphics, branding, movies, fine art, politics, city planning... you name it!

Today we are much more collaborative with our agencies; it's not about them going away with a brief and coming back with a finite solution. Looking back to times with other companies, some agencies acted as though they had the right to get regular briefs and would appear from their studios with work that wasn't good enough or was irrelevant to what was needed. Now we look for agencies to inspire us, who will offer us a killer insight, an aspect of surprise and delight that we would not have thought of on our own, which we can then embed into our internal work.

We want to be entertained and want designers and agencies who can bring something to the party that hasn't been seen before. Something worthwhile always comes from a humorous idea or from an element of eccentricity, which can be more difficult to generate within a corporate setting. At the point of first meeting an external designer or agency, the energy in the room, their engagement, their emotional reaction and connection with us rate as the most important ingredients on the list. The relationship that we seek with our external agencies is one of partnership, collaboration, and fun, so personality and trust are key.

Going forward, I believe collaboration with enlightened, inspiring, creative partners is paramount. And the more cross-discipline and removed they are from our own specific automotive world, the better. Inspiration is key. Unique market and customer insight is paramount. The automotive design world is beginning to mirror the greater context of immediacy, rapid communication, no-limits understanding and inspiration. So may it continue.

> Strategic Concepts Group at Ingeni is Ford's London design centre. It has a mixed-functional, in-house team across design, planning, marketing and engineering, and creates new product proposals.

XEROX EUROPE
Les Wynn
Manager of Industrial Design/Human Factors
www.xerox.co.uk

What I require from consultancies in the UK has changed over recent years. I have an internal design team, and I also put a volume of design work out to companies in the Third World, India for example. However, the work delivered tends to be strong on skill rather than knowledge and insight. I look to UK consultancies to have depth of understanding, to push the brief at an early stage, build the relationship and help define what needs to be done. It is no longer enough for a UK consultancy to rely on design skills alone; skills are a commodity and can be bought by the hour. Knowledge and understanding of the real needs of the client business, and delivery of solutions to fit that need, are core to survival.

If UK consultancies want to stay competitive they need to be integrated into the client's thinking. It's the difference between being a trade and a profession. Some of the good UK consultancies are aware of this new business model, where they sit on the same side of the table as the client. They do not produce multiple concepts for the client to choose from; they produce one concept with a well thought out rationale. This means that the agency cannot shirk responsibility by blaming the client for choosing the wrong one, and the client must listen and act on the input from the agency. It requires trust and honesty on both sides.

I need a consultancy to be integral to our business strategy. Unfortunately the word 'strategy' is over used. Often consultancies describe themselves as strategic, when what they are saying is simply that design is important. To be strategic, a consultancy must know our business better than we do, and identify real opportunities and solutions in the wider context of the global market. The best consultancies in the UK bring great design management to a project, not just raw creativity. They are adaptable in the tools and processes they use and are able to tailor them to the needs of our company.

Xerox is the global leader in document management, offering the widest range of technology, consulting services and solutions in the industry. Founded in 1906, it has over 57,000 employees and an annual revenue of $17.6 billion.

Section Eight:
The Design Bodies

The design bodies

Industry membership associations and design support bodies exist to make sure that the design sector grows and develops as it should, and they are well worth engaging with. As a taster, here are some thought-leadership views from a number of them. They were asked to consider what design businesses need to do in order to remain competitive for the future. Their responses are enlightening.

As well as advising design firms to make improvements in their strategic capabilities, commercial understanding and business planning, they propose a greater engagement in risk-taking for themselves. They suggest the delivery of higher-level work for their clients, helping them to transform their businesses and organisations. They highlight the importance of the global stage, and of international competition. They identify the need for collaboration with other design disciplines to meet clients' future needs. They recommend the constant monitoring of social and market trends. Finally, they make the case for much sharper professional practice skills, including more effective presentations.

Overall they caution that, if they are to succeed in future, design businesses need to become just that: businesses.

BRITISH DESIGN INNOVATION (BDI)
Maxine J Horn
CEO
www.britishdesigninnovation.org

Take a few entrepreneurial risks and become your own client. There is no better way of proving your creative ability and business acumen than by doing it for yourself, whether that is retail design firms trying their hand at pop-up shops, industrial, service innovation and digital firms developing their own products and propositions, or graphic firms developing and licensing material. Additionally, entrepreneurial collaboration across disciplines results in more rounded propositions, where it is recognised that no brand, product or service ever came to market without the core skills of several expert parties.

Many design firms have built excellent companies purely on 'fees for service', but this has always been a vulnerable model, subject to the ups and downs of economic climate where projects and income can disappear overnight. Design firms savvy enough to build a licensing structure or proposition brokerage model might just find new means of increasing their longer-term remuneration and building tangible assets, adding licenses and patents to their balance sheet.

BDI has enabled industrial and service design firms to move closer to the innovation space and to believe in themselves as knowledge providers and even investors (of skills and time) in start-up and Small and Medium Enterprise (SME) businesses and, through licensing, as investors in corporate brands. The 'Shared Risk and Shared Reward' model is making a more regular appearance at the negotiating table, and research and development (R&D) tax credits have opened up more opportunities for design firms to become their own client in a way barely considered before. There are few ways to truly future-proof a business, but taking risks and adopting a collaborative and entrepreneurial attitude certainly offers far more potential to earn more stable income than solely relying on fees for services.

Accredited by the Institute of Knowledge Transfer, BDI is the trade organisation for leading industrial designers, service designers and innovation professionals, promoting its members' creative expertise, knowledge and experience. Most BDI member company directors have ten years' minimum experience in their specialist discipline and sector: membership is by peer approval or recommendation. BDI is the most influential membership organisation of its kind. A cooperative not-for-profit trade body, owned and driven by its members, it represents those top-end strategic designers and design companies, R&D teams and innovation directors in industry and academia who deliver most value to industry and the consumer through product and service innovation. BDI facilitates accumulative industry-wide activity worth over £100 million per annum. It operates a national website and 12 regional portals, which together receive 18 million hits a year from 1.5 million unique visitors. BDI reaches an additional 30,000 companies through its free monthly *Newswire* subscription.

D&AD
Tim O'Kennedy
Chief Executive
www.dandad.org

For decades now, Britain has punched well above its weight in any competition decided by creativity, across pretty much all walks of design and communications in general. This is both a good thing, and a bad thing. Good, because the culture of creativity is firmly established here, and creativity has come to be relatively highly valued by our consumers and businesses alike. So the basic atmospheric conditions for design businesses are pretty good. But success can also lead to complacency, and a more insular perspective than is healthy. 'We've always been great, therefore we'll always be great' is a dangerous non-sequitur.

The UK is at a turning point: we must decide whether to be self-referential and perhaps a little smug, or to recognise and be energised by the fact that excellence in design is not our sole preserve. For many years, we've seen breathtaking design work from Germany, France, Italy, the Netherlands and the Nordic countries, to name just a few. And now, as the developing world evolves from manufacturing-led to creatively led economies (a process that is happening very rapidly) we're beginning to see startlingly fresh design thinking from further afield: Japan, of course, but now also South Korea, Singapore, China, India and South America among others.

UK design has the opportunity to re-assert itself on the global stage but, if that's going to happen, we'll need our work to compete on the global stage, and be informed by thinking, by influences, by design cultures and, yes, by technologies from far over our immediate horizon. A key survival skill for anyone in this business is this: judge your output not just against what's in your back yard, but against the very best design in the world.

D&AD exists to perpetuate brilliance in commercial creativity. Founded in 1962 by a group of London-based designers and art directors, including David Bailey, Terence Donovan, Alan Fletcher and Colin Forbes, the group was dedicated to celebrating creative communication, rewarding its practitioners and raising standards across the industry. D&AD continues that tradition to this day through its internationally renowned Yellow and Black Pencil awards, the Annual, and its Membership. Underpinning all activities is the fundamental belief that it is the responsibility of the industry to help nurture the next creative generation. As a not-for-profit organisation, D&AD invests in ambitious and influential education programmes that yield tangible benefits for industry and practitioners, both for students and for tutors and course leaders. The D&AD professional development programmes are about the practice of creativity, with workshops and training designed to encourage experimentation and exploration, to develop skills and challenge complacency.

DESIGN BUSINESS ASSOCIATION (DBA)
Adam Fennelow
Development Director
www.dba.org.uk; www.effectivedesign.org.uk;
www.dbaexpertsregister.org.uk

Design businesses are exactly that – businesses. Too many are started without any consideration for how the company will operate, just concern for creative freedom. Creativity obviously means a lot in this industry, but to remain competitive you need business acumen. Successful design businesses in the future will have to do what they have always done – only more so – as the range of competition increases.

The three main issues you will need to address are:

1. Business finances: your creativity counts for nothing if you are not making money. You need to track projects efficiently and be aware at all times of how much profit a job is worth to you. A sound financial advisor with a knowledge of the design industry is essential, someone who will ask awkward questions like 'why?' and 'how?' in Board/management meetings. Likewise business consultants are useful to give you an external view on what you are doing.

2. Measure your success: every project has a goal behind it, and the client will be measuring the success of your work. You need to understand the matrix they are using before you start work, and ask to be included in the reviews once completed. You will then build up a library of case studies illustrating your

effectiveness in a language that clients appreciate. These are worth their weight in gold for new business development.

3. Positioning: there is a plethora of design businesses in the UK, all claiming to be unique. To be successful, a design business actually has to do to itself what it does for its clients: you need to differentiate your business from your competitors. Clients are dazzled by the array of choice available to them and will always look for something different. What is your USP?

The Design Business Association (DBA) is the trade association for the UK design industry. It helps design consultancies become more professional and profitable by offering a range of industry specific membership services, training courses, events and awards. Its services for members range from free legal help to benchmarks on charge-out rates and salary levels. DBA training courses and events are for both design professionals and buyers of design: they cover business issues within design and are led by many of the contributors in this book. The annual DBA Design Effectiveness Awards are judged by clients and focus on the commercial impact of a design project. They are sought after by designers and clients alike because they are rewards for effectiveness rather than pure aesthetics. DBA member companies cover all design disciplines and are the cream of the UK design industry. A directory of members can be found on the DBA website.

DESIGN COUNCIL
David Godber
Deputy Chief Executive
www.designcouncil.org.uk

Design businesses have a lot to think about if they want to succeed. So what would I do?

I'd be optimistic. A lot of old ideas have stopped working, so business is unusually receptive to new ones.

I'd be realistic. A business can't run on creativity alone. It needs targets, future plans and a story for the bank manager. You owe your team nothing less.

I'd look at what's fantastic. There's some amazing work out there and many awards have been won. Start with 'That's brilliant' and you should be in about the right place.

I'd seek to understand a client's business and what it is they want to invest in. Everyone pitches credentials, but what value will you add to a client's business? Set tangible business objectives for your clients and you'll win business.

I'd make sure my presentation skills match my design skills. If you can't present an idea, a client won't buy it. Today, there's more competition and it's chasing fewer clients. A good first impression and pitch has never mattered more.

I'd join in with networks. Many networks exist to support businesses in general, and also in specific disciplines. There are also plenty of people out there who have been helped, and are now happy to help. Don't be afraid to ask for a little time over a large cup of coffee!

I'd be practical. Finance, IT and HR may not be fun, but getting it right makes all the difference. Time spent brushing up business skills is time well spent.

Finally, I'd be curious. The more you know about design, and also culture, industry, politics and everything else, the better you'll get at making great ideas work. To misquote Kipling (or was it Billy Bragg?), what do they know of design who only design know?

The Design Council helps designers, businesses and public services perform better to make Britain more creative, sustainable and competitive. As well as promoting the value of design, it provides:

- Coaching for private and public sector decision makers, through support programmes that give them the skills to spot design opportunities, brief designers and manage projects.
- Practical design responses to major national challenges by creating opportunities for designers, business people, public sector managers and others to come together and demonstrate design's potential in areas from healthcare and crime to water conservation.
- Backing for the design sector through leadership on improving design skills and education, and active investment in initiatives that strengthen the sector.

DESIGN MANAGEMENT INSTITUTE (DMI)
Dr Thomas Lockwood
President
www.dmi.org

The design organisation of the future will be one that is focused on collaboration and integration. Design per se is no longer about single discipline solutions to simple problems; rather, it involves multiple design disciplines, multiple touch points and diverse teams of people working together. This is because projects are rarely just 'stand alone'; more often they are part of a holistic customer experience. Design will be seen more as enabling experiences, and enabling innovations, so it must be considered as part of a larger initiative. Therefore, the designer and design manager must be skilled and committed to integrated work methods and processes in the future. In this way they can add value and be assured of a continuing important role in product, service and experience creations.

The other area for the design business to be focused on in the future is in business transformation. The global recession forced many executives to rethink their entire business models. The new innovations, and even new business focus, must be conceptualised, visualised, prototyped, tested and revised, often many times. This creates a significant opportunity for designers and design thinkers to play an important role. Much future work will be in conceiving new business scenarios, as much as individual project implementation. So the design business should be open to the fuzzy front-end, seemingly poorly briefed projects, and to expanding the scope of influence. Since everything needs to be designed, and the future is not likely to mirror the past, the future of the design business is deep and wide.

Since 1975, DMI has been committed to improving organisations worldwide through the effective integration and management of design and design principles for economic, social and environmental benefit. It connects the world's design leaders to the inspiration, knowledge and community they need to succeed. It connects design to business, to culture, to customers – to the changing world – and brings together educators, researchers, designers and leaders from every design discipline, every industry and every corner of the planet: the results are transformational. DMI has members in 44 countries, produces conferences and seminars, conducts research and publishes a practitioner magazine and an academic journal. It has produced over 800 articles about the role of design in business, 33 teaching case studies for Harvard Business School, five books and over 100 conferences. Over the decades, DMI has been the place where the world's most experienced, creative, and ambitious design leaders gather to share, distil and amplify their knowledge.

DESIGN PARTNERS
Andrew Summers CMG
Chairman
www.uktradeinvest.gov.uk

Data has shown that design companies and design-led companies which work internationally are also the most successful in their home markets. This comes from being open to much tougher competition and having to do everything better: marketing, finance, systems, people management, innovation and, of course, design.

For small businesses, there are considerable risks in working internationally, especially those of handling different market conditions and stretching scarce resource. But the benefits of greater market opportunities, of having to develop a clear competitive proposition, and of exposing yourself to worldwide influences are likely to put you in a stronger long-term position. And you don't have to be large to build a global reputation: some of the most successful UK-based design consultancies in the world have less than 50 people.

The UK has the benefit of providing a strong backdrop from which to pursue international business. We have a long design tradition and are known for being business-focused, good at problem-solving, and providing creative imagination, often quirky. London, especially, has the reputation as one of the world's great creative cities, and the profusion of creative activities in the capital – from theatre to TV, film to fashion, art to architecture, and design to digital media – creates something special which is valuable in promoting the UK around the world. We need to make sure this is done in an accessible, and not arrogant, way, but it is a good starting point to get through the door of prospective clients.

Much of this has grown up from the bottom. Government policy has helped, especially over the last decade, but the strength comes from the great creative abilities of so many people from so many cultures working in so many fields. Economics and politics have some short-term effect, but the underlying strengths of UK creativity and design are with us for the long term.

Design Partners works to increase the UK's international design business. It is a partnership of the main UK design bodies and Government bodies involved in supporting UK designers and design companies internationally. The main focus is on design consultancies (in the fields of product and industrial design, graphic design, branding, digital design, interior design and exhibition design) and on designer-makers (in the fields of furniture, lighting, ceramics, textiles, jewellery, metal, wood and glass). Design Partners acts as the advisory group on design to UK Trade & Investment, and is a key part of the international marketing strategy for the creative industries. It works mainly through British Embassies around the world, supporting exhibitions, seminars, outward and inward missions and providing information on market opportunities.

DESIGN WALES
Gavin Cawood
Operations Director
www.designwales.org; www.seeproject.org

Since 1994 we have acted as an independent honest broker in over a thousand meetings where clients were discussing a project with design consultants for the first time. On every occasion, what the client most wanted to see was the potential for their own project. The only way to do this is by showing aspirational examples of work from the same market sector they are in.

If designers get this right, clients will be prepared both to pay more and to seek them out to make use of their expertise within a specific market sector. This will not happen by accident.

Like any business, in order to remain competitive and realise growth design businesses must undertake proper business planning processes. This should not simply be for the amount of work they need to find to pay the bills, but to make the most of their strengths and to build a profile in specific target markets. In essence, they must give clients a strong reason to commission them over and above cost.

Design Wales is an international centre of expertise for design support and related national and regional policy. Activities include:

- Support services for business. Delivered on behalf of regional economic development offices and independent business organisations, these workshops, training courses and events support industry in understanding and managing design issues.
- Design policy and programme advice for regional economic development offices. Helping regional economic development offices understand the role of design, develop their own regional policy and support programmes, and train local business support staff.
- Design networks in the UK and Europe. Leading a number of design networks in Europe and the UK provides engagement with a broad spectrum of partners and insight to global best practice in supporting design within industry.
- Design policy research. Building understanding of the role of design support and promotion in economic development at a policy level. Since 2002, Design Wales has hosted the bi-annual International Workshop on Design Support.

NEW DESIGNERS
Isobel Dennis
Director, Upper Street Events
Event Director, New Designers
www.newdesigners.com; www.upperstreetevents.co.uk

Remaining competitive now and in the future follows simple rules, none of which is exhaustive.

Apart from the quality of your work, how you communicate with a client, customer or future employer – whether it be electronically, on paper or face-to-face – is critical. If they're not impressed with your personal presentation (and I don't mean how you dress) it will affect their opinion of you, and this may be before you've had a chance to present your work.

Do your research: gathering information, broadening your knowledge base, and looking outside the obvious will keep your work fresh, competitive and relevant.

If you're able to speak directly to the client before a presentation, ask open questions to gather more information: Who? What? Where? How? Why? Look at websites, including your client's competitors, and understand who they are. Look for a 'mission statement' as it can give you a simple, but important, insight into their long-term strategies. Prepare well.

Sign up to relevant e-newsletters, including city ones, as they will give you short, sharp, sound-bite news on issues that may affect, enhance and give the edge to the project you are working on. Differentiation is key in most projects whether it be a commission for jewellery or an architectural brief.

Try not to hide behind glossy technology. Don't dismiss the simple craft of drawing and the ability to drop ideas and sketches directly on to paper, as it still remains a powerful tool. It shows how you think, how in tune you are with the project and your level of energy for it.

Finally, relationship-building is critical, and will give you the competitive edge. Look after your clients: people like to work with someone they like, can trust, who is reliable, understands their needs, responds to their business, and who listens and delivers.

New Designers, organised by Upper Street Events, showcases the best in graduate design. The UK is a world leader in design education, and continues to produce talented design graduates. Every July in London at New Designers, some 3,500 newly graduated designers come together representing the top 200 design courses from across the nation to meet industry employers, the media, trend predictors and a design hungry public. It is seen as an essential resource for all who attend and an invaluable springboard for all who exhibit. The event runs for two weeks, with nine design zones and two prestigious awards evenings. It is supported by industry partners who recognise the importance of nurturing design and creativity for the future of their businesses. From animation to architecture, graphics to glass and fashion to furniture, New Designers is about vibrant content, celebration and reputation. It is an event for fresh thinking and aspiration.

ROYAL COLLEGE OF ART (RCA)
Paul Thompson
Rector and Vice Provost
www.rca.ac.uk

Like any professionals, designers must never let their antennae droop for one moment. They have to be acute observers of social and market trends. They must ensure that their studios draw from a strong well-spring of creative talent, and never become stale or complacent.

Whether in the field of architecture or communications, it is vital to manage growth: don't take on more projects than you can deliver at the highest creative and service levels. Being over extended, and delivering lacklustre projects because you're too busy to create something really fresh, kills reputation and ultimately competitiveness.

One of the world's leading universities of art and design, the Royal College of Art sits at the heart of an exceptional network, linking creativity with business innovation. Companies looking for ways in which to engage with the work of the College, whether working directly with students and staff on sponsored projects, supporting innovative research or using its facilities, have a number of opportunities:

- *InnovationRCA* enables the College's business partners to innovate more effectively, by accessing the knowledge and talent of the RCA.
- *Design London* combines world-class creativity and expertise in design engineering from the RCA, and engineering, technology and business from Imperial College London.
- *The Helen Hamlyn Centre* provides a multi-disciplinary focus for people-centred design and innovation by undertaking practical research and projects with industry.
- *Rapidform* brings together the College's digital design, prototyping and manufacturing technologies and makes them available to SMEs in the Greater London area.

ROYAL INSTITUTE OF BRITISH ARCHITECTS (RIBA)
Harry Rich
Chief Executive
www.architecture.com

The next few years are going to be challenging and increasingly competitive for UK design businesses, both in the UK and internationally. The Royal Institute of British Architects' (RIBA) surveys of the architectural profession and RIBA Chartered Practices, which operate internationally, reveal sea-changes to clients, forms of procurement and commissioning as well as environmental and technological changes and a global shift of economic power from West to East.

For any design business to survive, let alone be competitive and grow, it must think like a business:

1. Think radical. Conventional wisdom is less useful in changing times, so think differently and be counter-intuitive.
2. Be clear about value. Demonstrate real benefits and value to your clients and their customers and end-users. Don't compete on lowest cost, but on best value.
3. Be adaptable but focused. Be prepared to change, but keep to what you are good at or only diversify into areas you have something unique to offer.
4. Watch the bottom line. Carefully manage your costs and credit control. Invoice often and quickly. Have contingency plans in place to be able to deal quickly with a declining situation, including writing off bad debts and reducing staff and overheads.
5. Know your competition. Benchmark yourself against your competitors and peers. Competition will be much higher in tough times and in any attractive new markets, so you need to stay ahead of the game.
6. Look to the future. Learn new skills and develop new contacts. Market, network, keep on the look-out and set yourself up for any new opportunities and changing markets.
7. Keep positive. Hold on to an upbeat and 'can-do' attitude. Be the person with the solutions not the problems. Present yourself as an enabler, someone who adds value.

> As the voice of architecture in the UK since its foundation over 175 years ago, the Royal Institute of British Architects (RIBA) champions good design to Government, the public and the construction industry. It believes that everyday life can, and must, be improved through better-designed buildings and communities, and that the architect's role is crucial. The Institute provides support for its 40,500 members through a network of regional offices, nationally and worldwide, in the form of training, tailored services, publications and events, and it sets standards for the education of architects, both in the UK and overseas. Its annual award schemes recognise outstanding architecture and culminate in the RIBA Stirling Prize televised by Channel 4. At its London headquarters, the RIBA helps the public learn more about architecture through information services, a book shop and a world-class library that includes an unrivalled collection of books, photographs, drawings and manuscripts.

THE SORRELL FOUNDATION
Sir John Sorrell CBE
Co-Chair
www.thesorrellfoundation.com

Ask yourselves these questions:

1. *Uniqueness*. What is special about our business? Why should someone give us the job? What is our added value? Are we competing on price or skill? Do we have more expertise or market knowledge than our competitors? Are we better organised or more creative? Be brutally honest. If you don't know your point of differentiation you won't be competitive for long.

2. *Planning*. Why are we in business? Is it for lifestyle, money, to change the world or what? Where do we want to be in a year, three years, ten years? How are we going to get there? You need to understand your motivations and have a plan for getting to where you want to be.

3. *Creativity*. How can we embed a creative culture in the business? What can we do to help our people develop their skills? Creativity should be at the heart of your business. The best creative businesses don't just happen: they develop deliberate strategies which affect their values and culture.

4. *Systems*. Could we be more organised? Are our systems as good as they could be? Do we know our financial situation all the time? Are we good at the details of business? Do we have brilliant marketing and new business systems? If you have good systems in place for managing time, money, people and premises, you can approach your work for clients with absolute focus.

5. *People*. Have we got the right staff? Are they brilliant individually? Can they work as a team? What will we do if key players leave? What is our recruitment policy? People will make or break your business. Look after them, be generous and expect a lot in return. Build a team which wants to be successful together. And celebrate success when it happens.

The Sorrell Foundation aims to inspire creativity in young people and improve the quality of life through good design. It works with young people in primary and secondary schools, academies and universities, as well as with those not in school. The Foundation supports Building Schools for the Future, the Primary Capital and Academies programmes to help pupils create briefs for their new schools. Other work includes Designing Out Crime, an investigation with young people into issues concerning crime, and the Young Design Programme in which student designers work as consultants for pupils in schools. The Sorrell Foundation Young Design Centre at Somerset House, London, provides a base for hosting visits and workshops with young people from across England. The Foundation draws on an expert network of designers and architects, many of whom have worked with young people as clients.

UK DESIGN ALLIANCE
Lesley Morris
Head of Design Skills, Design Council
Director, UK Design Alliance
www.designcouncil.org.uk/gooddesignpractice

How can the UK design industry remain as world class in the future as it is today? You may well think the industry is doing fine, but in the face of increasing competition and new applications for design, designers need to be even better at what they do. They are increasingly called on to do more than just design. They need strategic business awareness to influence clients' thinking and a deeper understanding of the context for their work. They need to appreciate their role in environmentally sustainable production. They have to be comfortable working with non-designers in pursuit of innovation, be they technologists or users with ideas that need to be orchestrated and refined into tangible solutions to problems. And they need sharper business and professional practice skills alongside the craft and technical ability designers already have in abundance.

At the Design Council, we've been working with partners across the design sector to see how skills can be developed to address the industry's future needs. The UK Design Alliance is one of the results and its partners are supporting both industry and education to deliver the initiatives and projects necessary to trigger change. These practical ideas include linking design education more firmly to professional practice, making that practice more robust through training and rewarding the best design teaching in schools. The Good Design Practice campaign is raising awareness and promoting the need for these actions, particularly to designers who need to carry on learning after they leave education, so their careers stay on an upward trajectory and their businesses flourish.

The UK Design Alliance, founded by the Design Council and Creative & Cultural Skills, is a group of design sector bodies, working together to help develop the professional skills the industry needs. The Alliance is running the Good Design Practice campaign and its partners are supporting design education in schools and colleges as well as encouraging designers to undertake professional training and development.

Section Nine:
The Reference Library

The reference library

1 UK DESIGN MEMBERSHIP BODIES

The UK design sector is fortunate in having a number of excellent membership associations and organisations; some are for corporate members, others are for individuals. As well as those listed below, you can find details of many others, including discipline-specific and regional design networks, on the Design Council website: www.designcouncil.org.uk.

- BDI (British Design Innovation) For industrial and service designers, innovation professionals. Various membership options. www.britishdesigninnovation.org
- BIID (British Institute of Interior Design) For interior designers. Corporate and individual membership. www.biid.org.uk
- CSD (Chartered Society of Designers) Professional body for designers of all disciplines. Individual membership. www.csd.org.uk
- D&AD (British Design and Art Direction) For people in design and advertising. Individual membership. www.dandad.org
- DBA (Design Business Association) Trade association for the design industry, all disciplines. Corporate membership. www.dba.org.uk
- RIBA (Royal Institute of British Architects) For architects. Individual and Chartered Practice membership. www.architecture.com
- RSA (Royal Society for the encouragement of Arts, Manufactures and Commerce) Develops and promotes thinking on human fulfilment and social progress. Fellowship. www.thersa.org
- SBID (Society of British Interior Design) For interior design. Corporate and individual membership. www.thesocietyofbritishinteriordesign.org
- UKWDA (UK Web Design Association) For the web design and new media sector. Corporate and individual membership. www.ukwda.org

2 INTERNATIONAL DESIGN MEMBERSHIP BODIES

There are also many international design organisations which can supply useful information and knowledge, and which often provide networking opportunities through their events and conferences. Here is a selection.

For design professionals and design businesses

- DMI (Design Management Institute) For designers, educators, researchers, design leaders. Individual membership. www.dmi.org
- ICOGRADA (International Council of Graphic Design Associations) For graphic design. Membership: design associations, companies, individuals. www.icograda.org
- ICSID (International Council of Societies of Industrial Design) For industrial design. Membership: design associations, companies, individuals. www.icsid.org
- IFI (International Federation of Interior Architects and Designers) Organisation for interior design organisations. www.ifiworld.org
- IDSA (Industrial Designers Society of America) For industrial designers. Individual membership. www.idsa.org
- PDA (Pan-European Brand Design Association) For brand design agencies. Corporate membership. www.pda-europe.com

For design associations and other bodies

- BEDA (The Bureau of European Design Associations) The organisation for European design organisations. www.beda.org
- ICOGRADA (International Council of Graphic Design Associations) For graphic design. Membership: design associations, companies, individuals. www.icograda.org
- ICSID (International Council of Societies of Industrial Design) For industrial design. Membership: design associations, companies, individuals. www.icsid.org
- SEE (Sharing Experience Europe) European network on regional and national design policies. www.seeproject.org

3   UK DESIGN AND CREATIVE SECTOR SUPPORT

The UK also has an enviable level of design support organisations, largely Government-funded. Here are some of the bodies which operate in both the design sector and in the wider creative services arena. Again, the Design Council website contains details of other support organisations: www.designcouncil.org.uk.

Design

- Design Council UK national strategic body for design. www.designcouncil.org.uk
- Design Partners Design Partners works to increase the UK's international design business. www.uktradeinvest.gov.uk
- Design Wales Centre of expertise for design support and related national and regional policy. www.designwales.org

- Northern Ireland Design Alliance Supports designers in Northern Ireland. www.nidesignalliance.com
- UK Design Alliance Group of design sector bodies working to develop the industry's professional skills. www.designcouncil.org.uk and www.gooddesignpractice.org.uk.

Creative services

- British Council Organisation for educational and cultural relations. www.britishcouncil.org.uk
- Creative Choices Online service providing tools, knowledge and networks. www.creative-choices.co.uk
- Creative and Cultural Skills Sector Skills Council for advertising and design among others. www.ccskills.org.uk
- Creative Partnerships Government creative learning programme for young people. www.creative-partnerships.com
- Cultural Leadership Government-funded investment in leadership excellence in creative and cultural industries. www.culturalleadership.org.uk
- NESTA (National Endowment for Science, Technology and the Arts) Invests in companies, informs policy, encourages innovation culture. www.nesta.org.uk
- UK Creative Industries Marketing Toolkit UK Trade and Investment supported resource for international marketing activities. www.creative-industries.co.uk

4 UK BUSINESS ORGANISATIONS

In addition to becoming a member of a design association or organisation, you might consider joining a more general business body which can provide useful contacts and networking opportunities.

- Chambers of Commerce National body for Accredited Chambers of Commerce across the UK. www.britishchambers.org.uk
- CBI (Confederation of British Industry) Organisation supporting the needs of British business. Corporate membership. www.cbi.org.uk
- Federation of Small Businesses Promotes and protects interests of self-employed and owners of small firms. www.fsb.org.uk
- IoD (Institute of Directors) Organisation providing professional business support. Individual membership. www.iod.com

5 BUSINESS SUPPORT AND INFORMATION

There are several Government departments and other organisations which support UK businesses in general. Here are a few worth contacting if you need help, information and advice. Some also provide occasional development funding or can signpost you to other funding sources.

- Business Link Advice, information and resources to help businesses succeed. www.businesslink.gov.uk
- Companies House Incorporates and dissolves companies; stores and makes available company information. www.companieshouse.gov.uk
- BIS (Department for Business, Innovation and Skills) Key role: to build Britain's capabilities to compete in the global economy. www.bis.gov.uk
- DCMS (Department for Culture, Media and Sport) Responsible for government policy on arts, sport, media and other areas. www.culture.gov.uk
- UKTI (UK Trade and Investment) Government network dedicated to building British business success overseas. www.ukti.gov.uk

6   OTHER USEFUL ORGANISATIONS

There are times when we need particular information and advice, and other times when we need ideas and stimulation. Here is a selection of organisations which might help.

Design management

- Design London Joint initiative between Imperial College and Royal College of Art. Innovation-based. www.designlondon.net
- Design Research Society Multi-disciplinary international society for the design research community. www.designresearchsociety.org

Intellectual property

- ACID (Anti Copying in Design) Membership trade organisation to combat plagiarism in the design and creative industries. www.acid.uk.com
- UK Intellectual Property Office Grants Intellectual Property (IP) rights in the UK. www.ipo.gov.uk

The environment and design

- Envirowise Free, practical environmental advice to UK businesses. www.envirowise.gov.uk

Government and design

- APDIG (Associate Parliamentary Design and Innovation Group) Voice and advocate for design and innovation in UK Parliament. www.policyconnect.org.uk

The law and design

- Artlaw Helpful and accessible articles and information on law for visual arts practitioners. www.artquest.org.uk/artlaw

Education and development

- Helen Hamlyn Centre Focus for people-centred design and innovation. www.hhc.rca.ac.uk
- RCA (Royal College of Art) One of the world's leading postgraduate universities of art and design. www.rca.ac.uk
- The Sorrell Foundation Aims to inspire creativity in the young and improve the quality of life through good design. www.thesorrellfoundation.com

Investment

- BVCA (British Venture Capital Association) Industry body for the UK private equity and venture capital industry. www.bvca.co.uk

Standards

- BSI (British Standards) National standards body for the UK. www.bsi-global.com
- ISO (International Organisation for Standardisation) International standards body. www.iso.org

Staff recruitment and development

- Investors in People Supports and promotes staff training and development. www.investorsinpeople.co.uk
- National Occupational Standards Describe the skills, knowledge and understanding needed for particular tasks or jobs. www.ukstandards.org.uk

UK Data Protection Act

- HM Government Direct Gov www.direct.gov.uk
- Information Commissioner's Office www.ico.gov.uk

7   UK DESIGN EXHIBITIONS, EVENTS

Getting together with other design professionals is important; doing it during an event or an exhibition makes it interesting and enjoyable as well.

- Designer Breakfasts Regular networking events with speakers in London, and online forums. www.designerbreakfasts.co.uk

- Design Museum Contemporary design exhibition. London. www.designmuseum.org
- London Design Festival Annual Autumn design event in a range of venues. London. www.londondesignfestival.com
- London Festival of Architecture Annual summer event, city-wide. London. www.lfa2011.org (change year as appropriate).
- New Designers in Business Annual Summer event. Showcases the best in UK graduate design. London. www.newdesigners.com
- V&A Museum Design collections and exhibitions. London. www.vam.ac.uk

8 AWARD SCHEMES

Here is a selection of some of the many awards which operate in the design sector, compiled by Stef Brown (Chapter 5.9 *The Recognition*) and Shan Preddy; some cover wider categories than design alone. Please note that not all awards will apply to all design disciplines, and that entry costs and the complexity of entry requirements vary hugely. In addition, the awards marketplace changes frequently. The UK Design Council has an up-to-date list of national and international design competitions and awards schemes on www.designcouncil.org.uk.

Design and creative sector awards

- AIGA Annual Design Competition www.aiga.org.
- ADC (Art Directors Club) Awards www.adcawards.org.
- BIMA (British Interactive Media Association) Awards www.bima.co.uk.
- Cannes Lions Design Awards www.canneslions.com.
- Chip Shop Awards www.chipshopawards.com.
- Clio Awards www.clioawards.com.
- CorpComms Awards www.corpcommsmagazine.co.uk.
- Creative Review Annual www.creativereview.co.uk.
- D&AD Awards www.dandad.org.
- DADI Awards www.dadiawards.com.
- DBA Design Effectiveness Awards www.dba.org.uk and www.effectivedesign.org.uk.
- DBA/HHC Design Challenge www.dba.org.uk, www.hrc.rca.ac.uk.
- Designs of the Year Awards (Design Museum) www.designsoftheyear.com.
- Design Week Awards www.designweek.co.uk.
- Design Week Benchmarks www.benchmarkawards.co.uk.
- Dieline Awards www.thedieline.com.
- Ergonomics Design Award (Institute of Ergonomics and Human Factors) www.ergonomics.org.uk.
- Eurobest www.eurobest.com.
- European Design Awards (ED Awards) www.europeandesign.org.

- FAB Awards www.fabawards.tv.
- Fresh Awards www.freshawards.co.uk.
- FX Design Awards www.fxdesignawards.co.uk.
- GRAMIA Awards www.gramia.co.uk.
- ID Annual Design Review www.id-mag.com.
- IDEA (International Design Excellence Awards, from the Industrial Designers Society of America) www.idsa.org.
- IF Awards www.ifdesign.de.
- Innovation and Design Excellence Awards www.ideawards.co.uk.
- International Design Awards http:idesignawards.com.
- London International Awards www.liaawards.com.
- Marcom Awards www.marcomawards.com.
- Marketing Design Awards www.marketingdesignawards.com.
- MEGAs (MediaGuardian Innovation Awards) www.guardian.co.uk.
- Mobius Awards www.mobiusawards.com.
- New York Festivals www.newyorkfestivals.com.
- NMA (New Media Age) Awards www.nmaawards.co.uk.
- Pentawards www.pentawards.org.
- Red Dot Awards www.red-dot.de.
- Revolution Awards www.revolutionawards.com.
- Roses Design Awards www.rosesdesignawards.com.
- Spark Awards www.sparkawards.com.
- Starpack Awards, from IoM3 (Institute of Materials, Minerals and Mining) www.iom3.org.
- UK Packaging Awards www.ukpackagingawards.co.uk.

Marketing and communication awards

- CIM (Chartered Institute of Marketing) Marketing Excellence Awards www.cim.co.uk.
- Drum Marketing Awards www.thedrum.co.uk.
- Marketing Industry Network Awards www.marketingindustrynetwork.com.
- Marketing Society Awards for Excellence www.marketing-society.org.uk.
- Marketing Week Engage Awards www.marketingweekawards.co.uk.

Business awards

- Civic Trust Awards www.civictrustawards.org.uk.
- European Business Awards www.businessawardseurope.com.
- Queen's Awards for Enterprise www.businesslink.gov.uk and www.queensawards.org.uk.
- The Sunday Times Top 100 Companies to Work For www.business.timesonline.co.uk.

9   LIKE TO KNOW MORE?

If you've enjoyed the broader topics explored in this book, such as the size and scope of the design industry or where the future is going to take us, why not find out more? Some of the contributors have made suggestions for further reading and research.

For more information on the size and shape of the UK design sector, and for design casework, information and useful downloadable publications, **Shan Preddy** recommends:

- BDI (British Design Innovation) www.britishdesigninnovation.org.
- Creative and Cultural Skills www.ccskills.org.uk.
- DBA (Design Business Association) www.dba.org.uk and www.effectivedesign.org.uk.
- DCMS (Department of Media, Culture and Sport) www.culture.gov.uk.
- Design Council www.designcouncil.org.uk.
- Design Council Value of Design Factfinder www.designfactfinder.co.uk.
- Design Council Designing Demand Programme www.designingdemand.org.uk.
- Office for National Statistics www.statistics.gov.uk.
- UK Design Alliance www.gooddesignpractice.org.uk.

If you want to research international design, some of the organisations **Michael Thomson** mentions in his Chapter 1.3 *The Global Context* are:

- Centre for Innovation in Design, University of Art and Design, Helsinki www.taik.fi.
- Chartered Society of Designers (CSD) www.csd.org.uk.
- Danish Designers www.danishdesigners.com.
- Danish Ministry of Economic and Business Affairs www.oem.dk.
- Design Exchange, Toronto, Canada www.dx.org.
- European Commission, Enterprise and Industry ec.europa.eu.
- New Zealand Institute of Economic Research (NZIER) www.nzier.org.nz.
- Norwegian Design Council www.norskdesign.no.
- University of Cambridge Institute for Manufacturing www.ifm.eng.cam.ac.uk.
- World Economic Forum *Global Competitiveness Report* www.weforum.org.

To read more about the subjects examined in his Chapters 1.5 *The Future* and 2.10 *The Management Issues*, **James Woudhuysen** recommends:

- *Change by Design*, Tim Brown, HarperBusiness, 2009.
- *Designing Interactions*, Bill Moggridge, www.designinginteractions.com and The MIT Press 2007.
- *From Products to Services: insights and experience from companies which have embraced the service economy*, Laurie Young, John Wiley & Sons, 2008.

- Africa Research Institute www.africaresearchinstitute.org.
- Business Week, published by Bloomberg www.businessweek.com.
- CNN Money money.cnn.com.
- Forrester www.forrester.com.
- Gartner Technology www.gartner.com.
- INSEAD knowledge.insead.edu.
- Institution of Engineering and Technology www.theiet.org.
- McKinsey&Company www.mckinseyquarterly.com.
- MIT (Massachusetts Institute of Technology) Sloan Management Review sloanreview.mit.edu.
- Monitor www.monitor.com.
- Nature www.nature.com.
- New Scientist www.newscientist.com.
- Organisation for Economic Co-operation and Development www.oecd.org.
- Oxford Internet Institute, University of Oxford www.oii.ox.ac.uk.
- Science Magazine www.sciencemag.org.
- Scientific American www.sciam.com.
- Strategy and Business, published by Booz & Company www.strategy-business.com.
- Technology Review www.technologyreview.com.
- The Economist www.economist.com.
- The Research and Development Society www.rdsoc.org.
- The World Bank www.worldbank.org.
- UK National Statistics www.statistics.gov.uk and www.ons.gov.uk.
- Wharton University of Pennsylvania knowledge.wharton.upenn.edu.

If you'd like to explore financial management further **Mandy Merron**, author of the Chapters 2.6 *The Money (Part One)* and 3.13 *The Rewards*, suggests:

- British Business Angels Association www.bbaa.org.uk.
- Business Link www.businesslink.gov.uk.

For more information on the legal and taxation information covered in her Chapter 2.8 *The Law*, **Jo Evans** recommends:

- Companies House www.companies-house.gov.uk.
- HM Revenue & Customs www.hmrc.gov.uk.
- UK Border Agency www.bia.homeoffice.gov.uk.

And for more on the subjects identified in his Chapter 2.9 *The Intellectual Property*, **Darrell Stuart-Smith** suggests:

- *The Business of Invention*, Peter Bissell and Graham Barker, Wordbase, 1998.
- Intellectual Property Office www.ipo.gov.uk .
- World Intellectual Property Organisation www.wipo.org.

- GetOnLine for checking availability of domain names and registered owners. www.getonline.co.uk
- United States Patent and Trademark Office for searching and registering US trademarks and patents. www.uspto.gov
- OHIM (The Trademarks and Designs Registration Office of the European Union) for searching and registering EU trademarks and designs. www.oami.europa.eu

Ace networker **Phil Jones** signposts the following social event sites mentioned in his Chapter 2.13 *The Network*:

- www.bladderedagain.co.uk.
- www.digitalpodge.co.uk.
- www.longlunch.com.
- www.manchesterdigital.com.
- www.podgelunch.com.
- www.shesays.org.uk.
- www.typocircle.co.uk.

To find out more about the HR matters covered in Chapters 3.8 *The Incoming Resource* and 3.9 *The Outgoing Resource*, **Kim Briggs** would advise contacting:

- Chartered Institute of Personnel and Development www.cipd.co.uk.

To find out more details about the question of working abroad, **Christine Losecaat**, author of Chapter 4.3 *The Geography*, suggests:

- UKTI (UK Trade & Investment), the UK Government's international business development organisation www.ukti.gov.uk.
- Design Partners (UK) www.uktradeinvest.gov.uk.
- The European Commission's database, TARIC, holds information on classification for goods and duty rates for imports to the EU as well as other useful information ec.europa.eu.
- The Foreign and Commonwealth Office runs the global network of British embassies, high commissions and consulates www.fco.gov.uk.
- The Institute of Export is the professional membership body for those involved in importing, exporting and international trade www.export.org.uk.
- The World Chambers Federation (WCF) represents the interests of chambers of commerce and industry and has a directory of international chambers www.worldchambers.com.

For information and training on PR as introduced in Chapter *4.4 The Reputation*, **Julia James** suggests:

- The Chartered Institute of Public Relations www.cipr.co.uk.

And **Tina Fegent**, who wrote Chapter *4.11 The Procurement*, recommends the following for further information on procurement:

- Chartered Institute of Purchasing and Supply www.cips.org.
- Institute for Supply Management www.ism.ws.
- Supply Management www.supplymanagement.com.
- CPO Agenda www.cpoagenda.com.
- Procurement Leaders www.procurementleaders.com.
- Supply Excellence www.supplyexcellence.com.
- Office of Government Commerce www.ogc.gov.uk
- Supply2.gov.uk www.supply2.gov.uk.

For more on project management, **Lorna Dallas-Conte**, author of Chapter *5.4 The Projects* suggests:

- Project Management Institute www.pmi.org.
- Association for Project Management www.apm.org.uk.

If you want to know more about market research as explored in Chapter *5.5 The Research*, **Don Preddy** recommends:

- MRS (The UK Market Research Society), which has useful information on commissioning research from specialist companies, together with a directory of members www.mrs.org.uk.
- AQR (The Association for Qualitative Research), which has information specifically on qualitative research as well as a members' directory www.aqr.org.uk.

To liven up your meetings and make them more productive, as introduced in Chapter *5.6 The Meetings*, **Sean Blair** advises taking a look at:

- Mycoted for wiki-style ideas. www.mycoted.com

And to find out more about the ideas on sustainable design mentioned in Chapter *5.10 The Planet, Sophie Thomas* suggests:

- Greengaged, which offers thought-leadership, spaces for dialogue and opportunities for knowledge sharing www.greengaged.com.
- Three Trees Don't Make A Forest, a social enterprise with open-access tool for designers www.three-trees.org.
- Tree Hugger, an online media outlet with news, solutions, and product information www.treehugger.com.

- Worldchanging.com, a non-profit media organisation comprising a global network of independent journalists, designers and thinkers with innovative solutions, tools, models and ideas www.worldchanging.com.

10   WHAT ELSE HAVE WE WRITTEN?

All of the chapter authors work in the design sector as experts in their own field. Some have also written other books; if you enjoyed their work here, why not take a look at their other publications?

Kevin Duncan

So What? Capstone, 2007.
Start, Capstone, 2008.
Tick Achieve, Capstone, 2009.
Run Your Own Business, (second edition) Hodder & Stoughton, 2010.
Small Business Survival, Hodder Education, 2010.
Business Greatest Hits, A&C Black, 2010.
Marketing Greatest Hits, A&C Black, 2010.

Blair Enns

The Win Without Pitching Manifesto, Rockbench Press, 2010.

Louis Hellman

A is for Architect, Trend Publishing, 1975.
All Hellman Breaks Loose, Arcus, 1980.
Architecture for Beginners, Writers and Readers, 1988.
Archi-têtes: The Id in the Grid, John Wiley & Sons, 1999.
Do It With an Architect (with Barbara Weiss), Mitchell Beazley, 1999.
Architecture A-Z: A Rough Guide, John Wiley & Sons, 2001.

Liz Lydiate

Professional Practice in Design Consultancy (editor, co-author), Design Council, 1992.

Jeremy Myerson (selection)

Making The Lowry, The Lowry Press, 2000.
IDEO: Masters of Innovation, Laurence King, London 2001.
Rewind: 40 Years of Design and Advertising (with Graham Vickers) Phaidon, 2002.
The 21st Century Office (with Philip Ross) Laurence King, 2003.

Space To Work: New Office Design (with Philip Ross) Laurence King, 2006.
Gordon Russell: Designer of Furniture, second edition, Gower, 2008.
New Demographics New Workplace (with Alma Erlich, Jo-Anne Bichard), Gower, 2010.

Shan Preddy

How to Market Design Consultancy Services: Finding, Winning Keeping and Developing Clients, second edition, Gower, 2004.
Marketing en Acquisitie voor Ontwerpers (Dutch edition of How to Market Design Consultancy Services), BIS Publishing, 2006.

James Woudhuysen

Einstein: The First Hundred Years (with Maurice Goldsmith, David Mackay), Pergamon, 1980.
Central to Design, Central to Industry, Central School of Art & Design, 1983.
Robots (with Stephen Bayley), Conran Foundation, 1984.
Why is Construction so Backward? (with Ian Abley), Wiley, 2004.
Energise! A Future for Energy Innovation (with Joe Kaplinsky), Beautiful Books, 2009.

Section Ten:
The Contributors

The contributors

The people who have written the chapters in this book all work in design. The majority of them are specialist advisers, consultants and coaches to design businesses; others are design sector authors, journalists, academics and strategists. The cartoonist, Louis Hellman, whose work appears in the design press, trained as an architect.

Most of them know each other and many of them regularly work together, sharing complementary knowledge, experience and expertise. Even those who are, on the face of it, competitors understand that they have different capabilities and skills and will join forces on projects which would benefit from more than one input.

Some of them work exclusively in design; others spread their net wider into the creative services arena. Some are accredited consultants on the DBA Experts Register,[1] and some teach on the acclaimed DBA Professional Practice training programmes.[2]

All of them, however, are leading experts in their own field of activity.

GARY BAXTER, LIGHTBOX CONSULTING

www.lightboxconsulting.co.uk

Gary has worked with design consultancies since 1984, firstly as an external auditor and tax consultant, and then as Finance Director of The Partners for eight years. He has been an independent consultant for more than ten years, advising design businesses ranging from start-up firms to mature companies.

---

1   Design Business Association (DBA) Experts Register www.dbaexpertsregister.org.uk

2   Design Business Association (DBA) www.dba.org.uk

ANN BINNIE, PARTNER, AMETHIST

www.amethist.co.uk

Ann worked as Board Planning Director in top London advertising agencies before becoming an independent. She co-founded Amethist in 2000 to apply planning principles, consultancy and facilitation skills to strategy, positioning and development in the wider branding and design world; Amethist also has capabilities in international research and qualitative B2B segmentation. Ann has an MSc in Business Studies and is a qualified Enneagram teacher. She is a full member of the Market Research Society, a member of the Marketing Society and a Fellow of the RSA.

SEAN BLAIR, FOUNDER, PROMEET

www.promeet.co.uk

Sean trained and practised as an industrial designer before becoming Design Director of the UK Design Council. There, he advised ministers on the economic benefits of good design and regularly wrote about and lectured on good design, both in the UK and overseas. His career as a participative design leader led him to work on a wide range of projects from airports to cancer units, from start-up companies to corporations, and from regional development agencies to universities and government departments. His consultancy ProMeet improves meeting experiences. Sean is an Honorary Fellow in Enterprise at Durham University Business School, an Associate of the National School for Government and a Trustee of the RSA.

KATE BLANDFORD, MANAGING DIRECTOR, KATE BLANDFORD CONSULTING

www.kateblandfordconsulting.com

Kate has spent over 20 years in brand development and packaging, half agency-side and half client-side; this gives her a rounded view with insight into making agency-client relationships fruitful and enjoyable partnerships. Kate was Head of Packaging Design at Sainsbury's for eight years, creating brand strategy and implementing packaging. Kate now runs her own business, Kate Blandford Consulting, working as an independent consultant to both brand owners and design agencies on business development strategy and client presentations, as well as creative strategy and design leadership issues. Kate is a member of the DBA Experts' Register.

KIM BRIGGS, KIM BRIGGS HR

Kim worked in the software games industry before becoming Head of HR in a creative communications consultancy. She then set up Kim Briggs HR in 2002, specialising in working with smaller creative businesses. As a generalist, Kim is experienced in all areas of HR from recruitment and induction through to exit strategies, and she works with, and trains, senior management in best practice. Her work is varied, based on her clients' needs. Kim has a postgraduate diploma in HR Strategy and is fully CIPD (Chartered Institute of Personnel and Development) qualified. A BA Hons graduate, she also has a PGCE (Post-Graduate Certificate in Education).

STEF BROWN, MARKETING & BUSINESS DEVELOPMENT CONSULTANT, ON POINTE MARKETING

www.onpointemarketing.com

After 15 years as a senior marketer for agencies including Landor Associates, The Partners and Blue Marlin Brand Design, Stef formed On Pointe Marketing in 2009. Her work is geared towards building an agency's reputation in order to drive the business development pipeline for existing and new clients. Stef develops marketing plans and provides agencies with ongoing consultancy for implementation. She has written and marketed over 30 winning award entries, including seven DBA Design Effectiveness Awards, three Design Agency of the Year accolades (*Marketing Magazine*) and three Packaging Agency of the Year wins (GRAMIA Awards). Stef regularly speaks at design events and is a guest lecturer at the IED Comunicazione in Milan.

JAN CASEY, CONSULTANT

www.jancasey.co.uk

With over 25 years' experience in the creative industry, Jan has substantial expertise from both a business and consultancy perspective. Formerly a Board Director and shareholder at Lambie-Nairn, she is now an independent consultant, delivering a unique set of skills for clients and consultancies; she combines her experience as a brand consultant, project director, business advisor, coach and psychotherapist to build brands, implement projects and facilitate organisational change. Jan regularly chairs seminars on the creative industry including 'Meeting of Minds', an annual symposium held at the British Museum. She runs a training module for the DBA, and is a Fellow of the RSA.

MADELAINE COOPER, FOUNDER, HEROES

www.brilliantheroes.com

With a BA (Hons) in Film and Literature and an MSc in Adult Life Development, Madelaine is a talent broker and coach. She worked in branding, communication and the creative industries in the UK and New York before creating MCV Recruitment in 1995. Madelaine frequently participates in Career Forums, and provides coaching to individuals as well as to companies. She is the founder of Heroes, a talent agency which matches people and projects, giving agencies and businesses access to creative, branding and communications experts on an as-needed basis.

LORNA DALLAS-CONTE, CREATIVE CONSULTANT AND EDUCATOR

www.dallas-conte.co.uk

Lorna is a consultant and educator. Her work encompasses business creation, raising finance, research, project management, facilitation, mentoring and training activity. She has worked extensively in areas of regeneration in the South East and London, contributing to the building of creative communities and networks. Her clients range from large public and private bodies to smaller creative consultancies and individuals, and she is a consultant, principal lecturer and programme director for the University of the Arts. She has published research commissioned by the Arts Council of England. Lorna is unusual in that she holds an ACIB (Associate of the Chartered Institute of Bankers) as well as a MA in Design Studies.

DEBORAH DAWTON, CHIEF EXECUTIVE, DESIGN BUSINESS ASSOCIATION

www.dba.org.uk

Deborah graduated in industrial design from the University of Northumbria in Newcastle. She worked on the Student Design Awards at the RSA, before setting up her own business, Design Events, which delivered design-sector conferences, events and competitions all over Europe. In 2003, she became CEO of the Design Business Association (DBA), a membership organisation whose remit is to drive up the professionalism of the design industry and the profile of design's value in business. Deborah is President-Elect of BEDA (Bureau of European Design Associations), which liaises between its members and the authorities of the European Union in order to communicate and promote the value of design and innovation to the European economy.

PEERS DE TRENSÉ, TAPESTRY CONSULTING

www.tapestryconsulting.co.uk

Peers advises owners and managers of design companies on the growth and development of their businesses; he mentors partners and acts in an executive or non-executive role. Peers has over 20 years' experience in the design industry. From 1988 to 1996, he was a shareholder and Marketing Director of Worthington and Company, successfully selling the business to Havas subsidiary Conran Design Group (CDG). He became Executive Business Development Director at CDG, before leaving to set up his own consultancy in 2006. Peers is a Business Leader of the Marketing Society, and a member of the DBA Experts' Register and of Brilliant Heroes. He lectures for the DBA and the University of Wales.

KEVIN DUNCAN, OWNER, EXPERT ADVICE

www.expertadviceonline.com

Kevin is a business adviser, marketing expert, motivational speaker and author. After 20 years in advertising, he became an independent troubleshooter, advising companies on how to change their businesses for the better through change management programmes, non-executive work and better pitching.

BLAIR ENNS, FOUNDER, WIN WITHOUT PITCHING

www.winwithoutpitching.com

Blair is a Canadian-based business development consultant to marketing communication firms worldwide. He helps design firms transform from a high-cost, low-integrity, pitch-based business development strategy to one where the firm commands the high ground in the relationship and shapes how its services are bought and sold. Blair is the author of *The Win Without Pitching Manifesto*, published by Rockbench Press (2010), the self-published *Win Without Pitching Guidebook*, and the free *Win Without Pitching* Newsletter.

JO EVANS, PARTNER, LEWIS SILKIN

www.lewissilkin.com

Jo is a corporate lawyer at Lewis Silkin, acting for owner-managed businesses, particularly in the creative industries sector. She advises entrepreneurs at every stage of the corporate lifecycle, from inception of the business, through growth and fundraising to a trade sale or flotation. Lewis Silkin is a commercial law firm with an unrivalled client base in the creative and communications industries. As well as design, advertising, digital, PR and direct marketing agencies, the firm acts for brand and platform owners, advising and supporting clients with all of their commercial legal needs.

TINA FEGENT, MANAGING DIRECTOR, TINA FEGENT CONSULTANCY

www.tinafegent.com

Tina has a unique background, having worked in procurement for both clients and agencies. She set up and ran the Marketing Procurement teams for O2, GSK and Orange/France Telecom before joining Grey Advertising as their Commercial Director; this was followed by the same role at Lowe Advertising. She set up Tina Fegent Consultancy in 2006 to offer procurement support to clients and agencies. Tina chairs the CIPS (Chartered Institute of Purchasing and Supply) Specialist Knowledge Group on Marketing Purchasing, and developed and ran the 'Procurement for non-Procurement Managers' course for the IPA (Institute of Practitioners in Advertising). She is a trainer for the CIPS Marketing Collection courses.

LOUIS HELLMAN

www.louishellman.co.uk

Louis, who provided the cartoons for this book, studied in London and Paris before working as an architect; he then branched out on his own to design healthcare buildings and home adaptations for disabled people. His cartoons have appeared in numerous professional and national publications including *Design Week*. He has written for the press, lectured extensively in the UK, Australia and the United States and had exhibitions throughout Europe. He has shown his work at the Royal Academy Summer Exhibition every year since 1998. Louis received an MBE in 1993 for services to architecture, and an Honorary Degree from Oxford Brookes University in 2002.

JULIA JAMES, DIRECTOR, JULIA JAMES PUBLIC RELATIONS LTD

www.juliajamespr.com

Julia has over 15 years' experience within the design industry. She set up her own consultancy in 2006, providing PR and reputation management to the creative industry. Prior to this, Julia spent four years conducting a PR programme for the graphic design consultancy, Edward Briscoe Design, and then worked for six years as in-house Public Relations Manager for Conran Design Group. Julia conducts presentations and workshops on PR and profile raising, and is a Member of the Chartered Institute of Public Relations.

PHIL JONES

www.philjones.co.uk

One of the UK's digital pioneers, Phil founded APT, one of the UK's most successful typesetting companies, before becoming MD of Real Time; the business merged in 2000 with Evans Hunt Scott to become ehsrealtime and then EHS Brann. Since 2004, Phil has worked as a mentor and non-executive director. He was nominated for a lifetime achievement award in digital at the Net Imperative Awards in 2007, and he is a judge for *New Media Age* and *Revolution* magazine, and Chairman of the DADI Awards judges. Phil founded the annual Podge lunches for the design, digital and sports sectors and was the creator of Bladdered by Fax and its later digital replacement, Bladdered Again.

JONATHAN KIRK, BRAND CONSULTANT AND FOUNDER, UP TO THE LIGHT

www.uptothelight.co.uk

Jonathan held New Business Director positions at Fitch and EHS Brann before founding Up to the Light. He works with agencies on their competitive difference, new business and client development strategies and pitch effectiveness, and also provides training and mentoring across a range of skills. Jonathan interviews hundreds of clients each year, providing a unique perspective on the client-agency relationship. Jonathan is an accredited consultant on the DBA Experts' register.

CHRISTINE LOSECAAT, MANAGING DIRECTOR, LITTLE DIPPER

www.littledipper.net

With over 20 years' experience in the design and creative industries, Christine set up her consultancy, Little Dipper, in 2001. She is retained as Creative Industries Advisor to UK Trade & Investment (UKTI), working with the Creative Industries International Marketing Strategy Board and Design Partners. Christine chairs the Television Export Group and is Innovation Champion for the Olympic Legacy Unit. She has been actively involved in creative initiatives in the USA, Japan, Taiwan, South Korea and China, where she has driven the formation of the China Design Task Force, which helps introduce Chinese businesses to British design expertise. She now chairs UK China Partners.

LIZ LYDIATE

www.thehenrylydiatepartnership.com

Liz has been influential since the 1970s in professional practice teaching in art, design and communication colleges nationally. She devised, and acts as course director for, the DBA Professional Practice Courses, and established and managed BA and MA Design Management Programmes at The Surrey Institute, now University of the Creative Arts. She established the MA Enterprise and Management for the Creative Arts (MAemca) programmes at the University of the Arts London (UAL). Liz now runs her own development consultancy, working with creative individuals and organisations. She acts as an External Examiner, as a Specialist Subject Reviewer in art and design for the Quality Assurance Agency, and as a consultant for Sotheby's Institute of Art London and Singapore.

SIMON MAY, AUGUST

www.august.co.uk

With a Masters Degree in Design Strategy and Innovation and a background as a Management Consultant at PWC, Simon set up August in 1995 to deliver innovation, brand strategy and design management projects to large and small businesses and organisations in the public and private sectors, as well as to creative clients. Simon was Content Director for the DBA 'Design Does It' programme for public sector design buyers and, as part of the Design Council's '24/7 Manufacturing' project, he mentored UK manufacturing companies in design and innovation. Simon is a registered mentor at Nesta, including the 'Creative Pioneers' programme.

MANDY MERRON, PARTNER, KINGSTON SMITH W1

www.kingstonsmithw1.co.uk

Mandy is a partner of accountants Kingston Smith W1 which specialises in working with the media sector. Mandy focuses on creative, communications and consulting businesses, particularly design companies. As well as audit and tax work, her role involves general advice on a variety of commercial and technical issues such as employee incentives, developing business plans, mergers and acquisitions, fund raising, pre-sale tax planning, advising start-up businesses and succession planning.

BARRY MORRIS

Barry is a business consultant with over 25 years' experience working for and with small- and medium-sized companies, particularly in the design sector. He is an experienced manager, skilled in change management and organisational development, with a strong financial and general management background. He has practical knowledge and recent experience of mergers and acquisitions, and has been a trustee of several charities. Barry runs regular workshops for the DBA (Design Business Association) as part of their Professional Practice course, and is a consultant on the DBA Experts' Register.

JEREMY MYERSON, DIRECTOR AND HELEN HAMLYN PROFESSOR OF DESIGN, HELEN HAMLYN CENTRE, ROYAL COLLEGE OF ART

www.hhc.rca.ac.uk

Jeremy is Director of the Helen Hamlyn Centre at the Royal College of Art, London, where he holds the Helen

Hamlyn Chair of Design and is a member of the College's senior management team. A writer, academic and activist in design, he founded *Design Week* magazine in the UK and established Innovation RCA, the Royal College of Art's innovation network for business. The author of books on design, architecture and society, Jeremy has led a number of international research projects with industry and curated national exhibitions at the Design Museum and V&A. He is a Board Member of the Design Council and an adviser to a number of international design schools.

ROD PETRIE

www.rodpetrie.com

Rod graduated with a diploma in Illustration and Advertising from Bradford Regional College of Art before starting his career with Allied International Designers. He was promoted to the Board during the company's rapid growth and eventual listing as the first publicly quoted design group. In 1986, he was a founding partner and Group Creative Director of Design Bridge, one of the world's leading international branding agencies. In 2005, Rod started working as an independent coach with a specific insight into the creative sector, supporting emerging leaders to develop their personal and commercial vision and skills. Rod is a consultant on the DBA Experts' Register.

DON PREDDY, PARTNER, PREDDY&CO

www.preddy.co.uk

Don, an experienced researcher, is responsible for the client surveys which form part of Preddy&Co's consultancy programmes. After a career in television at the BBC and the Canadian Broadcasting Corporation, he worked in psychology as an academic researcher at the University of Manchester before entering the commercial sector. He was a founding Director of Consumer Insights, part of PAS (Public Attitude Surveys), before launching his own consultancy, Preddy Research, and is a former Board Director at The Research Business, now part of Synovate. Don is a full member of the MRS (Market

Research Society) and a member of AQR (Association for Qualitative Research), of which he is a previous Vice-Chair.

SHAN PREDDY, PARTNER, PREDDY&CO

www.preddy.co.uk

Shan has delivered strategic marketing consultancy and training programmes to design businesses around the world for over 20 years. A former MD of a Top 100 design company, she is a regular speaker at, and Chair of, international design conferences and is a skilled workshop and away-day facilitator. She sits on the UK Design Alliance Advisory Board, and is an accredited consultant on the DBA Experts' Register; many of the DBA training courses are also run by Shan. Her professional memberships include the Chartered Institute of Marketing and Institute of Directors, and she is a Marketing Society Business Leader, an Elected Associate of D&AD and a Fellow of the RSA. Her book *How to Market Design Consultancy Services*, a companion to this one, has become an industry standard.

ADRIAN RASDALL, PARTNER, REVENUE MATTERS

www.revenue-matters.com

Adrian is a seasoned businessman with over 30 years' experience in the design field. Having worked within design companies in a new business role, he progressed to managing, then forming, owning and selling design companies. With over 20 transactions to date, Adrian now advises a raft of successful companies, aiming to build their value for a future sale. He is an accredited DBA Experts' Register consultant.

LYNDA RELPH-KNIGHT, EDITOR, DESIGN WEEK

www.designweek.co.uk

Lynda has been editor of *Design Week*, the world's only weekly design magazine, since 1989; she oversees the magazine, its supplements and its website. Before taking up that role, she worked freelance, specialising in the built environment and design. In 2001 Lynda received an honorary MA from the Surrey Institute of Art & Design and is a fellow of the Royal Society of Arts. She became an honorary Fellow of the Royal College of Art in June 2007.

DARRELL STUART-SMITH, MEMBER, HUMPHRIES KIRK

www.hklaw.eu

Having graduated in law from University College London, Darrell began his solicitor training in London and finished it in the Channel Islands. He subsequently practised as a solicitor in London and Exeter, before joining the commercial team at Humphries Kirk in Dorset, where he now advises design and creative consultancies on all legal aspects of their business. Darrell has become an expert on IPR (Intellectual Property Rights). He leads the team which provides advice to both the DBA and its members, and regularly writes and presents on different aspects of business law.

SOPHIE THOMAS, DIRECTOR, THOMAS MATTHEWS

www.thomasmatthews.com

Sophie is director and founder of Thomas Matthews, UK pioneers in sustainable communication design. She plays a vocal part in promoting sustainable thinking in design education and regularly participates in conferences and workshops in the UK and internationally. She is co-founder of the social enterprise 'Three Trees Don't Make a Forest', set up to educate and inspire communication designers through practical tools and advice. She is also co-founder of Greengaged, which organises events to encourage debate around sustainable design. Sophie is an active mentor for up-and-coming designers and graduates; she writes regularly for the design press and is a trustee for the UK Design Council.

MICHAEL THOMSON, DESIGN CONNECT

www.designconnect.com

Trained in 3D design in Belfast and Germany and a seasoned international strategist, consultant and facilitator, Michael advises clients in design, manufacturing, media and finance. He has consulted on national and regional design, and is a former advisor to the Secretary of State for Arts and Media, Vienna. As President of BEDA (Bureau of European Design Associations) 2007–2009, he was instrumental in persuading the European Commission to initiate a European design policy. Michael served on the Board of ICSID (International Council of Societies of Industrial Design) 2001–2005, and in 2008 was named in *Design Week's* Hot Fifty. Programme Director for Torino World Design Capital 2008, he became an advisory committee member of Seoul World Design Capital 2010.

GEMMA WENT, DIRECTOR, RED CUBE MARKETING

www.redcubemarketing.com

Gemma has been a successful marketer within the design sector for over ten years. With a background in psychology, her model is grounded in understanding people's desires, their needs and what they need to hear from brands to make them connect. A believer in technological innovation, she was quick to adopt social media as a marketing tool and has merged this with more traditional methods. Gemma works with design companies on their marketing strategy, using a range of marketing, PR and social media tools to help them achieve their business objectives. She is an accredited DBA Experts' Register consultant.

JAMES WOUDHUYSEN, VISITING PROFESSOR OF FORECASTING AND INNOVATION, DE MONTFORT UNIVERSITY

www.woudhuysen.com

James helped to install Britain's first computer-controlled car park in 1968, before graduating in physics. He was Editor of *Design*, 1979–82, and co-founder of *Blueprint* magazine. Between 1983 and 1993, he delivered an instruction manual for word processing, led a study on e-commerce for Fitch and, while at the Henley Centre for Forecasting, proposed that the Web should be delivered through television. In 1995, he became Chief of Worldwide Market Intelligence at Philips Consumer Electronics in the Netherlands, before joining Seymour Powell as Director in 1997. Since 2001, he has worked independently. As well as lecturing, James regularly writes for print and online publications and is a contributor to BBC Radio 4.

Index

How to Market Design Consultancy Services
Finding, Winning, Keeping and Developing Clients

Shan Preddy

The fast-paced nature of the design business means that you probably spend most of your time, energy and resources looking after your clients' needs, not your own. In our current, increasingly competitive marketplace where supply far outstrips demand, no design business will survive for long – let alone grow and develop – without a really effective marketing programme. It is no longer enough for you to provide a good product and simply hope for the best. Potential clients need to know exactly what you can do for them and what makes you different from your competitors. Existing clients need to know exactly why they should develop and continue their business with you. Quite simply, you need to convince design buyers that you are unequivocally the right consultancy for them, time and time again.

This second, fully revised and updated, edition of Shan Preddy's popular book will help you to improve your marketing skills, no matter how large or small your design company, or which of the many disciplines you specialise in. Packed full of accessible, practical advice and information, this book is indispensable for all design consultancies.

Contents: Foreword. Preface; Part I The Principles – How To Do It: Introduction: getting started; Marketing and mousetraps; Looking backwards to look forwards; Where are you going? The vision thing; The marketplace: clients' selection criteria; What are you and what do you do? How to establish your market positioning; Who wants you? How to define your target markets; Why should they bother? Developing sales propositions; How will they find out about you? Approach media; I think, therefore I plan: putting it all together; Words and pictures: it's what you say and the way you say it; Life's a pitch: getting the business; Resources: man and machine; Just hang on to what you've got: client care and retention; Deeper and wider: client development. Part II The Practice – How It Is Done. Part III The Private Views – How It Could Be Done Better. Part IV The Priority – How Clients Would Like It To Be Done. Index.

238 pages   Paperback   978-0-566-08594-9 244 x 172 mm